THE CAMBRIDGE COMPANION T(

C000156022

This collection of essays by international
provides a lively and stimulating account
modern period. The first eight chapters c
from 1750 to the present day, while subse   ... .
and poetry in the twentieth century and explore a set of key identity questions:
ethnicity/migration, gender (writing by women) and sexuality (queer writing).
Each chapter provides an informative overview, along with closer readings of
exemplary texts. The volume is designed to be accessible for readers seeking an
introduction to the literature of Berlin, while also providing new perspectives for
those already familiar with the topic. With a particular focus on the turbulent
twentieth century, the account of Berlin's literary production is set against
broader cultural and political developments in one of the most fascinating global
cities.

ANDREW J. WEBBER is Professor of Modern German and Comparative
Culture at the University of Cambridge and has published widely on German
and comparative textual and visual culture. His books include *Berlin in the
Twentieth Century: A Cultural Topography* (Cambridge University Press,
2008). He has held visiting positions at a number of international institutions,
most recently the Erich Auerbach Visiting Chair in Global Literary Studies at the
University of Tübingen.

THE CAMBRIDGE
COMPANION TO
THE LITERATURE
OF BERLIN

EDITED BY
ANDREW J. WEBBER
University of Cambridge

31 augustus 2020

Voor mijn lieve zoon

Felix. Zie hoofstukken

12 en 13.

Veel plezier in Plymouth

Papa

CAMBRIDGE
UNIVERSITY PRESS

CAMBRIDGE
UNIVERSITY PRESS

University Printing House, Cambridge CB2 8BS, United Kingdom

One Liberty Plaza, 20th Floor, New York, NY 10006, USA

477 Williamstown Road, Port Melbourne, VIC 3207, Australia

4843/24, 2nd Floor, Ansari Road, Daryaganj, Delhi – 110002, India

79 Anson Road, #06–04/06, Singapore 079906

Cambridge University Press is part of the University of Cambridge.

It furthers the University's mission by disseminating knowledge in the pursuit of education, learning, and research at the highest international levels of excellence.

www.cambridge.org
Information on this title: www.cambridge.org/9781107062009
10.1017/9781107449466

First published 2017

Printed in the United Kingdom by Clays, St Ives plc

A catalogue record for this publication is available from the British Library.

Library of Congress Cataloging-in-Publication Data
NAMES: Webber, Andrew, editor.
TITLE: The Cambridge companion to the literature of Berlin / edited by Andrew J. Webber, University of Cambridge.
DESCRIPTION: Cambridge, United Kingdom ; New York, NY :
Cambridge University Press, 2017. | Series: Cambridge companions to literature | Includes bibliographical references and index.
IDENTIFIERS: LCCN 2016047816| ISBN 9781107062009 (hardback) |
ISBN 9781107661011 (paperback)
SUBJECTS: LCSH: Berlin (Germany) – In literature. | German literature – Germany – Berlin – History and criticism.
CLASSIFICATION: LCC PT149.G4 B474 2017 | DDC 830.9/35843155–dc23
LC record available at https://lccn.loc.gov/2016047816

ISBN 978-1-107-06200-9 Hardback
ISBN 978-1-107-66101-1 Paperback

CONTENTS

FIGURES

CONTRIBUTORS

JÜRGEN BARKHOFF is Professor of German (1776) in the Department of Germanic Studies and is Head of School of the School of Languages, Literatures and Cultural Studies at Trinity College Dublin, the University of Dublin. His main research areas are literature and medicine, science and psychology around 1800, contemporary Swiss literature and questions of identity in the German-speaking world and Europe. His major publications include *Magnetische Fiktionen: Literarisierung des Mesmerismus in der Romantik* (1995).

DAVID BARNETT is Professor of Theatre at the University of York. He is the author of *A History of the Berliner Ensemble* (2015); *Brecht in Practice: Theatre, Theory and Performance* (2014); *Rainer Werner Fassbinder and the German Theatre* (2005); and a monograph on Heiner Müller (1998). He has written several articles and essays on German- and English-language political and postdramatic theatre.

GERRIT-JAN BERENDSE is Professor of German at Cardiff University. Alongside four edited volumes and numerous articles on poetry, he has published four monographs: *Die 'Sächsische Dichterschule': Lyrik in der DDR der sechziger und siebziger Jahre* (1990); *Grenz-Fallstudien: Essays zum Topos Prenzlauer Berg in der DDR-Literatur* (1999); *Schreiben im Terrordrom: Gewaltcodierung, kulturelle Erinnerung und das Bedingungsverhältnis zwischen Literatur und RAF-Terrorismus* (2005); and *Vom Aushalten der Extreme: Die Lyrik Erich Frieds zwischen Terror, Liebe und Poesie* (2011). He is currently writing a monograph on surrealism in the German Democratic Republic.

CAROLIN DUTTLINGER is Associate Professor in German at the University of Oxford, Fellow of Wadham College and Co-Director of the Oxford Kafka Research Centre. She has published widely on modern German literature, thought and visual culture. Her books include *Kafka and Photography* (2007); *Walter Benjamins anthropologisches Denken*, ed. with Ben Morgan and Anthony Phelan (2012); and *The Cambridge Introduction to Franz Kafka* (2014).

MATT ERLIN is Professor and Chair of the Department of Germanic Languages and Literatures at Washington University in St. Louis. His most recent publications include *Necessary Luxuries: Books, Literature, and the Culture of Consumption in*

Germany, 1770–1815 (2014) and (with Lynne Tatlock) *Distant Readings: Topologies of German Culture in the Long Nineteenth Century* (2014). He is currently a co-investigator on the six-year, multi-university partnership grant 'Text Mining the Novel', which aims to produce a large-scale, cross-cultural study of the novel using quantitative methods.

ANNE FUCHS is Professor and Director of the UCD Humanities Institute. She has written widely on the literature and culture of Germany in the modern period. Her recent publications include *After the Dresden Bombing: Pathways of Memory, 1945 to the Present* (2012); *Transformations of German Cultural Identity 1989–2009*, special issue; *New German Critique* (co-edited with Kathleen James-Chakraborty, 2012); and *Time in German Literature and Culture, 1900–2015: Between Acceleration and Slowness* (co-edited with J. J. Long, 2016).

KATHARINA GERSTENBERGER is Professor of German and Chair of World Languages & Cultures at the University of Utah. She has published widely on topics concerning contemporary German literature. Her works include *Truth to Tell: German Women's Autobiography and Turn-of-the-Century Culture* (1999); *Writing the New Berlin: The German Capital in Post-Wall Literature* (2008); and *Catastrophe and Catharsis: Perspectives on German Culture and Beyond* (co-edited with Tanja Nusser, 2015). She is a member of the Transatlantic Environmental Humanities Network.

ANDREAS KRASS is Professor of German Literature at the Humboldt University Berlin, with a focus on pre-modern literature and culture, gender studies and queer studies. He is the Director of the Research Centre, Archive for Sexology, which investigates and reconstructs the cultural heritage of Magnus Hirschfeld's Institute for Sexology in Berlin (1919–33). His book *Meerjungfrauen* (2010) was concerned with the literary history of mermaids, and his most recent volume, *Ein Herz und eine Seele* (2016), deals with the literary history of male friendship.

ALISON LEWIS is Professor of German in the School of Languages and Linguistics at the University of Melbourne, Australia. She has published widely on postwar German literature and German cultural history, particularly on gender and women's writing, literature and politics; the GDR; German unification; the history of intellectuals; and, most recently, about secret police files and Stasi informers. Her most recent monograph is *Eine schwierige Ehe: Liebe, Geschlecht und die Geschichte der Wiedervereinigung im Spiegel der Literatur* (2009).

JOHN B. LYON is Professor of German at the University of Pittsburgh and has also taught at Duke University, Colby College and Carleton College. His research and teaching interests include German literature, philosophy and culture of the eighteenth and nineteenth centuries. He is the author of *Crafting Flesh, Crafting the Self: Violence and Identity in Early 19th-Century German Literature* (2006) and *Out of Place: German Realism, Displacement, and Modernity* (2013).

LYN MARVEN is Senior Lecturer in German at the University of Liverpool. Her research focuses on contemporary literature, with a particular interest in writing by women and Berlin literature. She is the author of *Body and Narrative in Contemporary Literatures in German* (2005) and is co-editor of *Emerging German-Language Novelists of the Twenty-First Century* (2011) and *Herta Müller* (2013), amongst other works. She is also the translator of the short story collection *Berlin Tales* (2009).

ANDREW J. WEBBER is Professor of Modern German and Comparative Culture at the University of Cambridge. He has published widely on modern German and comparative textual and visual culture. He is the author of several monographs, including *Berlin in the Twentieth Century: A Cultural Topography* (2008), and (co-)edited volumes, including *Cities in Transition* (2008, with Emma Wilson) and *Memory Culture and the Contemporary City* (2009, with Uta Staiger and Henriette Steiner). He is currently Principal Investigator for a major AHRC-funded project to provide digital critical editions of works by Arthur Schnitzler.

BENEDIKT WOLF wrote his PhD in German Literature at the Humboldt University Berlin, focusing on the figure of the penetrated man in twentieth-century fiction. He has published articles on gender, androgyny and identity, and on male and female images for the *Thomas Mann-Handbuch* (2015), and on Greek literary anti-gypsyism (2013).

YASEMIN YILDIZ is Associate Professor of German and Comparative Literature at the University of California, Los Angeles. She specializes in twentieth- and twenty-first-century German literature, literary multilingualism, minority discourses, transnational studies and gender studies. Her book *Beyond the Mother Tongue: The Postmonolingual Condition* won the MLA's 2012 Scaglione Prize and received Honorable Mention for the 2014 Laura Shannon Prize in Contemporary European Studies. She is currently working on a co-authored study of immigrants and Holocaust remembrance in contemporary Germany together with Michael Rothberg.

REINHARD ZACHAU is Professor of German at the University of the South in Sewanee, Tennessee. He is the author of numerous articles and books on twentieth-century German culture and literature, among them volumes on Hans Fallada, Heinrich Böll and Stefan Heym (with Peter Hutchinson). Zachau also edited Jakob Littner's Holocaust memoir, along with the volumes *Berlin and Modernism, Berliner Spaziergänge* and *German Culture through Film*. His latest publication is the co-authored textbook *Cineplex*.

EDITORIAL NOTE

All ellipses are editorial, unless otherwise indicated.

CHRONOLOGY

1237	First certified mention of the settlement of Cölln
1244	First certified mention of the settlement of Berlin
1280	Introduction of Berlin's new town seal, with two bears
1292	First mention of the Marienkirche (St Mary's Church)
1307	Berlin and Cölln form a union, with a joint council
1356	The Mark Brandenburg becomes an electorate of the Holy Roman Empire
1360	Berlin-Cölln joins the Hanseatic League
1415	The reign of the Hohenzollern dynasty in Brandenburg begins with Friedrich I as Elector and Margrave
1469	Completion of *Berliner Totentanz* (Berlin Dance of Death), Marienkirche
1486	The city castle in Cölln becomes the residence of the Electors of Brandenburg
1540	The Reformation takes hold in Brandenburg
1647	Between the city castle and the Tiergarten hunting ground, an avenue is established, later to develop into Unter den Linden
1671	Foundation of the Berlin Jewish community
1672	Foundation of the Berlin Huguenot community
1685	Friedrich Wilhelm issues the Edict of Potsdam, one of a series of edicts of tolerance
1688	Population reaches 20,000
1701	Coronation of Friedrich I of Prussia
1709	Friedrich I unites five separate towns to form Berlin as the royal residence, with a population of 55,000
1700–80	Construction of representative buildings around Unter den Linden, including the State Opera (1742) and the Old Library (1780)
1740	Accession to the throne of Friedrich II (Frederick the Great)

1743	Moses Mendelssohn arrives in Berlin from Dessau
1759–65	Publication by Mendelssohn, Lessing and Nicolai of the Enlightenment journal, *Briefe, die neueste Litteratur betreffend* (Letters Concerning the Most Recent Literature)
1761	Literary debut of Anna Louisa Karsch ('Die Karschin') in Berlin
1764	Opening of the first German-language theatre in Berlin
1767	G. E. Lessing, *Minna von Barnhelm*
1773–6	Friedrich Nicolai, *Das Leben und die Meinungen des Herrn Magister Sebaldus Nothanker* (The Life and Opinions of Master Sebaldus Nothanker)
1783–5	Friedrich Gedike, *Über Berlin, von einem Fremden* (On Berlin, by a Foreigner) in *Berlinische Monatsschrift* (Berlin Monthly)
1790	Rahel Levin (later Varnhagen) institutes her first salon in Berlin
1791	Dedication of the Brandenburg Gate
1793	Isaak Euchel, *Reb Henoch, oder Woß tut me damit* (Reb Henoch, or, What of It)
1798	First publication of the Romantic periodical *Athenaeum* in Berlin
1800	Population reaches 170,000
1805	Naming of the Alexanderplatz, for Tsar Alexander I
1806	Napoleon's troops occupy Berlin
1810	Opening of the Friedrich-Wilhelms-Universität (today, the Humboldt Universität), with Johann Gottlieb Fichte as Rector
1811–12	Publication of Kleist's journal, *Berliner Abendblätter* (Berlin Evening Pages)
1817	E. T. A. Hoffmann, *Das öde Haus* (The Abandoned House)
1818	Foundation of the Order of the Serapion Brethren, around Hoffmann
1822	E. T. A. Hoffmann, *Des Vetters Eckfenster* (My Cousin's Corner Window)
1824	With the expansion of industry, construction of the first *Mietskasernen* ('rental baracks' or tenements)
1830	Construction of the Altes Museum (Old Museum) by Karl Friedrich Schinkel
1847	Population reaches 400,000, with widespread poverty
1848	Revolution in Berlin, subsequently put down by Prussian troops
1871	Berlin becomes the capital and powerhouse of the new German Empire

1873   Economic crisis of *Gründerkrach* (Founders' Crash)
1877   Population reaches 1 million
1883   Opening of the Deutsches Theater
1888   Theodor Fontane, *Irrungen, Wirrungen* (Delusions, Confusions)
1889   Foundation of the Freie Bühne (Free Stage) in Berlin
1890   Social Democrats win the absolute majority of votes for the Reichstag
1892   Opening of the Neues Theater on Schiffbauerdamm, later home to the Berliner Ensemble
1893   Premiere of Hauptmann's *Die Weber* (The Weavers) at the Freie Bühne
1895   Theodor Fontane, *Effi Briest*
1897   Hirschfeld founds *Wissenschaftlich-humanitäres Komitee* (Scientific-Humanitarian Committee)
1903   Georg Simmel, 'Die Großstädte und das Geistesleben' (The Metropolis and Mental Life)
1925   Population reaches 4 million
1905–12   Robert Walser lives, writes and publishes in Berlin
1911   Gerhart Hauptmann, *Die Ratten* (The Rats)
1912   With an expansion of the city limits, the population of Greater Berlin reaches 2 million, with many living in *Mietskasernen*. Gottfried Benn, *Morgue* collection
1914   Opening of the Volksbühne Theatre
1914–18   Increasing hardship during the war years, leading to mass strikes
1917   Dada arrives in Berlin
1918   November Revolution in Berlin, abdication of the Kaiser, and proclamation of the Free Socialist Republic by Karl Liebknecht from the Berlin Castle
1919   Putting down of Spartakus uprising; murder of Karl Liebknecht and Rosa Luxemburg. Kurt Pinthus's Expressionist poetry anthology, *Menschheitsdämmerung* (Twilight of Humanity)
1920   Right-wing Kapp putsch, subsequently collapsing after general strike. Further expansion, with population rising to 3.8 million
1922   Assassination of Foreign Minister Walter Rathenau
1923   Inflation reaches its peak
1925   Development of first major architectural projects for new social living. Vladimir Nabokov, 'A Guide to Berlin'

1927   Bertolt Brecht, *Hauspostille* (Domestic Breviary) collection.
        Piscator's Berlin production of Toller's *Hoppa, wir leben!*
        (Hoppla, We're Alive!)
1928   Premiere of *Die Dreigroschenoper* (The Threepenny Opera)
        by Brecht and Weill. Mario von Bukovich's photobook, *Berlin*
1929   World economic crisis, high unemployment, violent demon-
        strations and street battles between left and right. Alfred
        Döblin, *Berlin Alexanderplatz*
1931   Erich Kästner, *Fabian*
1932   Irmgard Keun, *Das kunstseidene Mädchen* (The Artificial Silk
        Girl). Karl Aloys Schenzinger, *Hitlerjunge Quex* (Hitler Youth
        Quex)
1933   National Socialists take control of government; book burning
        in front of the Old Library; sacking of Hirschfeld's Institute for
        Sexual Research. Walter Benjamin leaves Berlin
1936   Staging of the Berlin Olympics. Jan Petersen, *Unsere Straße*
        (Our Street)
1937   Celebration of 700th anniversary of the city
1938   Reichskristallnacht, with burning of synagogues, terrorization
        of Jews and plundering of shops. Deportation of Gertrud
        Kolmar
1939   Second World War declared from Berlin. Christopher
        Isherwood, *Goodbye to Berlin*. Klaus Mann, *Der Vulkan*
        (The Volcano), published in Dutch exile
1942   Wannsee Conference, planning the 'final solution'
1943   Blanket bombing by Allied forces begins
1945   Battle of Berlin as Red Army attacks; surrender to the Allies
1946   Berlin, as 'city of rubble', split into occupied zones; onset of
        Cold War tensions
1947   Hans Fallada, *Jeder stirbt für sich allein* (Every Man Dies
        Alone, or Alone in Berlin)
1948   Blockade of Western sectors and airlift; formal division of city;
        foundation of Free University in West Berlin
1949   East Berlin becomes capital of new German Democratic
        Republic. Foundation of Berliner Ensemble, under Brecht
1953   Bloody putting down by Soviet troops of strike by East Berlin
        workers. Brecht finishes work on his adaptation of *Coriolanus*
1954   Berliner Ensemble takes up residence in Theater am
        Schiffbauerdamm
1957   International Building Exposition in West Berlin

1961	Following mass departures of GDR citizens from East Berlin, the Berlin Wall is erected. Uwe Johnson, *Das dritte Buch über Achim* (The Third Book about Achim)
1962	Development of Alexanderplatz and neighbouring Marx-Engels-Platz as representative centre of East Berlin
1963	John F. Kennedy's speech in front of Schöneberg Town Hall. John le Carré, *The Spy Who Came in from the Cold*. Christa Wolf, *Der geteilte Himmel* (Divided Heavens)
1966	First publication of Volker Braun's poem 'Die Mauer' (The Wall)
1967	Student protests against visit of Shah of Persia; development of extra-parliamentary opposition (APO)
1973	Aras Ören, *Was will Niyazi in der Naunynstraße* (What Does Niyazi Want in Naunyn Street)
1977	Heiner Müller, *Germania Tod in Berlin* (Germania Death in Berlin)
1978	Opening of Scharoun's new State Library in West Berlin
1982	Peter Schneider, *Der Mauerspringer* (The Wall Jumper)
1987	Separate celebrations of 750th anniversary of the city in East and West Berlin
1989	Following unrest and demonstrations, fall of the Berlin Wall
1990	Ian McEwan, *The Innocent*
1991	Decision to move the capital of the Federal Republic from Bonn to Berlin. Martin Walser, *Die Verteidigung der Kindheit* (The Defence of Childhood)
1993	First publication of Müller's poem, 'Mommsens Block'
1995	Wrapping of Reichstag by Christo and Jeanne Claude
1999	Inka Parei, *Die Schattenboxerin* (The Shadow-Boxing Woman). Peter Schneider, *Eduards Heimkehr* (Eduard's Homecoming).Tanja Dückers *Spielzone* (Playzone)
2001	Director René Pollesch's first season at the Prater stage of the Volksbühne
2002	Unveiling of restored Brandenburg Gate. Christa Wolf, *Leibhaftig* (In the Flesh)
2003	Emine Sevgi Özdamar, *Seltsame Sterne starren zur Erde: Wedding–Pankow, 1976/77* (Strange Stars Stare to Earth: Wedding–Pankow, 1976/77). Yadé Kara, *Selam Berlin*. Opening of Hebbel am Ufer (HAU) theatre
2005	Completion of Memorial to the Murdered Jews of Europe
2006	Berlin hosts final of World Cup; sculpture of stack of books by German authors, representing *Modern Book Printing*,

ANDREW J. WEBBER

Introduction

The literature of Berlin is a double category. It can at once reference literary writing that takes Berlin as its object and writing that, whether this is the case or not, belongs in Berlin, is attached to it, by virtue of being produced there. For the most part, this critical companion to the literature of Berlin will be concerned with the former: with writing, in a variety of genres and across the historical spread of modernity, that is concerned with the representation of this, one of the great cities of the modern world. But it will also incorporate consideration of the latter, of the sorts of habitation – and thus the conditions of possibility – that the city affords for the production of literature across its history.

Of course, given the chequered – often fraught – character of that history, in particular in the twentieth century, the conditions of literary production are not always hospitable. As we can see from the titles of two of the most prominent historical studies of the city, Alexandra Richie's *Faust's Metropolis* (1998) and Brian Ladd's *Ghosts of Berlin* (1997),[1] modern Berlin is at once a city dominated (on the Faustian model) by sometimes catastrophic fantasies and compacts of self-transformation and a haunting-ground for the phantoms of the resulting historical violence. Accordingly, the literature of Berlin has to negotiate both the operations of political power and, certainly for the period after the Second World War, their – often spectral – after-effects. At the same time, the city is not exclusively condi-tioned by those models, and it shares much with the other major cities of modernity. Indeed, the key generic themes that run through the broader canvas of the recent *Cambridge Companion to the City in Literature*, the socio-cultural dynamics and literary constructions that are sustained by cities, per se,[2] also feature in what follows, albeit in forms that are in significant respects site-specific.

While Berlin is a relative latecomer as a major urban centre, a status that the erstwhile provincial *Residenzstadt*, seat of the Hohenzollern dynasty since the fifteenth century, only really reached in the course of the eighteenth

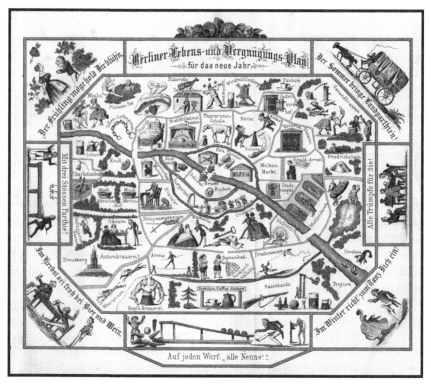

Figure 0.1: *Berliner Lebens- und Vergnügungs-Plan* (Berlin Map of Life and Entertainment), 1871. Photo © Dr. Jens Mattow, Berlin.

century, its ascendancy was remarkably dynamic. As discussed by Matt Erlin in Chapter 1 of this volume, it was with the reign of Frederick the Great (1740–86) that Berlin first became a significant centre of cosmopolitan thinking and cultural production. As traced by John B. Lyon in the opening of Chapter 3, in the last decades of the nineteenth century, the city then grew apace, becoming established as an imperial city of global significance and reach. An allegorical Berlin map of 1871 (Figure 0.1), representing such urban stations of life and entertainment as the city's theatres, shows that this burgeoning of the city also proceeded on a variety of cultural levels. And, as Anne Fuchs outlines at the start of Chapter 4, this development – in both broad civic and more cultural terms – was further accelerated at the start of the twentieth century, powered by the rapid industrialization of the city.

Notwithstanding the end of the Second Empire in the wake of the First World War, and the ensuing turbulence, Berlin continued to burgeon in the years of the Weimar Republic. As such, it became what the poet Else Lasker-Schüler – drawn to the city, like so many, from the provinces – called, in a short, lyrical prose text of 1922, a revolving 'Weltfabrik', or world factory. It was a dynamic industrial complex also in the field of cultural production: a magnetic attraction and an exacting time-piece, the 'clock of art' as Lasker-Schüler's dubs it,[3] for writers and other artists seeking the pulse of the times or wanting to play a part in setting its pace. In particular from its massive expansion around 1900, Berlin worked not just as a factory but also as an urban laboratory, a place of experimentation with the possibilities – and the excesses – of the modern city in social, political and cultural terms. This laboratory character applies, not least, to formative developments in the disciplinary, indeed intrinsically interdisciplinary, field of urbanology: the conceptually informed critical study of cities. In the first three decades of the twentieth century, first Georg Simmel, and then Siegfried Kracauer and Walter Benjamin, established the terms and the fundamental critical methods for the analysis of the modern urban condition. If, as Jürgen Barkhoff points out in Chapter 2, early nineteenth-century Berlin was the birthplace of the philosophical tradition of hermeneutics, then a century later, these pioneering urbanologists transferred its critical resources to the study of the city in its advanced, modern form. Not only did the city produce literary texts, but it was itself understood as an object of critical reading, a mobile and multiform text, requiring advanced skills of interpretation.

We might seek initial guidance here from one of the writers who can be said to have made a contribution through his literary work to the urbanological study of Berlin, an émigré visitor to the Weimar-period city of Kracauer and Benjamin: Vladimir Nabokov and his 'Guide to Berlin' ('Putevoditel' po Berlinu' (1925)). This text, one of the works in Russian that he wrote and published during his Berlin years, is also introduced by Yasemin Yildiz in her account of Berlin as a migratory setting in Chapter 11. In its style, it is close to the kind of short prose text, the urban narrative miniature, which Fuchs discusses in Chapter 4, principally through close analysis of the exemplary case of Robert Walser, and which Carolin Duttlinger follows in its further developments in Chapter 5. Like Walser, in Fuchs's account, Nabokov is at once concerned to conjure up the experience of the contemporary city across a variety of external and internal environments, and to apply critical understanding to its workings. Here, the literary work of such as Walser or Nabokov converges with the urban cultural analysis of Kracauer or Benjamin, both of whom indeed also contributed to creative writing on the city in the short reportage form of the *Feuilleton*.

Perhaps above all, what Nabokov's 'Guide' shows is a constitutive tension that is also fundamental to Benjamin's study of nineteenth-century Paris or early twentieth-century Berlin, whereby the progressive dynamics of modernity are always also turned back towards the past. This dialectical turn is introduced in the second of the five urban vignettes – or, with Benjamin, Kracauer, Bloch and Adorno, *Denkbilder* (literally, 'think images') – that make up the 'Guide': 'The Streetcar'. The first person narrator muses on this contemporary mode of transport, which has superseded the horse-drawn cabs of his youth in St Petersburg, but – in its turn – is set for supersession. The 1920s urban observer projects through time onto 'some eccentric Berlin writer in the twenties of the twenty-first century', who will study the museum-bound remains of the age of the tram and, with their help, give account of 'Berlin streets in by-gone days'.[4] And for the narrator of the Berlin guide, Nabokov's proxy, this is the function of literary creation in the mode that he pursues: an attentive viewing of the contemporary world as if from the future. It is the view that also draws the 'Guide' to a close, that of 'future recollection',[5] as the narrator sees himself, as a persistent memory image in the making, through the eyes of a young boy in a Berlin bar.

This distinctive turn to the future in order to experience the present as past is arguably proper to the ambiguous temporal structures of cities in general. Cities are structures that, as they expand and contract over time, project into the future and recall the past, rise and fall, often in non-synchronic ways. But the sense of multiple timescales has particular resonance for the city of Berlin, more especially in its Weimar years. And it is especially in evidence in the sort of 'thickening' that Yildiz attributes, following Aydemir and Rotas, to the migratory setting, as space becomes layered, after the fashion of a palimpsest, through time. The migratory subject, always coming from another place at another time, is perhaps especially liable to thicken the experience of the city in this way.

This complex temporality is also the disposition of the writings of another expatriate literary guide to Berlin in those years: Christopher Isherwood. Isherwood captures at once the setting of the stage for the violence of National Socialist Berlin, which Reinhard Zachau outlines in Chapter 6 of this volume, and a melancholic sense of a present that can only be the object of retrospection when he says 'goodbye to Berlin', and the march of history takes over. The 'Welcome to Berlin' that Andreas Kraß and Benedikt Wolf adopt from Bob Fosse's 1972 screen version of the musical *Cabaret* to open Chapter 10 also anticipates a 'goodbye', in particular to the kinds of sexual and socio-cultural liberties that Weimar Berlin cultivated and that drew Isherwood, W. H. Auden and others to the city. If Isherwood, famously, casts his literary work as that of a first-person camera,[6] recording views of late Weimar Berlin, his literary version of photography is marked by the kind of mixed tense that Roland Barthes attributes to that medium, capturing the

4

compound temporality of the future anterior, as '*This will be* and *this has been*' are melded into what will have been.[7] This is the character, for instance, of the darkening city scenes that open two of the sections of his *Goodbye to Berlin*: 'A Berlin Diary (*Autumn 1930*)' and 'A Berlin Diary (*Winter 1932–3*)'.[8] As Duttlinger shows in Chapter 5, there is a particular, intermedial alignment between the writing of Weimar Modernism and the genre of the photobook, and also the medium of film. Lyn Marven's reading of Irmgard Keun's late Weimar classic, *Das kunstseidene Mädchen* (The Artificial Silk Girl (1932)), in Chapter 9, provides a nice illustration of the latter.

What this triangular relationship between literature and other media implies is a tension between the future-oriented drive of the city as recorded by the camera (in particular the film camera) or by the photographically disposed literary text and the prospect of its loss. Photography, like Nabokov's streetcar, is a technology that is already marked by the anticipation of its passing. And observational urban writing modelled on it has a similar predicament. We are reminded of a scene from another of Nabokov's Berlin writings, where a puddle encountered 'in the middle of the black pavement resembled an insufficiently developed photograph'.[9] It is the paradox of this form of writing that it presents that sense of loss (inflected, for the émigré Nabokov, with that of the other city, the place of origin, behind Berlin) with compelling presence.

This volume stakes a claim for Berlin as a city that has produced a compelling series of literary presences in the last 250 years, even as it registers the narrative of what has been lost or not fully developed. The sort of companionship that the volume offers to the reader in the exploration of the iterations of the literary city over that period is of a particular kind. While visitors to the city, like Nabokov or Isherwood, make appearances in the volume, most of the authors considered here are German, and most of the literary works originally written in German. And while some readers will be familiar with at least some of what is discussed and with the original language of the German texts, no such familiarity is assumed. Rather, the authors of its thirteen chapters have sought to be genuine critical companions to the interested reader, offering orientation through different dimensions of the city's literary map and introductions to a set of its most significant locations, its landmark features and key historical developments.

While a significant part of the corpus of texts that feature here is canonical, in that sense also with landmark status, this companion equally seeks to introduce readers to less mainstream writing. These categories may not fully align with the more and the less familiar territories of the city, but the literature of Berlin has certainly done much to shape the way in which the city has come to be known, both internally and at large. Given that the experience of a city is always mediated as much through the texture of its localized spaces as through its focal points of orientation, the experience of the city in literature needs to encompass something of both types of encounter. For Berlin in particular, this means giving adequate attention to the less conspicuous category of the *Kiez*, the local 'patch' or neighbourhood, as an informal level of civic organization, informing the identification of Berliners with their city. Cumulatively, the chapters of this volume draft a literary map that is at once marked out by key reference points, places and monuments, some of them encountered on multiple occasions, and the more local domains, on the model of the *Kiez*.

By way of introduction to this double form of mapping, we might consider perhaps the best-known landmark example of the literature of Berlin. It is one that is recurrently referenced in this volume, most substantially in Duttlinger's reading in Chapter 5: Alfred Döblin's Modernist masterpiece, *Berlin Alexanderplatz* (1929). Döblin's epic narrative is at once centred upon and named for one of the major civic squares of the city, and it undertakes an exploration of the more informal spaces that surround it. The Alexanderplatz is, to use the terms developed by the urban theorist Henri Lefebvre, representative in a double sense here. It is at once a 'representational space' (the space, that is, of lived experience and the practical negotiation of everyday existence as representational practice, a production of meaning) and the object of 'representations of space' (of plans and designs relating to the conceptual shaping of the city).[10] The Alexanderplatz is perhaps paradigmatically representative of modern Berlin in that double sense. As I have argued elsewhere, it is a kind of agora for the modern city of Berlin, a marketplace and site of social interaction. In that sense, Döblin's view of the Alexanderplatz in 1929 is a mobile equivalent to that of E. T. A. Hoffmann, from a self-consciously fixed point, upon the social congregation of the Gendarmenmarkt square a century earlier, as discussed by Barkhoff in Chapter 2. At the same time, the Alexanderplatz has been the object of a series of master plans for the political, architectural and logistical organization of urban life.[11] The relationship between the two levels of space, in turn, determines the forms of spatial practice that emerge on and around the square: practice at the level of everyday life and at the level of the march or the demonstration, that is, of more orchestrated forms of political representation. We could think of the rally on 4 November 1989, when leading GDR writers, such as Heiner Müller and Christa Wolf, both of whom feature in this volume, were amongst those who occupied this marching-ground of the state in order to lend their voices as literary intellectuals to the calls for political change that would prove to be tectonic. Wolf invoked the idea of the ruling cadre marching past the people in the 1 May parade on the Alexanderplatz, and Müller the idea of demonstrations with dancing if the government should resign.[12]

The Alexanderplatz of today with its architectural silos, from the fourteenth-century Marienkirche (St Mary's Church) at its southern boundary, via the Weimar Modernism of Peter Behrens, to such heroic Soviet-era implants as the Television Tower, and the banal, generic mall constructions of the post-unification years, represents the history of the city in a remarkably assorted, almost archival constellation. Yet, there is a sense that the archive is not properly configured, that the elements are not placed in cultural-historical terms, but rather in the mode of what Marc Augé famously called the non-place, the generic site without distinctive identity.[13] While Augé's principal focus is on the exchangeable, globalized spaces of airports and hotels, there is also every reason to consider the 'place', or square, on the model of the Alexanderplatz, as non-place, in his sense. Indeed, it is perhaps indicative that Augé's anthropological term of art has entered into popular discourse, with a recent Berlin television feature on an online public dialogue around the tribulations of urban planning in the case of the Alexanderplatz and the adjacent historical centre of Berlin dubbing it a 'Nicht-Ort', a non-place.[14] And while Augé develops the term for the particular conditions of what he calls 'supermodernity', it arguably already applies to the historically unsettled scene of construction and reconstruction that gives its name to Döblin's Modernist novel.

This tension between a settled sense of place and forms of non-placement is perhaps what gives *Berlin Alexanderplatz* its paradigmatic status for the literature of Berlin. Notwithstanding its character as a text inhering in a particular time – the late Weimar years – as well as occupying a particular, eponymous location, this text can serve as a more developed kind of second-order guide for the literary mapping that is undertaken here across a variety of periods and urban environments. If different contributors to this volume, dealing with very different chapters in the story of Berlin in literature, have made reference, unbidden, to *Berlin Alexanderplatz*, this indicates something of its potential as a landmark text. In particular, as Katharina Gerstenberger notes in Chapter 8, it has been a yardstick for the efforts to capture the so-called *Wende*, or 'turn', of unification in 1990, and the city's new status as the capital of the 'Berlin Republic' that has followed. The notion of the *Wenderoman*, or novel of that national and civic turn, has recurrently been measured against Döblin's epic narrative, and the contenders, for all their individual interest, invariably found wanting. *Berlin Alexanderplatz* has accordingly been invested with a powerful nostalgia for its encompassing representation of the life of the city in dynamic and unsettled times. It is, in other words, a particular site of memory for the literary culture of Berlin.

Of course, the literary mapping undertaken here cannot itself pretend to be encompassing. It cannot entirely represent the literary life of Berlin in spatial terms – the imaging of the city in the synchronic dimension – or in temporal terms – the diachronic dimension of developments in its literary culture. And it can certainly not do full justice to the interaction between the two, how the spatial organization of the city – what I have called elsewhere its cultural topography – is modified along the timeline of its modern history.[15] The history of the literature of Berlin is represented here through a set of its key chapters, ranging from the eighteenth century to the present day. That the account could have started earlier is clear, and indeed this is illustrated in striking form by the *Berliner Totentanz* in the Marienkirche, the city's version of the generic, medieval *danse macabre*, as presented by Gerrit-Jan Berendse to set the scene for Chapter 13. However, the volume spans most of the city's more significant literary production. There are points in this histor-ical span where the account is thickened, the mappings compounded and, so, complicated. This is the case, in particular, for the first decades of the twentieth century, when Berlin emerged as what the discourse of the time called a *Weltstadt*, or city of the world. And the Weimar period, as perhaps the heyday of the city's literary and broader cultural life, and the apogee of its global cultural influence, is thus given particularly sustained attention across several chapters, as indeed in this Introduction.

While the historical sequence that governs the larger part of the volume gives prominence to narrative writing, albeit also with some reference to other genres, individual chapters are also dedicated to drama and to poetry. As David Barnett argues in Chapter 12, Berlin is a leading city of theatre, less as a developed setting for the plots of dramas than as a place of their production and performance. Indeed, Berlin theatre has played a particular role in the creative re-production of literary texts, from the pioneering work of Brecht and his Berlin Ensemble (Barnett particularly explores the example of Brecht's adaptation of Shakespeare's *Coriolanus*) to the innovations of *Regietheater* or 'directorial theatre', which holds sway in the Berlin theatre culture of today.

In the dramas most associated with the city of Berlin since the beginning of the twentieth century, life and death sit closely together. This is most evident in the postwar theatre of Heiner Müller, as in *Germania Tod in Berlin* (Germania Death in Berlin (1977)), one of Barnett's focal texts. But it is already fundamental to the Naturalist drama of Gerhart Hauptmann, as also explored in Lyon's reading of *Die Ratten* (The Rats (1910)) in Chapter 3. And with the medieval *Totentanz* as his point of departure, Berendse, in Chapter 13, shows that this proximity of death to life in Berlin is also a key characteristic of the modern city's relationship to poetry. It is seen there to extend from visceral versions of the high lyric mode in the post-Baudelairean sonnets of Gottfried Benn, through the *Gebrauchslyrik*, or utilitarian lyric, of Brecht's urban poetry, to the popular verse of David Bowie's Berlin songs.

Bowie's association with Berlin is, one might say, identitarian, in a special sense. That is, it has to do with the particular frame that the city in certain forms and at certain times – in this case West Berlin in the late 1970s – has provided for a living out of counter-normative, creative identities. Three chapters of this volume are also assigned to a set of identity questions that have particular salience for Berlin and have made distinctive contributions to the vitality of the city's literary identity in the period since 1900: questions of gender (Marven on writing by women in Chapter 9), of sexuality (Kraß and Wolf on queer writing in Chapter 10) and of ethnicity and migration (Yildiz in Chapter 11). This – in certain senses interrelated – set of identity categories, which could certainly have been extended further, has a special function, not only in the practical life of the city but also in what we could call its cultural imaginary – the ways in which ideas of Berlin have been constructed. It is a measure of both the inclusiveness that the city has achieved and the exclusions that it has imposed, or that have been imposed by powers of state, across its history. To use a term coined by Henri Lefebvre, what is at issue here are the 'rights to the city':[16] the extent to which different social and cultural groups can freely inhabit it by right and, thereby, also co-constitute its conditions of living. And, as further developed by Michel de Certeau, this is the basis of 'habitability' as the 'production of an area of free play (*Spielraum*) on a checkerboard that analyzes and classifies identities'.[17]

Chapters 9, 10 and 11 of this volume each investigate the contours of that area of free play, what one of the texts discussed in Gerstenberger's account in Chapter 8 (Tanja Dückers' *Spielzone* (1999)) titles a Play Zone. These chapters trace both the possibilities and the limits of an alternative space of urban occupation, extending beyond the governing discourse and structural economy of what de Certeau calls the 'local authority'.[18] While these questions of the right to the city – as extended to the literary rights to the city – are particularly in focus in those three chapters focusing on identity formations, they also feature in other contributions to the volume from its first steps. The great thinker, Moses Mendelssohn, who is a focal protagonist in Erlin's account of Berlin as a centre of the Enlightenment in Chapter 1, had to enter the city via the Rosenthaler Tor, a gate designated for non-resident Jews, when he migrated there from Dessau in 1743. The networks of urban intellectual and cultural sociability that sustain the developments of the Berlin Enlightenment in Erlin's account, and subsequently Berlin Romanticism, as discussed by Barkhoff in Chapter 2, were never fully inclusive. As Barkhoff shows, while the literary life of early nineteenth-century

Berlin was enlivened by salons that were sustained by Jewish women, the more general culture of the city in the Romantic period was marred by anti-Semitism. Equally, any emancipation that it afforded for women was strictly limited. Much as the Romantics were attached to certain freedoms of the imagination and literary creation, they often also infringed others; and as the volume recurrently shows, this ambivalent constellation of progressive and reactionary thinking and activity is a regular feature of the literary history of Berlin.

The history of anti-Semitism and of other forms of identity-based coercion and exclusion also indicates a level of experience that is not always readily visible in the surface appearances of the city. And another theme that recurs in this volume is the underground, inhabited with varying degrees of choice, often by those who have forcibly deprived of any right to the city they might have enjoyed. Here, too, a more general characteristic of the literature of cities takes on a particular form, in keeping with the historical specificity of Berlin. It is most acute, of course, in the period of the most intense civic constraint, that of National Socialism as shown in Chapter 6 and signalled by the title of the only recently published testimonial narrative of survival against the odds by Marie Jalowicz with which Zachau's account concludes: *Untergetaucht* (Gone Underground (2014)). But, what Gerrit-Jan Berendse calls, after Julia Kristeva, abjection – the driving out or underground of the inherent 'other' – is in evidence at other times too. There are, for instance, the rats – archetypal species of urban abjection – that run underground, as it were, from Hauptmann's drama, as discussed by Lyon, to Annett Gröschner's *Walpurgistag* (Walpurgis Day (2011)), set against the contemporary gentrification of the *Kieze* of East Berlin, which features amongst the texts by women writers given special attention by Marven. These Berlin rats, hosted by different texts, embody at once the precarity and the potential resilience of underground existences in the city.

Between the two rat texts and in the wake of National Socialism, which mobilized the figure of the urban rat for its own ideological purposes, there is Cold War Berlin, as adumbrated indeed in Robert Siodmak's 1955 film of Hauptmann's play, transposed to the postwar, pre-Wall city. As Alison Lewis shows in her account of the literature of Cold War division in Chapter 7, the imposition of the Wall upon Berlin radically reorganized its space for authors writing on either side of it and projecting the possibility of border-crossings. The Wall imposed upon the city a split psycho-geography, which prompted fantasies of crossing to the other side, in the wall-jumping that Lewis discusses, but also, in many cases, tunnelling. We could here invoke another foreign visitor as a writer of and in Berlin, Ian McEwan, following in the tradition of adopting Berlin as setting for hard-boiled Cold

War thrillers. In his *The Innocent* (1990), the Cold War city is embodied through a double topographic constellation: that of the Wall and the tunnel. McEwan registers this in an epigraph drawn from German literature and a tale by Franz Kafka, an earlier writer who was also an occasional visitor to Berlin and spent six months there in the last year of his life.[19] Kafka's 'Der Bau' (translated as 'The Burrow' (1923/4)), written during his Berlin time, is a story with no evident location, and a badger-like rather than rat-like protagonist. It is adopted by McEwan as an allegory for the sort of blocked and underground existence that subsisted in Cold War Berlin. Overground existence is also always attached to the underground in such conditions. We might be reminded of the fantasy architecture that was constructed in the name of a group of writers from a very different period: the nineteenth-century 'Tunnel over the Spree', discussed by Lyon in Chapter 3. As represented by a leading light of that literary club, Theodor Fontane, Berlin Realism – while not having to respond to the sort of division that characterized the postwar city – was also intently concerned with what is hidden or made to go underground in the social reality of things and what is encoded, symptomatically, in surface appearances.

From Nabokov and Isherwood to McEwan, we see that Berlin offers complicated and often ambivalent forms of hospitality to the visiting writer. At the same time, it is also variable in its hospitability for home writers, as is most acutely in evidence for authors driven away from this, their home – or adoptive – city by the National Socialists. The first writer named in this introduction, Else Lasker-Schüler, can stand for many here. Lasker-Schüler was at once part of the cultural networks of Berlin around the avant-garde journal *Der Sturm* (The Storm) and an idiosyncratically independent operator who adopted the city as an invigorating arena for the performance of her writerly personae, before being forced into an unhappy exile in Palestine as the National Socialists took control.

Throughout the volume, a question that arises is what types of habitability the writers of Berlin literature can achieve for themselves and their protagonists, and, in turn, offer to their readers. Berlin has certainly provided advanced forms of sociability and support networks for writers – salons, clubs, collectives and ensembles – and a space of sustenance or of provocation for some remarkable individual literary work. But, the licence that the city has given has also been subject to conditions that have often been uncongenial – sometimes, indeed, life-threatening – for the work of writing and, at least, for certain classes of writer. Against this context, the thirteen chapters of this *Companion to the Literature of Berlin* show the range of what has been achieved by writing in and of this city in exploring, interrogating and enabling forms of literary habitation – for writers, for protagonists and, not least, for readers.

NOTES

1. Alexandra Richie, *Faust's Metropolis: A History of Berlin* (London: HarperCollins, 1998); Brian Ladd, *The Ghosts of Berlin: Confronting German History in the Urban Landscape* (Chicago: University of Chicago Press, 1997).
2. Kevin R. McNamara, ed., *The Cambridge Companion to the City in Literature* (Cambridge: Cambridge University Press, 2014).
3. Else Lasker-Schüler, 'Die kreisende Weltfabrik' (The Revolving World Factory (1922)), in *Werke und Briefe: kritische Ausgabe*, ed. Norbert Oellers et al., vol. 4.1 (Frankfurt am Main: Jüdischer Verlag, 2001), pp. 24–6 (p. 26).
4. Vladimir Nabokov, 'A Guide to Berlin', in *Details of a Sunset and Other Stories* (London: Weidenfeld and Nicholson, 1976), pp. 89–98 (pp. 93–4).
5. Ibid., p. 98.
6. Christopher Isherwood, *Goodbye to Berlin* (Harmondsworth: Penguin, 1974), p. 7.
7. Roland Barthes, *Camera Lucida: Reflections on Photography*, trans. Richard Howard (London: Vintage, 2000), p. 96.
8. Isherwood, *Goodbye to Berlin*, pp. 7 and 184–5.
9. Vladimir Nabokov, 'The Return of Chorb', in *Details of a Sunset*, pp. 57–70 (p. 64).
10. Henri Lefebvre, *The Production of Space*, trans. Donald Nicholson-Smith (Oxford: Blackwell, 1991), p. 33.
11. Andrew J. Webber, *Berlin in the Twentieth Century: A Cultural Topography* (Cambridge: Cambridge University Press, 2008), pp. 188–228.
12. Transcripts and recordings at: www.dhm.de/archiv/ausstellungen/4novem ber1989/cwolf.html, www.dhm.de/archiv/ausstellungen/4november1989/ mulr.html (accessed 30 July 2015).
13. Marc Augé, *Non-Places: Introduction to an Anthropology of Supermodernity*, trans. John Howe (London/New York: Verso, 1995).
14. Laurence Thio, 'Ergebnisse der Stadtdebatte zu Berlins Mitte' (27 July 2015), www.rbb-online.de/abendschau/archiv/20150727_1930 (accessed 29 July 2015).
15. Webber, *Berlin*, pp. 22–6.
16. Henri Lefebvre, *Le Droit à la ville* (1967), translated as 'The Right to the City', in Lefebvre, *Writings on Cities*, trans. and ed. Eleonore Kofman and Elizabeth Lebas (Oxford: Wiley-Blackwell, 1996), pp. 147–59.
17. Michel de Certeau, *The Practice of Everyday Life*, trans. Steven Rendall (Berkeley: University of California Press, 1988), p. 106.
18. Ibid.
19. Ian McEwan, *The Innocent* (London: Jonathan Cape, 1990), no page number.

I

MATT ERLIN

Literature and the Enlightenment

Athens on the Spree?

In October 1785, the journal *Berlinische Monatsschrift* published an anonymous article with the title, 'Ein Wort über die vielen Anti-Berlinischen Schriften in unsern Tagen' (A Word on the Many Anti-Berlin Writings That Have Appeared of Late). Its author takes his fellow Germans to task for the many misrepresentations of the city that have appeared in recent travelogues and in the periodical press. While it is true, for example, that Berliners like to talk politics, their outspokenness should not be mistaken for dissatisfaction with their king. Nor should one believe, as one critic of the city has claimed, that the male residents are all 'withered, pale, and emaciated', and the women of a 'pale, yellow' complexion.[1]

Berlin was a hot topic in late eighteenth-century Germany, with plenty of advocates as well as detractors, and for good reason. In less than a century, the city had been transformed from a provincial backwater into one of Europe's leading metropolises. Part of this transformation was demographic. Berlin's population exploded in the eighteenth century, growing from roughly 16,500 residents in 1685 to 90,000 in 1740 and then almost doubling again to reach 170,000 by the end of the century.[2] Moreover, as a result of the population policies of the Prussian kings, Berlin was a relatively cosmopolitan city for the period, home to a sizable Huguenot and Bohemian population, as well as an unusually wealthy and prominent Jewish community. Equally central to Berlin's prominence in the 1780s, however, was its emergence as a leading intellectual and cultural centre of the German-speaking world, one closely associated with the idea of enlightenment. It is no coincidence that the famous debate on enlightenment that exercised German intellectuals in the 1780s had its origins in the discussions of the Berliner Mittwochsgesellschaft (Berlin Wednesday Society) and found its first articulation in print in the pages of the *Berlinische Monatsschrift*.

For most eighteenth-century Germans, Berlin's rise was inextricably entwined with the rule of the Hohenzollern kings and especially with the accession to the throne of Frederick the Great in 1740. Twenty-first-century scholars will continue to debate whether and to what degree Frederick's variant of absolutist rule was, in fact, enlightened and whether the Francophile inclinations of the king and his court stimulated or hindered the development of indigenous literary and intellectual traditions. Most contemporaries, however, had no doubt that Frederick had ushered in a new era of cultural vibrancy, not to mention political prestige and economic prosperity. While the designation of the city as *Spreeathen* (Athens on the Spree) was first coined to celebrate the achievements of Frederick I, it was his grandson who tended to be most closely associated with the phrase, especially after Voltaire asserted in a letter that Berlin, under his protection, would become 'the Athens of Germany, perhaps of Europe'.[3]

In many respects, Berlin's eighteenth-century literary and cultural renaissance appeared to play out on two stages operating independently of each other.[4] The first was both directed and populated by the king and his court. Frederick the Great was not only a patron of the arts and letters, famous or infamous for his French academy of sciences, his sometimes tumultuous relationship to Voltaire and his support of the French materialist philosopher La Mettrie, but he was also a prolific poet and essayist, whose works (written almost entirely in French) fill some thirty volumes in the definitive edition.

Appearing on the other stage were those non-courtly authors and intellectuals who have constituted the focus of most scholarship on the literary culture of eighteenth-century Berlin, generally under the rubric of the Berlin Enlightenment or *Berliner Aufklärung*. These individuals were typically, but not exclusively, members of the middle classes, most of whom admired the king but were sceptical of his Francophile tendencies. The principal players in this group were the publisher and author Friedrich Nicolai, the Jewish philosopher Moses Mendelssohn, the celebrated Enlightenment dramatist and critic Gotthold Ephraim Lessing, and, somewhat later, Karl Philipp Moritz, who is best known for his novel *Anton Reiser*, his editorship of the *Magazin für Erfahrungsseelenkunde* (Magazine of Experiential Psychology) and his contributions to the development of modern aesthetic theory. Supporting roles were played by less canonical figures who made successful careers in Berlin but who have since received only sporadic attention from literary and cultural historians: Christlob Mylius, editor of the *Berlinische priviligierte Zeitung* (Chartered Newspaper of Berlin) and collaborator with Lessing; the poets Karl Wilhelm Ramler, Johann Ludwig Wilhelm Gleim and Anna Louisa Karsch; the Swiss philosopher Johann Georg Sulzer, author of the *Allgemeine Theorie der schönen Künste* (General Theory of the Fine Arts); the illustrator Daniel Chodowiecki; the editors of the *Berlinische Monatsschrift*, Friedrich Gedike and Johann Erich Biester; and representatives of the Jewish

Enlightenment or Haskala such as the doctor and Kant-protégé Markus Herz, the author and educational reformer Naphtali Herz Wessely and the philosopher Lazarus Bendavid.

Equally important for the non-courtly aspect of Berlin's reputation in the period were a variety of publications that appeared in the city. Between 1759 and 1765, Nicolai, Mendelssohn and Lessing co-edited the *Briefe, die neueste Litteratur betreffend* (Letters Concerning the Most Recent Literature), a review of contemporary letters that introduced a new literary-critical idiom and established the Berliners as an alternative to the two dominant literary schools of thought, associated with Johann Christoph Gottsched in Leipzig, and Johann Jakob Bodmer and Johann Jakob Breitinger in Zurich.[5] Even more influential was Nicolai's encyclopedic review journal, the *Allgemeine Deutsche Bibliothek* (Universal German Library), which published over 60,000 reviews in 256 volumes during its forty-year run.[6] Berlin's status as a centre of the German and the Jewish Enlightenment, particularly in the 1780s, is closely linked to two further publications. From 1783 until 1792, when a tightening of censorship forced the editors to publish in Jena, the *Berlinische Monatsschrift* provided a forum for wide-ranging discussions of everything ranging from aesthetics to book piracy, religious tolerance, press freedom and, most famously, the question of enlightenment itself. And *Hame'assef* (The Collector), the leading periodical of the Haskala, was published in Berlin beginning in 1787, having been founded in Königsberg in 1783.[7]

Berlin, finally, was also a centre of the new modes of sociability that took shape around the print culture of the eighteenth century, even before the founding of the famous salons of Henriette Herz, Rahel Varnhagen and others. Learned societies such as the Montagsklub (Monday Club (1748)) and the Gelehrtes Kaffeehaus (Learned Coffeehouse (1755)) provided a forum for the presentation and discussion of material both prior to and after publication. These were later supplemented by large-scale public lectures such as those delivered on ancient and modern art by Karl Philipp Moritz between 1789 and 1793.[8] Although its meetings took place in secret, the Gesellschaft der Freunde der Aufklärung (Society for the Friends of the Enlightenment), founded in 1783 and later known as the aforementioned Berliner Mittwochsgesellschaft, nonetheless contributed to the resonance of Berlin's literary activities due to the fact that its discussions often found their way into the articles of the *Berlinische Monatsschrift*. Less connected to print culture but also important in terms of fostering unconstrained interaction across class boundaries were the three masonic lodges operating in the city, the first of which had been founded in 1740.[9] Commentators both inside and outside Berlin remarked on these institutions as well as on other forms of literary sociability that figured prominently in city life, especially lending libraries and reading societies.

The lines of communication between city and court have recently begun to be addressed in greater detail, and it has become clear that the two stages mentioned above only appeared to be separate.[10] In fact, Berlin literary culture in the eighteenth century comprised a complex network of individuals and institutions with multiple interconnections. This network grew especially dense in the 1780s and 1790s, when key members of the Mittwochsgesellschaft also occupied positions in the state bureaucracy, but it came into existence well before then, whether in the meetings of the masonic lodges or the houses of prominent Jewish families. The Berlin Academy of Sciences, whose reform Frederick had undertaken immediately upon his accession to power, provides an additional example. At least in the early years of Frederick's reign, the Academy was a predominantly French institution. Its president, Pierre Louis Moreau de Maupertius, was a French philosopher, and many of the most renowned members were French. Business was conducted and publications appeared in French.[11] Nonetheless, the essay competitions hosted by the academy generated numerous submissions from Berlin intellectuals (e.g. Lessing, Mendelssohn and Johann August Eberhard) as well as discussion and debate that filtered into the Berlin print culture and Berlin social life more generally. The same can be said of many of the other elements of the city's 'courtly' literary culture, from Frederick's previously mentioned support of La Mettrie to his negative pronouncements on German literature in the essay *De la Littérature Allemande* (On German Literature (1780)).

As this complexity makes clear, no brief discussion of Berlin literary culture in the eighteenth century can do justice to the full range of personalities, publications and practices that constituted literary life in the city. The remainder of this chapter will thus focus on a particular facet of the topic, namely on what authors of the *Berliner Aufklärung* had to say about the city itself, and more specifically, whether they viewed metropolitan life as facilitating or frustrating the progress of their Enlightenment aims of greater religious tolerance; moderate social, political and cultural reform; and individual self-cultivation. Three key features that appear repeatedly in representations of the city will provide conceptual scaffolding for the discussion. Section one will focus on the metropolis in general, and Berlin more specifically, as a paradigmatic site for evaluating the consequences of the civilizing process, for cataloguing the pros and cons of modern life. Section two will consider the new forms of urban sociability or *Geselligkeit* understood as characteristic of Berlin and the degree to which they are seen to help foster a cosmopolitan outlook. The third and final section will address metropolitan life as an inspiration for new, more universalistic models of literary production. While the primary focus will be on the period of Frederick's reign, from 1740–86, certain literary topics will require us to extend past these rather arbitrary historical boundaries.[12]

Urban Modernity and Its Discontents

Perhaps the most compelling testimony to Berlin's dynamism in the late eighteenth century is the sheer volume of travel literature devoted to describing it. In the case of Berlin, authors writing in the late 1780s already cast themselves as critical revisionists of earlier texts; by 1785 one can identify a sense of market saturation.[13] Attitudes towards the city range from enthusiasm to contempt. The most vocal advocates of Prussia's new metropolis are proud residents like Gedike and Nicolai. Non-residents, in contrast, often seem intent upon taking the Berliners down a peg. Clearly, the city's rapid rise to prominence elicited strong reactions from both insiders and outsiders attempting to make sense of its growth. While German travel writers evidently recognize that Berlin is not Paris or London, they have no difficulty considering all three within a common framework of metropolitan life, as the multiple comparisons among them make clear. Regardless of the city, they focus on such topics as public hygiene, the attractiveness of public buildings, the character of the residents, and the number and quality of political, educational, religious and cultural institutions. Within these categories, a number of unique topics also appear with regularity in texts about Berlin: the dust and muck, the influence of French culture, the extent of religious toleration, the strong military presence, the outspokenness of city residents, the beauty of the Tiergarten park, the large number of prostitutes, the relaxed atmosphere of the social clubs and the problems of poverty and begging. What really distinguishes the descriptions of Berlin in such reports, however, is the underlying sense that the city is in a state of flux, that its institutions, policies and even concrete structures have been established recently and face an uncertain future.

Virtually all commentators, in other words, view Berlin as a quintessentially 'modern' space, modernity being understood in the eighteenth century less in terms of rationalization, technology or science than in the Rousseauian sense of 'civilization' or 'cultivation'. Furthermore, the phenomena associated with this urban modernity, such as the mixing of estates or the emergence of cultural consumerism, come into focus against the backdrop of competing models for interpreting temporal change. At one end of the spectrum is a notion of rapid and meaningless fluctuation whose only long-term significance is to indicate the capriciousness of human activity. Eighteenth-century authors tend to identify this type of change with fashion (*Mode*) and luxury, which in texts from the period are often interpreted through the lens of an older Christian vanitas discourse. At the other end is an idea of progress, that is, of gradual evolutionary change according to a stadial model of development. The controversy over Berlin as a historical phenomenon is largely played out in the space created by these opposing conceptual frameworks.

The tension between these two categories structures positive and negative representations of Berlin, as can be seen in the series of twenty-eight letters that appeared between 1783 and 1785 in the *Berlinische Monatsschrift* under the title, 'Über Berlin, von einem Fremden' (On Berlin, by a Foreigner). In fact, the letters were penned by Friedrich Gedike, who was not only co-editor of the journal but also served in a variety of civil service positions related to religious and educational policy. His letters reflect these interests, covering a wide array of topics. Not all of these topics are related to the urban experience as such, but Gedike's letters do include frequent meditations on the evolution and impact of modern urban life, depicting Berlin as the culmination of a long-term process of historical development with generally positive consequences.

Gedike's brief description of the city topography in the first letter offers a case in point. Over the course of the letters, it becomes clear that he shares many of the concerns of his contemporaries regarding the rapid pace of change in the city, but here the emphasis is on those steady improvements that have transformed Berlin into the most beautiful city in Europe. That Berlin deserves this title is, he claims, incontrovertible.[14] He then continues with a discussion of how the city has developed, reaching all the way back to the origins of Berlin and Cölln in the thirteenth century in order to set up a contrast between the narrow, crooked streets that remain from that era and more recent neighbourhoods. One can discern in his narrative an underlying framework of linear progress through a series of stages. The chaos of the medieval city gives rise to the simple utilitarianism of the Friedrichswerder, built by the Great Elector in the late seventeenth century, when one had to focus on 'Nutzen' ('utility') rather than 'Schönheit' ('beauty' (*ÜB*, p. 7)). The symmetry and linearity of the Neustadt (also known as the Dorotheenstadt) and Friedrichsstadt indicate a higher degree of reflection, thus revealing their more recent origins under the careful supervision of Friedrich Wilhelm I (see Figure 1.1). Gedike then goes on to emphasize the active participation of the Berlin residents, whose independent industriousness was the primary impetus for the gradual expansion of this urban core by the four suburbs. Finally, he turns to the more ornamental building projects of the most recent period – 'many large, beautiful houses' – and the various

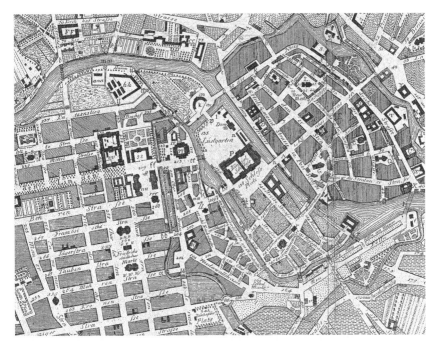

Figure 1.1: Detail from map of central Berlin, 1786 (Zentral- und Landesbibliothek Berlin, 2011).

public buildings commissioned by Frederick the Great, as well as the many beautiful public and private gardens that grace the city (*ÜB*, p. 7).

The notion of historical stages that finds expression in Gedike's description of Berlin offers perhaps the most immediately apparent link between the urban experience and a modernity conceived in positive terms. Gedike represents the cityscape as concrete evidence of a historical evolution, one that suggests a progression on two fronts. It indicates a movement from basic to more refined needs as well as from absolute monarchical control to cooperation between the monarch and the citizens. With regard to the latter, Gedike's emphasis on the 'eignen Fleiß' ('independent industry') of the residents suggests that the Berliners have evolved along with their city and are now in a position to take greater control of their destiny (*ÜB*, p. 7). This motif reappears at various points in the letters, as when Gedike, in a criticism of the most recent construction in the city, states his objection to top-down development, or when he celebrates the positive impact of the king's tolerance on the citizens (*ÜB*, p. 20). Indeed, the entire dynamic of big-city life as described in the letters, the diversity of experience and the exposure to a diverse population, is seen to encourage self-reliance and toleration.

Gedike presents Berlin as a kind of laboratory of enlightenment in the Kantian sense of maturity or *Mündigkeit*, and in doing so he implicitly links the urban experience to a narrative of universal human development. If Gedike's Berlin testifies to the positive consequences of the civilizing process, however, it also points to what eighteenth-century commentators saw as its limits. The narrative of linear progress articulated in the city topography is counterbalanced by the all-too-prevalent reminders of unenlightened elements that remain: cramped and unattractive public buildings, swamp-like roads and dilapidated bridges, not to mention such repugnant practices as emptying chamber pots directly onto the streets. To be sure, these aspects of metropolitan life are more suggestive of an incomplete project of modernization than of its negative consequences, those alleged pathologies of civilization so hotly debated by European intellectuals in the wake of Rousseau. Rousseau himself viewed the metropolis as the epitome of modern decadence ('full of scheming, idle people'),[15] and his views were shared in whole or in part by many German authors who addressed the topic. The Berlin clergyman Friedrich Zöllner, for example, refers in an essay on metropolitan life to a series of vices unique to large cities.[16] Gedike has a less sceptical attitude, but such vices make an appearance nonetheless, as when he refers in his lengthy discussion of the Berlin Jewish community to the 'Üppigkeiten der Hauptstadt' ('excesses of the capital city') to which Jewish residents are allegedly falling victim (*ÜB*, p. 146).

The idea of the metropolis as a site of decadent excess is virtually ubiquitous in the period; the political-economist Johann Heinrich Justi goes so far as to argue that opulence is both the mother and child of the big city.[17] Thanks in no small part to the hardscrabble reputation of Frederick the Great, Berlin was less frequently associated with luxury than other cities, such as Vienna, at least with regard to king and court. The spread of luxury nonetheless continued to be seen as a threat, as Gedike's comments reveal. For the most part, his treatment of the Jewish community aligns with the narrative of progress implied by his discussion of the urban topography. He describes the current generation of Jews, Moses Mendelssohn and Markus Herz among them, as signalling a new era in Jewish history. Borrowing much of his argument from the ground-breaking treatise *Über die bürgerliche Verbesserung der Juden* (On the Civic Improvement of the Jews (1781)) by Christian Wilhelm Dohm, a fellow Berliner, Gedike insists on the integrity of an original Jewish character and claims that the high level of Jewish depravity (which he accepts without question) stems from oppression and intolerance that are slowly giving way to enlightenment. Such positive indicators notwithstanding, however, Gedike expresses his concern that the newfound affluence and the sociable pleasures associated with it may represent too much too soon, causing enlightened cultivation to shade over into fashionable 'Seelenluxus' ('spiritual self-indulgence') and 'Schöngeisterei' ('aestheticism' (*ÜB*, p. 146)). Ultimately, for Gedike, the battle between progress and decadence remains undecided, both as regards the Jewish community and the city as a whole. In the penultimate letter on public amusements, after insisting on the general decency and restraint that characterizes the Berliners, he points to the insidious spread of 'Luxus, Spielsucht, Freßliebe, Sinnlichkeit' ('luxury, addiction to gambling, gluttony, and sensuality') and wonders whether the passage of time will wash away the lessons and the example of the enlightened men of the present (*ÜB*, p. 155).

The Perspective of Humanity

In the travel literature of the eighteenth century, capital cities often appear as states in microcosm. In this incarnation, they function as privileged sites for the acquisition of certain kinds of knowledge (of social, political and religious institutions) and as reference points for claims about the superiority of one nation over another. Gedike's letters are no exception, describing Berlin at one point as an 'emblem' of the Prussian monarchy and, though not without critical moments, generally celebrating the achievements of the Hohenzollerns (*ÜB*, p. 9). Passages such as the one describing the Berlin Jewry, however, highlight a different aspect of the city, one no less crucial to eighteenth-century conceptions of Berlin as a laboratory of enlightenment. Such passages imply that Berlin can be best understood within the supranational framework of the metropolis or *Großstadt*. In these cases authors often emphasize the diversity of experiences available in the big city and especially the exposure to individuals of different backgrounds and estates (*Stände*).

According to some, this exposure leads to a lamentable disrespect for distinctions of rank; the previously mentioned Zöllner remarks that the candour encouraged by metropolitan life can degenerate into 'Ungezogenheit' ('rudeness') on the part of the common man.[18] In contrast, positively inclined commentators depict the unconstrained sociability that characterizes urban life, and the encounter with multiple viewpoints that it enables, as a means towards the achievement of a more universal perspective. As Gedike succinctly puts it, 'Alles schleift sich hier an einander ab, die Stände sind vielfacher, der Umgang vermischter; und so kommt man endlich zu dem gesunden Menschenverstand: Männer nicht zu verachten' ('Everything is kept in check by everything else here; the ranks are more various, intercourse is more mixed; and so one eventually comes to the healthy conclusion: not to scorn one's fellow man' (*ÜB*, p. 80)). In such representations the urban experience is associated with the Enlightenment ideal of self-improvement, often in a variant that combines refined manners with an extensive experiential knowledge of the human condition.

A similar interest in metropolitan perspectives can be discerned in two popular dramatic works from the late eighteenth century: Lessing's *Minna von Barnhelm* (Minna of Barnhelm (1767)) and Jewish author Isaak Euchel's *Reb Henoch, oder: Woß tut me damit* (Reb Henoch, or, What of It (1793)). Indeed, although the novel has long been considered the urban genre par excellence, the drama, as the most conversational literary form, seems particularly well suited to convey eighteenth-century conceptions of the metropolis as a space of unregulated sociability. Both plays include a highly socially differentiated cast of characters, and in both cases this differentiation appears as a function of the urban context. In Lessing's case, the play is also explicitly set in Berlin and includes multiple references to the city, both as an 'emblem' of the Prussian monarchy (as in his depiction of the Prussian practice of using innkeepers as informants) and as representative of the big city more generally (as in Franziska's objection to the noise of the 'verzweifelten' ('accursed') big cities').[19] It is well known that Lessing himself had ambivalent feelings towards Berlin; in *Minna von Barnhelm*, however, he depicts the metropolitan experiences of the main characters as challenging but ultimately constructive.

The play relates the reunion of the separated lovers Minna von Barnhelm and her fiancé, the Major von Tellheim. At the beginning of the action, set at the end of the Seven Years' War, Tellheim is camped out at a Berlin inn, both wounded and dishonoured as a result of an unjust accusation of corruption in connection with Saxony's contributions to the war effort. As a result of his poverty and especially his disgrace, he feels that he can no longer marry Minna, and only a complicated series of coincidences and a deception on the part of Minna make a happy ending possible. Scholars have tended to view this resolution as evidence of the triumph of Enlightenment optimism in a play that often appears on the verge of tragedy. Ultimately, Minna's spunky persistence overcomes the nihilistic misanthropy that threatens to overwhelm Tellheim, and the joyful resolution of all conflicts seems to point to Lessing's faith in some form of providence.

Regardless of whether one accepts this interpretation of Lessing's views on religion, there can be no doubt that the play ends with a full reconciliation of all parties. One can, moreover, link this positive outcome to the urban setting. Both Tellheim and Minna experience Berlin as a site of increased autonomy; the time they spend in Berlin is time spent outside of those institutional contexts (e.g. the family, the military and the court), that had previously provided them with a sense of social identity. In Tellheim's case this autonomy initially appears as a threat. Having been discharged from the army, he can no longer pay for his room at the inn where he has taken up residence. He finds himself on the street as a result, sharing much in common with the rootless and impoverished urban rabble that appear frequently in the travel reports from the period. Minna's metropolitan experience is more positive, even if she never manages to undertake the sightseeing tour mentioned in Act Three. When Minna arrives in the city to track down her estranged fiancé, she is accompanied only by her chambermaid and occupies none of the subordinate familial roles with which women are most often associated in eighteenth-century literature: she is neither mother, wife, daughter nor sister. On the contrary, she confidently asserts her independence in response to the innkeeper's nosy inquiries as to the purpose of her visit, stating, 'Ich bin lediglich in meinen eigenen Angelegenheiten hier' ('I am here solely to look after my own affairs').[20]

It is hard to imagine the kind of independence claimed by Minna existing anywhere but in the metropolis, and it may be that her independence has a specific Berlin inflection in the play. In a journal article of 1779, the author notes that he visited a coffeehouse in the city where three unaccompanied women 'of the best reputation' drank their coffee without causing the least disturbance, and he takes this fact as evidence of the liberal atmosphere in the city.[21] This same freedom, moreover, serves as the enabling condition for her deception, a mock tragedy in which she plays the lead, pretending that she has been disinherited so as to reawaken Tellheim's belief in the possibility of positive action. In *Minna von Barnhelm*, in other words, for both characters, the temporary autonomy made possible by the unregulated space of the city gives rise to a self-estrangement that opens up new perspectives and creates new possibilities for agency. The achievement of these new perspectives, moreover, also owes much to chance, unscripted encounters with the diverse cast of characters, both admirable and unappealing, that populate Berlin.

New possibilities for agency are also explored in Isaak Euchel's play, but with less encouraging results. The urban moment in *Reb Henoch* is even more pronounced than in Lessing; the social differentiation of the cast, which already in *Minna von Barnhelm* marked a departure from an earlier comedic tradition, is taken here to an entirely new level. Euchel includes no fewer than twenty-five different roles, ranging from Henoch, his wife and his four children, to the English doctor, Sir John, and the French tutor, Deschamps. Euchel foregrounds this social diversity by coupling it with linguistic diversity (Yiddish, German, French and English) and also peppers the play with references to the sometimes dubious pleasures of big-city life: masked balls, gambling, dance halls, opera, theatre and bordellos. While there can be no doubt that *Reb Henoch* is a play about late eighteenth-century metropolitan life, however, the question as to whether it is actually set in Berlin remains a matter of debate.[22] Some scholars have argued for Königsberg, where Euchel was a student and leading light of the Haskala movement in the city until he moved to Berlin in 1787. In fact the play contains elements that link it to both cities as well as other large German cities, but it was written while Euchel was in Berlin and clearly engages with the preoccupations of the Berlin Jewish community.

The action centres on the family of Reb Henoch, a family caught between tradition and modernity. Henoch himself is firmly situated on the side of Jewish orthodoxy, but his four children represent a range of responses to the lure of assimilation. Over the course of the drama, the family more or less unravels, and Henoch's dogmatism and prejudice are revealed as the ultimate source of the trouble. His son Hartwig (Herzsche) has meandered into a life of dissipation and debt, thanks to a misdirected religious education and his father's refusal, for reasons of tradition, to apprentice him in any of the trades in which he expresses an interest. Hartwig's older sister Elizabeth (Elke) had the good fortune of spending three years with her enlightened uncle Nathan, who did much to educate her, but she was then forced into an unhappy marriage and very nearly takes refuge in the arms of a cynical German Lieutenant. Hartwig's second sister Hedwig (Hodeß) is a good-natured but rather simple young woman whom he has unintentionally corrupted by trying to impart to her philosophical principles that she understands even less than he does. As Henoch discovers the details of their various situations and transgressions, he responds with rigidity and hardheartedness, blaming everything on the new ways and comparing himself to Job. His comeuppance occurs just before the curtain falls, when he discovers that his much-beloved Schmuel, who appears throughout the play as the loyal son and as deeply steeped in Jewish tradition, has in fact impregnated the Christian housekeeper.

Despite the modernity of its urban setting and many of its thematic preoccupations, in terms of its dramaturgy, one could argue that *Reb Henoch* reaches back past Lessing to the poetics of the *sächsische Typenkomödie* (Saxon comedy of types) in its focus on casting Henoch largely as an object of derision for the audience. The play ends not with a reconciliation and wedding but with the ultimate slap in the face. Some of the other characters, however – especially Hartwig and Elizabeth – are depicted with an impressive sense of the psychological turmoil that lies behind the decisions of young Jews to break with tradition and to step out of their pre-scripted roles.[23] As with Lessing, moreover, the possibility of making such a break proves to be a function of the city. Most notable in this respect are those leisure opportunities that enable unconstrained social contact among different ranks as well as between Jewish and non-Jewish residents of the city. On the one hand, the exposure to what Gedike in his letters referred to as the 'excesses of the capital city' certainly does encourage negative behaviours on the part of the children. Hartwig refers to his own biography in these terms, claiming, 'So hat aber meine Aufklärung einen verkehrten Gange genommen' ('And so my enlightenment proceeded in the wrong direction').[24] One should note, however, that the urban setting is no less closely connected to the true enlightenment embodied in the positive figure of 'The Doctor', a compassionate, highly educated, reform-minded Jew who is largely responsible for salvaging the hopes and happiness of Henoch's children after the father has more or less disowned them. Indeed, the play's presentation of the metropolis as the site of a confrontation between 'true' and 'false' enlightenment places Euchel in close proximity to those non-Jewish Berlin *Aufklärer* who engaged in similar debates in the pages of the *Berlinische Monatsschrift*. All the same, the authentically urban institutions in Euchel's play seem to be more closely associated with vice than virtue, and it is noteworthy that Elizabeth acquired her education while residing with her uncle Nathan, a provincial deputy, suggesting a more sceptical view towards the freedom of the metropolis than is to be found in Lessing. Nonetheless, for the reader at least, the clash of multiple perspectives in the metropolis reveals the limitations of each, enabling a more panoramic view.

The Metropolitan Style

Scholars of twentieth-century Berlin literature, especially those interested in European Modernism, have often stressed the connection between urban experience and innovations in tone, style or narrative technique, that is to say, in elements that go beyond the question of whether or not a work is set in Berlin or contains a metropolitan cast. Whereas one can easily discern the connection between the shocks of modern metropolitan life and the montage technique in Alfred Döblin's novel *Berlin Alexanderplatz* (1929), however, the situation in the eighteenth century is less clear-cut. The previous section raised the possibility of an elective affinity between the socially differentiated dramas of Lessing and Euchel and the social diversity of the metropolis, but the evidence is indirect. Other scholars have suggested other ways in which the experience of life in eighteenth-century Berlin might have influenced literary production, from contributing to a 'new realism' in the works of authors from the Berlin circle to shaping a Berlin style informed by journalism and essay-writing and strongly suspicious of anything that smacked of pedantry, jargon or pompous erudition.[25]

The question of whether one can identify a distinctly urban aesthetic among Berlin authors remains productive for twenty-first-century scholars, but it proves difficult to answer definitively. We can, however, describe with some certainty how those authors themselves understood the relationship between metropolitan life and literary production, since they described this relationship in a number of different contexts. A case in point is the discussion surrounding the poet Anna Louisa Karsch, the innkeeper's daughter who was 'discovered' by Rudolf Gotthard von Kottwitz and made her Berlin literary debut in 1761. Karsch (known as 'die Karschin'), who first made an impression with her occasional poetry and her patriotic hymns to Frederick the Great, was celebrated as a 'natural talent' and especially admired for her capacity to improvise. With regard to the impact of metropolitan life on artistic production, however, it proves instructive to consider Moses Mendelssohn's response to her poetry. He writes, 'Die Dichterin lebt nunmehr in unsrer Hauptstadt und genießt die Vorteile, die Muße und Umgang dem angeborenen Genie verschaffen' ('The poetess now lives in our capital city and enjoys the advantages that leisure and social intercourse can provide to the natural genius'). She needs to take advantage of these opportunities, because her genius requires 'mehrere Cultivierung' ('a good deal more cultivation').[26] Here again we have an association of the city and an affirmative conception of civilization, in this case with an explicit connection to the arts rather than to the more general category of personal development.

Such associations were common among the representatives of the *Berliner Aufklärung*, but there was in the period no more vocal advocate for urban refinement in the arts than Friedrich Nicolai. Unlike the majority of those authors and intellectuals who have come to be associated with eighteenth-century Berlin literary culture, Nicolai was a lifelong resident who also published three editions of a massive compendium on Berlin entitled *Beschreibung der königlichen Residenzstädte Berlin und Potsdam* (Description of the Royal Residences Berlin and Potsdam).[27] An interest in the question of how city life influences the arts can be found in some of his earliest publications. In his first major work, for example, the *Briefe über die jetzigen Zustand der schönen Wissenschaften in Deutschland* (Letters on the Current State of the Fine Sciences in Germany (1755)), Nicolai blames the disappointing state of German literature partly on the absence of a national capital like Paris or London, and Germany's lack of a capital city also appears as a topic in Nicolai's contributions to the multi-authored *Briefe, die neueste Litteratur betreffend*. In the 200th letter of the collection, he asserts that German drama will remain in a state of childhood for as long as Germany is comprised of different territories, each with its own capital city.[28] The reason, as he has already explained, is that 'ein Mensch, der sich auf die geringe Anzahl von Ideen einschränken will, die eine Universität, oder eine Provinzialstadt darbieten, kann unmöglich mit gutem Erfolge für die Schaubühne arbeiten' ('a person who intends to restrict himself to the small number of ideas that a university or provincial city has to offer can never write successfully for the stage').[29]

Variations of this criticism appear repeatedly in Nicolai's contributions to these letters, where he takes German authors to task for their inability to create characters with universal appeal, their reliance on imitation and their eagerness to praise each other. He attributes all of these faults to a lack of familiarity with 'the world', and the implication is that a genuine capital city – were it to exist in Germany – would enable such familiarity. Nicolai, in other words, conceives the metropolis as a universalizing space, a world in miniature, both because of its diversity and the possibilities it presents for human interaction. But one finds nothing explicit in Nicolai's early works to indicate that he thought Berlin could or would fulfil this role. In fact, some of his publishing projects, especially his long-running review journal the *Allgemeine Deutsche Bibliothek*, seem designed to create textual surrogates for the absent metropolis. On the other hand, the idea of exposure to 'the world', which Nicolai connects to the capital city and others associate explicitly with Berlin, clearly informs his own literary practice in his most popular novel, *Das Leben und die Meinungen des Herrn Magister Sebaldus Nothanker* (The Life and Opinions of Master Sebaldus Nothanker (1773–6)), and nowhere more so than in the section of the work that is set in the city.

The novel relates the fate of the country pastor Sebaldus, whose idiosyncratic religious views lead to dismissal and disaster at the beginning of the tale. After losing his position as well as both his wife and one of his daughters to illness, he spends the rest of the novel wandering through Germany and the Netherlands, trying to patch his life back together. Despite a kind-hearted and humble disposition, however, his outspokenness makes it impossible to stay out of trouble. Only after a long series of setbacks and misadventures is he reunited with his second daughter, Marianne, at which point a lucky lottery ticket allows him to purchase a small property and settle down.

Nicolai's commitment to a 'worldly' literature finds expression in the novel as a whole, which has long been recognized for the sober realism with which it depicts a range of social classes and conditions. In addition, by exposing the reader to a variety of perspectives on highly topical debates, especially regarding religion, the novel clearly seeks to foster in the reader such enlightened values as independent thought and a commitment to reasoned debate. Nicolai's general orientation towards a cosmopolitan rationalism, moreover, acquires a particular inflection in the passages set in Berlin, which appear in the first several chapters of the second volume. Berlin is only one of the stations on Sebaldus's journey, but is a particularly important one for understanding Nicolai's aspirations as a novelist.

The protagonist has set off for the city in order to make his fortune but is robbed along the way and now finds himself with little more than the clothes on his back. Nonetheless, having nowhere else to go, he continues on towards his original goal. The representation of Sebaldus's arrival in the city contains elements that anticipate tales of the naive country bumpkin coming to Berlin that become so prominent in the latter nineteenth and early twentieth centuries. Sebaldus makes his first stop at the Tiergarten, where he confronts an impressive bustle of Berliners on foot and on horseback, dressed in the latest fashions and enjoying a Sunday in the park. Later he wanders door to door, first seeking assistance from a young priest who balks at his heterodox views on eternal damnation and then from a *Separatist* who refuses to help him because he belongs to the clergy. Next he stumbles into a tavern where four wastrels try to ply him with alcohol and make a fool of him. He finally ends up on the streets, begging for help from the indifferent passers-by until a humble schoolteacher takes pity on him and brings him into his home.

This subplot on the attractions and the challenges of metropolitan life anticipates nineteenth- and twentieth-century Berlin novels and films, but it also has a decidedly eighteenth-century twist. Sebaldus is clearly naive and ill-prepared for the metropolis, but his naiveté is of a particular variant, one that hearkens back to Nicolai's earlier critical writings. In some respects, Sebaldus is already enlightened when he arrives in the city. As he approaches Berlin in the company of a devout pietist he has met along the way, they discuss the state of life in the city, and Sebaldus responds to the pietist's dogmatic condemnations of Berlin's irreligiosity with a healthy dose of common sense. How is it possible, he wonders, in an allusion to the positive impact of Frederick the Great, for a state (Prussia) and its capital to have become so affluent if it is filled with such immoral residents? He remarks that Berlin in particular is said to have prospered significantly in the past thirty years.[30] And later, in the Tiergarten, when the pietist responds to the scene with a comparison of Berlin to Sodom and Gomorrah, Sebaldus exclaims that there is nothing sinful in enjoying a beautiful day.

The common sense of the protagonist has its limits, however. When asked by the charitable schoolteacher how he plans to support himself, Sebaldus responds that he had intended to teach philosophy, in particular that of Christian August Crusius and his popularizer Julias Elias Wüstemann. A large court city like Berlin, after all, must contain many residents in need of philosophical instruction. The schoolteacher, not surprisingly, has never heard of either, and remarks, 'Ich habe schon mehrmals bemerkt, daß Leute, die auf Universitäten für sehr berühmt gehalten werden, in Berlin keinem Menschen bekannt sind. Ich glaube überhaupt nicht, dass Sie in Berlin durch Philosophie Ihr Glück machen werden. Da hilft Gunst und Protektion, tiefes Beugen und langes Warten mehr, als das beste System' ('I have already noticed on several occasions that people who are considered very famous at universities are totally unknown in Berlin. I really don't think you will make your fortune in Berlin with philosophy. Here, favour and patronage, the ability to bow deeply and wait patiently are of greater value than the best philosophical system').[31] Sebaldus, in other words, resembles one of those previously mentioned writers who possess only those ideas 'that a university or provincial city has to offer'.[32] He needs to develop practical abilities and to learn the ways of the world in order to find his way in the city. Ultimately, they come to the conclusion that his limited skills as a piano teacher will take him further than his arcane philosophical training.

As was the case in Gedike's letters, Nicolai's passage contains elements that are quite specific to eighteenth-century Berlin as well as those that suggest an engagement with metropolitan life more generally. In both cases, however, the primary preoccupation is with the question of whether the urban context fosters a more universal perspective, free of prejudice and committed to practical efforts at social reform rather than fruitless speculation. With regard to Sebaldus himself, this passage at least suggests a connection between the urban experience and an expansion of horizons. In a later passage, however, the multiplicity of perspectives in the city actually appears as a hindrance to enlightenment. In the course of a conversation with his new friend Herr F., Sebaldus remarks on the religious tolerance that characterizes the city, referring to Berlin as a bastion of freedom.[33] Herr F. is quick to point out to Sebaldus that this religious enlightenment has developed unevenly. Noting that progress in thought is registered far more quickly in texts than in the minds of the inhabitants, he remarks that the religious views of many Berliners have not changed in forty years. In a description best characterized as a topography of tolerance, Herr F. then goes on to discuss discrepancies in the relative dogmatism of various Berlin neighbourhoods. The city proper and the Berlin suburbs are among the most orthodox, whereas one finds free-thinkers in Cölln and in the area around the palace. The Herrnhüter congregate around the Hospital Church of Saint Gertraut, and various species of 'enthusiasts', including the pietists, can be found in the Friedrichsstadt. Significantly, this topography reveals a clear correlation between tolerance and political authority, explicitly linking the proximity of the court to the fact 'dass die Leute hier freyer denken' ('that the people here are more free-thinking').[34] In other words, enlightenment radiates outward from the centre, rather than arising from pockets of autonomy made possible by the heterogeneity of the city. On the contrary, it is this very heterogeneity that allows enclaves of orthodoxy to exist.

Like all of the texts addressed in this chapter, then, Nicolai's novel depicts Berlin with a certain degree of ambivalence with regard to its contribution to the project of enlightenment. The city appears on the one hand as a kind of anthropological training ground, where new modes of unscripted sociability are seen to foster tolerance as well as the experiential knowledge of man and the world so crucial to the Enlightenment ideal of self-cultivation. But the urban context can also foster resistance to progress, and modern urban sociability also has a darker side. The same societal advancements that make true cultivation possible can sabotage it if the individual is exposed to these advancements before he or she has reached the appropriate level of maturity. The question of authentic versus false enlightenment, in other words, one of the central areas of contention in the debate that unfolded in the pages of the *Berlinische Monatsschrift* and elsewhere, has for these authors a concrete point of reference in the dynamic, restless capital of the upwardly mobile Prussian state. And regardless of whether a particular author comes down in favour of or against Berlin, the attempt to make sense of it proves highly productive for the literary culture of the period.

NOTES

1. 'Ein Wort über die vielen Anti-Berlinischen Schriften in unseren Tagen', *Berlinische Monatsschrift* 2 (1785), p. 319.
2. Helga Schulz, *Berlin 1650–1800: Sozialgeschichte einer Residenz* (Berlin: Akademie-Verlag, 1987), pp. 61, 172, 296. Other sources have slightly different totals.
3. Voltaire to Frederick the Great, Leiden, December 1736, in *Œuvres de Frédéric le Grand – Werke Friedrichs des Großen, Digitale Ausgabe der Universitätsbibliothek Trier*, vol. 22, ed. Johann D. E. Preuss (Berlin: Rudolph Ludwig Decker, 1853), pp. 25–6. http://friedrich.uni-trier.de/de/oeuvres (accessed 3 June 2015).
4. Klaus Hermsdorf, *Literarisches Leben in Berlin: Aufklärer und Romantiker* (Berlin: Akademie-Verlag, 1987), pp. 51–2.
5. Ursula Goldenbaum and Alexander Košenina, 'Vorwort der Herausgeber', *Berliner Aufklärung: Kulturwissenschaftliche Studien* 1, 2nd ed. (2011), pp. 7–8.
6. Ibid., p. 8.
7. Steven M. Lowenstein, *The Berlin Jewish Community: Enlightenment, Family, and Crisis 1770–1830* (New York: Oxford University Press, 1994), p. 38.
8. Yvonne Pauly, 'Aufgehoben im Blick: Antike und Moderne bei Karl Philipp Moritz', *Berliner Aufklärung* 1, p. 195.

9. Horst Möller, 'Enlightened Societies in the Metropolis: The Case of Berlin', in *The Transformation of Political Culture: England and Germany in the Late Eighteenth Century*, ed. Eckahrt Hellmuth (London: Oxford University Press, 1990), p. 221.

10. See Ursula Goldenbaum, 'Im Schatten der Tafelrunde: Die Beziehungen der jungen Berliner Zeitungsschrieben Mylius und Lessing zu französischen Aufklärern', *Berliner Aufklärung* 1, pp. 69–99.

11. Adolf Harnack, *Geschichte der Königlich Preussischen Akademie der Wissenschaften zu Berlin*, vol. 1.1 (Berlin: Reichsdruckerei, 1900), pp. 295–7.

12. Sections of the following discussion have been adapted from my book, *Berlin's Forgotten Future: City, History, and Enlightenment in Eighteenth-Century Germany* (Chapel Hill, NC: UNC Press, 2004). I would like to thank UNC Press for allowing me to make use of this material.

13. Karl Heinrich Krögen, *Freie Bemerkungen über Berlin, Leipzig, Prag* (1785; repr., Leipzig: Gustav Kiepenheuer, 1986), p. 5.

14. Friedrich Gedike, *Über Berlin: Briefe 'Von einem Fremden' in der* Berlinischen Monatsschrift *1783–1785*, ed. Harald Scholtz (Berlin: Colloquium Verlag, 1987), p. 6 (henceforth *ÜB*).

15. Jean-Jacques Rousseau, *Letter to D'Alembert and Writings for the Theater*, vol. 10 of *The Collective Writings of Rousseau*, ed. and trans. Allan Bloom, Charles Butterworth and Christopher Kelly (Hanover, NH: University Press of New England, 2004), p. 293.

16. Johann Friedrich Zöllner, 'Beitrag zur Charakteristik der großen Städte und des Großstädters', *Lesebuch für alle Stände* (1783), p. 116.

17. Johann Heinrich von Justi, 'Die große Stadt in verschiedenen Verhältnissen betrachtet', *Gesammelte Politische und Finanz-Schriften*, 3, p. 464 (1764; repr., Aalen: Scientia Verlag, 1970).

18. Zöllner, 'Charakteristik', p. 111.

19. Gotthold Ephraim Lessing, *Gesammelte Werke*, ed. Paul Rilla, vol. 2 (Berlin: Aufbau-Verlag, 1957), p. 153.

20. Ibid., p. 158.

21. Ludwig Friedrich Günther von Göckingk, 'Briefe eines Reisenden an den Drost von LB', *Deutsches Museum* 2 (1779), p. 273.

22. Delphine Bechtel, 'Hybride Sprache, Zwittergestalten: Kulturen im Kontakt in einer jüdischen Komödie der Aufklärungszeit', in Isaak Euchel, *Reb Henoch, oder: Woß tut me damit*, ed. Marion Aptroot and Roland Gruschka (Hamburg: Helmut Buska Verlag, 2004), pp. 24–6.

23. Bechtel, 'Hybride Sprache', pp. 28–9.

24. Euchel, *Reb Henoch*, p. 198.

25. Hermsdorf, *Literarisches Leben*, pp. 125–6. Alexander Košenina, 'Der Journalist Lessing als Wegbereiter der Berliner Aufklärung', in *Berliner Aufklärung: Kulturwissenschaftliche Studien* 4 (2011), pp. 50–1.

26. Moses Mendelssohn, 'Allgemeines Urtheil über die Gedichte der Fr. Karschin', *Briefe, die neueste Litteratur betreffend* 17 (1764), p. 125.

27. Friedrich Nicolai, *Beschreibung der königlichen Residenzstädte Berlin und Potsdam und aller daselbst befindlichen Merkwürdigkeiten* (Berlin: Friedrich Nicolai, 1769). The second edition appeared in 1779 and a much expanded third edition in 1786.

28. Friedrich Nicolai, 'Von den Ursachen, warum die deutsche Schaubühne immer bisher in der Kindheit geblieben', *Briefe, die neueste Litteratur betreffend* 11 (1761), pp. 303–4.
29. Ibid., p. 301.
30. Nicolai, *Sebaldus Nothanker*, p. 172.
31. Ibid., p. 188.
32. Ibid., p. 301.
33. Ibid., p. 203.
34. Ibid., p. 206.

2

JÜRGEN BARKHOFF

Romantic Sociability, Aesthetics and Politics

German Romanticism was quintessentially an urban and a modern movement, despite its strong and at times anti-modern idealization of nature and the past. Between the early 1790s and the late 1820s, its various constitutive groupings, circles of friends and collaborators came together in many of the intellectual centres of the politically fragmented German speaking world: Jena and Heidelberg, Dresden and Munich, Vienna and Berlin. This Romantic *Wanderlust* of course had to do with the dynamism and the intellectual and social energy of the movement, yet it was more fundamentally owing to the unstable social and political situation into which this Romantic generation of the 1770s was born. Its members experienced an era of unprecedented political turmoil and rapid change between the French Revolution in 1789, the crumbling, under the Napoleonic onslaught, of the venerable but now entirely dysfunctional Holy Roman Empire of German Nations between 1803 and 1806, the French occupation of Germany after 1806, the 1812–15 wars of liberation and the restoration period after the Congress of Vienna in 1815.

At different junctures between the 1790s and 1820, Berlin became one of the defining centres of Romanticism. While Vienna remained the most populous and most important capital of the German-speaking world, Berlin was in transition from the residence of Frederick the Great to one of the most vibrant modern urban centres of Europe, counting around 180,000 inhabitants in 1800. It was also, as many visitors, including Madame de Staël, observed, one of the most modern and most beautiful cities in Europe. Its opera and its many theatres, its museums and concert halls, its reading circles and coffee houses, its societies, literary salons and wine taverns all provided venues for a vibrant intellectual and cultural life of great energy and conviviality. It attracted at various junctures within this period the most important German writers and intellectuals of the time, who exerted a crucial influence not only on the culture but, as we will see, also the political life of Berlin, Prussia and the whole of Germany.

Within Berlin Romanticism we can distinguish three distinct phases and groupings, which can be identified with different forms of Romantic sociability, different constellations of protagonists (though with considerable continuities and overlaps), and diverging aesthetic concepts, political orientations and practical objectives. They also correspond roughly to the three phases of early, high and late Romanticism as a whole. The first, from around 1790 to 1806, was centred around the liberal and tolerant literary salons of educated Jewish women, who practised and celebrated an aesthetic and social utopia of sociability that was at once exclusivist and egalitarian. With the Napoleonic occupation of Berlin, a more patriotic spirit began to dominate, in which Romantic cultural nationalism turned political, anti-French, and in parts militarist and chauvinistic. The Christlich-Teutsche Tischgesellschaft (Christian-German Table Society) of 1811–13, which now explicitly excluded Jews and women, is the most representative Romantic circle for this period. After 1815 the Serapionsorden, a circle of artistically minded friends around the multitalented Romantic and Prussian judge E. T. A. Hoffmann, provided a Romantic critique of the philistine political and cultural climate of the restoration period. In distinct ways, these three interrelated circles made Berlin, during this crucial period of transition into modernity, a focal point not only of Romanticism, but of the aesthetic, social and political constellations of the time.

'Free Sociability' in the Romantic Literary Salons of Jewish Women (1790–1806)

The establishment of literary salons, run by educated and culturally sophisticated Jewish women, the wives and daughters of wealthy Jewish businessmen and professionals, is rooted in the specific conditions of late eighteenth-century Berlin. During the reign of Frederick II, Berlin was one of the European cities most tolerant towards Jews; it had no ghetto, Jews had fewer legal and economic restrictions imposed on them, and the enlightened ideals of tolerance, equality and education increasingly informed the cultural climate of the time. Many Jews attained considerable wealth and influence. In addition, Moses Mendelssohn, the popular philosopher and pioneer of the German Haskala, the Jewish enlightenment, who tirelessly worked towards the civil and political emancipation of the Jews, opened up within the Jewish community the desire for emancipation from narrow and restrictive customs and traditions.

Based on the French model and conditional on the existence of a national literature, which for Germany, with Lessing, Goethe, Schiller and the Romantics, was a relatively new phenomenon, these literary salons offered a unique opportunity for women to participate in the literary and intellectual life of their time and provided a limited and clearly framed, but also liberating sphere of social and intellectual experimentation. Literary salons in general were the first social groupings outside the family and the court where women and men could come together in an informal manner, where barriers of class, social standing and religion were less rigid and could be overcome, and where women, in an extension of their traditional role as housewives, could – as hostesses – be the centre of attention. The most innovative part of the intellectual life of Berlin before 1806 was substantially sustained by women such as Henriette Herz and Rahel Levin, who ran the two most famous of these salons, where commoners and noblemen, writers and thinkers, actresses and musicians came together for animated conviviality, intellectual stimulation and networking across social barriers. Established during the Enlightenment, they took on a distinctly Romantic flavour in the 1790s, when a younger generation began to dominate the guest lists and the discussions. The southern German Romantic Jean Paul, visiting Berlin in 1801, characterized their unconventional conviviality as follows: 'Gelehrte, Juden, Offiziere, Geheime Räthe, Edelleute, kurz was sich an anderen Orten ... die Hälse bricht, fället einander um diese, und lebt wenigstens freundlich an Thee- und Esstischen beisammen' ('Scholars, Jews, officers, privy councilors, aristocrats, in brief all those who elsewhere ... are at each other's throats, here hug one another und live together amicably at least around tea and dinner tables').[1]

Henriette Herz created the prototype of the Berlin literary salon. She was the wife of the medical doctor, philosopher and man of science Markus Herz and established her salon as a pendant to her husband's enlightened scientific colloquia. Her literary salon initially focused on the new literature of the *Sturm und Drang* (Storm and Stress) and was also one of the centres of the Berlin Goethe cult. In the 1790s famous Romantics such as Friedrich Schlegel and his brother August Wilhelm, the theologian Friedrich Schleiermacher, the brothers Wilhelm und Alexander von Humboldt and the Idealist philosopher Johann Gottlieb Fichte were among her guests. The salon of Rahel Levin, the most famous Berlin *salonnière* of all, was established in the 1790s and became one of the centres of early Romanticism. The hostess, who later, after marrying the Romantic Varnhagen von Ense, became the prolific writer Rahel Varnhagen von Ense, was the daughter of a wealthy jeweller and the first unmarried woman in Berlin to have her own salon. In her famous 'attic' in Jägerstrasse 54, off the Gendarmenmarkt, she too brought together some of the most illustrious names of German Romanticism, such as the Schlegel and Humboldt brothers, Schleiermacher or Friedrich Gentz, with theatre people, government officials, officers and the nobility. Levin, who re-established her salon after returning to Berlin in 1819 and maintained it throughout late

Romanticism until 1833, later remembered its uniquely free and spirited atmosphere during these early years as an alluring mixture of 'Schönheit, Grazie, Koketterie, Neigung, Liebschaft, Witz, Eleganz, Kordialität' and the 'Drang, Ideen zu entwickeln' ('beauty, grace, coquetry, inclination, flirtation, wit, elegance, cordiality' and the 'urge to develop ideas').[2]

Clearly the atmosphere in the salons was charged not only intellectually, but also erotically, and many Romantic liaisons originated there, for example the controversial marriage between Friedrich Schlegel and Dorothea Veit, one of the daughters of Moses Mendelssohn. Schlegel, the most prominent figurehead of early Romanticism and editor of the movement's Romantic periodical, *Athenaeum* (published in Berlin between May 1798 and August 1800), perhaps best represents the confident claim of the Romantics of being a revolutionary literary and philosophical avant-garde. The early Romantics, who built their group identity in the Berlin salons, were a typical youth movement with a characteristic sense of mission and a delight in provocation. They also wanted to challenge the narrow social conventions of enlightened Prussian society. The couple's highly controversial novels, Schlegel's *Lucinde* (1799) and Veit's *Florentin* (1801), were much more than a literary scandal, as they were intended to make their relationship public and propagate individual freedom, including free love or at least a much freer and more equal relationship between the sexes based on complementarity. To the delight of their authors and other Romantics, they outraged, among others, the figurehead of enlightened Berlin, Friedrich Nicolai, who was a close friend of Dorothea's father, Moses Mendelssohn.

The early Romantics saw themselves as the avant-garde of a rebellious counter-culture, and the salons were in many ways their laboratory of intellectual, emotional and social experimentation and emancipation. The protagonists attempted to establish innovative aesthetic practices of communal creation of thought and literature, which they characterized with the neologisms of 'symphilosophy' and 'sympoesy'. The relationship between the artist as an exceptional subjectivity and the demands and confines of society and convention were a prime concern throughout Romanticism. The Berlin salons were a Romantic project, not least in the way they aimed at a utopian fusion of life and art, in which art as the expression of a self-determined life and the art of living became one.

In typical Romantic fashion, this social practice was complemented and enhanced by theory. Schleiermacher, a frequent visitor to the salons, in 1799 presented his *Versuch einer Theorie des geselligen Betragens* (Toward a Theory of Sociable Conduct), which had the self-proclaimed aim 'to construe social life as a work of art'.[3] It is a heady and idealized theory of the salon as a utopian counter-world, achieving reconciliation between the freedom of the individual and a sense of community which does not limit and restrict but, on the contrary, enhances, enriches and extends true individuality. 'I am to offer my individuality, my character, and I am to assume the character of society. Both . . . should be one and be united in a single operation.'[4] Based on this premise, the Romantic salon is constructed by Schleiermacher as a place

> where the sphere of the individual is present in such a way that it is intersected by the spheres of others as diversely as possible and where one's own outer limits afford one the view into a different and alien world. In this manner, one can come to know all the appearances little by little, and even the most alien persons and relations can grow familiar and become, as it were, neighbours. This task is accomplished by the free association of rational and mutually-cultivating persons.[5]

This is nothing less than a theory of networked inter-subjectivity, which is based on an egalitarian and dialogic understanding of personhood and therefore can negotiate diversity and alterity to mutual benefit. On this basis, sociality is a key ingredient for the development of a rounded individual. With its view that sociality 'addresses nothing less than the entire person',[6] it firmly situates itself in the context of the epoch's belief in rounded education as the best way to achieve societal change and political reform in an evolutionary way, and also as a therapy against the alienation and fragmentation of the modern world, the increasing specialization in intellectual life and the division of labour in bourgeois society. It echoes Fichte's Idealism, Kant's notion of 'Zweckfreiheit' (freedom from purpose) as elucidated in his *Critique of Judgement* (1790) and, in particular, Schiller's *Letters on the Aesthetic Education of Humankind* (1795). While Schleiermacher's theory of 'free sociability' is of course as euphoric as the salons were exclusivist, there can be no doubt that the salons were visionary and utopian not only in atmosphere and spirit, but also in the way in which they practised and pre-empted many elements of the liberal post-1806 Prussian reforms.

The Friedrich-Wilhelms-Universität as Romantic Institution
(1806–10)

The tolerant climate of the cultural life of Berlin changed dramatically and suddenly with the Napoleonic occupation after the battles of Jena and Austerlitz of 14 October 1806. Since the 1795 Peace of Basel between Prussia and France, Prussia had maintained a politically difficult and uneasy neutrality between France and Russia, but had also enjoyed a period of relative calm which allowed the cultural, intellectual and social life of Berlin to flourish. This ended, however, when in 1806 Prussia declared war against France after the victory of the anti-French party in government. Within one week, the proud and once formidable army of Frederick the Great succumbed to the onslaught of Napoleon's military might. The king and his beautiful and popular Königin Luise, the Prussians' queen of hearts and much-adored icon of national resistance, fled to Königsberg, while the population of Berlin anxiously awaited the emperor and his army. On 27 October 1806 Napoleon paraded triumphantly through the recently built Brandenburg Gate, and immediately the harsh realities of the occupation were felt. In the subsequent peace diktat of Tilsit Prussia was reduced almost by half and subjected to crushing reparations and occupation. These conditions formed the political and economic backdrop to the Romantics' turn away from aesthetics and elitism to politics and populist appeal.

Among the political elites, the reaction to defeat and humiliation was a determination to rebuild the spirit of the nation through thorough reform of the outdated and dysfunctional Prussian institutions. The famous liberal Prussian reformers such as State Chancellor von Hardenberg and Minister von und zum Stein were all anti-French, and they pushed through a comprehensive modernization of state and society to instil Prussia with a new sense of confidence and purpose. Within a few years, this 'revolution from above' achieved a set of reforms, including the progressive edict of emancipation for the Jews in 1812.

The reform project most directly informed by a Romantic spirit was the establishment of a university for Berlin, pushed through by the philosopher, linguist and educational reformer Wilhelm von Humboldt, who became minister of education in 1809. The need for a new university was directly linked to military defeat, as Prussia had lost three of its five universities. Within his sixteen months in office he energetically reformed all branches of education, established the German Gymnasium high school and in 1810 founded the Friedrich-Wilhelms-Universität, which since 1949 has borne his name and that of his brother, the explorer, geographer and natural scientist, Alexander von Humboldt. Already in 1807 the king was said to have declared about the university project, 'the state has to replace with intellectual powers what it had lost in physical ones'.[7]

Humboldt defined the university as the place 'in which comes together everything that contributes directly to the moral culture of the nation'.[8] His ideas were largely based on an earlier treatise by Schleiermacher on the subject, *Gelegentliche Gedanken über Universitäten im deutschen Sinn* (Occasional Thoughts on Universities in the German Spirit (1808)), which spelled out how developing the independence of mind of the individual student, pursuing original research and renewing the spirit of a downtrodden country were to work hand in hand. For Schleiermacher, the ultimate aim of university education is 'the learning of learning' ('das Lernen des Lernens'), the acquisition of a 'general overview of the range and interrelatedness' of knowledge,[9] and the 'immediate unity of all cognition'.[10] These programmatic objectives constituted a radical departure from the prevailing utilitarian view of university education as the acquisition of specialized and immediately applicable knowledge and as preparation for a profession or a career. Instead they provided a novel blueprint based on a synthesis of enlightened insistence on self-thinking, Romantic hopes for the unity of science and encyclopedic comprehensiveness and idealist aspirations to educate the whole person. The famous Humboldtian principles derived from these foundations, academic freedom of enquiry and the unity of teaching and research, became an enormously influential model which informed most university systems across continental Europe for almost 200 years.

The importance of this new educational institution for the state and the nation was aptly expressed by the prestigious building it was given and where it still is: the Prince Heinrich Palace, part of the Forum Fredericianum opposite the opera house at the top of Unter den Linden. Its first elected rector was the idealist philosopher Johann Gottlieb Fichte, and the professors appointed were the leading intellectuals of their time: Fichte in philosophy, Schleiermacher in theology, Karl von Savigny in law and Christoph Wilhelm Hufeland and Johann Christian Reil in medicine, to name just those particularly close to the Romantics. It is no exaggeration to say that the new university in Berlin was, in terms of its conceptual foundations, its spirit and its personnel, a Romantic institution. Two leading Berlin Romantics, Achim von Arnim and Clemens Brentano, wrote festive cantatas to mark its opening, and in its momentous first year, Schleiermacher developed his thoughts on hermeneutics, which were to become the foundation of this most influential theory of interpretation.

Cultural and Political Nationalism around the Christlich-Teutsche Tischgesellschaft (1806–13)

The most important field of activity for the Berlin Romantics during these years was their involvement in turning cultural nationalism into a tool for mobilizing national sentiment for armed resistance against the French. A distinct sense of German identity did not exist at the end of the eighteenth century, but it was invented by the Romantics as a response to Napoleonic domination and oppression. In the absence of political sovereignty and national unity, the project of creating a sense of German identity, of belonging together with a common purpose, was realized first and foremost in the sphere of culture. Drawing on Johann Gottfried Herder's concept of the distinctiveness of all cultures, and his insistence that they have to be appreciated on the basis of the specific forces that shaped them, the Romantics sought to establish, highlight and celebrate unifying factors such as a common language, a common culture and a shared history and tradition.

This construction of shared cultural memory included the idealization of the Middle Ages instead of antiquity as a period of distinct German greatness and influence, with the revival of the gothic style in the visual arts and architecture. Another important element of the invention of tradition was the turn to *Volkspoesie*, the literary heritage of the common people. In sharp contrast to the aesthetic elitism of early Romanticism, the search for the authenticity and uniqueness of German culture aimed to draw on the tastes and resources of the common people, fuse them with an advanced Romantic aesthetic and appeal to as broad a public as possible.

The most famous of these Romantic projects and the one with worldwide influence until today is of course the collection of the *Kinder- und Hausmärchen* (Children's and Household Fairy Tales) by the brothers Grimm in 1812, but even more popular and influential at the time was the collection of folk songs and poetry *Des Knaben Wunderhorn* (The Boy's Magic Horn) that Achim von Arnim and Clemens Brentano assembled in three volumes in 1805 and 1808. Like the Grimm fairy tales, these collections were purportedly largely drawn from the oral traditions of the common people and preserved for posterity in written culture by their Romantic collectors. In reality, they were primarily from literary sources and the redacting influence of the editors was enormous, but this recourse to the oral tradition strengthened the claim that they provided a connection to the roots of 'genuine' Germanness. *Wunderhorn* literally means 'cornucopia', the magic vessel that never ceases giving. It suggests literature and culture as infinite sources of nourishment for the German soul and as an inexhaustible reservoir of national strength. Until 1806 Heidelberg was the centre of this Romantic cultural nationalism, but the protagonists gradually moved to Berlin and made it the place where, under the pressurized conditions of the occupation, cultural nationalism quickly turned political, ideological and decidedly anti-French.

This shift can be traced through the Berlin of these years in various ways. August Wilhelm Schlegel's highly acclaimed public lectures on *Schöne Literatur und Kunst* (Fine Literature and Art) in 1801 and 1804 advanced a typically romantic, self-reflective synthesis of theoretical and historical perspectives on art. At the same time, they laid the foundations of a future German national philology in presenting the integrative sum of German cultural achievements as 'Deutschheit', as distinctly and specifically German. However, in a spirit of intercultural openness that again echoes

Herder, Schlegel insisted that one of the German characteristics was cosmopolitanism, which made Germans uniquely able to empathize with and therefore respect other cultures.

A few years later in 1807–8, Johann Gottlieb Fichte's public *Addresses to the German Nation* took a decidedly less tolerant and open view. Even more so than Schlegel's, they were important public events with great resonance in cultural and political life. They represent the most influential intellectual contribution to the shift from cultural to political nationalism and have been described as 'the foundational text of modern nationalism'.[11] Fichte lent all the authority of his rhetoric and his heavy-duty idealistic philosophy to an ultimately essentialist and supremacist definition of Germanness, which understood national identity not, like Herder, as a set of historically and culturally acquired characteristics, but as an ethical and almost metaphysical quality. Fichte saw the nation as a community across time and history, rooted in a common past, connected by a common language and morally obliged to embrace transgenerational solidarity and commitment. Furthermore he postulated the identity of nation, language and state, a figure of thought that in the course of the nineteenth and twentieth centuries became the blueprint for ethnic nationalism all over Europe. Like Schleiermacher and von Humboldt, he saw education as the pathway to a strong sense of national identity and the necessary strengthening of resolve for this civilizing mission, and many of his addresses are devoted to a plan for educating the German people in the new spirit and preparing them for action. However, with Fichte, the project of emancipation from French oppression for the whole of Germany, with the formation of a strong, unified nation state and political and cultural dominance in Europe, had taken on a distinctly supremacist and xenophobic edge. In the subsequent development of Romantic nationalism, a dualism of national 'essences' was constructed that declared the fight against the French as a clash of civilizations. This radical 'othering' would poison Germany's relationship with France and dominate politics and culture in the heart of Europe for 150 years.

The social equivalent to Fichte's nationalistic philosophy was the Christlich-Teutsche Tischgesellschaft, a conservative dining club founded by Achim von Arnim at the beginning of 1811. It existed until 1813, when the club's kitty was donated to equip a volunteer in the Prussian cavalry. In this grouping, leading figures of Berlin Romanticism such as Brentano, Fichte, Savigny, Schleiermacher, Heinrich von Kleist, the reactionary political philosopher Adam Müller, the composer Zelter, the architect Schinkel and the highly popular author Baron de la Motte Fouqué mixed with prominent members of the Prussian nobility and military. Nothing exemplifies their new spirit of intolerance better than the statutes of the club, which explicitly and provocatively excluded women, Jews, Frenchmen and 'philistines' from membership. Philistines, narrow-minded, materialistic and intolerant bourgeois, had been the Romantics' favourite enemy and target for relentless caricature throughout. In now excluding most of the social groups that had made the earlier Romantic salons such vibrant and exciting places, the members of the Christian-German Dining Club turned rather philistine themselves. They presented a radical and bigoted counter-model to the inspirational gatherings of Romantics around Jewish women which most of its members had frequented earlier and, in part, continued to visit.

In highly polemic after-dinner speeches and pamphlets, such as *Der Philister vor in und nach der Geschichte* (The Philistine before, in and after History) and *Über die Kennzeichen des Judentums* (On the Characteristics of Jewry), which were meant to be humorous and satirical, but were in fact deeply offensive and divisive, Brentano and Arnim used their biting wit to revive and propagate centuries-old, ugly anti-Semitic stereotypes, which in turn also featured in some of their literary works. In part, these anti-Semitic sentiments have to be seen as an ingredient of the wider resistance of this conservative group to the new liberal political spirit. As an impoverished Prussian Junker, Arnim was, like most of his class, highly indebted to Jewish financiers and felt threatened by the agrarian and tax reforms of the Prussian reformers. Many members of the dining club opposed the edict on the emancipation of the Jews, fearing increased Jewish influence in the economy and public life. Adam Müller wrote in Heinrich von Kleist's *Berliner Abendblätter* against the Prussian reforms and the liberal spirit of the new university, demanding a more politically applied nationalistic curriculum.

The ambitious and short-lived *Berliner Abendblätter*, published daily between October 1810 and March 1811, are a good example of the ambiguities and contradictions of the Romantic projects during this period. In journalistic terms, the publication was highly innovative in that it was the first daily in Berlin and, by including summaries of police reports, had a focus on crime aimed to entice a broader readership in a manner not dissimilar to today's tabloids. Overall, it was part of the Romantic drive to influence public thinking via more applied literary forms. At the same time it also contained some of Kleist's most intricate, aesthetically radical and challenging novellas and essays such as 'Die heilige Cäcilie' (Saint Cecilia) or 'Über das Marionettentheater' (On the Puppet Theatre), thus staying true to the experimental and somewhat elitist orientations of the movement. Because of censorship, the *Berliner Abendblätter* could not be openly political and presented themselves as a literary and philosophical journal, yet they nevertheless became a mouthpiece for the archconservative Adam Müller and alienated the Prussian reformers.

As a member of the Prussian nobility, Kleist saw the Prussian capital and residence of his king as something of an anchor place in his restless life. When he returned to Berlin in early 1810 he had high hopes that he would be able to contribute to the nationalist cause and find public acclaim. Yet his patriotic drama *Prinz Friedrich von Homburg*, which he had completed that year, was too ambivalent for Prussian tastes. On one level, it is a homage to Queen Luise, a celebration of Prussian militarism and an attempt to reconcile military discipline and obedience with the enlightened and idealist notion of free will. Yet his portrayal of the somnambulist protagonist, who brings military triumph by defying orders and then is terrified to face the consequences, in a typically Kleistian (and indeed Romantic) fashion undermined aesthetically and psychologically what it propagated politically. Before coming to Berlin, Kleist had written the propagandistic play *Die Hermansschlacht* (The Battle of Hermann (1808)), in which he revived the Germanic foundational myth of Arminius and his heroic resistance against foreign Roman occupation as his contribution to inciting a public uprising against the French. It was not printed during his lifetime, but is a deeply problematic text, dripping with bloodthirstiness and hatred of the French, and was, in later periods of German history, instrumentalized as a call to total war. The same applies to the most controversial and arguably most influential of all Kleist's texts, his ode 'Germania an ihre Kinder' (Germania to Her Children), which contains the lines:

> Wachst du auf, Germania?
> Ist der Tag der Rache da?
> . . .
> Dämmt den Rhein mit ihren Leichen,
> Laßt gestaut durch ihr Gebein,
> Schäumend um die Pfalz ihn weichen,
> Und ihn dann die Grenze sein.[12]
> (Are you rising, Germany?,
> Is the day of vengeance here?
> With their corpses dam the Rhine,
> Fill its foaming waters with their bones.
> Divert its stream around the Pfalz,
> And then let it be the border!)

Such obsessed incitement to hatred today seems shocking and also very much at odds with the conventional view of Romanticism, yet it represents the spirit of a particularly heated historical moment. Arnim, Ernst Moritz Arndt and Theodor Körner, the celebrated nationalist poet who joined the famous Lützow Free Corps and died in battle, penned similarly vicious verses of war propaganda that relied, as the genre always does, on a fiercely reductive and brutally simplistic othering of the enemy. It fed into a *Zeitgeist* during which Prussia, under the suspicious eyes of the French, organized a militia for the war against Napoleon and prepared the minds, hearts and bodies of its citizens for war.

Another important facet of this was the gymnast's movement of Turnvater Jahn, a deeply nationalistic activist who coined the term 'Volksthum', which went on to have a fateful career in essentializing ethnicist concepts of national identity. His gymnasts' association was a paramilitary organization under the guise of sport, and the opening of the first gymnast's field on the Hasenheide (Hares' Heath) in the spring of 1811 was arguably as significant an event for the mobilization of Prussian fighting power as the opening of the university half a year before. After the defeat of Napoleon's *grande armée* in Russia, Prussia at the beginning of 1813 changed sides, and only 30,000 men, around 12.5 per cent of the army, were volunteers. Of those, 6,500 came from Berlin, and the proportion of students, academics and artisans among their free corps was particularly high. The military contribution of the free corps to the liberation of Berlin in March 1813 and to the decisive Battle of the People in Leipzig in October 1813 might have been small, but the sentiment – or myth – that the determination of the people as a whole drove the enemy from their own territory so that they could live free and self-determined lives, created enormous momentum. How important the contribution of Romanticism to the development of political nationalism and a German national identity really was can perhaps best be illustrated with the words of a Prussian general. When the king, sceptical as to the revolutionary potential of a people's army, dismissed suggestions of a popular insurrection as 'fit for poetry', Gneisenau replied: 'Religion, prayer, love of the ruler, of the fatherland, of virtue: all that is nothing but poetry. But there is no enthusiasm without a poetic disposition. If we act only from cold calculation, we become rigid egoists. The security of the throne is founded on poetry.'[13]

E. T. A. Hoffmann and the Uncanny Side of Berlin

A very different Romantic circle to the ones discussed so far constituted itself around E. T. A. Hoffmann after he arrived in Berlin in the autumn of 1814 and settled first in the Französische Straße and then in the Taubenstraße. Hoffmann kept a distance from the social circles of official Berlin, which on occasion he ridiculed mercilessly in his writings, and instead preferred the wine taverns around the Gendarmenmarkt square. Especially in his favourite haunt, Lutter & Wegner, he brought together old friends to recreate and revive the informal and inspiring conviviality of earlier Romantic groupings, among them Ludwig Tieck; Fouqué; Adelbert von Chamisso, the exiled French aristocrat and author of *Peter Schlemihls wundersame Geschichte* (Peter Schlemihl's Wondrous Story (1814)); Hoffmann's long-time friend Eduard Hitzig; the writer Carl Wilhelm Contessa; and the controversial Romantic doctor, personal physician of State Chancellor von Hardenberg and mesmerist, David Ferdinand Koreff.

In October 1814 Hoffmann founded with his friends the 'Seraphinenorden' and in November 1818 the order of the Serapion-brethren, named after the poetological patron saint of the group. Out of this circle emerged the most important testimony to this experimental late phase of Berlin Romanticism, Hoffmann's four-volume collection of novellas, *Die Serapions-Brüder* (The Serapion-Brethren (1819–21)). Its framing narrative is similar to that of earlier collections that also owe their existence to Berlin Romantic sociability, such as Arnim's *Der Wintergarten* (The Conservatory (1809)), the framing narrative of which is situated in a country house in the Tiergarten, and also Ludwig Tieck's *Phantasus* (1812–16). But, in this case the link between life and literature is particularly close, as the five fictitious friends, who in the framing narrative in a typically Romantic self-reflexive manner discuss the aesthetic merits or demerits of each tale, can be identified directly with Hoffmann's associates.

In many ways Hoffmann can be described as the archetypal Romantic artist. The opposition between internal and external worlds, between the rich inner realm of fantasy and prosaic outer reality, between the perilous existence of the artist as a fragile and endangered subjectivity and the orderly and narrow world of middle class respectability, is his dominant theme. His own biography also reflects a similar 'chronic dualism', to use one of Hoffmann's favourite phrases. On the one hand we have the disciplined, hard-working and highly efficient Prussian civil servant and judge, who in his later career is a courageous defender of civil liberties. On the other, we have the multi-talented Romantic, the highly sought after author and contributor to year-books and almanacs, the sketch artist who humorously exposes the spleens of his contemporaries in his drawings and the composer who came to Berlin not least with the ambition that he could establish his opera *Undine*, based on a libretto by his friend Fouqué, as the ultimate Romantic synthesis of text and music. The opera was indeed premiered in 1816 in the national theatre at the Gendarmenmarkt, but failed to convince, and Hoffmann instead excelled with his writings, becoming one of the most popular authors of his time.

The city of Berlin provides the backdrop for many of Hoffmann's tales. Moreover, his Serapiontic poetology of 'inneres Schauen' (inner vision'), the ability to transcend, through imagination, the everyday in order to achieve inner depths and subjective authenticity without losing contact with reality, penetrates the topography of the cityscape to provide his readers with an unsettling glimpse into the dark side of bourgeois identity, the deep Romantic 'dissatisfaction with normality',[14] and the position of artists, minorities and other outsiders as endangered and liminal subjectivities. One of the poetological musings among the Serapion-brethren pinpoints precisely the importance of anchoring Romantic flights of the imagination in the lived reality of the contemporary city. They discuss the advantage of 'laying the scene of your story in Berlin', and 'of giving the names of streets, squares etc.': 'It not only gives an element of historical truth which helps a sluggish fancy', but 'the story gains greatly in life and vigour', especially for those who know the city.[15] Walter Benjamin, in a radio feature called 'Demonic Berlin', went so far as to describe Hoffmann as 'the physiognomist of Berlin' and 'the father of the Berlin novel'.[16]

Hoffmann's very first published literary work, *Ritter Gluck: Eine Erinnerung aus dem Jahre 1809* (Knight Gluck: A Memory from the Year 1809), opens with the first person narrator observing a tableau of a lively Sunday afternoon in the centre of the city:

> eine lange Reihe, buntgemischt – Elegants, Bürger mit der Hausfrau und den lieben Kleinen in Sonntagskleidern, Geistliche, Jüdinnen, Referendare, Freudenmädchen, Professoren, Putzmacherinnen, Tänzer, Offiziere usw. durch die Linden, nach dem Tiergarten ziehen. Bald sind alle Plätze bei Klaus und Weber besetzt; der Mohrrüben-Kaffee dampft, die Elegants zünden ihre Zigaros an, man spricht, man streitet über Krieg und Frieden usw.[17]
>
> (a long, motley row – men-about-town, citizens with their wives and their dear little ones in Sunday clothes, clergy, Jewesses, articled clerks, prostitutes, professors, milliners, dancers, officers and so on moving through the Linden toward the Tiergarten. Soon all places at Klaus and Weber are occupied; the carrot coffee is steaming, the men-about-town light their cigars, there's conversation, argument about war and peace and so on.)

Against this backdrop of humming contemporary life, a story unfolds of the artist as outsider, embodying a critique of society. The narrator meets a mysterious composer who finds it difficult to relate to his time and the society he lives in and instead is caught up in a solipsistic realm of musical inspiration and madness, gripped by the *idée fixe* that he is the eighteenth-century composer Christoph Willibald Gluck, who reformed opera and gave it a hitherto unknown complexity and depth. The fundamental ambiguity around the identity of this uncanny stranger prefigures one of the central themes of Hoffmann's entire *oeuvre*, which made him an early master of the fantastic in Todorov's terms: is he a madman, thus highlighting the closeness between artistic ingenuity and mental endangerment, or is he a ghostly revenant of the composer, thus opening the idyllic Berlin scene towards the realm of the uncanny and supernatural? The first reading would highlight the dangers of artistic obsession, whereas the second would make the stranger into an allegorical representation of a more profound and sincere musical genius of earlier times, haunting the shallow bourgeois entertainment culture. The unresolved ambiguity of the tale demonstrates that these dimensions are inseparable.

Similarly, the story *Das öde Haus* (The Abandoned House (1817)) revolves around a seemingly abandoned and dilapidated haunted house on Unter den Linden, which starkly stands out against the splendour of the street with all its new and shiny city residences and palaces. With his 'sixth sense' the young Romantic enthusiast Theodor is curiously attracted to the house and yearns to uncover the dark secret that seems to be hidden in the middle of the buzzing capital. 'Sixth sense' here operates as a cypher both for poetic inspiration and a higher form of sensibility that seeks to reach beyond the surface of people's bourgeois roles to access their hidden motives and desires. Berlin at the time was particularly fascinated with phenomena that allowed such a glimpse into the subconscious like somnambulism, spiritism or mesmerism, an early form of hypnosis and a branch of Romantic medicine practised by the Serapion-brother and star physician Koreff.

As Theodor is drawn into a web of mesmeric manipulation which leads him to the brink of madness himself, he visits Koreff's fictitious twin brother 'Doktor K., berühmt durch seine Behandlung und Heilung der Wahnsinnigen, durch sein tieferes Eingehen in das psychische Prinzip' ('Dr K., famous for treating and curing the insane and for his deeper engagement with psychological phenomena').[18] The secret of the house revolves around a vengeful old woman with strong mesmeric powers who was driven into madness by a lover's betrayal and plotted with a gypsy sorceress to engineer her revenge. The uncanny house, then, is a symbol for the ugly and unsettling power dynamics that lie hidden behind the splendid facades of respectability. Theodor's insistence upon uncovering those dynamics presents a critique of the shallow rationalistic and prosaic spirit of a modern age that refuses to acknowledge their influence. In pre-modern times they found expression in the belief in magic and the supernatural, which explains Hoffmann's fondness for this realm as a literary device; later, in advanced modernity, they would find their discursive home in psychoanalysis, of which Hoffmann's writings are acknowledged as important precursors.

Die Brautwahl (The Choice of a Bride (1819)) is explicitly called 'a Berlinese tale' and features many Berlin landmarks with which the contemporary reading public would be familiar. It presents a more satirical perspective on the shallow materialism of a society obsessed with rank, title and status, in which neither love nor artistic inspiration can flourish, and needing the assistance of the supernatural in order to attain some degree of happiness. In this contemporary fairy tale, only the magical interventions of an alchemist revenant from sixteenth-century Berlin can stop the pedantic bureaucrat, bookworm and Clerk of the Privy Chancery Tusmann from pursuing his planned marriage with the young and beautiful Albertine Vosswinkel, the daughter of an old school-friend. Albertine becomes the love interest of three parties: Tusmann, the young painter Edmund Lehsen, and the rich but greedy and repulsive Jewish Baron Benjamin Dümmerl, the portrayal of whom shows Hoffmann not to be immune to the anti-Semitic stereotypes of his time. Albertine's father is only interested in wealth and status and refuses to allow the marriage with the charming and talented artist – until he discovers that Edmund is heir to a substantial fortune.

In order to prevent a catastrophe that would ruin everybody's reputation, the alchemist Leonhard designs a ritual in which the three wooers have to choose one of three magic boxes. They contain what each of them most desires: further riches, acquired in a not entirely honest way for the Jew, and a book out of which any book he can think of pops up for Tusmann. This gift for the voracious reader and polyhistor realizes – and ridicules – in comic form one of the daring utopian projects of early Romanticism: to create the absolute book, an all-encompassing encyclopaedia which comprises the totality and unity of all knowledge. Edmund could get his beloved bride, but he chooses to go to Italy instead in pursuit of artistic perfection like his great role model Sternbald from Ludwig Tieck's Romantic artist's novel *Franz Sternbald's Wanderungen* (Franz Sternbald's Wanderings (1798)). There, he quickly forgets his Berlin bride; Albertine, however, finds a promising and handsome civil servant instead. The message is clear: modern Berlin is not a place where true artistic talent can flourish, and it needs miracles in order to be saved from itself.

The most famous Berlin story by Hoffmann is also the last literary work he published, shortly before his death: *Des Vetters Eckfenster* (My Cousin's Corner Window) of 1822. Here, two cousins observe a busy market morning on the Gendarmenmarkt from the superior vantage point of a window high up above the hustle and bustle beneath them, fixing upon particular scenes and characters within the crowd. One of the two, the Gendarmenmarkt resident, is a writer, now wheelchair-bound and close to the end of his life. In surveying the 'most varied scene of town life',[19] he invites his visiting cousin to cultivate the inspired and penetrating mode of observation of the artist in order to develop 'the art of seeing'.[20] Observing a motley group of interesting characters from all social strata and walks of life – with a noticeable voyeuristic preference for oddballs and attractive young women – the cousins read their appearances, their dress codes and their behaviours physiognomically, in search of a character and his or her particular life story. As they do not know these people, they have to invent narratives around them, fantasizing about their fate and constructing in some cases competing stories around the market women and housewives, elegant ladies and servants, actresses and students, retired military men and farming families. In other words, the superior, but also isolated vantage point of the artistic imagination problematizes and multiplies the identities of the real life persons and gives the societal portrait of contemporary city life an iridescent and unsettling complexity and ambiguity.

In this story there is, however, no hint of the dangerous and uncontrollable powers of the unconscious or of the supernatural. Instead, in a rare explicit reference to politics in Hoffmann's work, the two cousins reflect on how the traumatic experience of the French occupation has left a positive legacy, in that the people had come to a new appreciation of their distinct identity as Berliners, and how as a result, behaviour in society overall has become more relaxed and more refined. As the cousin of the narrator observes: 'The Berlin populace has undergone a remarkable change since that unfortunate period when an insolent and overbearing enemy inundated our country and laboured in vain to suppress the popular spirit, which soon rebounded with new strength.'[21]

Some commentators read this tale as Hoffmann's late shift to Realism, marking the historical closure of Berlin Romanticism. Against that we must note that the Romantic obsession with auto-poetological reflection is still at its core, as it is all about the isolated position of the writer towards the city, allowing him privileged insight. But the ground in this respect is shifting too, and the tale leaves a strikingly modern legacy. Only one of the scenes that the two cousins discuss is not a product of their imagination: the writer tells his cousin of an earlier encounter with a flower girl on the market, whom he found reading one of his books. Flattered, he revealed himself as the author but was met with utter incomprehension, as 'she had no idea that such things as writers or authors existed' and in return 'asked frankly and naively whether I made all Mr Kralowski's books?'[22] Kralowski was a well-known Berlin lending library for entertainment literature, and this statement is much more than merely a blow to the author's vanity. It signals, as Detlef Kremer has convincingly shown, the dawning of a new era in which the Romantic cult of genius and the illusion of authorial autonomy will be replaced by the realization that literature and culture have become commodities and that the writer sells his wares on the marketplace of public taste in just the same way as the Berlin flower-girls.[23]

NOTES

1. Letter from Jean Paul Friedrich Richter to Karoline Herder, 12 January 1801, in Jean Paul, *Sämtliche Werke: Historisch-kritische Ausgabe,* 3, vol. 4, *Briefe 1800–1804,* ed. Eduard Berend (Berlin, Weimar: Böhlau, 1960), p. 41. All translations, unless otherwise noted, are by the author.

2. Letter from Rahel Varnhagen von Ense to Karl Gustav von Brinckmann, 30 November 1819, in Rahel Varnhagen von Ense, *Gesammelte Werke,* ed. Konrad Feilchenfeldt, Uwe Schweikert, and Rahel E. Steiner, vol. 2.2 (Munich: Matthes & Seitz 1983), pp. 609f.

3. Friedrich Schleiermacher, 'Toward a Theory of Sociable Conduct', *Friedrich Schleiermacher's 'Toward a Theory of Sociable Conduct' and Essays on its Intellectual-cultural Context,* ed. Ruth D. Richards (Lewiston, Queenstown, Lampeter: Mellen, 1995), pp. 20–39 (p. 22).

4. Ibid., p. 28.

5. Ibid., pp. 20f.

6. Ibid., p. 26.

7. Max Lenz, *Geschichte der Königlichen Friedrich-Wilhelms Universität zu Berlin,* vol. 1, *Gründung und Ausbau* (Halle an der Saale: Verlag der Buchhandlung des Waisenhauses, 1910), p. 78.

8. Wilhelm von Humboldt, 'Über die innere und äußere Organisation der höheren wissenschaftlichen Anstalten in Berlin', in *Werke in fünf Bänden,* vol. 4, *Schriften zur Politik und zum Bildungswesen,* eds Andreas Flitner and Klaus Giel (Darmstadt: Wissenschaftliche Buchgesellschaft, 1993), p. 255.

9. Friedrich Schleiermacher, 'Gelegentliche Gedanken über Universitäten im deutschen Sinn', in *Fichte, Schleiermacher, Steffens über das Wesen der Universität,* ed. Eduard Spranger (Leipzig: Verlag der Dürrschen Buchhandlung, 1910), pp. 105–203 (p. 127).

10. Ibid., p. 129.

11. Joep Leerssen, *National Thought in Europe: A Cultural History* (Amsterdam: Amsterdam University Press, 2006), p. 112.

12. Heinrich von Kleist, 'Germania an ihre Kinder', p. 4. Fassung, in *Sämtliche Werke und Briefe,* vol. 1, ed. Helmut Sembdner (Frankfurt am Main: Insel, 1978), pp. 713, 715.

13. Fritz Lange (ed.), *Neidhardt von Gneisenau: Schriften von und über Gneisenau* (Berlin: Rütten & Loening, 1954), p. 260.

14. See Lothar Pikulik, *Romantik als Ungenügen an der Normalität* (Frankfurt am Main: Suhrkamp, 1979).

15. E. T. W. (sic) Hoffmann, 'A Fragment from the Life of Three Friends', in *The Serapion Brethren,* vol. 2, trans. Alex Ewing (London: George Bell and Sons, 1892), pp. 151f.

16. Walter Benjamin, 'Demonic Berlin', in *Radio Benjamin,* ed. Lecia Rosenthal (London, New York: Verso, 2014), p. 27.

17. E. T. A. Hoffmann, 'Ritter Gluck', in *Fantasie- und Nachtstücke,* ed. Walter Müller-Seidel (Munich: Winkler, 1976), p. 14.

18. Hoffmann, 'Das öde Haus', in *Fantasie- und Nachtstücke,* p. 474.

19. E. T. A. Hoffmann, 'The Cousin's Corner Window', in *The Golden Pot and other Stories,* trans. Ritchie Robertson (Oxford: Oxford University Press, 1992), p. 380.

20. Ibid.
21. Ibid., p. 399.
22. Ibid., pp. 388f.
23. Detlef Kremer, 'Des Vetters Eckfenster', in *E. T. A. Hoffmann: Leben – Werk – Wirkung*, ed. Detlef Kremer (Berlin: de Gruyter, 2009), pp. 394–406 (pp. 405f).

3

JOHN B. LYON[1]

Literary Realism and Naturalism

During the nineteenth century, Berlin grew from a provincial city into a modern industrial metropolis. Two very significant literary movements, Realism and Naturalism, emerged at this time, and while both responded to changes in the city, their emphasis, focus and intensity varied dramatically. Both claimed that their art was mimetic, that is, that their literary works imitated reality. Yet with contrasting philosophical, political and aesthetic approaches, these movements agreed neither on the nature of reality nor on how to represent it. While the first highlighted a hidden reality with elaborate and symbolic prose, the second focused on the detailed grain and neglected margins of external reality with near-photographic precision. It was as if they used two mirrors, one concave, the other convex, to reflect the same object, Berlin. Their contrasting modes of reflection mirror two different Berlins during the same era.

Growing Pains

In 1805, Berlin was the sixth largest city in Europe,[2] but it retained a decidedly provincial, even feudalistic character. On one hand it was the residence of the Prussian monarchy; on the other, there were farms and fields within the city walls, and some farmers still kept livestock in the city, herding the animals through the city streets. Over the ensuing century, Berlin attracted large-scale industry and a growing unskilled proletariat, transforming both the size and character of the city into a modern metropolis. It grew at more than double the rate of its European counterparts and most intensely between 1850 and 1900. In 1800 the city had just over 172,000 inhabitants; by 1850 this had more than doubled to over 418,000; in the late 1870s, the population passed the milestone of one million; and by 1900 there were almost 1.9 million residents. Immigration was a primary driver: by 1864, 50.4 per cent of the Berlin population had not been born in the city, and by 1895 that number increased to 58 per cent.[3] For the latter half of the nineteenth century, Berlin was a city of immigrants.

Modern industry both attracted immigrants and determined where they lived. Beginning in the 1840s, the city differentiated itself into three major regions that were associated with specific economic functions: factories and industrial centres on the northern outskirts of the city, business and service industries in the city centre, and textile and clothing industries in the southern parts. The population resided predominantly in the southern, the southeastern and, to some extent, the northern outlying suburbs.[4] Such functional differentiation of work and living space reflected a departure from a pre-modern, pre-industrial world, where workplace and residence had belonged together.

As the population expanded, so too did the geographical footprint of the city: previously rural and peripheral towns were incorporated into the metropolis, first in 1861 and again in 1920 as the city limits were redrawn. The population in these areas, demarcating Berlin's police district, increased by more than sixty-seven times in the course of the nineteenth century. And the rapidly growing population also spawned a rash of real estate speculation. Investors, aiming to reap quick rewards, bought properties in Berlin without plans to develop them. Properties would change hands frequently before being developed. This produced two notable outcomes. The first was the infamous Berliner *Mietskaserne* (rental barracks, comparable to tenements in the USA and the UK), where, in order to recoup the initial financial investment, a developer would pack as many apartments as possible into a single building. Upper and lower classes were thrown together in apartment buildings where many rooms lacked adequate light, air and space. The *Mietskaserne* became the iconic symbol for urban modernity and its woes. The second product of unsustainable real estate speculation was a recession, a financial crash. The *Gründerkrach* (Founders' Crash) of 1873 affected stock markets around the world and burst the housing bubble in Berlin, leaving the city with multiple *Krachruinen* (ruins of the crash) – unfinished buildings abandoned by their bankrupt owners.

Whereas Berlin at the beginning of the nineteenth century was divided along feudal lines of social groups or estates (*Stände*) such as aristocracy, citizens and farmers, by the end of the nineteenth century the rising industrial middle class challenged the aristocracy for pre-eminence and found itself in conflict with the burgeoning proletariat. Society, economy and politics were reorganized less around social *Stände* and more around class. In 1849 a three-class voting system was introduced, which disenfranchised the lowest class by dividing the voting populace into groups according to the amount of taxes they paid. Those paying the most taxes had the largest proportion of votes. The growing politically disenfranchised proletariat fostered the rise of socialism in Germany. In 1875, the Socialist Workers' Party of Germany

(Sozialistische Arbeiterpartei Deutschlands) was formed from a merger of two workers' parties. Otto von Bismarck, Chancellor of Germany after its unification in 1871, perceived socialism as a threat to the landed aristocracy, who still held political sway in Prussia, and he outlawed the Socialist Party in 1878.

In short, Berlin's identity as a city was changing through competition between the aristocracy, the bourgeoisie and the proletariat, through clashes between older and newer ways of living and working, and through a rapid shift from a feudalistic to a capitalistic economic and social order.

Realism

German Realism, also labelled Bourgeois or Poetic Realism, reflected these tensions and conflicts in Berlin. On a symbolic level, Berlin embodied the confluence of multiple features of modernity: urbanization, industrial capitalism, class conflict and a mobile populace. On a material level, it provided a context for writers' own experiences of modernity and a setting for many of their works. Many Realist authors, even those associated with other regions in the German-speaking world, drew on their experiences in Berlin for inspiration. These authors included Theodor Fontane, Wilhelm Raabe, Gottfried Keller, Gustav Freytag, Theodor Storm, Karl Gutzkow, Julian Schmidt, Friedrich Spielhagen, Paul Heyse, Felix Dahn and Georg Ebers. Berlin was home to the literary group 'Tunnel über der Spree' (Tunnel over the Spree), to which Fontane, Storm, Heyse and others belonged.

Historical convention maps the starting and ending points of this epoch onto political events: the failed Revolution of 1848 and the year of Bismarck's resignation as Chancellor, 1890, respectively. Yet, since Realists such as Adalbert Stifter and Karl Gutzkow published before this forty-two-year span, and Fontane and Raabe wrote after it, it is more accurate to situate German Realism in relation to cultural epochs and contemporary authors. It followed Romanticism and preceded Modernism, and its authors were contemporary with European Realists such as George Eliot, Charles Dickens, Honoré de Balzac, Gustave Flaubert, Leo Tolstoy and Fyodor Dostoevsky.

The term 'Realism' can be misleading, as it suggests an unfiltered, mimetic representation of the world. Yet German Realism was far from this, as its modifying adjectives suggest: its view was mediated by aesthetic ('poetic') and political ('bourgeois') ideals. Realist authors represent bourgeois norms and values during a time of rapid social and economic transformation; some portray these values as timeless, others show how such values are changing with the onset of urban modernity. Realists thus used poetic means to represent the dominant bourgeois ideology in the years before 1900.

In particular, Realism attempted to bring together the seemingly incongruous philosophical traditions of idealism and materialism. For example, Julian Schmidt, editor of the journal *Die Grenzboten* (The Border Envoys), fused spiritualistic motifs with materialistic means.[5] Schmidt distinguishes Realism from earlier epochs by arguing: 'The belief of the past era was that the ideal was the enemy of reality and would suspend it; our belief, in contrast, is that the idea realizes itself in reality and we hold this belief as the principle of the future.'[6] Realists thus embraced a unique blend of materialism and idealism.

Realists distanced themselves from 'coarse reality',[7] and thus eschewed Naturalism and other attempts to imitate reality with photographic accuracy. Rather than strive for impartial objectivity, Realists asserted a practice that was deliberately representational – that is, they presented a world that did not correspond perfectly to that of their readers. Fontane asserted that Realism is fundamentally *interested*, that it represents a biased position or 'Interessenvertretung'.[8] He described this as 'Läuterung' (refinement),[9] and Julian Schmidt justifies a similar practice in his well-known dictum: 'Truth cannot be represented by one who does not know reality, nor by one who is its slave.'[10] This notion of Realism frames the author as one who perceives reality clearly, refines or transfigures it so as to identify its true essence and then conveys that essence in poetic form. The Realist perceives the ideal and lets it shine through.

The means by which Realist writers conveyed such a view of reality differed from those of past epochs: their techniques were more spatial than dynamic. That is, plot often became secondary to setting, context, milieu, character and historical circumstance. Commenting on new novelistic techniques, Karl Gutzkow writes in his novel, *Die Ritter von Geiste* (Knights of the Spirit (1850/1)): 'The novel of the past ... represented the *succession* of artistically intertwined events.'[11] But Realist novels are different:

> the new novel is the novel of simultaneity. The whole world lies there! Kings and beggars meet there! ... No segment of life any more, but the complete, round, full circle lies before us; the poet builds a world or at least contrasts his illumination to that of reality. He looks down from the perspective of an eagle hovering in the air and has a *worldview*, new, peculiar. Unfortunately it is a polemic one.[12]

For Gutzkow, the Realist novel should give a bird's-eye perspective on the 'truth' of reality. But that view is more subjective than objective. While Realist novels subsume plot to the highlighting of relationships in space, as if seen from above, these relationships reflect a slanted, polemic worldview. Because Realism preferred artistic forms that enabled such a bird's-eye view, narrative prose is the most prevalent genre in this epoch.

Novels represented bourgeois morals and aesthetics in a variety of frameworks: the contemporary business world, as in Gustav Freytag's *Soll und Haben* (Debit and Credit (1855)); historical contexts, as in Fanny Lewald's *Prinz Louis Ferdinand* (1849) or Louise von François's *Die letzte Reckenbürgerin* (The Last Reckenbürger (1871)); exotic lands and experiences (Karl May, Charles Sealsfield, and Friedrich Gerstäcker wrote novels set in America); and even tales of crime or mystery, such as Wilhelm Raabe's *Stopfkuchen* (Stuffcake (1891)).

Both poetry and shorter prose forms flourished during Realism, although drama did not. Storm, Keller and Conrad Ferdinand Meyer were important poets, often treating rural and agrarian life in lyrical as well as narrative forms. An important subgenre of short prose was the 'Dorfgeschichte' or village tale – such as in Berthold Auerbach's *Schwarzwälder Dorfgeschichten* (Black Forest Village Stories (1843)) or Gottfried Keller's *Die Leute von Seldwyla* (The People of Seldwyla (1856–75)) – which portrays an agrarian way of life in contrast to the increasingly industrialized and urbanized modern world. Such tales, often told at a narrative remove, as a tale within a tale, suggest that the agrarian world of the past is now a distant memory for an urban reading public.

Theodor Fontane's *Irrungen Wirrungen* (1888)

Theodor Fontane (1819–98) is perhaps the best-known Realist author associated with Berlin. He was born of French Huguenot stock in 1819 in Neuruppin, a town in the rural March of Brandenburg, northwest of Berlin. After attending trade school in Berlin, he began writing literature while working as a pharmacist's apprentice, and in 1844 joined the literary group 'Tunnel über der Spree'. In 1849 he abandoned his career as a pharmacist to pursue writing. Working for many years as a journalist, he polished his skills in reportage and detailed descriptions of locales. Yet he did not write his major novels until the late 1870s, after many of the dramatic demographic, architectural and social transformations in Berlin had already taken place. Since he had spent most of his life in Berlin, he would have witnessed these changes firsthand. And although he published a multivolume collection cataloging his journeys in rural areas around Berlin, *Wanderungen durch die Mark Brandenburg* (Wanderings through the March of Brandenburg (1862–89)), his novels do not preserve a lost sense of an agrarian lifestyle threatened by modernity, as works of early Realists tend to, but instead they represent the impact of modernity as a given, a tendency more typical of later Realists. His major novelistic work acknowledges, sometimes wistfully, the decline of the landed aristocracy and the ascendance of both bourgeois industrialists and the urban proletariat. Many of his novels are set in Berlin and the rural periphery on which it encroaches, and represent the struggle between the declining aristocracy and the rising middle class. His major works include *Vor dem Sturm* (Before the Storm (1878)), *Irrungen Wirrungen* (Delusions, Confusions [On Tangled Paths]), *Frau Jenny Treibel* (1893), *Effi Briest* (1895) and the posthumous *Der Stechlin* (The Stechlin (1899)).

Irrungen Wirrungen offers us the broadest view of Berlin and thus merits detailed discussion here. The novel, set against the background of Berlin in the 1870s, describes a failed romantic relationship between Baron Botho von Rienäcker and the seamstress Lene Nimptsch. The first half of the novel relates how they fall in love, have a relationship and then separate when social convention and financial pressures prohibit their union. The second half of the novel focuses primarily on Botho and his efforts to resign himself to life without Lene. It describes how he and Lene each marry partners more appropriate to their respective social stations (for Botho, his cousin Käthe von Sellenthin, also from the nobility, and for Lene, budding industrialist Gideon Franke), yet it also suggests that they have relinquished true love in the process. By focusing on the personal and the romantic, Fontane softens his portrayals of modernity with both irony and sympathy.

In the novel, Berlin is an arena of multiple illusions and delusions. These result from historical changes, specifically a more modern, urban environment that, on one hand, levels the distinctions between individuals (what Walter Müller-Seidel labels 'Gleichmacherei'),[13] and, on the other, brings together competing social groups: the waning aristocracy and the ascendant bourgeoisie. Classes and social groups produce illusions to sustain their power, akin to Marx's notion of illusion and ideology (as set out in *The German Ideology* (1845)), although Fontane does not reference Marx explicitly. The fundamental question of both the novel and modern urban life is how to live genuinely within these myriad illusions.

Fontane points to the tension between ascendant modernity and declining aristocratic tradition throughout the novel. In the second half of the narrative, for example, Botho visits the grave of Lene's adoptive mother, Frau Nimptsch, and on the way back he passes a *Mietskaserne*, while the driver of his horse-drawn cab is a Silesian immigrant. Fontane references these signs of urban modernity without discussing them. Similarly, a prime motivation for Botho to abandon Lene is his family's financial need; his uncle Osten points out that, like many of the Prussian nobility, they are gradually losing their country estates and that he will have to marry a woman from a wealthy family to shore up his own family's position. For Fontane, the aristocracy is headed towards bankruptcy, both literally and figuratively, although he treats this more as a historical inevitability than a form of social pathology.

These historical tensions are accompanied by those between classes, invariably couched in the local colour of Berlin. For example, urban locales are identified explicitly. These are places of leisure (an officer's club, a resort, multiple restaurants), commerce (market squares), transportation (train stations), work (a factory, a market garden) and residence (rented apartments and country estates), each of which contemporary readers would have recognized and associated with a specific class or social group. We also see various neighbourhoods in Berlin: Tiergarten, associated with the aristocracy, the lower-class neighbourhood on the Luisenufer and middle-class areas such as Wilmersdorf and Charlottenburg. And we hear characters from lower classes speak in Berlin dialect. The local colour of Berlin reminds us repeatedly of institutionalized class and social distinctions in the city.

Fontane casts these distinctions as illusions, as evident in the opening scene, where a building that looks like a castle, a symbol of the aristocracy, turns out to be the home of a market gardener who deceives his customers by mixing in bad asparagus with the good. Fontane suggests here both that the distinctions between classes, as much as they shape people's lives, are illusory, but also that within a specific class or social grouping, illusion and deceit are essential to success. We see the same message when Fontane portrays the affairs that the nobility conduct with lower-class women: we learn that aristocratic officers mask their identities when socializing as a group with lower-class women. On the one hand, the aristocratic officers want to nourish the illusion of no class boundaries within such relationships, but on the other, they employ pseudonyms to preserve these boundaries. As this example demonstrates, Fontane shows the workings of class and historical conflicts less through social malaise and more through personal relationships and character development. Individuals from all echelons generally embrace the illusions necessary to sustain class and social distinctions.

At the beginning of the novel, Botho embraces illusions more readily than Lene. For example, he leaves his apartment and walks into the street, 'wo sich, wie auf einem Camera obscura-Glase, die Menschen und Fuhrwerke geräuschlos hin- und her bewegten. „Wie schön. Es ist doch wohl eine der besten Welten"' ('where, as if on the screen of a camera obscura, people and vehicles silently moved back and forth. "How beautiful. Really, I suppose it probably is one of the best of all possible worlds"').[14] For Botho, it is not the actual experience of reality and empirical truth that makes the world ideal, but the appearance, as if through the artificial lens of a viewing device.

Lene, by contrast, identifies illusions as such. When she learns that Botho's pseudonym is Gaston, a reference to the man in the iron mask, she does not laugh, but tells him that he does indeed wear a mask. And this is the chief problem of their romance and the novel. Unlike the 'masks' that his comrades wear to hide their loveless, lower-class romantic liaisons, Botho finds himself in a lower-class relationship, but also in love. He is torn between the social demand for illusion and his individual desire for authenticity. Lene struggles with this, as well. On one hand, she denies giving in to delusions when she tells Frau Dörr: 'Ich bilde mir gar nichts ein. Wenn ich einen liebe, dann lieb ich ihn. Und das ist mir genug. Und will weiter gar nichts von ihm, nichts, gar nichts; und daß mir mein Herze so schlägt und ich die Stunden zähle, bis er kommt, und nicht abwarten kann, bis er wieder da ist, das macht mich glücklich, das ist mir genug' (*IW* 106) ('I'm not getting any ideas at all. If I love somebody, I just love him. And that's enough for me. And I don't want anything else from him, nothing, not a single thing. Just that my heart beats like it does and that I count the hours until he comes and can't wait until he comes again – that's what makes me happy. That's enough for me' (*DC* 17)). Unlike Botho, Lene openly recognizes that her relationship with him cannot last, but appreciates it nonetheless.

On the other hand, however, Lene desires to escape with Botho, even briefly, 'in Gottes freier Natur, möglichst fern von dem großstädtischen Getreibe' (*IW* 143) ('as far as possible from the bustle of the city in God's free and open spaces' (*DC* 61)), suggesting that one might escape the tensions inherent in Berlin by fleeing into nature. Fontane demonstrates, however, that an idealized notion of nature and separation from the city is also a modern delusion. Botho and Lene pursue this illusion by making an excursion to Hankel's Depot, a resort outside Berlin. When Botho asks the resort owner about its name, the difference between city and country vanishes. His host explains that 'Depot' refers to its earlier role as a loading and receiving post, when it had been a large crown domain under earlier Prussian monarchs. There were probably about thirty villages that belonged to it, and they had exports and imports, and thus needed a port or market-place for both: 'diese Bucht wurde Hafen, Stapelplatz, "Ablage" für alles, was kam und ging' (*IW* 150) ('This inlet became a port, marketplace, a "depot" for everything that came or went' (*DC* 69)). The resort owner's description contrasts with the naturalness and seclusion that Lene and Botho had envisioned in Hankel's Depot. In this regard, it mirrors Berlin, one of the largest river ports in Germany, in microcosm, for it too was based on commerce, exchange and the frequent interaction of large groups of people and commodities. Hence, the seclusion and distance from the bustle of the metropolis is a delusion. Fontane reinforces this not only by describing the boatloads of Berliners who visit regularly, but also by having Botho's comrades and their mistresses arrive to drive the couple out of paradise.

In this instance, we see that both Botho's and Lene's illusion of an idyllic getaway clashes with the reality of modern urban life. This event, where both Lene and Botho were seduced by an illusion of life free from the social restrictions of the metropolis, precipitates their separation.

After their separation, Botho marries his cousin, Käthe, who is more superficial than Lene – she has learned to live in a world of illusions. In the latter half of the novel, Botho must resign himself to live in that world of illusions, even as those that sustain his class lose their power. An important lesson for him in this regard comes from Lene's fiancé, the industrialist Gideon Franke. After he learns of Lene's past, he seeks out Botho to determine if she has been honest with him. Botho confirms that she has and then Franke expounds on the importance of honesty, asserting that there are many ways that lead to God, but that they all must be honest and open: 'Aber jeder gute Weg muß ein offner Weg und ein gerader Weg sein und in der Sonne liegen, und ohne Morast und ohne Sumpf und ohne Irrlicht. Auf die Wahrheit kommt es an, und auf die Zuverlässigkeit kommt es an und auf die Ehrlichkeit' (*IW* 206) ('But every good road has got to be an open road, and a straight road, and lie in the sun and not have any morass or swamp or will-o'-the-wisps to lead you astray. It all depends on truth and on reliability and on honesty' (*DC* 134)). Franke's appeal to honesty reiterates bourgeois ideals and it appeals to Botho, as well. At the same time, though, it references Berlin's topography, for the city was built on a swamp with groundwater still encroaching upon its foundations. In a way that is characteristic for his symbolic investment of environmental conditions, Fontane implies that an honest way of life that avoids 'swamps', whether figurative or literal, is impossible in Berlin.

And so Botho must choose either to live genuinely at the expense of the illusions that maintain his financial and social position, or to resign himself to these illusions at the expense of his happiness and integrity. Botho expresses this dilemma to one of his military compatriots, who asks whether he should make his own liaison with a lower-class woman permanent. Botho advises him against this and tells him that he can choose between two options: either break with tradition and marry her and eventually 'sich selbst ein Gräuel und eine Last sein' (*IW* 221) ('become a horror and a burden to yourself' (*DC* 153)) or follow tradition, leave her, and 'dann ist der Jammer da, dann muß gelöst werden, was durch glückliche Stunden und ach, was mehr bedeutet, durch unglückliche, durch Not und Ängste verwebt und verwachsen ist. Und das tut weh' (*IW* 221) ('then you've got to sever something that has become intertwined and interwoven through all kinds of difficulties and worries, through good times and – my God, what's even more important – hard times as well. And that hurts' (*DC* 153)). There is no happy medium here: either he can embrace illusions and live according to social rules but without love, or he can pursue love and lose his place in society, ultimately ruining his happiness. Botho has chosen illusion. Although we see Lene's and Gideon's wedding at the conclusion of the novel, narrated from a distance, the final focus is on Botho, highlighting his difficult choice as a product of life in modern Berlin.

Fontane's text is thus resigned to the rise of a modern, materialist world, even as it looks wistfully on the fading world of the aristocracy. He finds illusions in both worlds and does not offer his modern readers a world free of the same, only a choice of which illusions to live by. Such compassion and understanding of both the aristocracy and middle-class is typical for Realism, but, as we will see, it contrasts with the disposition of Naturalism. For although Naturalism also recognized delusions and deception in society, it focuses less on sincerity and feeling and more on the material realities of the lower classes of society.

Naturalism

Although Naturalists, like Realists, aimed to represent reality, the similarities between the two movements end there. Naturalists opposed Realism's idealist whitewashing of the harsh aspects of reality. Rather than palliate the ills of reality, Naturalists insisted on highlighting them, and for this reason they considered themselves, in contrast to the Bourgeois Realists, as more rigorous in their realism, that is, more engaged with social realities. Where Realists represented bourgeois ideals, Naturalists focused on the ailments of the modern metropolis, such as poverty, homelessness, sickness, insanity, alcoholism, incest and abuse.

Naturalism drew on influences from outside Germany. Prominent among these was the French historian and philosopher, Hippolyte Taine, whose milieu theory asserted that human creations are products of biology and nationality ('race'), environment and social context ('milieu'), and situation or temporal context ('moment'). This deterministic worldview resonated with scientific developments, specifically Darwin's theory of evolution (championed in Germany by Ernst Haeckel and Wilhelm Bölsche), which highlighted the powerful influence of biology and genetics. Taine influenced Émile Zola, often considered the founder of European Naturalism, whose novels portray characters determined by heredity, their social milieu and their historical circumstances. Also influential was Norwegian dramatist Henrik Ibsen, whose plays criticized moral and social codes in nineteenth-century bourgeois culture. In his drama *A Doll's House* (1879), for instance, the protagonist, Nora, confronts the inequality and emptiness in her seemingly ideal bourgeois marriage and subsequently abandons her husband and children.

German Naturalism's aesthetic program found clearest formulation in a volume, *Die Kunst, ihr Wesen und ihre Gesetze* (Art, its Essence and its Laws (1891)), by Arno Holz and Johannes Schlaf. They laid out a plan for a 'rigorous Naturalism' and offered the formula 'Kunst = Natur – X' ('art = nature – X'), where X is the author's input. The author should minimize his or her own contribution and make art as close to nature as possible. Such an aesthetic program valued exact reproduction of reality, whether in language that relies on dialect and colloquial speech instead of more formal or refined speech, in exhaustive descriptions of social misery in all of its minutiae, or in a literary device known as *Sekundenstil* (literally, 'second style' – where the time of the literary representation should match actual time telegraphically, down to the second). There is no effort to transfigure reality to show a deeper truth, as one finds in Realism, but instead the aim is to represent unvarnished, blemished reality.

Whereas Realism offered subtle criticisms of bourgeois and aristocratic culture, Naturalism was forceful and incisive in its censure. Yet the aim of Naturalism was not specifically political; Naturalists wanted reform more than revolution. As much as they criticized the unjust practices of Wilhelmine Germany, its militarism, censorship of art, and policies that reinforced rather than alleviated social inequality, they offered no real political alternative. During a period when Socialism was establishing footholds in Germany, Naturalists focused less on allegiance to a political party and more on eliciting *Mitleid* (pity, compassion) from their readers or viewers. For example, after Gerhart Hauptmann's drama *Die Weber* (The Weavers (1891/2)) was initially banned from the Prussian stage for depicting a revolt among Silesian weavers (see also Chapter 11 in this volume), Hauptmann proclaimed that this drama was not a social-democratic treatise, but a poetic appeal for *Mitleid*. Later critics of Naturalism, such as Bertolt Brecht, would thus accuse Naturalism of depicting the superficial symptoms in society while ignoring their deeper political and economic causes.

Naturalism was at home among the exploited workers of the countryside as well as in the industrial metropolis with its concomitant maladies. In Germany, Naturalism concentrated in Munich and Berlin. The Munich Naturalists gathered around a newspaper, *Die Gesellschaft* (Society), founded in 1885 by Michael Georg Conrad, and included writers such as Hermann Conradi, Karl Bleibtreu and Detlev von Liliencron. In Berlin, the Freie Bühne (Free Theatre) was founded in 1889 and premiered Gerhart Hauptmann's drama *Vor Sonnenaufgang* (Before Sunrise) in the same year.

Apart from Hauptmann, Naturalists in Berlin included figures such as Arno Holz, Johannes Schlaf and Clara Viebig and clustered around the journal *Kritische Waffengänge* (Critical Clashes) and the literary association, Durch! (Through!).

Naturalist literature began with lyric poetry, particularly 'Großstadtlyrik' (poetry of the metropolis), and was usually socially critical in tone, with Arno Holz as perhaps its best-known exponent. Naturalist prose established itself around 1890, with shorter forms such as the novella, the sketch, the study and the generic short narrative, often experimental and relying on literary techniques such as *Sekundenstil* and early experiments in stream of consciousness. Well-known examples include Hauptmann's *Bahnwärter Thiel* (Flagman Thiel (1888)) and Holz and Schlaf's *Papa Hamlet* (1889). In the 1890s, drama became the most important medium for Naturalists, and introduced to Germany what we today consider modern drama. Stage directions were exhaustive, the focus was on milieu and character, and both beginnings and endings of dramas were often open in form, thwarting an audience's desire for closure. Naturalist drama focused not on heroes, but on victims of injustice, social inequality and determinism.

Gerhart Hauptmann's *Die Ratten* (1911)

Gerhart Hauptmann (1862–1946) was born in Obersalzbrunn in Silesia and spent much of his youth in that region. He took up and broke off studies in agriculture, sculpture, philosophy, literature, drawing and law. Beginning in childhood and subsequently throughout his life, he suffered lung ailments, which prevented him from living in large cities on a long-term basis – he would often escape to the Villa Lassen in Erkner, outside Berlin, or to a cloister on the Baltic island of Hiddensee.

He began to establish himself as a writer in the mid to late 1880s and found success with the aforementioned novella, *Bahnwärter Thiel*, and drama, *Vor Sonnenaufgang*. This drama's unvarnished representation of social misery caused a scandal in Berlin and led to a breakthrough for both Hauptmann and Naturalism. He went on to become the best-known representative of German Naturalism and an international cultural figure. In addition to countless German prizes, in 1912 he won the Nobel Prize for Literature, and in 1932 received an honorary doctorate from Columbia University in New York City. His drama *Die Ratten* (The Rats (1911)), the last play in what is referred to as his Berlin trilogy, demonstrates clearly his relation to both Berlin and Naturalism. The first parts of this trilogy, *Der Biberpelz* (The Beaver Coat (1893)) and *Der Rote Hahn* (The Conflagration [literally The Red Cockerel] (1901)), are set in the rural outskirts of Berlin and represent efforts by a conniving lower-class woman to gain social and economic advantage through self-interest and corruption. In *Die Ratten*, the entire drama is set in the 1880s in a large *Mietskaserne* in the eastern, proletarian portion of Berlin.

The drama is founded on a duality, as Hauptmann himself explained: 'The idea of the drama consisted of the contrast between two worlds and had these two worlds as its point of departure.'[15] The only two settings in the play are the apartment of the proletarian couple, Herr and Frau John, and the apartment and storage room of the theatre director, Harro Hassenreuter and his family. Typically for Naturalist drama, the milieu plays as much of a role in the drama as do the characters: Hauptmann gives the stage and scenic directions in exhaustive detail. The two settings contrast in a variety of ways: the Johns live lower in the building, while Hassenreuter's apartment is connected to the attic; the Johns's apartment is light, while Hassenreuter's is poorly illuminated and dusty, its light uncertain ('ungewiss');[16] and the proletarian apartment is Spartan in its appointment but clean, whereas Hassenreuter's is cluttered with numerous props and costumes from his work in the theatre.

These two contrasting settings point to the two plot lines of the drama, the first of which focuses on the John family. Frau John, the wife of a blue-collar worker and Socialist sympathizer, still grieves for the loss of their first child, who died years earlier when only a few days old. She persuades a suicidal young woman, Pauline Piperkarcka, who is pregnant with an illegitimate child, to give birth and entrust the infant to her care. After the child is born, Frau John convinces her husband and neighbours that the child is her own. But Pauline returns, asking to see the baby, and Frau John treats her harshly, claiming the child is now hers. Pauline tells her that she has reported the birth of the child to the local authorities, who will visit to determine its welfare. Frau John leaves with Pauline's child, misleading the authorities to assume that the neglected, dying child of a disreputable woman across the hall is Pauline's. Frau John then asks her thuggish brother to ensure that Pauline does not pursue the matter with the authorities. Her brother murders Pauline. As the truth gradually emerges and the authorities close in, Frau John's activities are exposed to both her husband and her fellow residents, her husband leaves her, and she kills herself in the street in front of their building.

In contrast to this tragic plotline, typical for Naturalism, Hauptmann gives us the story of the theatre director, Hassenreuter, which is closer to a romantic comedy. Hassenreuter's daughter, Walburga, falls in love with Eric Spitta, her tutor and a theology student who decides to pursue acting, much to Hassenreuter's dismay. Hassenreuter's approach to theatre is steeped in the classical tradition of Goethe and Schiller, whereas Spitta finds this tradition artificial and bound to the interests of the upper class. Echoing Naturalist sentiments, he calls for theatre that can find tragedy in a lower-class washerwoman and that eschews artificial diction and sentiment. Hassenreuter is thus shocked to learn that his daughter and Spitta have a secret romance. Yet he has no moral high ground from which to condemn them, for his daughter catches him in an affair with an actress. Despite Hassenreuter's best efforts to keep them apart, Spitta and Walburga are united at the end; the insinuation is that they will marry and follow Hassenreuter to his new appointment as theatre director in Strasbourg.

Hauptmann intertwines these supposedly unrelated stories so that the stark contrasts between upper and lower classes, high culture and low culture, corruption and morality, and theatre and reality, begin to blur. In effect, Hauptmann shows these dualities to be false, ultimately criticizing not only the individuals in the play, but also the city of Berlin itself. Hauptmann wrote about the drama: 'Perhaps I can, with at least one work, hold up a mirror to this city. It must see itself as I see it (...): filled with demons, an inferno.'[17]

Die Ratten indeed holds up a mirror to many aspects of Berlin life. Hauptmann fills the drama with countless details that evoke the city. The setting in a *Mietskaserne* suggests not only the military history of Berlin (this *Mietskaserne* was formerly a cavalry barracks), but also the real estate speculation during the nineteenth century that led to construction of such buildings. It points to the housing crisis that was typical of Berlin and to which Pauline Piperkarcka refers when she tells Frau John that she has lost her 'Schlafbodenstelle' (*DR* 739), that is, a rented sleeping space in a larger household, a phenomenon found in nearly 20 per cent of Berlin households at this time.[18] Another characteristic feature of the *Mietskaserne* was the combination of multiple classes within one building – in *Die Ratten* we see representatives of the proletariat, the bourgeoisie and the Berliner underworld (prostitutes, ruffians, etc.) within the same house. The living space embodies the class conflicts inherent in Berlin at the time, and class conflict emerges as an issue in the drama. For example, when Herr John denigrates students and intellectuals, in characteristic Berlin dialect: 'Aber keener will wat Reelles anfassen' (*DR* 802) ('But none o' you wants to put your hand to some reel work' (*TR* 460)), Spitta responds that he is a 'Geistesarbeiter' ('brain worker'), asserting that 'Ihre Herrn Bebel und Liebknecht sind auch Geistesarbeiter' (*DR* 802) ('your Socialist leaders – your Bebels and your Liebknechts – are brain workers too' (*TR* 461)). August Bebel and Wilhelm Liebknecht founded the Social Democratic Workers' Party of Germany in 1869. And just as we see confrontation between workers and students here, so we also see a conflict between the student, Spitta, and the established theatre director, Hassenreuter, who recoils at the thought of Spitta leaving his theological studies to pursue a career in the theatre. Throughout the drama, tension between the classes persists.

Hauptmann reflects Berlin and its class differences not just in space, but also in sound. This is evident in the sounds of the city that repeatedly intrude on the action within the *Mietskaserne*. Traffic sounds, an organ grinder, children's voices, bells and a military march establish the scene as an urban drama. The sounds of the city are inescapable and are also evident in characters' language, which reflects distinctions between classes: while the lower-class figures speak a strong Berlin dialect, as we climb the social ladder, middle-class characters speak a more standard German and, at the top, Herr Hassenreuter speaks an academic, syntactically complex German peppered with French, English and Latin phrases.

Hauptmann's mirror of Berlin focuses on the city's entrance into the modern era, which he portrays in ambivalent terms. This is evident in urban modes of transportation. There are frequent references to the omnibus and the *Pferdebahn*, a system of horse-drawn streetcars created in 1871. Spitta saves Frau Knobbe from being trampled to death by these horses early in the drama, so that modern transportation systems not only bring convenience, but also danger. And modern technology is similarly ambivalent. Herr Hassenreuter donates a Soxhletsche milk apparatus (invented in 1886) so that Frau John can sterilize milk for her new child. In sterilizing milk, this apparatus replaces the mother in both milk production and nursing; technology disrupts the bonds between humans. And modern bureaucracy functions similarly. On the one hand, Pauline can appeal to the registry office and to social services to fight for her lost child. On the other hand, when Herr Hassenreuter considers adopting Pauline's newly orphaned child at the drama's conclusion, the landlord, Quarquaro, warns that he will lose both time and money to the bureaucracy of the adoption process. Herr Hassenreuter relinquishes the child to the foster system where, Quarquaro tells us, ten out of twelve children usually die. Modern bureaucracy may bring more rights, but it does so at great human cost.

And finally, modern urban life brings with it decadence and decay. Frau Knobbe, the neighbour of the Johns, is a drug-addicted prostitute, fallen from a higher station earlier in life. Frau John's brother, Bruno Mechelke, is a petty thug who not only steals, but also murders Pauline Pieperkarcka. Yet, as much as Hauptmann condemns this decadence, he also condemns the religious and moral intolerance that exacerbates it: Spitta's sister had become pregnant outside of marriage and was subsequently ostracized from her

strictly religious family, resulting in her suicide. Decadence is the dark under-
belly of the modern metropolis, yet intolerance and inhumanity are its
bourgeois counterparts.

The Naturalist mirror that Hauptmann holds up to Berlin reflects a city
riven by class distinctions, plagued by capitalist greed and social ills, and
suffering, as much as it benefits, from the technological, bureaucratic and
social developments of modernity. Hauptmann portrays this in terms of
duplicity and false appearances, for whatever level of refinement or
humanity is manifested on its surface, it only veils corruption, decay and
decadence. Towards the end of the drama, for example, Herr John recognizes duplicity within his own family, as well in the *Mietskaserne* and
Berlin at large. He exclaims: 'Horchen Se ma, wie det knackt, wie Putz
hinter de Tapete runterjeschoddert kommt! Allens is hier morsch! Allens
faulet Holz! Allens unterminiert, von Unjeziefer, von Ratten und Mäuse
zerfressen! ... Allens schwankt! Allens kann jeden Oochenblick bis in
Keller durchbrechen' (*DR* 824) ('Listen to the crackin'! Listen how the
plasterin' comes rumblin' down behind the wall-paper! Everythin's rotten
here, everythin's worm-eaten! Everythin's undermined by varmint an' by
rats an' by mice ... Everythin' totters! Any minute the whole business
might crash down into the cellar' (*TR* 506)). Vermin, rats and mice have
undermined the veneer of order and propriety. Hauptmann is not specific
about exactly who or what these vermin, rats and mice might represent,
but they abound in the drama. When we first meet Bruno Mechelke, he is
tinkering with a mousetrap. Early in the drama Hassenreuter labels his
apartment and storage chamber 'mein Motten-, Ratten- und Flohparadies'
(*DR* 744) ('my paradise of moths and rats and fleas' (*TR* 344)), and later in
the drama he labels Spitta a rat after hearing his ideas about theatre and
complains that rats undermine the newly created glorious German empire
(a jab at socialism). Clearly, Hauptmann associates rats and the parasitic
decay they represent with all classes and all realms of society. His drama is
an indictment of the modern metropolis, where everyone contributes to
the demise of the other and where decadence and decay fester beneath
a veneer of social and technological progress.

Yet Hauptmann trains his mirror not only on Berlin, but also, self-
reflexively, on Naturalism itself. *Die Ratten* is a work of late Naturalism,
written decades after the beginnings of the movement in the 1880s and after
Hauptmann had begun to experiment with romantic and mythical subject
matter in dramas such as *Hanneles Himmelfahrt* (Hannele's Ascension
(1893)), *Die versunkene Glocke* (The Sunken Bell (1896)) and *Und Pippa
tanzt* (And Pippa Dances (1905)). In Die *Ratten*, Hauptmann reflects on
Naturalist drama and its practices. The bifurcation of the drama into two

levels – a tragedy that plays out in the painful reality of the lower classes of Berlin, typical of Naturalism, and a romantic comedy that plays out in the middle-class realm of an unemployed theatre director – allows one level to comment on the other. Spitta criticizes Hassenreuter's classical conception of theatre of 'der Schiller-Goethisch-Weimarischen Schule der Unnatur' (*DR* 752) ('the Goethe-Schiller-Weimar school of idealistic artifice [literally 'unnature']' (*TR* 359)) from a Naturalist perspective, whereas Hassenreuter mocks Spitta's idolization of the lower classes: 'Sie haben neulich behauptet, daß unter Umständen ein Barbier oder eine Reinmachefrau aus der Mulackstraße ebensogut ein Objekt der Tragödie sein könnte als Lady Macbeth und König Lear' (*DR* 778) ('You asserted the other day that, in certain circumstances, a barber or a scrubwoman might as fittingly be the protagonist of a tragedy as Lady Macbeth or King Lear' (*TR* 413)). By the end of the drama, both Spitta and Hassenreuter have changed positions, however, for in observing the plight of the orphaned child, Spitta focuses not on material inequity, but on 'ein wahrhaft tragisches Verhängnis' (*DR* 831) ('a genuinely tragic fatality' (*TR* 522)). Hassenreuter, in response, asserts, 'Die Tragik ist nicht an Stände gebunden. Ich habe Ihnen das stets gesagt' (*DR* 831) ('Tragedy is not confined to any class of society. I always told you that' (*TR* 522)). Both have changed their position on tragedy and realism in the course of the drama, as if Hauptmann questions the absolute validity of both the Naturalist and the more classical dramatic traditions.

Along similar lines, Hauptmann incorporates many non-naturalist elements into this drama, pushing the boundaries of Naturalism at the same time as he enacts its most standard tropes. And so, in a drama focused on representing reality in harsh detail, we find frequent references to spirits and ghosts, supernatural elements that should have nothing to do with reality. Overlaying a bourgeois love comedy upon a tale of kidnapping and murder similarly enhances the dissonance between the Naturalist worldview and the bourgeois world that it criticizes, yet simultaneously implies their co-existence. For Hauptmann, the focused Naturalist worldview has expanded to account for the variety of perspectives that will characterize the metropolis of the twentieth century.

Realist and Naturalist representations of Berlin share a mimetic impulse, a desire to represent realistically a city in tension with an agrarian, aristo-cratic past and a fast-developing urban present. And both focus on delusion and deception as essential to modern life. Yet these similarities yield funda-mentally different results due to differing aesthetic regimes – one that would reflect an unseen reality and another that would magnify seen reality – and divergent objects of representation: the bourgeoisie and the proletariat. As such, the urban reality of Realism contrasts starkly with that of

Naturalism. Realist authors portray the waning of feudal society with nostalgia and the rise of a new modernism with resignation. The deceptions and delusions of the metropolis are milder; they point to larger social transformations but result only in a sense of personal resignation and bankrupt aristocratic estates. Naturalist authors, in contrast, share neither nostalgia for the past, nor a resigned acceptance of the present: they represent the modern metropolis as dangerous and threatening, for by the end of Hauptmann's drama we have a murder, a suicide, a child dead from neglect and another bound for foster care, where it will likely die. Naturalism in Berlin concludes with a pessimistic view of a divided metropolis and agitates for social reform. At the end of the nineteenth century, then, Berlin is a city divided not only economically and socially, between feudalism and capitalism, upper and lower classes, but also artistically, between the aesthetic regimes of Realism and Naturalism.

NOTES

1. Thanks to Holly Yanacek for research assistance with this essay.
2. Paul Clauswitz, *Die Städteordnung von 1808 und die Stadt Berlin*, reprint 1986 (Berlin: Julius Springer, 1908), p. 4.
3. Ingrid Thienel, *Städtewachstum im Industrialisierungsprozeß des 19. Jahrhunderts: Das Berliner Beispiel*, vol. 39, *Veröffentlichungen der Hist. Kommission zu Berlin* (Berlin: de Gruyter, 1973), p. 398.
4. Ingrid Thienel, 'Verstädterung, städtische Infrastruktur und Stadtplanung: Berlin zwischen 1850 und 1914', *Zeitschrift für Stadtgeschichte, Stadtsoziologie und Denkmalpflege*, 4.1 (1977), pp. 55–84, 59–63.
5. Julian Schmidt, 'Der neueste englische Roman und das Princip des Realismus', in *Roman und Romantheorie des deutschen Realismus*, eds H. Ruckhäberle and H. Widhammer (Athenäum Verlag: Kronberg, 1977), p. 207.
6. Julian Schmidt, *Bilder aus dem geistigen Leben unserer Zeit* (Leipzig: Duncker & Humblot, 1870), p. 34.
7. Arnold Ruge, 'Idealismus und Realismus im Reich des Ideals – Als Vorläufer zu Schillers Hundertjährigem Geburtstage', in *Deutsches Museum: Zeitschrift für Literatur, Kunst und öffentliches Leben*, 8.15 (8 April, 1858), p. 529.
8. Theodor Fontane, 'Unsere lyrische und epische Poesie seit 1848', in *Deutsche Annalen zur Kenntnis der Gegenwart und Erinnerung an die Vergangenheit* I (Leipzig: Avernarius & Mendelssohn, 1853), pp. 353–77 (p. 359).
9. Ibid., p. 358.
10. Schmidt, 'Der neueste englische Roman', p. 209.
11. Karl Gutzkow, 'Der Roman des Nebeneinander', in *Romanpoetik in Deutschland: Von Hegel bis Fontane*, ed. Hartmut Steinecke (Gunter Narr Verlag: Tübingen, 1984), p. 113.
12. Ibid., p. 114.
13. Walter Müller-Seidel, W., *Theodor Fontane: Soziale Romankunst in Deutschland*, 2nd edition (Stuttgart: J. B. Metzler, 1980), p. 257.

14. Theodor Fontane, *Irrungen, Wirrungen, Sämtliche Werke*, ed. Edgar Gross, vol. 3 (Munich: Nymphenburger Verlagsbuchhandlung, 1959), p. 122 (henceforth *IW*). Translations from: Theodor Fontane, *Delusions, Confusions and The Poggenpuhl Family*, ed. Peter Demetz, trans. William L. Zwiebel (New York: Continuum, 1989), p. 35 (henceforth *DC*).

15. Cited in Klaus Hildebrandt, *Naturalistische Dramen Gerhart Hauptmanns* (Munich: Oldenbourg, 1983), p. 70.

16. Gerhart Hauptmann, *Die Ratten*, Sämtliche *Werke*, vol. 2 (Frankfurt: Propyläen Verlag, 1965), p. 735 (henceforth *DR*). Translations from: Gerhart Hauptmann, *The Rats*, The *Dramatic Works of Gerhart Hauptmann*, vol. 2, *Social Dramas*, ed. and trans. Ludwig Lewisohn (New York: B. W. Huebsch, 1913), p. 325 (henceforth *TR*). Translations without a page number are my own.

17. Journal entry of 19/20 February 1909, cited in Peter Sprengel, 'Gerhart Hauptmann: *Die Ratten*: Vom Gegensatz der Welten in einer Mietskaserne', in *Dramen des Naturalismus*, ed. W. Bellmann (Stuttgart: Reclam, 1988), pp. 243–82 (pp. 268–9).

18. Thienel, *Städtewachstum*, pp. 387–90.

4

ANNE FUCHS

Short Prose around 1900

I feel lost in Berlin. It has no resemblance to the city I had supposed it was ... The bulk of the Berlin of today has about it no suggestion of a former period. The site it stands on has traditions and a history, but the city itself has no traditions and no history. It is a new city; the newest I have ever seen. Chicago would seem venerable beside it; for there are many old-looking districts in Chicago, but not many in Berlin.

Mark Twain[1]

Modernist Short Prose and the Metropolitan Environment

Mark Twain was not alone in being struck by the patent modernity of Berlin around 1900. In his excellent study, *Reading Berlin 1900*, the historian Peter Fritzsche analyzes the emergence and impact of Berlin as a text-producing and text-consuming metropolis. By the turn of the century Berlin had morphed from a provincial backwater into a modern metropolis, as evident in its substantial population growth (from 400,000 inhabitants in 1848 to two million in 1905), the expansion of the city boundaries and the development of a modern transport system and infrastructure. 'A rich stream of texts', comments Fritzsche, 'guided and misguided its inhabitants, and, in large measure, fashioned the metropolitan experience'.[2]

On their daily journeys through the bustling city, Berliners encountered a myriad of print forms and images in mass circulation newspapers, posters, advertisements on the omnipresent *Litfaßsäulen* (advertising pillars), schedules, announcements and traffic signs that, in Fritzsche's words, brought forth a 'word city' which overlaid the built city with heteroglossic text.[3] New print technologies had boosted the newspaper industry in Imperial Germany: in the period from 1881 to 1897, the market expanded from 2,437 printed daily papers to 3,405,[4] and in Berlin alone approximately ninety newspapers were in circulation.[5] By 1920 the three main publishers – Ullstein, Scherl and Mosse – all published midday, evening and night editions on top of their regular morning editions of the *Berliner Morgenpost*, the *Berliner Lokal-Anzeiger* and the liberal *Berliner Tagblatt*, in which the Swiss modernist writer Robert Walser published his *Feuilletons* and short prose sketches.[6] The metropolitan city thus constituted itself through a continually evolving text world that orchestrated the exciting and unnerving dynamic of modernity through a polyphony of dissonant voices.

The prime locus for the continual traffic between the city as lived texture and published text was the literary *Feuilleton*, which appeared 'unter dem Strich' (below the line), topographically separated from the more important news items. A marginal genre dedicated to broadly cultural affairs, it seemed to lack the weight and importance of political news coverage. Günter Oesterle observes that from its inception in the nineteenth century, the *Feuilleton* was therefore engaged in a perpetual discourse of legitimation that interrogated its form and function.[7] However, by around 1900 the *Feuilleton* had finally established itself as modern genre that was especially suited to capturing the cultural dynamic of modernity. It secured its place in the newspaper by taking care of seemingly non-political affairs, including articles on fashion, art and culture, everyday observations and subjective impressions about modern life. The author of a detailed history of the *Frankfurter Zeitung*, published in 1911, highlights the enhanced importance of the *Feuilleton* as a dynamic form that now competed with the *Leitartikel* (the lead article) for the reader's attention.[8] This is echoed by Joseph Roth – a prolific *Feuilletonist* with the *Frankfurter Zeitung* who reported from Berlin during the early 1920s – who asserts with great panache that his contribution is no mere 'pudding' ('Mehlspeise') to follow the politics, but the 'main meal' of the newspaper.[9]

Roth not only challenges here the old hierarchy between political analysis and the marginal *Feuilleton* but also queries the supposedly apolitical nature of the small form: in his view, the *Feuilleton* brings forth radically new modes of articulation that can be more hard-hitting than conventional news coverage. Precisely because it seemed so marginal to mainstream political news coverage, it became an experimental field where the boundaries between fiction and autobiography, reality and imagination, the city as material environment and the city as text were constantly crossed. As a dynamic forum for cultural commentary, the *Feuilleton* thus occupies a central role in the archive of modernity's cultural history, tracking, as Christian Jäger and Erhard Schütz put it, the 'self-perception of the age'.[10] In the same vein, Andreas Huyssen observes that 'the modern miniature as a specific mode of writing may indeed be more central to the new in literary Modernism than the novel or poetry'.[11]

As a genre 'beyond' conventional genre boundaries,[12] the miniature prose sketch defined itself programmatically through a heightened self-reflexivity that accentuates the subjective experience of modernity. Its brevity, or smallness, made it particularly germane to exploring and advancing new modes of attention and perception in the metropolitan environment. Reflecting on his prolific production of 'kleine Sachen' ('small pieces'), the Austrian author Peter Altenberg famously compared his miniature sketches with a beef stock cube, 'extracts of life' that required liquefaction in the reader's mind before turning into a tasty broth.[13] Altenberg's humorous analogy draws attention to a paradoxical feature of the small prose piece: even though it homes in on contingent, accidental and ephemeral aspects of everyday life, it employs the principle of condensation to achieve poetic effect. However, here the principle of condensation is no longer the effect of poetic inspiration but the outcome of the mass-production of a modern consumer product, i.e. the practical stock cube. It is precisely the paradoxical structure of what I would like to call condensed contingency that for Altenberg mobilizes the reader's imagination. For Althaus, Bunzel and Göttsche, the genre's intrinsic marginality is thus its driving engine: by combining cultural analysis with everyday observations and a heightened self-reflexivity, the genre became the playing field par excellence for literary innovation in German Modernism.[14]

Beyond such poetological considerations, the boom of modern short prose around 1900 has to be understood as an effort of resistance to the heightened pace of modernity. In his study *Suspensions of Perception*, the art historian Jonathan Crary has analyzed how, in the course of the nineteenth century, the effects of rapid technological and social change in modernizing society produced radically new conditions for our sensory experiences, which, by the end of the century, were being negotiated through a far-reaching debate on attention.[15] The collapse of classical models of vision and of the stable subjects these models had presupposed motivated an empirical-scientific approach to the notion of the human sensation. From the 1880s onwards, attention features in a range of discourses that deal with a precarious subjectivity that appears to be threatened by the force of modernity's dazzling visual sensations. In the period from 1900 to the 1930s, short prose became a particularly productive literary field for the exploration of new modes of short-lived attention and distraction in the metropolitan environment, and not least in the burgeoning metropolis Berlin.

Writers of short prose not only experimented with the fast-paced transitoriness of modern life in form and content, but they also had to grapple with the newspaper as an information-driven medium that continually produces its own obsolescence. Unless collected in book form, the *Feuilleton* piece was excluded from literary canonization. The irresolvable tension between the fast-paced newspaper landscape and the poet's aspiration for longer-term recognition features prominently in the writings of Robert Walser who, in many of his prose pieces, reflects with characteristic humour on the unstable publishing conditions of the modern writer of short prose. For example, in 'Was aus mir wurde' (What Became of Me), an autobiographical sketch published during his Berlin phase in 1912, the self comically discloses an eccentric trajectory: 'Und so schleuderte mich das barsche Leben in die Bahnen eines exekutierenden Feuilletonisten. O hätte ich nie ein Feuilleton geschrieben' ('And thus harsh life has catapulted me into the orbit of a prolific writer of *Feuilletons*. Oh, if only I had never written a *Feuilleton*.').[16] Alongside his well-known 'Für die Katz' (literally 'For the Cat', which means 'in vain') and 'Meine Bemühungen' (My Efforts) from his later Berne phase, Walser's piece 'Die Glosse' (Annotation) continues this self-conscious and comical exploration of the low cultural capital of the writer of *Feuilletons*. At the beginning of the piece the author is depicted as a mere 'Glossenschmied', a toiling blacksmith of notes whose exhausted 'Skizzenhervorbringerseele' ('sketch-producing soul') has to contend with a contemptuous literary public. Towards the end, however, Walser then proclaims with considerable verve that, against all odds, he has managed to obtain a real 'Glossensieg' ('victory with the sketch'), with the 'angels of prose-poetry' now serenading him (*SW* XIX: 289). And he goes on to declare that while the sketch may represent a form of depravity, as seen from the 'upholstered chair of writerly morality', it has the smallness of stature to be comfortably placed at will and so to achieve universal appeal (*SW* XIX: 289).

In 'Die Glosse', Walser aggrandizes the genre's perceived inferiority by invoking established topoi that have accompanied the history of the prose sketch, including the pressurized production of the piece, its pithiness, transitoriness and low cultural capital, only to overturn these seeming deficits by elevating it to the more noble form of the *poème en prose* in the tradition of Baudelaire's *Le Spleen de Paris* (Paris Spleen) of 1868. In a final move, he further boosts the genre's status by linking its smallness with enhanced versatility and flexibility, two traits that should appeal to the modern metropolitan reading public. As we will see in what follows, these are the distinguishing characteristics of Walser's engagement with Berlin through a range of prose miniatures written between 1907 and 1912.

Short Prose Topography

Walser's short prose about Berlin stands at the beginning of a large body of writing that graphically captures the often-contradictory dynamic of a rapacious process of modernization that produced different kinds of speed alongside titillating entertainment and visual spectacles. Berlin as a site of a dazzling modernity is mostly associated with the Weimar period and the so-called Golden Twenties. Joseph Roth, Egon Erwin Kisch, Victor Auburtin, Franz Hessel, Alfred Polgar, Siegfried Kracauer and Gabriele Tergit are amongst the most prominent writers of *Feuilletons* who mapped out a dynamic topography of modernization that vividly captured the New West area of the city with the stylish Kurfürstendamm, as well as the ceaseless traffic patterns at Potsdamer Platz, the magical or seedy night life in Friedrichstraße, the vast building site of Alexanderplatz and the oasis of the Tiergarten. As Christian Jäger and Erhard Schütz have pointed out, this trajectory dissolved in the *Feuilleton* into a confusing mosaic, made up of a multitude of attractions such as the Panoptikum, the coffee house culture of Café Größenwahn or the Romanische Café, the thrills of Lunapark with its big wheel and merry-go-rounds, the screenings in the vast film palaces, the excitement of sporting events, such as the famous six-day-cycling races or boxing matches, and the titillating eroticism of the Varieté culture.[17]

However, it is important to emphasize that the idea of Berlin as electrifying metropolis predates the First World War. Besides Georg Simmel's seminal essay 'Die Großstädte und das Geistesleben' (The Metropolis and Mental Life (1903)) and the large body of Expressionist city poetry, there is Robert Walser's Modernist novel *Jakob von Gunten* (1908).[18] The novel presents itself as the diary of the eponymous hero who, although he is of aristocratic origins, enters a school for servants which is located in a city identifiable as Berlin. While the novel is often read as an anti-*Bildungsroman* which deliberately perverts the idea of self-realization through *Bildung*, that is, a process of social and cultural education, it is also a Berlin novel which offers regular snapshots of Jakob's dazzling experiences in the city. In a striking diary entry Jakob captures the rhythm of movement at street level through a range of alliterations and onomatopoeic words that mimic the continual traffic noise and traffic patterns, evoking the city as a social space in perpetual commotion.[19] In the moving crowd, social differences are lessened by the experience of a novel proximity: the old and the young, men and women, the elegant and the crippled walk side by side, orchestrating the rhythm of city life at the democratic street level.

After briefly attending a school for servants and spending a stint in service at Schloß Dambrau in Upper Silesia, Robert Walser returned briefly to Switzerland before moving to Berlin in 1905 for several years. His brother Karl, who had already made his name as a stage designer for Max Reinhardt,[20] introduced him to the literary and cultural elite, including, for example, the publishers Bruno Cassirer and Samuel Fischer, and the head of the Berlin Secession Max Liebermann. During his time in Berlin, Walser produced more than one hundred short prose pieces, which appeared in leading newspapers and journals, including *Die Schaubühne*, *Die neue Rundschau* and the *Berliner Tagblatt*. Thematically, these pieces cover a broad territory, ranging from fictionalized literary portraits, unconventional reviews of theatrical productions, short dialogic sketches, re-imaginings of literary characters and sketches about food and fashion to topographical explorations of the city environment.

Urban Codes of Conduct and the Construction of Social Space

On 7 January 1906, the brothers Karl and Robert Walser were invited to dinner by the publisher Samuel Fischer along with twenty-four illustrious guests, amongst them the actress Tilla Durieux; the theatre critic and director of the Deutsches Theater Otto Brahm; journalist and critic Arthur Eloesser and his wife, Margarete; the translator and journalist Max Meyerfeld; the publisher Georg Bondi; and the director of the Märkische Museum Otto Pniower.[21] Walser's 'Dinerabend' (Dinner Evening), which appeared in the *neue Rundschau* in March 1908, provides a running commentary on the required mastery of a particular social etiquette. Recalling how he entered his host's abode, the Walserian self establishes early on the intrinsic connection between his own mannered linguistic register and the expected social protocol:

> Der Diener öffnete die gastliche Pforte. Gastliche Pforte? Ein etwas feuilleto-nistischer Ausdruck, aber ich liebe es, mich im Stil kleiner Tagesware zu bewegen. Ich gebe mit so viel Manier, als ich kann, Hut und Mantel ab, streiche mein ohnehin glattes Haar vor dem Spiegel noch ein wenig glätter, trete ein, stürze mich dicht vor die Herrin des Hauses, möchte ihr die Hand gleich küssen, gebe indessen den Gedanken auf und begnüge mich damit, eine vollen-dete Verbeugung vor ihr zu machen. (*SW* III: 73)

> (The servant opened the hospitable gate. Hospitable gate? An expression straight from the *Feuilleton* pages but I love adopting the style of small daily goods. I hand over my hat and coat with as much manner as I can muster, further pat down my already smooth hair in front of the mirror, enter, plunge myself into close proximity with the lady of the house, want to kiss her hand straightaway but abandon that idea and content myself with executing a perfect bow before her.)

Both the *Feuilleton* and the dinner are introduced here as highly stylized affairs, demanding proficiency in a particular social code that fuses established class consciousness with modern attention to fashion and the cultivation of the 'right' social pace and tone. Re-enacting the dinner evening from arrival to departure in the present, the self in this piece is shown to practice an alien style. Astonished by his unaccustomed worldly demeanour, which 'enables me to transport food to my mouth with such style, while chatting away' (*SW* III: 74), he self-consciously highlights his status as born imitator ('geborner Nachahmer') of a society conditioned by 'fortlaufende Nachahmung' ('continuous imitation' (*SW* III: 74)). Mimicry appears here as a quintessential social tool that, on the one hand, enables the proletarian or rural self to adapt to this high-class metropolitan setting through role-play, while, on the other, also serving the exposure of the authoritarian and disciplinary function of such social etiquette. The humorous slippage in this piece therefore continually disavows the very social rules that it appears to uphold, as the Walserian self's performance surreptitiously displaces the mechanisms of social surveillance and power. Red-faced and increasingly inebriated, the self eventually reveals his proletarian background as he greedily devours large quantities of food and drink, surprised by the seemingly never-ending sequence of courses:

> O ich freue mich über das alles, ich Proletarier, was ich bin. Mein Gesicht ist ein wahres hochrotes Eßgesicht, aber essen Aristokraten etwa nicht auch? ... Was? Auch noch Käse? Und noch Obst und jetzt noch einmal einen See von Sekt.
>
> (*SW* III: 75)

> (O, I am so delighted with everything, proletarian that I am. My face is a truly and deeply red dining face, but don't aristocrats have to eat too? ... What? There is even cheese? And fruit and now a whole lake of sparkling wine.)

Even though the self continues to claim metropolitan 'Weltsicherheit' ('wordliness'), as he traverses the reception rooms smoking a cigar, the slippage in his role-play pinpoints his separation from the social and symbolic capital of metropolitan high society.

An altogether different mode of sociality finds articulation in Walser's prose piece 'Aschinger', which was published in *Die neue Rundschau* in December 1907. The piece describes the self's bustling observations of the comings and goings during a visit to one of the popular Aschinger beer halls. Originally founded in 1892 by the brothers August and Karl, the first Aschinger establishment introduced the principle of the fast delivery of food and beverages: besides drawing the beer for the first time openly behind a counter in the beer hall, they introduced raised tables that allowed customers to consume their beers quickly while standing up. The brothers also devised a fast-food menu, offering simple fare such as 'Erbsensuppe mit Speck' (pea soup with bacon) or 'kalte Mamsell',[22] at affordable prices. With their appeal to mass consumerism and affordability, as underlined by their motto 'billig und schnell' (cheap and fast), Aschinger restaurants and beer halls quickly established themselves in the surroundings of the big railway stations Friedrichstraße, Zoo and Alexanderplatz; others could be found at Spittelmarkt, Potsdamer Platz, in Friedrich- and Leipziger Straße, in Gesundbrunnen and in Neukölln. The brothers later expanded their business by adding a chain of stylish patisseries and restaurants to their portfolio. By the beginning of the 1930s the Aschinger empire comprised twenty-three beer halls, fifteen patisseries, eight restaurants and twenty food stalls. Every day some 40,000 customers frequented one of the Aschinger food and drink outlets.[23]

In his 'Aschinger' piece Walser interweaves the description of the self's ostentatiously relaxed consumption of beer and food with considerations that concern the regulation of behaviour in an environment that stands for the modern production of time as a prized resource. While the employment of the present tense throughout the piece accentuates the hustle and bustle of continual arrival and departure in the restaurant, the self is introduced as a calm participant-observer who, with a good measure of 'Seelenruhe' ('serenity' (SW III: 67)), consumes his fare, while observing the locality and people around him with an anthropological eye. In contrast to 'Dinerabend' where Walser self-consciously mimicked an upper class code, in the fast consumption environment of Aschinger his behaviour appears as habitualized and well-practised, conversational in style: smearing mustard on a slice of bread with a small spoon, he declares that at Aschinger's, one soon adopts a tone of familiarity while eating and drinking ('einen Eß-und Trink-Vertraulichkeitston' (SW III: 67)). And yet, even though the two pieces represent opposite ends of modern food culture, both enact an anthropology of observation that foregrounds the regulation of social conduct through location-specific scripts. Hence the self's role as social anthropologist who, having satisfied his basic needs, can now engage in 'all sorts of observations ... One wants to have registered exactly how the Berliners eat' (SW III: 67). As he annotates the customers' routines, he also foregrounds the role of the furnishings that manage and regulate movement through space:

> Die Unbefriedigten finden rasch an der Bierquelle und am warmen Wurstturm Befriedigung, und die Satten springen wieder in die Geschäftsluft hinaus, gewöhnlich eine Mappe unter dem Arm, einen Brief in der Tasche, einen Auftrag im Gehirn, einen festen Plan im Schädel, eine Uhr in der offenen Hand, die sagt, daß es jetzt Zeit ist. Im runden Turm in der Mitte des Gemaches thront eine junge Königin, es ist die Beherrscherin der Würste und des Kartoffelsalates (SW III: 68)

(The dissatisfied can soon enough satisfy their desire at the beer tap and the warm sausage mountain, and those who are replete can bounce back into the world of business, usually equipped with a folder under their arm, a letter in their pocket, an order on their brain, a real plan in their head, a watch in their open hand, which tells them that it is now high time. In the round tower in the middle of the chamber a young queen sits on her throne, she is ruler over the sausages and potato salad.)

The description of the locality in terms of a 'Gemach' (chamber), which is overseen by a 'junge Königin' (young queen), produces characteristic narrative irony, but it also serves to ennoble a modern and intrinsically democratic establishment that levels the relevance of social class. Accordingly, the self humorously notes the embarrassment of a fine lady as she awkwardly picks up her 'Kaviarbrötchen' (caviar roll) with her two fingers instead of the accustomed fork (SW III: 68). The self's observations of people are punctuated by comments that foreground his own presence in the restaurant while also recording the leisurely passage of time. As a modern fast-food establishment with a high turnover, Aschinger provides the self with the right conditions for experiencing a heightened sense of laissez-faire and of an individuality that is paradoxically based on anonymity: 'And the best of all is that you can stand there in the same spot for hours on end; nobody minds, not a single one of those who come and go find this strange. He who takes a liking to humbleness, can get by here, he can live, nobody will stop him' (SW III: 70). In 'Aschinger' Walser represents not so much the malaise of an alienating metropolitan culture and modernity's inexorable time regime, but rather a buzzing node of connectivity between an observant self and a world in flux that levels social differences. For Walser, the fast-food restaurant is a metropolitan institution that fosters a democratic form of individuality by introducing egalitarian codes of behaviour.

Walser's 'Gebirgshallen' (Mountain Halls), published under the title 'Reklame' (Advertisement) in Die Schaubühne in February 1908, adds a further facet to his anthropology of urban conduct: the piece choreographs a visit to the eponymous tavern that was situated Unter den Linden and offered garish dance-hall performances in front of a tacky stage set of papier-mâché glaciers and alpine mountains. Parodically adopting the style of an advertisement or tourist guidebook, 'Gebirgshallen' enacts close proximity to the reader: 'Kennen Sie die Gebirgshallen unter den Linden? Vielleicht probieren Sie einmal einen Gang dorthin. Der Eintritt kostet nur dreißig Pfennig' ('Do you know the Gebirgshallen on Unter den Linden? Perhaps you might venture there one day. Admission is only thirty Pfennig' (SW III: 42)). The piece then exposes the commodification of the longing for authentic experience in modernity by intertwining the worn rhetoric of the modern tourist and entertainment industry with descriptive elements that evoke the long tradition of nature discourse in German literature and thought. Accordingly, the reader is invited to the Gebirgshallen, where she encounters the owner in Swiss costume before meeting the female dancers and waitresses who are dressed up in alpine outfits as they perform their acts or deliver drinks. The kitschy alpine decorations and costumes are indispensable accessories of a particular choreography of eroticism that connects the vaudeville tradition with the idea of Swiss 'Urtümlichkeit' (earthiness), that is, rural authenticity. While in 'Dinerabend' parodic slippage was produced through the role-play of the Walserian self, here that slippage is a design feature of a metropolitan locality that, in today's parlance, would be called a 'themed pub'.

In his seminal *Eine Theories des Tourismus* (A Theory of Tourism), Hans Magnus Enzensberger tracked the emergence of modern tourism around 1800 at a time when Romanticism projected the desire for freedom and happiness onto a nature that had seemingly escaped the disappointing and alienating conditions of the post-revolutionary age.[24] The Romantic poetic imagination and ideology, argues Enzensberger, simultaneously preserved and betrayed the revolutionary ideal of freedom by projecting it onto a nature that was conceived as the untainted other of culture. Modern tourism emerges in the same period to then take advantage of the enduring identification of freedom with nature by commodifying, repackaging and reinventing the modern longing for authenticity. This is precisely the cultural-historical background of Walser's prose piece 'Gebirgshallen' which challenges and overturns the binary dichotomy between the perceived inauthenticity of modern culture and a seemingly authentic nature. Even though Walser's piece clearly parodies the gaudy kitsch of the Gebirgshallen establishment, he suggests here that kitsch is a modern variant of the Romantic longing for authenticity. And so it is that the artificiality of the world of the Gebirgshallen can indeed engender authentic longing. In line with this, at the end of the piece the narrating self drops the role of the tourist guide, as he retreats into his inner world of longing and dreams:

> Gehen Sie doch mal hin, ich kann Ihnen sagen, na! Vielleicht treffen Sie dort auch mich wieder einmal an. Ich aber werde Sie gar nicht kennen, ich pflege dort, von Zaubereien gebannt, stillzusitzen. Ich lösche dort meine Dürste, Melodien wiegen mich ein, ich träume. (*SW* III: 44).

> (Why don't you go there one day – I am telling you! Perhaps you will meet me there too. But I won't recognize you, as I tend to sit still spellbound by magic. I quench my thirsts there, melodies cradle me and I dream.)

The three texts discussed here gesture towards an anthropology of urban conduct by foregrounding the production of urban sociality through location-specific scripts. While 'Dinerabend' parodically explores the display of class-consciousness amongst the metropolitan elite, 'Aschinger' stages the modern fast-food restaurant as the democratic site par excellence of a new form of individuality that flourishes through anonymity. Here the self exercises control over social time by prolonging his stay in an otherwise fast-paced environment. His leisurely observations of the flow of activity from a stationary position accentuate the polychronic temporality of the metropolis: the city not only observes the modern script of synchronized acceleration and the Taylorian time regime, but it also brings forth new forms of asynchronicity that appeal to the poetic imagination. And this extends from Walser's captivation by urban sociality in interior spaces to the Walserian experience of perambulation and street life in Berlin.

Urban Street Life

In his *Practices of Everyday Life*, Michel de Certeau argues that the view from the modern skyscraper across the metropolis is an optical illusion that resembles the visual simulacra or models created by urban planners. Both perspectives offer totalizing top-down vistas that are divorced from the everyday practice at street level where the footsteps of urban walkers weave places together, enacting 'a mobile organicity' that resists panoptical surveillance.[25] For de Certeau, urban walking thus belongs to a set of spatial practices that 'elude discipline without being outside the field in which it is exercised'.[26] He further defines urban walking as akin to the performance of language, where the walking subject can divert and displace the rhetorical system, the moves and turns, that the regulation of city space imposes.[27]

De Certeau's translation of walking as urban practice into a subversive language resonates with Robert Walser who, in complementary fashion, turned the production of prose sketches into a form of leisurely walking. In the longer prose narrative *Der Spaziergang* (The Walk (1917)) the reader encounters a self whose leisurely excursion into the suburbs of an unnamed Swiss town is replicated by a meandering narrative voice which is evidently unperturbed by the economy of speed.[28] Surrounded by a working population that has internalized the time management of modern life and is therefore quite hostile to this walking misfit, the Walserian peripatetic self stimulates his poetic imagination through deliberate desynchronization. While the inhabitants of the small Swiss town demonstrate their disapproval of the self's anti-social and displaced behaviour, the enactment of social censorship is much more complicated in the metropolis. The continual flow of traffic and people at street level not only impedes the identification of misdemeanours, it also creates new energizing multiplicities, dynamic intersections and dazzling visual attractions. 'Großstadtstraße' (Urban Street), 'Guten Tag, Riesin!' (Good Day, Giantess), 'Berlin W', 'Auf der Elektrischen' (On the Tram) and 'Friedrichstraße' are examples of short prose pieces that thematize the creation of a new urban sensibility through continual mobility.

'Friedrichstraße' appeared in *Die neue Rundschau* in August 1909 and begins with a vertical upward perspective that is drawn towards large-lettered advertisements at roof level before zooming in on the street as metropolitan site of a ceaseless flow of movement. Note how Walser's description combines elements of a metropolitan modernity that is designed to create visual spectacle with nature imagery that captures an invigorating vitality:

> Bis zu den Dächern hinauf und über die Dächer noch hinaus schweben und kleben Reklamen. Große Buchstaben fallen in die Augen. Und immer gehen hier Menschen. Noch nie, seit sie ist, hat in dieser Straße das Leben aufgehört zu leben. Hier ist das Herz, die unaufhörlich atmende Brust des großstädtischen Wesens. Hier atmet es hoch auf und tief nieder, als wenn das Leben selber über seinem Schritt und Tritt unangenehm beengt wäre. Hier ist die Quelle, der Bach der Fluß und das Meer der Bewegungen. (*SW* III: 76).

> (Right up to roof level, and even beyond, advertisements hover and cling. Large lettering catches the eye. And people incessantly walk along. Never since this street has existed has life come to a standstill here. It is the heart, the continually breathing bosom of metropolitan organism. Here, life itself breathes deeply in and out as if it were uncomfortably restricted on every step of the way. Here is the source, the stream the river and the ocean of all movement)

The typically Walserian anthropomorphism evokes the street as a theatre of a dynamic totality of life. His description taps into *Lebensphilosophie*, a school of thought that, inspired by Nietzsche's and Schopenhauer's anti-rationalism, combined the rejection of Western intellectualism with a search for a more intuitive and mystical understanding of the world and all its phenomena. In 'Friedrichstraße', social antagonisms and differences are neutralized by way of an organic proximity of people and things. For Walser, the choreography of crowd movement on the street produces a new form of social tolerance and acceptance, 'weil jeder einzelne, durch den Zwang des zusammengeknebelten Verkehrs genötigt, ohne Zaudern alles, was er hört und sieht, billigen muß' ('because by force of the tightly controlled and gagged traffic everyone must willy-nilly tolerate everything that he hears and sees' (*SW* III: 77)). Even though this new mode of mutual toleration is brought forth by 'Zwang', it carries the utopian promise of social inclusiveness. Rather than a locus of anonymity and alienation, the street is the true 'Heimat der Nichstwürdigen, der Kleinen' ('home of the undeserving, the little people' (*SW* III: 78)). It is not moral conviction or political consensus that inspires this new form of tolerance but merely the steady footfall of rushed pedestrians and traffic flow patterns. The small form is particularly suited to paying attention to the little people even in their metropolitan massification.

At the same time the production of a specifically metropolitan code of toleration also comes with new modes of self-discipline and uniformity that ache for release. Friedrichstraße is thus shown to morph at night into a titillating stage for entertainment and amusement, unleashing pent-up passions. As people chase their unfulfilled desires, 'ein wollüstig auf und nieder atmender Körpertraum' ('a bodily dream, voluptuously breathing up and down' (*SW* III: 79)) descends on the street. With this final and strikingly anthropomorphic image, Walser envisages the urban street as a vital organism pulsing with the flow of desire and life.

While 'Friedrichstraße' unfolds a chronological schedule that takes the reader from day time activity to the electrifying night life, 'Guten Tag, Riesin!' delves into the polychronicity of urban life in the early morning hours: here, the pathways of blue collar workers, small salesmen, early travellers and girls from all walks of life cross with an assortment of late night revellers who are being catapulted out into the streets (*SW* III: 65). Such dissonances invite fleeting engagement that favours the fragmentary detail above and beyond a totalizing panoramic view. The impressionistic annotation of a world in flux takes the place of the authoritative description of a stable urban physiognomy. As Peter Fritzsche comments, the *Feuilletonists* of the early twentieth century 'did not nail down city matters but merely alerted readers to detail and fluctuation. As a result, the city became equally unknowable and equally astonishing to all its readers.'[29]

Walser's itinerary also takes him to Kurfürstendamm and Tauentzienstraße in West Berlin where everybody seems to know 'was sich schickt' ('what is in' (*SW* III: 79–80)). Accordingly, 'Berlin W' which was published in October 1910 in *Die neue Rundschau*, unfolds a topography of style and stylization which contrasts sharply with the street democracy of 'Friedrichstraße'. The 'elegance of the West' enlists precisely the 'gewisse Kälte' ('a certain coldness' (*SW* III: 79)) that, according to Georg Simmel, is a hallmark of modern city life. In his seminal essay 'Die Großstädte und das Geistesleben' of 1903, Simmel scrutinized the psychological effects of the city dweller's exposure to quickly changing stimuli and fractured sensations that succeed each other in sharp discontinuity.[30] According to his argument, the metropolitan environment propagates a dramatic 'intensification of nervous stimulation' that necessitates the development of a protective mechanism.[31] In reaction to the perpetual onslaught of visual and aural sensations modern man mutates into a hardened self who cultivates indifference to all genuine individuality, hence his strikingly blasé attitude, which – according to Simmel – shields him from the incessant impact of disparate images, impressions and sounds. In line with Simmel's analysis, Walser's prose text introduces West Berlin as the proper habitat of a modern masculinity that shuns the display of feelings and gallantry of old in favour of a code of behaviour which is driven by capitalist interests: 'The gentlemen's world of today is the world of business, and he who has to earn money has little or no time to behave particularly nicely. That's the reason for the rather rough and disparaging tone.' (SW III: 80). A theme of many of Walser's prose pieces, 'Ritterlichkeit' (gallantry) connotes not so much the social and gender differences of the now obsolete feudal order but rather a form of theatrical role-play that makes room for adventure, poetry and the possibility of parodic slippage. Because the modern masculinity of the Kurfürstendamm services capitalist aims, the self promptly turns his poetic attention to a range of odd characters who stand out in the crowd, such as 'die Emporkömmlingin' ('female social climber'), 'die Kleine vom Kurfürstendamm' (presumably a well-known prostitute) or the 'Lebegreis' ('the aged bon vivant' (SW III: 80)). And yet, in spite of this typology of difference, West Berlin exemplifies the capitalist impoverishment of imagination: 'Die hiesigen Frauen sind schön und anmutig! Die Gärten sind sauber, die Architektur ist vielleicht ein wenig drastisch, was kann mich das kümmern' ('The local women are beautiful and charming! The gardens are clean, the architecture perhaps a little bombastic but what do I care!' (SW III: 81)). For all its stylishness and youthfulness, Berlin West leaves the self ultimately unmoved. In line with this, 'Berlin W' passes over well-known landmarks such as the Kaufhaus des Westens, the famous Café des Westens where the likes of Max Liebermann, Alfred Kerr, Christian Morgenstern, Frank Wedekind and Max Reinhardt socialized, or any mention of the Lunapark, which had opened in 1909 at the end of the Kurfürstendamm in Halensee as Europe's biggest leisure park. Unlike in 'Friedrichstraße' or 'Guten Tag, Riesin!', the self in 'Berlin W' does not adopt the street perspective of the flâneur, who as Benjamin remarked, spends his time 'botanizing on the asphalt',[32] but rather a digressive style that indicates a degree of unmistakable boredom with his topic. At the end of his piece he self-consciously reproduces the somewhat exhausted register of the tourist guide, albeit with a twist:

Aber wie schwenke ich da nur ab? Darf man das? Es gibt einen sogenannten alten Westen, einen neueren Westen (rund um die Gedächtniskirche) und einen ganz neuen Westen. Der mittlere ist vielleicht der netteste. Ganz bestimmt trifft man in der Tauentzienstraße die höchste und meiste Eleganz; der Kurfürstendamm ist reizend mit seinen Bäumen und seinen Kaleschen. Ich sehe mich mit großem Bedauern schon an den Rahmen meines Aufsatzes anstoßen in der fatalen Überzeugung, daß ich vieles, was ich unbedingt habe sagen wollen, gar nicht gesagt habe. (*SW* III: 81–2).

(But how I have deviated from my topic! Is that allowed? There is the so-called old West, a newer West (around the Memorial Church) and the very latest West. Perhaps the middle one is the nicest. But you will definitely find the highest level of elegance in Tauentzienstraße; Kurfürstendamm is charming with its trees and coaches. It is with great regret that I see myself bumping in to the frame of my essay in the fatal knowledge that I have not said much of what I really wanted to say.)

This hyperbolic declaration of regret at having reached the frame, i.e. the end of his essay, reminds the reader that this version of West Berlin is a 'word city', to appropriate Fritzsche's phrase, produced by a writing self under the constraints of the modern literary market that requires parceled digestibility.

Walser's Berlin pieces delve into specifically urban modes of behaviour, attention and distraction, alongside class and gender positions. They stand at the beginning of a particularly fertile literary tradition that offers multifaceted, vivid and contradictory representations of Berlin as the European theatre par excellence of an explosive process of modernization. On the one hand, they tap into the tradition of Impressionism by foregrounding the instability of fleeting visual impressions that dissolve objects into a fascinating constellation of shapes and forms. On the other, however, these prose pieces clearly reveal Walser's keen awareness of the city as a socially contested space in which established class and gender positions can be confirmed, challenged and over-turned. These sketches work towards an anthropology of urban conduct, foregrounding precisely the location-specific scripts which are normally part of tacit social knowledge. By exploring these scripts through a humorous and highly self-conscious style, Walser employs a Brechtian technique of alienation *avant la lettre*, thereby exposing the irresolvable tension between the capitalist production of class differences on the one hand and the anarchic democratic impulse of modern urbanization on the other. Walser's vertical social perspective is therefore often undercut by a hori-zontal line of experience that showcases street life in pre-war Berlin as a paradigmatic site of practised democracy.

Even though Imperial Berlin was undoubtedly politically ossified and repressive, the practice of everyday life, as presented in Walser's prose, creates surprising proximities, connections and juxtapositions at street level that point to a radically modern urban sociality. Perhaps Walser's observations about metropolitan life are so astute because they remain latently shadowed by his Swiss background and his status as outsider. This is most evident in 'Gebirgshallen' where the false alpine stage props unleash longing for an authentic nature. Such moments regularly puncture a topography of modernity that, in its fast-paced forward drive, inevitably brings forth a whole range of conflicting temporalities. Accordingly, Walser's prose piece 'Auf der Elektrischen' foregrounds not so much the thrill of speedy transport as habitual boredom, marshalling new strategies of attention in the observing self.[33] Berlin West and especially the Kurfürstendamm, at the time of Walser's stay becoming established as 'Inbegriff urbaner Asphaltkultur' ('the incarnation of urban asphalt culture'), appear in his prose piece as a gendered locus of accelerated capitalism that leaves the observing self unmoved.[34] By contrast, Friedrichstraße and Tiergarten appear as exhilarating sites of a democratic heterogeneity that brings forth fresh modes of social proximity. Walser's exemplary topography of early twentieth-century Berlin is thus uneven: it showcases the city as a heterogeneous social space that is 'always under construction'.[35] As a fluid and highly dynamic genre that advances new modes of attention the short prose sketch is particularly suited to capturing the evolving city through 'a simultaneity of stories so far'.[36]

NOTES

1. *Mark Twain's Travel Letters from 1891–92*, with original illustrations by Dan Beard and Harold R. Heaton, *Chicago Daily Tribune*, 3 April 1892. See http://twainquotes.com/Travel1891/April1892.html (accessed 27 August 2014).
2. Peter Fritsche, *Reading Berlin 1900* (Cambridge, MA: Harvard University Press, 1996), p. 1.
3. Ibid., p. 5.
4. Werner Faulstich, *Medienwandel im Industrie- und Massenzeitalter 1830–1900* (Göttingen: Vandenhoeck & Ruprecht, 2004), p. 31.
5. Christian Jäger and Erhard Schütz, *Städtebilder zwischen Literatur und Journalismus: Wien, Berlin und das Feuilleton der Weimarer Republik* (Wiesbaden: Deutscher Universitätsverlag, 1999), pp. 9–10.
6. Fritzsche, *Reading Berlin 1900*, p. 29.
7. Günter Oesterle, '"Unter dem Strich": Skizze einer Kulturpoetik des Feuilletons', in *Das schwierige neunzehnte Jahrhundert: Germanistische Tagung zum 65. Geburtstag von Eda Sagarra im August 1998*, eds Jörgen Barkhoff et al. (Tübingen: Niemeyer, 2000), pp. 230–50 (p. 235).
8. *Geschichte der Frankfurter Zeitung von 1856 bis 1906*, ed. Verlag der Frankfurter Zeitung (Frankfurt a. M.: August Osterrieth, 1911), p. 919.

Short Prose around 1900

9. Letter by Joseph Roth to Benno Reifenberg, 22 April 1926, in Joseph Roth, *Briefe 1911–1939*, ed. Hermann Kesten (Cologne, Berlin: Kiepenheuer & Witsch, 1970), p. 87.

10. Christian Jäger and Ehrhard Schütz (eds), *Glänzender Asphalt: Berlin im Feuilleton der Weimarer Republik* (Berlin: Fannei & Waltz, 1994), p. 336.

11. Andreas Huyssen, 'Modernist Miniatures: Literary Snapshots of Urban Spaces', *PMLA* 122/1 (2007), pp. 27–42 (p. 29).

12. Thomas Althaus, Wolfgang Bunzel and Dirk Göttsche, 'Ränder, Schwellen, Zwischenräume: Zum Standort Kleiner Prosa im Literatursystem der Moderne', in *Kleine Prosa: Theorie und Geschichte eines Textfeldes im Literatursystem der Moderne*, eds Th. Althaus, W. Bunzel, D. Göttsche (Tübingen: Niemeyer, 2007), pp. IX–XXVII (p. IX).

13. Peter Altenberg, 'Selbstbiographie', in P. Altenberg, *Auswahl aus seinen Büchern*, ed. by Karl Kraus (Frankfurt am Main: Insel, 1997), p. 59.

14. Althaus, Bunzel, Göttsche, 'Ränder Schwellen, Zwischenräume', p. XX.

15. Jonathan Crary, *Suspensions of Perception: Attention, Spectacle, and Modern Culture* (Cambridge, MA: Harvard University Press, 2001).

16. Robert Walser, 'Was aus mir wurde', in R. Walser, *Bedenkliche Geschichten: Prosa aus der Berliner Zeit 1906–1912. Sämtliche Werke in Einzelausgaben* (Frankfurt a. M.: Suhrkamp, 1985), vol. XV, pp. 73–4 (henceforth *SW*).

17. Jäger and Schütz, *Glänzender Asphalt*, p. 343.

18. Georg Simmel, 'Die Grossstädte und das Geistesleben', in *Gesamtausgabe*, ed. Rüdiger Kramme (Frankfurt am Main: Suhrkamp, 1995), vol. 7, pp. 227–42. Robert Walser, *Jakob von Gunten: Ein Tagebuch, Sämtliche Werke in Einzelausgaben*, ed. Jochen Greven (Frankfurt am Main: Suhrkamp, 1991), vol. 11.

19. Walser, *Jakob von Gunten*, pp. 37–8.

20. Karl Walser's work included the set for Reinhardt's production of *A Midsummer Night's Dream*, which used a revolving stage for the first time. See Bernhard Echte and Andreas Meier (eds), *Die Brüder Karl und Robert Walser: Maler und Dichter* (Zurich: Rothenhäusler Verlag Stäfa, 1990), pp. 178–82.

21. The complete guest list is cited in ibid., p. 200 (footnote 172).

22. The 'kalte Mamsell' or 'Kaltmamsell' was the female kitchen employee responsible for arranging all cold food, and the term refers to cold buffet food, such as sandwiches and salads.

23. Hans Aschenbrenner, 'Bei Aschinger – fast wie früher'. See http://www.luise-berlin.de/bms/bmstxt99/9906nova.htm, (accessed 2 April 2014).

24. Hans Magnus Enzensberger, 'Eine Theorie des Tourismus', in H. M. Enzensberger, *Einzelheiten I & II* (Hamburg: Spiegel Verlag, 2009), pp. 177–203 (p. 188).

25. Michel de Certeau, *The Practice of Everyday Life*, trans. Steven Rendall (Berkeley, London, Los Angeles: University of California Press, 1988), p. 99.

26. Ibid., p. 97.

27. Ibid., p. 100.

28. Robert Walser, 'Der Spaziergang', in *Sämtliche Werke in Einzelausgaben*, ed. Jochen Greven, 20 vols (Zurich, Frankfurt am Main: Suhrkamp, 1986), vol. 5, pp. 7–77. A slightly edited version appeared in *Seeland* (see *SW* VII: 83–151).

29. Fritzsche, *Reading Berlin 1900*, p. 94.

30. Simmel, 'Die Grossstädte und das Geistesleben', p. 229.

31. Ibid., p. 228.
32. Benjamin, 'Paris in the Second Empire in Baudelaire', cited in Fritzsche, *Reading Berlin 1900*, p. 91.
33. Robert Walser, *Drucke im Berliner Tagblatt*, ed. Hans-Joachim Heerde, in Robert Walser, *Kritische Ausgabe sämtlicher Drucke und Manuskripte*, eds Wolfram Groddeck and Barbara von Reibnitz (Frankfurt am Main, Basel: Stroemfeld, 2013), vol. 3.1, pp. 21–4.
34. Jäger and Schütz (eds), 'Nachwort', p. 340.
35. Doreen Massey, *For Space* (London: Sage, 2005), p. 9.
36. Ibid.

5

CAROLIN DUTTLINGER

Modernist Writing and Visual Culture

The (In)visible City

In his foreword to Mario von Bucovich's 1928 photobook *Berlin*, Alfred Döblin explores the fundamental difficulties of representing the modern city. As a result of faster lenses, lighter cameras and more sensitive film, photography in the early twentieth century had become synonymous with the snapshot, a medium ideally suited to capture the fast-changing urban environment. And yet, as Döblin argues, photographers were likely to miss the 'real' Berlin:

> Berlin consists, first, of the bequest of a number of deceased people and, second, of that which people are doing today.
> The former can be accessed by means of a cemetery visit (sightseeing tour), and the individual parts of this wardrobe of remains [die einzelnen Stücke der Nachlaßgarderobe] can easily be photographed. Most of the latter, however, cannot be photographed at all, or isn't worth photographing. In other words: Berlin is mostly invisible.[1]

Berlin comprises two cities: that of the living and that of the dead. Monarchs and rulers have left their mark through architectural landmarks – remnants of a past both glorious and oppressive – while the 'invisible' lives of the current inhabitants will leave no lasting trace and cannot, Döblin claims, be captured on camera. While this situation of unequal visibility applies to all cities of all ages, it takes on a particular significance in the case of early twentieth-century Berlin, where tradition and modernity sat uneasily side by side. After 1871, the young German Empire projected its ambition through grand building projects such as the Reichstag, the Kaiser Wilhelm Memorial Church and the Berlin Cathedral, thereby obliterating much of the historical character of the old Prussian capital. If Paris was, according to Walter Benjamin, the 'capital of the nineteenth century', then Berlin, the latecomer and upstart, was arguably the capital of the twentieth,[2] the quintessential modern city. This modernity harboured both challenges and opportunities. For the seasoned traveller, Döblin argues, Berlin could be rather disappointing, particularly when compared to such cities as Paris or London. Döblin sees Berlin as 'an unpoetic and not very colourful city, but a very true one',[3] a view shared by writers both German and international:

> At 3 A. M. the people of Berlin will light another cigar and embark afresh and refreshed upon discussions regarding Proust, or Rilke, or the new penal code, or whether human shyness comes from narcissism ... The eyes that in London or Paris would already have drooped in sleep are busy in Berlin, inquisitive, acquisitive, searching, even at 4 A. M., for some new experience or idea.[4]

Berlin's youthful energy is one recurrent theme; another one is tempo, or rhythmic speed: 'Tempo is linked to a city's layout. Can someone adopt a Berlin pace in Paris, even when he's in a hurry? He can't.'[5] Siegfried Kracauer, one of Weimar Germany's most incisive cultural commentators, was also a trained architect, and his remarks touch on issues of urban planning. Between 1900 and 1920, Berlin's population doubled from two million to four million, and by the late 1920s the city was short of about 200,000 dwellings. This prompted ambitious construction projects, such as the Hufeisen Siedlung in Britz and the Waldsiedlung in Zehlendorf – large-scale suburban garden settlements overseen by Bauhaus architect Bruno Taut. Inevitably, these building projects attracted criticism for being too vast, too uniform and too starkly modern. For Döblin, however, they embodied Berlin in its essence and at its best. As he argues, a traveller entering the city by train, preferably at night, could not help but realize that this was 'a truly modern city, a great city, the dwelling of current people'.[6]

By looking at Berlin through the photographer's lens, Döblin touches on issues which also concerned writers, painters and filmmakers. Not all shared his vision of the anonymous, quotidian city, but the challenge of how to depict Berlin in ways which captured its modernity – a modernity both febrile and prosaic, vibrant and invisible – underpinned creative responses to the city in the first decades of the twentieth century, from Expressionism via Dada to New Objectivity. These decades, arguably the richest and most internationally resonant in the life of Berlin, saw a veritable explosion of styles, schools and movements which coexisted, often in a state of conflict, against the backdrop of seismic political change, which led from the Wilhelmine Empire via the lost war to the short-lived democratic experiment of the Weimar Republic, which was terminated by National Socialism. By depicting Berlin in a state of flux and conflict, Modernist writers and artists actively intervened in its (cultural) politics, although such interventions manifested themselves in different ways and were pursued with very different agendas.

Double Visions: Berlin in Expressionist Poetry

In Germany, the 1910s are known as the 'Expressionist decade'. Expressionism was a youth movement united by rebellion against the institutions of Wilhelmine Germany and by an (albeit loosely defined) agenda of individual change and social transformation. This agenda is encapsulated in the title of Kurt Pinthus's famous anthology of Expressionist poetry, *Menschheitsdämmerung* (Dawn of Humanity (1919)). Berlin was the centre of the movement, the site of a vibrant literary and cultural scene. The Berlin-based periodicals *Die Aktion* (The Action) and *Der Sturm* (The Storm) published literature, essays and visual art. Their international list of contributors included emerging as well as established writers, thinkers and artists, with a particular emphasis on the dialogue between French and German Expressionists. To celebrate the publication of the hundredth issue of *Der Sturm* in 1912, its editor Herwarth Walden opened the Sturm-Galerie, which became a centre of international art for over a decade. A key literary forum was the 'Neue Club' (New Club) near Hackescher Markt, whose public events, the so-called 'Neopathetisches Cabaret' (Neo-Pathetic Cabaret), were explosive and rather short-lived, ending after just two years in 1912.

The city is a key theme in Expressionist writing, and Berlin a major inspiration. The focus is usually on the negative aspects of urban life – poverty, prostitution and disease, sensory overload, anonymity and loneliness. In this, Expressionism was influenced by Naturalism, although Naturalist quasi-scientific exactitude gave way to subjectively distorted visions of city life and transformational, allegorical modes of writing.

One of the hubs of the movement was the Café Josty on Berlin's Potsdamer Platz, which is the subject of Paul Boldt's 1912 poem 'Auf der Terrasse des Café Josty' (On the Terrace of the Café Josty):

> Der Potsdamer Platz in ewigem Gebrüll
> Vergletschert alle hallenden Lawinen
> Der Straßentrakte: Trams auf Eisenschienen,
> Automobile und den Menschenmüll.
>
> (Potsdamer Platz in an endless roar
> Glaciates all echoing avalanches
> Of the street complex: trams on iron rails,
> Automobiles and the refuse of mankind.)[7]

Writers and artists were attracted by the Josty's bustling location, and Boldt's sonnet highlights the deafening noise and perpetual traffic of vehicles and bodies. In this environment, the individual becomes expendable and worthless, 'Menschenmüll' (the refuse of mankind). But at the same time, the poem also depicts Berlin as an enchanted place shot through with natural imagery. The city becomes a forest and the square a cave, where people move 'Ameisenemsig, wie Eidechsen flink' (quick as ants, nimble as lizards).

In trying to capture the dynamism of Berlin, Modernist writers often focused on its unresolved contradictions: between the individual and the masses, nature and technology, dynamism and stasis. In Boldt's poem, the noise of the streets is 'vergletschert' (glaciated), suspended in time and space. Looking at Berlin often involves looking beyond or away from it – from the bustle of the centre to the stillness of the margins, or from the present to a past either recent or archaic. Both techniques are central to the poetry of Georg Heym, one of Expressionism's most resonant voices.

Heym was born in Lower Silesia and moved to Berlin in 1900. A sense of detachment pervades his 'Berlin' sonnets written in 1910, in which the city is explored through a series of vignettes revolving around a dialectic between dynamism and stasis. In 'Berlin I' the speakers, the anonymous 'we', see 'the city loom far in the fading light'; stretched out by the dusty roadside, they look on as vehicles and people are moving

> Dem Riesensteinmeer zu. Doch westlich sahn
> Wir an der langen Straße Baum an Baum,
> Der blätterlosen Kronen Filigran.
>
> (Towards the giant stone sea. But we looked west,
> saw tree on tree lining the road's long rim,
> the filigree of crowns whose leaves were lost.)[8]

The poetic perspective is bifocal, looking both inwards and outwards; but in both directions, movement ends in deadly stillness. The traffic of 'Automobiles, smoke, horns with their roar' is headed for the 'giant stone sea' of the city, a quasi-natural habitat ossified by modernity, while in the opposite direction, skeletal trees line an avenue leading out into the country-side. This liminal perspective recurs in Heym's other 'Berlin' poems. In 'Berlin VIII', a skyline of chimneys is cast against the 'darkening palace' of the evening sky, whose 'low seam is burning like a golden step' ('Wie goldne Stufe brennt sein niedrer Saum'), an image both beautiful and ominous.[9] As in 'Berlin I', the gaze is drawn away from the city into a bleak countryside, where 'on icy rails a long freight train / is dragging itself heavily along'. In 'Berlin III', the speakers are themselves on a train, which in the final stanza enters into the city:

> Der Zug fuhr an. Wir brausten in die Halle
> Des Bahnhofs ein, die voll war von dem Toben
> Des Weltstadtabends, Lärm und Menschenschwalle.

(The train drew slowly in. We thundered loud
into the station concourse and its crazed
clangour of city sunset, surging crowds.)[10]

In Modernism, the city loses its 'thematic specificity', dissolving into 'a kind of cosmic, random, background noise'.[11] This is particularly true of early Expressionism. While Boldt's and Heym's texts are at least nominally rooted in Berlin, other poems are abstracted from any identifiable location, exploring the city as an archetypal site of modernity, a space both timeless and apocalyptic. In Heym's 'Der Gott der Stadt' (The God of the City (1910)), the big cities are ruled, as well as embodied, by a vengeful pagan god, while Alfred Wolfenstein's 'Städter' (City Dwellers (1914)) focuses on the psychological effects of urban life – on anonymity and solitude, but also a lack of privacy. This poem abounds with images of fragmentation and penetration, whereby boundaries – of buildings, bodies and the mind – become porous and collapse. Houses appear to strangle the street running between them, and inside the trams passengers face each other like 'façades', tied together by voyeurism and desire. Walls are skin-thin, so that 'everyone is involved when I weep', but this solicits no empathy. The city as a space of violated boundaries only highlights the individual's isolation 'in a hidden cave / Untouched and unregarded'.[12]

Dada: 'The Din of the Street'

Expressionist visions of the modern city were bleak and often startling in their focus on violence and destruction. For all their shock value, however, they remained rather abstract, using present-day Berlin as a springboard for archaic, allegorical scenarios. A radically different approach to city life was taken by the Dadaists, the self-declared successors and opponents of Expressionism. At first sight, Dada and Expressionism have a lot in common. Both are youthful movements informed by a strong group identity, an identity shaped by and around the spaces of the city. But while the First World War spelled the end of the first, early phase of Expressionism – many of whose members had naïvely welcomed the war as a catalyst of change, with many subsequently dying in action – Dada emerged during the war and was closely bound up with its trauma. The birthplace of the international Dada movement was the Cabaret Voltaire in Zurich, but from there the writer Richard Huelsenbeck brought it to Berlin in early 1917. War-torn Berlin was a very different location from neutral Zurich, home to wealthy profiteers. Although front-line fighting happened far away, Berlin was deeply scarred by the war. Following severe food rationing, the population was ravaged by hunger and illness; in the freezing winter of 1917–18, when temperatures plummeted to −18°C, people died in their thousands.[13] Having remained physically untouched by the fighting, Berlin subsequently witnessed a succession of attacks from the Left and Right, from the (failed) November Revolution of 1918 to the right-wing Kapp Putsch of 1920, which foreshadowed Hitler's rise to power. The most traumatic of these was the communist Spartacist uprising of January 1919, which resulted in scenes of civil war: street fighting between revolutionaries and government troops, and the siege and shelling of buildings such as the Mossehaus in the publishing district and the police headquarters on Alexanderplatz.

The city's volatile atmosphere offered a fertile ground for Dada's radical politics. At the first Berlin Dada evening in April 1918, Huelsenbeck read out his 'Dadaistisches Manifest' (Dadaist Manifesto), in which he denounced Expressionism as inward-looking and elitist: 'The hatred against the press, the hatred against advertising, the hatred against the sensational is characteristic of people who treasure their armchair more than the din of the street.'[14] So how did Dada engage with the 'din of the street'? The movement did not simply embrace popular culture but rather used it to subversive effect. To this end, Dada appropriated the spaces and institutions of the city. In a parody of commercial language, the movement operated as its own advertising agency, and Dada slogans were posted in shop windows and coffee houses. Raoul Hausmann's poster poems, made up of arbitrary sequences of letters put together with the help of a professional typesetter, were displayed all over Berlin; they too emulated street advertising, while at the same time exposing the arbitrariness of language and meaning.

The key technique of Berlin Dada, however, was photomontage. Dadaists used images found in newspapers and magazines, combining them into subversive and witty artworks. But this montage technique also had a more serious psychological dimension. As Huelsenbeck declared:

> The highest art will be that which … has let itself be thrown by the explosions of the last week, which time and again gathers its limbs together after the crash of the previous day. The best and most extraordinary artists will be those who every hour snatch the tatters of their bodies out of the frenzied cataracts of life, tenaciously holding on to the intellect of their time, bleeding from hands and hearts.[15]

Dada's practices were deeply shaped by the war's effects on individual and society. As Brigid Doherty argues, Dada photomontage aimed to be 'mimetic of traumatic shock in such a way that the materialization of shock experiences would be effected in the bodies of both the maker and the beholder of the dada object'.[16] Yet while Dada montage reflects the trauma of the war, it also points forward towards practices of intermediality in the Weimar Republic. Though Berlin Dada was short lived, culminating in the International Dada Fair of 1920, its members continued to shape Weimar culture. One prominent example is ex-Dadaist John Heartfield, whose photomontages mocking Nazi ideology found a wide circulation through the Berlin-based *Arbeiter Illustrierte Zeitung* (Workers' Illustrated Newspaper); with the writer Kurt Tucholsky, he produced the equally satirical photo-text-book, *Deutschland, Deutschland über alles* (Germany, Germany, Above All (1929)).

In its engagement with the 'din of streets', Berlin Dada laid the foundations for cultural practices which shaped the Weimar Republic, where the separation between 'high' and 'popular' culture became permeable. Weimar Berlin was a centre of 'modernist intermediality', a space 'where artists, writers, film directors and theatre producers experimented with the aesthetic potentials and social effects created by the interaction of various traditional and avant-garde media'.[17] Such encounters, however, were not always harmonious, but reflected an equally volatile social and political climate.

Cool Conduct: The Novels of 'New Objectivity'

The sudden and rather unexpected flourishing of Berlin in the 1920s is a central part of the city's narrative. By common consent, Weimar Berlin was the capital not only of the newly founded German republic but also of international Modernism, attracting writers and artists from all over the world. But this narrative about Berlin in the 'Golden Twenties' eschews the many continuities between pre- and postwar culture, as well as the combination of political and economic crises which shook the city. Political attacks from Left and Right were followed, in 1921, by a hyperinflation from which Germany only emerged in early 1924. After a few years of relative stability, the New York City stock market crash of November 1929 and the ensuing world economic crisis plunged the country into another, even deeper depression.

These events had a profound effect on Berlin's cultural life. The predominant artistic movement of the Weimar Republic, in literature, painting, photography and film, was Neue Sachlichkeit. Often translated as 'New Objectivity', the term gestures back to the 'old' objectivity of nineteenth-century realism but infuses it with a new, modern edge. 'Sachlich' also means factual, matter-of-fact, the opposite of emotional. In this, New Objectivity, like Dada, marked a deliberate move away from the pathos of Expressionism, favouring instead sober, detached modes of representation. Art should be relevant to people's everyday lives, reflecting their experiences and concerns; in literature, the ethos of precise, dispassionate observation reflects the influences of sociology and journalism, the genre of reportage. Many writers turned to journalism to supplement their income, and Weimar newspapers and magazines became a key forum for intellectual debate. This new ethos is summarized by the Prague-born, Berlin-based journalist Egon Erwin Kisch, the self-styled 'rasende' (racing/raving) reporter, writing in 1924:

> Nothing is more startling that the simple truth, nothing more exotic than our own environment, nothing more fantastical than objectivity. And there is nothing more sensational in the whole world than the times in which we live.[18]

The Weimar Republic has been termed the period of 'cool conduct'.[19] In the jungle of the modern city, a space both antagonistic and anarchical, the individual needs to be on the lookout for potential dangers. This need for perpetual vigilance was already highlighted by the sociologist Georg Simmel in his seminal 1903 essay 'The Metropolis and Mental Life', and it recurs in Weimar debates about the modern city, as emblematized by Berlin. One theme that dominated contemporary accounts was Berlin's status as capital of mass entertainment; another, closely related aspect was its perceived moral corruption. The currency devaluation of 1921–4 precipitated a decline in traditional, bourgeois, moral values. Gambling and illicit night-life were thriving. In 1926, 100,000 prostitutes were counted in Berlin, and vice laws were only selectively enforced. As one 1920 article declared, 'Berlin is Becoming a Whore'.[20] Economic deprivation led many middle-class girls and women into prostitution; 'though often associated with glamorous decadence and titillating depravity, Weimar's common prostitution in fact bespeaks the republic's severe economic and juridical inequalities for women'.[21]

The world of crime and prostitution features prominently in Weimar art and culture, where it often serves as the backdrop for modern morality tales tracing an individual's struggle against corruption both external and internal. Döblin's *Berlin Alexanderplatz* is such a story, as is Erich Kästner's bestselling novel *Fabian*, subtitled *Roman eines Moralisten* (The Story of a Moralist (1931)). Kästner's Berlin, as seen through the eyes of a single young man, is the site of erotic adventures, some of which were omitted from the original, censored edition. The opening chapter sets the tone for the rest of the novel:

> The city was like a fair-ground. The house-fronts were bathed in garish light to shame the stars in the sky. An aeroplane droned above the roofs. Suddenly there was a shower of aluminium talers. The passers-by looked up, laughed and bent to pick them up. Fabian fleetingly recalled the fairy tale of the little girl

who lifted her chemise to catch the small change that fell from heaven. Then he took one of the talers from the stiff brim of a stranger's hat. It bore the words: 'Come to the Exotic Bar, 3 Nollendorfplatz, Beautiful girls, Nude tableaux, Pension Condor in the same house'.[22]

This early scene evokes the Brothers Grimm fairy tale about 'The Star Talers', in which a destitute girl, having given away all her possessions to the poor, is showered with gold coins from above. The advertising ploy turns Berlin into a fairy-tale city, an Aladdin's cave of wealth and riches, but once the coins' inscription is revealed, the tale takes a different turn. A girl lifting her chemise can indeed make money in this city, but at what price?

As this opening vignette implies, Kästner's Berlin is a city of surfaces whose deceptive glamour enthrals and corrupts, particularly the naïve newcomer: the novel's original title was *Der Gang vor die Hunde* (Going to the Dogs). Weimar novels often feature outsiders, people who come to Berlin from the provinces and who are both fascinated and repulsed by it. Fabian initially shares this response, but as he frequents Berlin's nightclubs, brothels and bohemian circles, he evolves from a 'moralist' into a realist, who observes events with an air of ironic detachment. And yet Fabian cannot suppress a certain residual idealism. Disillusioned with Berlin and disappointed by love, he moves back to his hometown of Dresden, where he has a sudden revelation: 'Was there not always, everywhere, a stage for those who wished to act? For what had he been waiting all these years?'[23] The opportunity to act presents itself almost immediately, but when Fabian jumps into a river to save a drowning child, this gesture is not heroic but tragicomically futile:

> The little boy swam ashore, howling.
> Fabian drowned. Unfortunately he could not swim.[24]

In his preface to the 1950 edition, Kästner claimed that the book's intended purpose had been to warn against the threat of fascism, but this warning is ambiguous at best. The novel's conclusion presents heroism, individual sacrifice, as outdated, eroded by the moral relativism of the modern city.

A complementary female perspective on Berlin is offered in Irmgard Keun's bestselling novel *Das kunstseidene Mädchen* (The Artificial Silk Girl) of 1932 (see also Chapter 9). It traces the experiences of Doris, a young woman who moves from Cologne to Berlin hoping to become a film star, where she moves from one unhappy affair to the next. As Doris reveals, she normally only gets to travel by taxi 'with men who like to smooch', but today I rode in a taxi alone, like rich people, leaning back in my seat and looking out of the window – lots of cigar stores on the corners – and movie theaters – *The Congress Dances* – Lilian Harvey is blonde – bakeries . . . yellow trams gliding past me and the people inside could tell I was a star – I'm leaning way back in my cushions and I don't watch how the fare is adding up . . . blue lights, red lights, millions of lights – shop windows – dresses, but no models.[25]

The luxury of this taxi ride is the privacy it offers, and yet it remains a vehicle of seeing and being seen. It turns its passenger into a spectacle, her self-perception refracted in the images of a commodity culture which offers only surfaces without a (human) core. Protagonists such as Doris and Fabian are heirs of the flâneur, the nineteenth-century figure who walked the city in leisure. *Flânerie* offered a mobile, proto-cinematic view of the city, but in Modernist narratives, this view is both accelerated and fragmented by modern (transport) technology. Keun's novel recounts the decentred experiences of her protagonist. For Doris, however, this outlook is a deliberate choice: 'I want to write like a movie, because my life is like that and it's going to become even more so . . . And when I read it later on, everything will be like at the movies – I'm looking at myself in pictures.'[26]

Doris's narrative echoes Siegfried Kracauer's analysis of Weimar mass culture. He described its music halls and movie theatres as 'temples of distractions', whose glamour offers momentary respite from the daily struggle for survival, particularly for a new, predominantly urban class of white-collar workers, who lacked a sense of collective identity. Unlike many of his contemporaries, however, Kracauer saw the subversive potential of this situation. The disjointed spectacles of mass entertainment, he argued, held up a mirror to their audience, confronting them with their own isolated existence and hence with the need for greater solidarity. And this cautiously optimistic outlook is mirrored in Keun's novel. Despite a string of ultimately unhappy relationships, Doris is no passive victim but feisty and unsentimental. Her craving for glamour and romance can be read as a textbook case of self-delusion fed by the mass media, but her gaze through the imaginary camera also has a distancing effect, making Doris a typical exponent of cool conduct and a figure of identification for readers of both genders.

Between Animation and Stillness: Ruttmann's *Berlin* Film and the Weimar Photobook

Keun's Doris is enthralled by the cinema and its glamorous fantasies of wealth and romance, an intermedial fascination, also extending to still photography, that is characteristic for the literature of the period. Weimar

Berlin became the centre of German film production, with the headquarters of the UFA (Universum-Film AG) in nearby Babelsberg. Filmmakers used Berlin as the setting for stories of vice, crime and social deprivation, but the late 1920s also saw the emergence of a different, documentary way of filming the city, whereby Berlin became the setting, and indeed the protagonist, of films which focused on the everyday lives of its inhabitants. They include Wilfried Basse's *Markt in Berlin* (Market in Berlin (1929)) and Robert Siodmak's *Menschen am Sonntag* (People on Sunday (1930)). The most prominent of these city documentaries, however, is Walter Ruttmann's *Berlin: Die Sinfonie der Großstadt* (Berlin: The Symphony of a Great City (1927)). It gives its name to the cinematic genre of the 'city symphony' – films which tried to emulate aspects of musical composition, such as rhythm, polyphony and recurring themes, to create a visual structure which eschewed traditional plot and instead tried to organize the many, often incongruous facets of city life into one overarching whole.

Not everyone was convinced by this approach. Siegfried Kracauer criticized the film as insufficiently coherent and analytical, arguing that it was made up of 'scraps' strung together without any underlying purpose. That said, to view the film as straightforwardly realist would be to misunderstand its agenda. In his Bauhaus manifesto *Malerei, Fotografie, Film* (Painting, Photography, Film (1925)), the photographer László Moholy-Nagy argued that film and photography should not simply reproduce reality but should be mobilized in new artistic techniques and genres which showcase the technical media's creative potential, in turn facilitating new modes of perception. Ruttmann's film opens with images of light playing on water, followed by an abstract pattern of moving black and white shapes which evokes a rising and setting sun. It then proceeds with that classical opening of Modernist city narratives: the train journey into the city. Here, the footage of the train and the passing scenery continue the abstract dimension of the opening shots as wheels, tracks, pylons and railway bridges are filmed at close distance and at great speed. The film reflects the experience of the earliest train passengers whose perceptual habits had yet to catch up with the new speed of transport. This focus on the mechanisms of modern technology is a structuring device throughout the film. In capturing a city at the height of modernity, the camera work reflects the achievements, but also the ongoing challenges, of technological acceleration. Having passed meadows, forests and suburban industrial estates, the train eventually enters the city, where advertisements painted onto the facades of tenement houses give a first taste of commodity culture, another recurring theme, until the camera comes to a halt in front of a station sign announcing the destination: 'Berlin'.

While the opening sequence maps a spatial trajectory from the periphery into the centre, the following five 'acts', a nod to classical drama, are structured temporally, tracing a day in the life of Berlin from the early morning until late at night. The first act shows the city waking up, its empty streets gradually populated by animals and people. The speed picks up as factory gates open to admit workers, and the doors of a train depot open to release a train. Throughout the film, the movement of people is juxtaposed with the dynamism of traffic: of trams, cars, trains, bicycles and horse-drawn carriages, which form geometric patterns and lend the film its varied tempi, though every so often 'the visual regime of the city symphony threatens to exceed compositional control'.[27] The speed of the modern city is exhilarating but also potentially destructive, for such technology always harbours the risk of errors and accidents.

The film lacks a conventional narrative plot but is structured around a complex network of recurring but varied motifs edited to produce effects of similarity and contrast. A recurring theme is class. In the lunchtime sequence (Act IV), an outdoor shot of a proletarian mother and her shaven-headed young boys is followed by lavishly arranged food displays and diners in a high-ceilinged restaurant, and then by the two middle-class girls and their mama, all dressed in white, posing for a photographer in the park. Children are a prominent group. They are shown at school and at play; their day mirrors the adult working day, but they also form self-contained little communities with their own rules. In one amusing but puzzling sequence, a young child, perhaps part of circus troupe, is seen playing with some lion cubs.

Indeed, animals form another group which is contrastingly juxtaposed with the human adult sphere. The first living creatures to populate the empty streets in the opening scene are a dog being walked, a cat and a pigeon. Later on, in a scene which prefigures Döblin's *Berlin Alexanderplatz*, a shot of cows being herded into an abattoir is followed by workers arriving at the factory. In amongst the bustle of modern transport, horses are a recurring sight, a reminder of city life in its previous, more sedate incarnation, but also of more recent history. For contemporary viewers, the sight of a horse lying on the ground, eventually struggling back on its feet, would have carried resonances of the recent war, where the plight of horses had poignantly embodied the creatureliness of human suffering, and it is no coincidence that this is followed by a military line-up.

Alongside domestic animals, the film also contains various shots from the Berlin zoo. A sequence showing the frenzied pace of modern communication – of a telephonist shouting into the receiver – is interspersed with images of fighting dogs and monkeys. The latter shot recurs in a vertiginously accelerated sequence which leads up to the film's dramatic climax: the suicide of a woman who jumps from a bridge into the river. While the camera usually shows people from mid-distance, maintaining a documentary detachment, the close-up of the woman's face, her eyes bulging in a state of panic, harks back to the cinema of Expressionism.

The suicide sequence is preceded by a succession of newspaper headlines ('Crisis', Murder', 'Money') and images of a rising storm. The shot of a hat being blown away by the wind recalls the opening of Jakob van Hoddis's famous Expressionist poem 'Weltende' (End of the World (1912)):

> Dem Bürger fliegt vom spitzen Kopf der Hut,
> In allen Lüften hallt es wie Geschrei.
> Dachdecker stürzen ab und gehn entzwei
> Und an den Küsten – liest man – steigt die Flut.
>
> (The burgher's hat flies off his pointed head,
> All airs are echoing like a scream.
> Roofers come crashing down and break apart
> And on the coasts – one reads – the flood is rising.)[28]

Ruttmann's vision of Berlin film is quotidian rather than apocalyptic, but it too contains moments of barely suppressed panic in the face of a looming crisis. One of its harbingers is objectification. In van Hoddis's poem, the image of roofers shattering – like roof tiles – indicates that the boundary between human beings and objects has become blurred. Ruttmann's suicide sequence does not involve the shattering of the body, but the film is full of moments which challenge the dividing line between people and objects. From the early-morning sequence, where the deserted streets are animated only by a piece of paper blown around by the wind and where factory doors open apparently without human agency, his camera is repeatedly drawn to a Berlin devoid of people, a space where objects lead an uncanny life of their own. Shop-window mannequins, dolls and other humanoid figures are a recurrent motif in Ruttmann's film. In a nod to German Romanticism, a period fascinated by apparatuses and automata, Berlin appears as a city populated by human effigies which are associatively, uncannily, connected to the lives of its human inhabitants. In one short sequence, the arrival of a bride at a wedding reception is immediately followed by a shop window full of naked child mannequins arranged in a circle, as if on a merry-go-round and accompanied by a wooden swan (Figure 5.1). The word reflected in the shop window, 'Maschinen' (machines), functions as a kind of caption, alluding to the technologically enhanced

Figure 5.1: Shop-window mannequins, from Walter Ruttmann, *Berlin: Die Sinfonie der Großstadt* (Berlin: The Symphony of a Great City, 1927)

spectacles of urban modernity as well as their filmic representation. And yet, here and throughout Ruttmann's film, the bustle of the metropolis is stalled by lifeless tableaux which reflect a fetishistic fixation on the world of objects but also an uncanny reversal of perceptual agency. The shop window, designed to attract the gaze of passers-by, doubles as a space of surveillance, whereby street life is covertly overseen from its margins.

The world of commodity culture was also a favourite motif of Modernist photography, from Eugène Atget's Paris street scenes to the images of Berlin-based photographers such as Otto Umbehr (Umbo) and Friedrich Seidenstücker. Despite the competition from film, photography remained a central part of Berlin culture during the Weimar years, and images documenting the life of the city and its inhabitants were very popular. Illustrated magazines and newspapers catered to this interest; another prominent medium, however, was the photobook. Innovations in printing technology meant that, for the first time in the history of the book, photographs could be reproduced in high quality and at relatively moderate cost. The Weimar Republic was a golden age of the photobook, and in the late 1920s, several publishers brought out photobooks about Berlin. In addition to Mario von Bucovich's *Berlin* (1928), they

Figure 5.2: 'Grünfeld's Stores, Kurfürstendamm', from Mario von Bucovich, *Berlin* (Berlin: Albertus, 1928)

include Sasha Stone's *Berlin in Bildern* (Berlin in Pictures (1929)) and Laszlo Willinger's *100 x Berlin* (1929). In trying to capture the many facets of the city, these books juxtapose contrasting motifs, moods and techniques. Thus all three try to strike a balance between famous sights and the less conspicuous aspects of city life. In von Bucovich's book, photo sequences of great monuments, often captured without people, are counterbalanced by more contemporary, everyday scenes, such as an illuminated department store on Kurfürstendamm and an image of pedestrians, seen from above, which resembles a film still in its evocation of movement (Figures 5.2 and 5.3). Indeed, movement is a central organizing principle in these books. Reversing the spatial trajectory of Ruttmann's film, all three photobooks lead the viewer from Berlin's

Figure 5.3: 'Pedestrians', from Mario von Bucovich, *Berlin* (Berlin: Albertus, 1928)

centre to its outskirts, in an arrangement which, as Hake argues, 'imitates the act of walking in the city and, in so doing, suggests both a narrative of progress, or progression, and an experience of individual agency akin to photographic flanerie'.[29]

This sense of agency, however, is arguably tied to one of detachment. Stone, Willinger and von Bucovich were all foreign-born and, having been drawn to Berlin during the 1920s, all three left the city again after 1933. Their engagement with the city stands for that of countless international writers, thinkers and artists who shaped the cultural life of Weimar Berlin. The ambulatory mobility, combined with a keen eye for detail, which underpins their photographs, is the productive result of their outsider status, a perspective also central to literary depictions of Berlin during the Weimar years.

The Face of the Whole: *Berlin Alexanderplatz*

The most iconic of Weimar novels about Berlin is Alfred Döblin's *Berlin Alexanderplatz*. Published in 1929, it is often described as the literary counterpart to Ruttmann's city symphony; indeed, Döblin here draws on a literary approach which he had laid out much earlier, in 1913. In his so-called 'Berliner Programm' (Berlin Programme), Döblin calls for literature to emulate the montage technique of film, which makes it possible to depict 'fast processes' with the 'greatest precision'. Rejecting psychological narration as amateurish and imprecise, Döblin also advocates psychiatry as a more rigorous discourse.[30]

Even as the techniques of film advanced, the agenda of this 1913 essay still underpins *Berlin Alexanderplatz*, whose title highlights the precarious balance to be struck. It foregrounds the city, metonymically represented by one of its most prominent squares, and it is only in the subtitle, *Die Geschichte vom Franz Biberkopf* (The Story of Franz Biberkopf), that the protagonist is introduced, almost as an afterthought. This tension between title and subtitle sets the tone for a narrative where the stories of Biberkopf and Berlin are closely, often also antagonistically, intertwined, and where the city – personified, in Old Testament terms, as the Whore of Babylon – is host to a whole set of forces intent on leading the protagonist astray.

The theme of moral corruption, familiar from other Weimar novels, thus recurs, as does the central figure of the outsider. Biberkopf is a Berliner, but he has become estranged from city life during a prison sentence served in Tegel Prison, outside the confines of the city. Opening with his release, the first chapter introduces the novel's main themes through a montage of personal and impersonal narration. It gives us an insight into Biberkopf's inner turmoil after his release: his instructions to himself ('Stand up straight you scrawny bugger, pull yourself together or you'll feel my fist'), and interjections by an unnamed second voice ('dreadful, Franzie, why dreadful?').[31] Compared to the simple routines of prison life, Berlin seems overwhelmingly intense, but also strangely hollow: 'In the shop windows stood figures in suits and coats, with skirts, stockings and shoes. Outside everything was moving, but behind it all was nothing [aber – dahinter – war nichts!]! It – was – not – alive!' (*B*, p. 2). In a form of narrative slow motion indicated by the dashes, Döblin, like Ruttmann, points to the deadness which underpins and, in an uncanny way, animates city life.

As Biberkopf enters the city, excerpts from the prison manual outlining clear structures and routines are juxtaposed with a mêlée of urban sound bites, from newspaper titles to train announcements. While working on the novel, Döblin gathered together a vast archive of material, from newspaper cuttings to weather forecasts, which he pasted into his notebook opposite his own text, a physical manifestation of his own narrative montage technique. Only at one point in the novel does this montage technique become visually manifest, namely at the beginning of the second book, which includes a list of icons associated with different municipal departments, such as 'Transport', 'Fire', 'Department of Health' and 'Civil Engineering', all headed by the Berlin Bear, the city's heraldic animal (B, pp. 42–3). Here the novel resembles a kind of primer, teaching us how to read the city-text, though the apparent simplicity of these icons is belied by what turns out to be a polyphonic and fundamentally ambiguous space that resists decoding.

Why, then, did Döblin choose the Alexanderplatz as the central site of his novel? The square, one of Berlin's largest, was a building site for nearly two decades, starting from the construction of the underground system begun in 1913 until the more general modernization of the space undertaken between 1929 and 1932. As such, it encapsulates what Hake calls 'the dream of a modern society defined by mobility, adaptability, and uniformity and a modern metropolis ruled by efficiency, functionality, and rationality'.[32] The square's surrounding areas, however, were largely unchanged, and Alexanderplatz remained associated with petty crime, poverty, vice and left-wing activism. Thus, the square also embodied 'the underside of the modernization project', acting as a 'locus of resistance and an emblem of alterity'.[33]

How does Döblin utilize these conflicting associations? Construction – the alteration or erasure of the old – is a key principle in the novel, extending from the city to the protagonist. The preface describes Biberkopf as a 'former transport and cement worker', and his roots in construction work anticipate the end of the novel, when he will emerge, after multiple crises, 'much altered and battered about, and yet knocked into shape [zurechtgebogen]' (B, p. xi). Human nature is subject to conflicting associations in the novel. As in van Hoddis's poem, the human body is a thing to be broken; when Biberkopf loses his arm in a traffic accident, it is replaced by a prosthesis, alluding to the maiming and mutilation of (male) bodies during the First World War. In Döblin's novel the body becomes an assemblage, a composite of organic and man-made parts, but the text also foregrounds its creaturely dimension. The protagonist's surname, Biberkopf ('beaver-head'), performs a merging of human and animal parts, suggesting that the head is no longer the seat of reason but the site of pre-rational, animalistic urges. Indeed, one of the novel's most haunting episodes is an extended scene set in an abattoir, which represents the culling of different animals. The slaughterhouse is a microcosm of the city, a space where 'the transaction of human life into its bare, creaturely other state is enacted'.[34] The way the animals are inexorably driven towards their death is an allegory for the fates of the human characters.

The protagonist is both the perpetrator and the victim of violence. Shortly before Reinhold pushes him out of the car, he strikes Biberkopf's arm with an 'iron blow' (B, p. 249), a formulation which echoes the slaughter of an ox with hammer blows to its head (B, p. 158). Biberkopf's murder of his girlfriend Ida is described in defamiliarizing terms; the laws of Newtonian physics are used to describe his blows to her ribcage. Mieze's murder by Reinhold is recounted with greater immediacy, alternating between Mieze's and Reinhold's perspective. Underlining the creatureliness of violence, a flashback to the slaughterhouse scene replaces the actual description of her death.

Döblin's Berlin is a city of violence and death, and the language used to depict it is provocatively eclectic. For all its discursive montage effects, however, Döblin's text also presents itself as an old-fashioned morality tale. The preface anticipates the three increasingly severe blows which Biberkopf is dealt. After Mieze's murder, he retreats from the world ready to die. He is hospitalized in the mental asylum of Berlin-Buch; like Mieze's murder, this episode takes place outside the city. Contrasting the city with the countryside was a common theme in Weimar cultural debates; right-wing commentators in particular presented the rural regions as the authentic heart of Germany, a space to be protected from the corrupting effects of urbanity. By setting the turning points of his novel outside Berlin, Döblin hints at a more complex, dialectical relationship between city and countryside, one already at play in Expressionist poetry. While the city is a jungle barely controlled by the rule of law, it is in the countryside that these atavistic forces fully break through.

For Biberkopf, however, the countryside is also a space of self-realization. Having faced Death and his own shortcomings, he returns to Berlin and becomes a doorman in a factory; as the text concludes, 'There is nothing further to report about his life' (B, p. 559). And yet the novel remains open-ended. The narrative returns once more to Biberkopf as he watches a parade or march passing the factory: 'Biberkopf looks coldly out of his door and stays quietly at home for a long time' (B, p. 561). His reserve, which resonates with the Weimar survival strategy of 'cool conduct', is followed by an imaginary dialogue in which a voice beckons him to join. Biberkopf initially resists, fearing that 'if I join, I'm going to have to pay later with my head for something other people have thought up'. At the end of the novel, however, his voice is submerged into a collective chorus:

> And forward march, and right and left and right and left, marching, marching, we're marching off to war, there's a hundred pipers marching at our side, they blow the pipes and beat the drums, rat-a-tat-tat, a smooth path for one man,

rough luck for another, one man's still standing, the next one falls over, one
man keeps running, the next's silent for ever, rat-a-tat-tat. (B, p. 562).

Superseding both Franz Biberkopf's anguished inner monologue and the impersonal montage of city voices, the novel ends with an unspecified 'we' fused together through physical as well as linguistic uniformity. This is a scene of departure, leading away from Berlin into an unspecified war against an unspecified enemy. This new collective is marked by a chilling indifference to the fate of the individual, just as the marching rhythm of '*and right and left and right and left*' implies that its political orientation is uncertain, perhaps irrelevant.

In his preface to von Bucovich's *Berlin* photobook, Döblin remarks, 'Only the whole has a face and a meaning: that of a strong sober modern city.'[35] The end of the novel gestures towards such a collective vision, but this outlook remains supremely ambivalent. As Döblin writes in another essay, a preface to August Sander's famous photobook, *Antlitz der Zeit* (The Face of the Time (1929)), 'Society is changing, the cities have grown huge, a few individuals remain, but already new types [of identity] are emerging.'[36] *Berlin Alexanderplatz* depicts the city as site and agent of change, where categories of language, place and identity are constantly being erased and rewritten. Like other Modernist writers, Döblin pays tribute to Berlin's power of self-reinvention, but he also registers the anxieties this produces, which manifest themselves in calls for homogeneity and, conversely, for exclusion. A sentence close to the end uncannily echoes the Expressionist rhetoric of a new beginning, while also foreshadowing events to come: '*The path leads to freedom, to freedom we march, the old world must perish, arise, a new day dawns* [*wach auf, die Morgenluft*]' (B, p. 562). The changes – political, social and cultural – undergone by Berlin between the 1910s and the 1930s were as traumatic as they were productive; just as striking, however, are the continuities.

NOTES

1. Alfred Döblin, 'Berlin', in *Kleine Schriften*, vol. 3, ed. Anthony W. Riley (Zurich/Düsseldorf: Walther, 1999), pp. 153–9 (p. 154).
2. Thus Andrew Webber's characterization, which, as he concedes, includes 'an element of speculation and provocation'. *Berlin in the Twentieth Century: A Cultural Topography* (Cambridge: Cambridge University Press, 2008), p. 11.
3. Döblin, 'Berlin', p. 153.
4. Harold Nicholson, 'The Charm of Berlin', in *The Weimar Republic Sourcebook*, eds Anton Kaes, Martin Jay and Edward Dimendberg (Berkeley, CA: University of California Press, 1994), pp. 425–6 (p. 426).

5. Kracauer, 'Ein paar Tage Paris', in *Schriften*, vol. 5.2, ed. Inka Mülder-Bach (Frankfurt am Main: Suhrkamp, 1990), p. 298.

6. Döblin, 'Berlin', p. 156.

7. Paul Boldt, *Junge Pferde! Junge Pferde! Das Gesamtwerk: Lyrik, Prosa, Dokumente*, ed. Wolfgang Minaty (Olten: Walter, 1979), p. 70; trans. Richard Pettit, http://germanhistorydocs.ghi-dc.org/sub_document.cfm?documen t_id=729 (accessed 18 December 2014). Here and elsewhere, published English translations are on occasion silently amended.

8. Georg Heym, *Gedichte 1910–1912: Historisch-kritische Ausgabe aller Texte in genetischer Darstellung*, eds Günter Dammann, Gunter Martens and Karl Ludwig Schneider (Tübingen: Max Niemeyer, 1993), vol. 1, pp. 265–6; *Poems*, trans. and intro. Antony Hasler (London: Libris, 2004), p. 21.

9. Heym, *Gedichte*, pp. 622–3.

10. Heym, *Gedichte*, p. 295; Heym, *Poems*, p. 25.

11. Burton Pike, 'Images of the City', in *The Cambridge Companion to the Modern German Novel*, ed. Graham Bartram (Cambridge University Press, 2004), pp. 110–22 (p. 111).

12. Kurt Pinthus (ed.), *Menschheitsdämmerung: Dawn of Humanity: A Document of Expressionism*, trans. and intro. Joanna M. Ratych, Ralph Ley and Robert C. Conard (Columbia, SC: Camden House, 1994), pp. 68–9.

13. See Alexandra Richie, *Faust's Metropolis: A History of Berlin* (New York, NY: Carroll & Grave, 1998), p. 276.

14. Richard Huelsenbeck, 'Dadaistisches Manifest', in *Dada Almanach* (Berlin: Erich Reiss, 1920), pp. 35–41 (p. 37).

15. Huelsenbeck, 'Manifesto', p. 35.

16. Brigid Doherty, '"See: We are all Neurasthetics!" or, The Trauma of Dada Montage', *Critical Inquiry*, 24.1 (1997), pp. 82–132.

17. Rolf J. Goebel, 'Media Competition: Ruttmann's *Berlin: die Symphonie der Großstadt* and Hessel's *Ein Flaneur in Berlin*', in *Topography and Literature: Berlin and Modernism*, ed. Reinhard Zachau (Göttingen: V&R unipress, 2009), pp. 111–24 (p. 112).

18. Egon Erwin Kisch, *Der rasende Reporter* (Cologne: Kiepenheuer & Witsch, 1983), p. 10.

19. Helmut Lethen, *Cool Conduct: The Culture of Distance in Weimar Germany*, trans. Don Reneau (Berkeley, CA: University of California Press, 2002).

20. Thomas Wehrling, 'Berlin Is Becoming a Whore', *Weimar Republic Sourcebook*, pp. 721–3.

21. Ibid., p. 718.

22. Erich Kästner, *Going to the Dogs: The Story of a Moralist*, trans. Cyrus Brook, intro. by Rodney Livingstone (New York, NY: New York Review of Books, 2013), p. 6.

23. Ibid., p. 174.

24. Ibid., p. 175.

25. Irmgard Keun, *The Artificial Silk Girl*, trans. Kathie von Ankum, paperback edition (New York, NY: Other Press, 2011), p. 111.

26. Ibid., p. 3.

27. Webber, *Berlin*, p. 170.

28. Jakob van Hoddis, *Dichtungen und Briefe* (Zurich: Arche, 1987), p. 15.

29. Sabin Hake, *Topographies of Class: Modern Architecture and Mass Society in Weimar Berlin* (Ann Arbor, MI: University of Michigan Press, 2008), p. 193.

30. Alfred Döblin, 'An Romanautoren und ihre Kritiker: Berliner Programm', in *Schriften zur Ästhetik, Poetik und Literatur*, ed. Erich Kleinschmidt (Olten: Walter, 1989), pp. 119–23 (p. 121).

31. Alfred Döblin, *Berlin Alexanderplatz*, trans. Anne Thompson (North Charleston, SC: Create Space Independent Publishing, 2014), pp. 1–2 (henceforth *B*).

32. Hake, *Topographies*, p. 197.

33. Ibid., p.198.

34. Webber, *Berlin*, p. 206.

35. Döblin, 'Berlin', p. 156.

36. 'Von Gesichtern, Bildern und ihrer Wahrheit', in Döblin, *Kleine Schriften*, pp. 203–13 (p. 213).

6

REINHARD ZACHAU

Writing under National Socialism

After the National Socialists consolidated their power on a broad political level, they quickly established their rule in Germany's cultural politics by staging one of their first cultural events in Berlin. The notorious burning of books 'against the un-German spirit' ('wider den undeutschen Geist'), was coordinated by the Nazi student organization and enacted at many universities across Germany. University libraries had been asked to comb through their shelves for 'anti-German' and Jewish books, which were put in huge piles, before torches carried in the nocturnal parade were used to burn them. The Berlin ceremony took place on 10 May 1933 in the arena of Berlin's Opernplatz or Opera Square, close to the buildings of the Humboldt University. Joseph Goebbels accepted the student organization's invitation to give a public address, which established his reputation as Germany's premier Nazi censor and propagandist.

The Nazis embodied the cultural political antithesis of the Weimar Republic. While many authors had felt inspired by Weimar's artistic energy, the Nazis swiftly censored their creativity in 1933 and replaced individual experimentation with formulaic art. Much as many Weimar writers realized the Nazi horror instantly, others were slower to comprehend its magnitude. One of those was Victor Klemperer, who asked in 1933, 'Where was I and how did it happen that nobody paid attention to this sudden rise of the Nazis?'[1] While the first authors who left Germany were Hitler's more express political opponents, most others dug in and believed that the Nazi government would be just another episode in the attempt to set up a stable government. Germans as a whole did not realize that the regime had a monstrous master plan, one that used the weak economy and the Reichstag fire as pretences to push through arrest warrants against left-leaning intellectuals, journalists and writers.

The Nazis hated urban life, especially in the form it took in Berlin, and shifted their literary interests to historical topics and to mythical concepts of nature, commonly known by the slogan, 'Blut und Boden' (blood and soil).

Goebbels reviled contemporary urban literature as 'Asphaltliteratur' and described Berlin as 'the reddest city in Europe besides Moscow'.[2] And Hitler is said to have 'despised Berlin's greed and frivolity ... he stood baffled and alienated by the phenomenon of the big city, lost in so much noise, turbulence, and miscegenation'.[3] But the Nazis soon realized that a complete break with Weimar literature was not in their interest, as a discussion about city life in Alfred Rosenberg's periodical *Bücherkunde* in 1941 showed. Here, the critic Hans Franke maintained that modern life could indeed only be found in cities, demanding in true Nazi spirit an organic, *völkisch* perspective to capture modern life, not a multifaceted view as Weimar authors had given. The wartime debate reveals the increasing tension between Rosenberg's ideology, with its 'blood and soil' watchword, and that of Goebbels, who wanted National Socialist writers to have the 'courage to engage with the present' and occupy the domain of urban literature.[4] And this was conducted against the background of Hitler's desire to destroy Berlin as it stood and transform it into Germania, a heroically super-scaled metropolis. In stark contrast to Weimar Berlin's aggregated, informal districts, or *Kieze*, Hitler planned to recreate a classical city that would erase one thousand years of history in favour of a concept borrowed from the Roman Empire. It is an irony of history that, while Hitler's plans for Germania never materialized, the firebombing of Berlin almost achieved the city's extinction by other means.

Party Lines

The first example of a Nazi propaganda novel is Karl Aloys Schenzinger's *Hitlerjunge Quex* (Hitler Youth Quex (1932)), which subsequently also became a popular feature film. The book is based on the life of Herbert Norkus, who died in Moabit's Beussel Kiez while being confronted by members of the Communist youth organization. Schenzinger fictionalized the case of Norkus to show how Heini Völker (the surname translates as 'Peoples'), the son of an unemployed Communist, does not join the youth organization of his father's party (the 'Commune'), but instead the Hitler Youth. Heini befriends a Nazi teenager who invites him to his upscale Hansa Quarter home, where he explains how German society has become crippled by its class system. Heini then warns the Nazis of a Communist plan to bomb their assembly hall, and when his mother finds out, she is so afraid of the Communists that she turns on the gas to kill herself and the boy. After awakening in a hospital, Heini finds himself surrounded by Hitler Youths who present him with a uniform. The energetic Heini then works all night to print Nazi leaflets and distributes them in the Beussel Kiez. After Heini falls in love with a member of the Nazi BDM organization (the Bund deutscher Mädchen, or Association of German Girls), they practise kissing at a play rehearsal. When the thrilled boy is attacked by Communists on his way home, he never recovers from the injuries and dies a week later. His last words are those of the Horst Wessel song, which would become the unofficial Nazi anthem, and the novel concludes with the scene of 75,000 boys singing the same song the martyr sang on his deathbed, as they parade before Hitler.

The prototype for Schenzinger's story is evidently Erich Kästner's *Emil und die Detektive* (Emil and the Detectives (1929)), with the idea of solidarity among the boys an important factor in negotiating Berlin's various classes and neighbourhoods. Like Kästner's world, Schenzinger's is divided into Manichean categories of good and evil. But where Kästner shows adults as corrupt, Schenzinger singles out the Communists for their dubious morals: the girls are lax, while the boys engage in theft and violence. After an excursion, the book takes on a different tone, as the Berlin teenagers are happy to get away from the city and its decadent atmosphere. While the Communists simply use nature for drinking and vulgar games, for Schenzinger, the Nazis are shown to need nature for their military games, as Nazi ideology romanticized a return to the natural state for political renewal.

Hitlerjunge Quex can be compared to Jan Petersen's *Unsere Straße* (Our Street (1936)), the Communist version of a Berlin *Kiez* battle. *Unsere Straße*, one of the most influential Communist novels written in Berlin during the Nazi period, was smuggled out of Germany to enable its publication. Petersen was the Berlin leader of the Association of Proletarian-Revolutionary Authors (Bund Proletarisch-Revolutionärer Schriftsteller), founded in 1928. The BPRS counted among its members many of Germany's prominent left-wing writers, such as Bruno Apitz, author of the Holocaust novel *Nackt unter Wölfen* (Naked amongst Wolves (1955)), Johannes R. Becher (who later became the GDR's Culture Secretary), the journalist and writer Egon Erwin Kisch, the theatre director Erwin Piscator, the writer Anna Seghers, and Friedrich Wolf, whose *Professor Mamlock* (1933) is among the best-known plays written in exile. Petersen was able to keep the BPRS active as an underground organization until 1935, when it was betrayed to the Gestapo. In *Unsere Straße* he tells the story of his own Berlin *Kiez* and how his comrades tried to survive Nazi aggression by engaging in acts of active and passive resistance. The book portrays the Wallstraße, a proletarian street where the workers and servants of the middle-class Charlottenburg district lived. To disguise the identities of his comrades, Petersen fictionalized his diary entries and followed the pattern of the 'barricade novels' of the early 1930s which were popularized by Klaus

Neukrantz's *Barrikaden am Wedding* (Barricades at Wedding (1931)), a Marxist novel of street conflicts in the working-class Wedding district.

Whereas Weimar's flâneur culture had been decidedly bourgeois and often apolitical, the BPRS-rooted novel of the streets became the prototype for illegal writing during Berlin's Nazi occupation. *Unsere Straße* is a self-reflective narrative, cast between reportage and novel, with the author's creative hand visible in the narrative arc he creates out of the diary-style accounts. The text has the character of a political thriller, with its suspenseful scenes centring on the struggle between the Communists and the Nazis for control of the eponymous street. The story begins with a shooting on 30 January 1933, when a troop of armed SA-men march through the Wallstraße to claim the Communist territory as theirs and accidentally shoot one of their own number and an accompanying Berlin policeman. It ends with the trial of local Communists, when the twenty-eight accused are all sentenced to prison, while no Nazi is indicted. The Nazi terror on the streets of Berlin and in the early days of the concentration camps is described in full detail, including the torture and murder of the writer Erich Mühsam at the Brandenburg concentration camp. After an appearance at the First International Writers' Congress for the Defence of Culture in Paris in June 1935, Jan Petersen was hunted by the Nazis, but was able to avoid capture and to emigrate first to Switzerland and then to England.

Outside Views

Other, less famous Berliners also emigrated from Hitler's terror, among them Konrad Merz, whose autobiographical novel *Ein Mensch fällt aus Deutschland* (A Human Being Falls out of Germany (1936)) is one of the first exile books written from the perspective of a Jewish Berliner. It is a very touching literary document of the existential struggle Germans endured during the 1930s, when every day was finely balanced between survival and death. Merz's various notes are not merged into a continuous text in the same way as Petersen's, but they are left in their original form, as this example shows: 'Gestern früh sind wir aus Berlin gekippt. Ungewaschen, ungekämmt. Wie ausgespuckt. Mit 6 Mark und 5 Pfennigen durch die Stunden gekrochen, durch die Nacht geschlichen ... Jetzt soll Heiligabend sein.' (Yesterday morning we were pitched out of Berlin. Unwashed, uncombed. As if spat out. With 6 marks and 5 pfennigs we crawled through the hours and crept through the night ... Apparently it's Christmas Eve now.)[5] The experience of enforced emigration is recounted with sober immediacy.

Several well-known Weimar authors who were on the Nazis' Black List left Germany quickly but felt compelled to write about life in Berlin as they imagined it from exile. It is interesting to consider the degree of authenticity in those émigré texts, as compared to the accounts of eyewitnesses. Lion Feuchtwanger was already in exile when he wrote his novel *Die Geschwister Oppermann* (translated as *The Oppermanns*) in 1933. A Jewish writer, Feuchtwanger had been one of Weimar Germany's most popular authors. He was in exile in southern France when the SA raided his house and destroyed his manuscripts and most of his library of over 10,000 books. *Die Geschwister Oppermann*, one of the first books about Nazi activities in Berlin to be published in exile, provides narrative accounts of torture in concentration camps that were predictions of what was to come. And Bertolt Brecht also left Germany in 1933 and, in *Furcht und Elend des Dritten Reiches* (translated as *The Private Life of the Master Race* (1938)), gave his own reconstruction of the ideological conditions of life in Germany. In his scenic montage he shows the country as a land of poverty, violence, fear and pretence that has fallen into the hands of greedy capitalists.

While many of Weimar Germany's leftist authors left Berlin quickly in the early 1930s, the city was becoming increasingly interesting for a number of foreign authors, providing the perspective of the outsider. While Christopher Isherwood's *Goodbye to Berlin* (1939) is known for the prototypical use of the viewpoint of a foreigner, using ironic distance to show the emergence of Nazi terror, there were others who gave a more chilling perspective on the ascendancy of the new regime. Thomas Wolfe, who was America's best-known author in Germany at that time, recognized the brutality behind Berlin's splendid façade and expressed the change in his attitude from naiveté to eventual understanding of the evil nature of the regime. Wolfe's *I Have a Thing to Tell You* (1937) is a novella about a conversation between a fictitious Berlin writer and a German friend. The latter's quiet voice 'touched somehow, for an American, with unfathomed depths of living, with a resignation that had long since passed despair, a fortitude that had gone far past both pride and hope',[6] with which he wants to master his life in these difficult times. When the narrator realizes that the friend is Jewish, the novella provides a classical peripeteia, or turning point, to reveal his misconceptions about Nazi Germany, and he finally grasps the country's tragic destiny.

In *Through Embassy Eyes* (1939), Martha Dodd chose another classic German literary form for her autobiographical text: a version of the *Bildungsroman*. Dodd describes her encounter with a number of famous writers, among them Hans Fallada and Thomas Wolfe, and the effect they had on Berlin in the 1930s. According to Dodd, Wolfe's early uncritical attitude towards the Nazis was not unlike her own, which created an awkward situation for her father, the American ambassador in Berlin. Martha Dodd met Hitler through a friend, Putzi Hanfstengel, who suggested she become Hitler's girlfriend, and Dodd gives us here one of the earliest descriptions of the Nazi leader: 'The first glance left me with a picture of a weak, soft face with pouches under the eyes, full lips and very little bony facial structure. The moustache didn't seem as ridiculous as it appeared in pictures – in fact, I scarcely noticed it.'[7] She was, however, impressed by Hitler's 'startling and unforgettable' eyes that could contain 'fury and fanaticism and cruelty'.[8] Although initially scared of him, Dodd warmed to Hitler's 'quiet charm' and his 'tenderness of speech and glance',[9] before she eventually became the girlfriend of Rudolf Diels, the first head of the Gestapo.

Klaus Mann also wrote about a Nazi fellow-traveller in his *Mephisto, Roman einer Karriere* (Mephisto – Novel of a Career (1936)), which became the most influential of the early exile novels. After failing to write his autobiography, Mann decided to write a novel about the director of the Prussian state theatre, Gustaf Gründgens. Hendrik Höfgen, the Gründgens character in the novel, is a man obsessed with becoming a famous actor. When the Nazis come to power, he renounces his Communist past and deserts his wife and mistress in order to continue performing. His diabolical performance as Mephistopheles proves to be the stepping-stone he yearned for, attracting the attention of Hermann Göring. The rewards – public esteem, a castle-like villa, a place in Berlin's highest circles – are beyond his wildest dreams, but the moral consequences of his betrayal begin to haunt him, turning his dream world into a nightmare. This betrayal built into the pact with power is at the core of the novel and, with its Mephistophelean theme, gives insight into the lives of artists under the Nazis and their reasons for collaboration. Klaus Mann was able to reconstruct Gründgens' motivations, since he knew him very well. The climactic scene, where Höfgen tries to save a friend from Nazi persecution, contains Mann's blunt warning to anybody considering working with the ruthless Nazis not to enter into a pact with them.

Staying On

Mann's advice sounds like the motto for those writers who stayed in Germany and would become known as the authors of Inner Emigration. One of them was Sebastian Haffner (Raimund Pretzel), a relatively unknown journalist in 1933 who would later become a major historian of the Hitler period with his books *Germany – Jekyll and Hyde* (1940) and *Anmerkungen zu Hitler* (translated as *The Meaning of Hitler* (1978)). Haffner began his career during the Nazi period as a reporter for fashion magazines and, by following Weimar's celebrated reportage tradition of the pragmatic journalist, painted a colourful picture of life in Berlin during the 1930s in a collection later published as *Das Leben der Fußgänger* (The Life of Pedestrians (2004)). Superficially, everything looks normal in Haffner's texts, but with each short essay the reader is challenged to discover the truth beneath the surface of the reports he presents.

The books published by Heinrich Spoerl during the Nazi period are an established part of Germany's cultural heritage, beginning with the publication of *Die Feuerzangenbowle* (The Fire Tongs Punch) in 1933. Unlike many entertainment novels at this time, Spoerl's *Der Gasmann* (The Gas Man (1940)) contains a number of references to contemporary life in Berlin. The protagonist Hermann Knittel sells his business suit for the exorbitant sum of 10,000 marks to a man on a train. As is later revealed, the man's identity had to be protected since he had spent the night with a woman on the train. The result of this transaction is disastrous for Knittel, as everyone suspects illegal activities behind this huge amount of money. In Knittel's escape to Berlin's entertainment district, Spoerl furnishes a critique of Berlin's decadent life style, which had been at the core of Weimar Berlin's frenzied culture and which the Nazis despised. Knittel's conflict with the justice system offers a caricature of Nazi bureaucracy as he gets lost in a Kafkaesque police building where he ends up in a Gestapo-like interrogation, where no one knows why he is being questioned. The book captures the sinister atmosphere of the 1930s in which someone is assumed to be guilty if questioned by the police. It is full of telling Berlin city scenes, illustrating the murky dynamics of power under the regime, including a woman bragging about her relationship with a Nazi party member and a neighbour reporting Knittel's wealth to the police when he buys a piano.[10]

Although Erich Kästner is mainly known for his children's literature and his belief in the regenerating powers of youth, he was put on the Nazi Blacklist. However, unlike many fellow authors who were critical of the dictatorship, he did not emigrate. When the Nazis assumed power, Kästner traveled to Italy and Switzerland, where, after meeting with exiled fellow writers, he decided to return to Berlin, arguing that he could chronicle the times better from there. He later described this in a poem:

Ich bin ein Deutscher aus Dresden in Sachsen.
Mich läßt die Heimat nicht fort.
Ich bin wie ein Baum, der – in Deutschland gewachsen –
wenn's sein muss, in Deutschland verdorrt.

(I'm a German from Dresden in Saxony.
My homeland won't let me go.

> I'm like a tree that – grown in Germany –
> if needs be, will wither in Germany too.)[11]

Although Kästner was one of the few writers who watched his books burn in 1933, he did not speak up and chose instead to publish apolitical entertainment novels such as *Drei Männer im Schnee* (Three Men in the Snow (1934)). In 1942, Kästner received a special exemption to write the screenplay for the prestigious *Münchhausen* film for the UFA studios, on the occasion of the production company's twenty-fifth anniversary.

Kästner's *Die verlorene Miniatur* (The Lost Miniature (1935)) is considered one of his apolitical books. As with Spoerl, however, we recognize subtle criticism of the Nazis, as in the fact that the protagonist in the story is fighting against gangs of criminals located in Berlin. Also, one of the novel's characters wants to live in a world where the sun only shines on the just while the unjust stand in the shadow. The pleasant and naïve owner of butcher's shops in Berlin, Oskar Külz, is on vacation in Copenhagen when he gets involved in a crime case concerning stolen art. In this comedy of errors, the stolen miniature changes hands frequently, which is made more complicated by the fact that there is an exact replica in circulation. Eventually, nobody is sure anymore which is the real miniature and which the fake. In this adult variation of *Emil and the Detectives*, everything ends well; the miniature is returned to its rightful owner and the robbers are punished. And just as Kästner's children's books are fairly light fare, with a simple lesson to impart, *Die verlorene Miniatur* has a straightforward conclusion: keep your positive disposition, even in times of difficulty, and things will work out for you. That seemed to be the attitude with which Kästner himself survived the Nazi years. In his *Notabene 45*, Kästner described his literary experience in Nazi Germany as one in which the country resembled a destroyed anthill, with his writings as the observations of a 'thinking ant'.[12]

Alongside Kästner, Hans Fallada was the Weimar Republic's best-known author in the sober observational style of Neue Sachlichkeit or New Objectivity. His books were not burned, and he remained in Germany, keeping a low profile. However, in 1937 he produced one of his most important books, *Wolf unter Wölfen* (Wolf among Wolves), which describes Berlin's economic and political crisis in the 1923 inflation and contrasts it with the situation in the Prussian countryside. Fallada gives a realistic portrait of both Berlin and rural life to show how both parts of Germany were equally guilty of promoting fascist thinking. Fallada had experienced life both in the city and on Prussian country estates, since he had worked as an estate manager in Pomerania. In this novel, he deploys montage elements with a film-like technique and abandons his journalistic perspective for a balanced, multifaceted approach. By limiting the first part of *Wolf unter Wölfen* to one day and one night, Fallada gives close attention to the hectic atmosphere of the time, which was exacerbated by the continuously rising dollar exchange rate and the frantic search for money. The narrative starts with a desolate scene that seems directly modelled after Hemingway's bleak novels; a man and a woman sleep in a miserable backyard apartment in one of Berlin's tenement buildings near the Alexanderplatz. The precise and unemotional description shows the two bodies as objects placed in their historical context.

In a scene that shows Fallada's intention of building up his female protagonist, Petra, the shabbiness of the tenement building is contrasted with her attempt to escape the environment. Although Petra has worked as a prostitute, she realizes that the time has come to establish her independence. In confronting her landlady and coworkers, she insists on acting with sophistication and not in the downtrodden manner of these working class women. Although her coworkers challenge her attitude as arrogant and ridicule her belief that she can free herself from her current situation, she takes the first step towards her independence. Eventually, she manages a life as a reputable middle-class citizen. At first sight, Petra's story would fit well with the Nazi ideology of branding the city as the source of all evil, as most characters leave the city to go to the country, where they hope to find a wholesome atmosphere. Instead, however, they find even more intrigue and poverty there than in the slums of Berlin, where people were more inventive in overcoming their misery. In the country they found ultra-right groups preparing a coup against the vilified political system of the Weimar Republic. Fallada's description is similar to George Grosz's surreal drawings, a description of a perverse time for a Germany that had not found its bearings. This perversity extended in all directions, both left and right, with the 'romantic' domain of the country as fertile breeding ground for the latter. And so it was no surprise that this novel, with its subversion of the ideological fantasy of blood and soil, was quickly banned in Nazi Germany.

Like so many others, Fallada also turned from the dangerous ground of contemporary life to historical subjects, as in his *Der Eiserne Gustav* (Iron Gustav (1938)). It was first conceived as a film treatment and relates the true story of the Berlin horse-cab driver Gustav Hartmann, who took his carriage to Paris in the 1920s in order to show that he could compete with the burgeoning motorized taxi business. The book reveals Fallada's increasing dependence on the Nazis for the opportunity to publish: the main characters all have to convert to National Socialism.

Victims

Another novel turning on the depiction of a unique urban character was Georg Hermann's *Rosenemil* (Roses Emil (1936)). After the publication of his novels *Jettchen Gebert* and *Henriette Jacoby* in 1906, Hermann had been one of Berlin's principal authors of city novels, introducing to his substantial readership such distinctive characters as Kubinke and Doktor Herzfeld. *Rosenemil* was published not in Berlin, where it clearly belonged, with its portrayal of one of the city's petty criminals, but in Amsterdam, to where Hermann had emigrated. The narrative takes place in the Eastern part of Berlin with which Hermann was very familiar: the Lothringerstraße, now Torstraße, where the peddlers, prostitutes and petty criminals meet. The book was Hermann's last and a superb dedication to the old Berlin that he had made so famous in his earlier novels. Hermann, who was Jewish and died in Auschwitz, has been almost completely forgotten by post–Second World War generations.

From October 1941 to April 1943, Berlin's remaining Jews were deported and many of them killed in the concentration camps in Eastern Europe. The poems of Gertrud Kolmar are some of the most significant literary documents of the Holocaust in the German language. She was born into a middle-class Jewish Berlin family and grew up in the Charlottenburg district. In November 1938, after the Kristallnacht, Kolmar and her father were forced to sell their spacious home in Finkenkrug, a rural suburb of Berlin, and move to a *Judenhaus* in the Schöneberg district, where Gertrud pined for what they had lost. In 1941 she was compelled to do forced labour in the German armaments industry, and in February 1943 she was arrested and then deported to her death in Auschwitz (Figure 6.1).

In her letters, Kolmar described the mundane aspects of her life, such as walking long distances through the city in disguise, and the lack of privacy and solitude brought about by the constant presence of others in the close quarters of the *Judenhaus*.[13] Kolmar's unusual ability to render her traumatic experiences in lyric form makes her one of the most important poets in German literature and places her amongst the greatest lyrical poets of Jewish descent. Her poetry reveals how she consciously selected other spaces, other times and other self-representations than those either forced upon her by the Nazi regime or chosen by the other Jews in her environment. Thus, in 'Abschied' (Farewell (1932)), she sends her face forth in a self-constructed exile to the East:

> Nach Osten send' ich mein Gesicht:
> Ich will es von mir tun.
> Es soll dort drüben sein im Licht,

Figure 6.1: *Stolperstein*, or stumbling-stone, commemorating the deportation of Gertrud Kolmar, in front of Münchener Straße 18a
(Photo by OTFW, Berlin, licensed under CC BY-SA 3.0, via Wikimedia Commons).

Ein wenig auszuruhn

. . .

Und wenn ich dann nur leiser Schlag
An blasse Küsten bin,
So roll ich frühen Wintertag,
Den silbern kühlen Sarkophag
Des ewigen Todes hin,
Darin mein Antlitz dünn und leicht
Wie Spinneweben steht,
Ein wenig um die Winkel streicht,
Ein wenig flattert, lächelnd bleicht
Und ohne Qual verweht.

(Into the East I send my face:
I'm giving it away.
And in some distant sunlit place
A moment it should stay.

...
And finally, when I fade away,
A wave on pale coasts,
I'll wash to sea a winter's day,
A sepulcher of frigid gray,
Death's everlasting ghost.
Inside, my fragile face will stay
As I sail round the bend,
And I will smile and drift away,
And disappear in wind and spray
To meet a painless end.)[14]

Kolmar's poetry relies on the use of metaphorical landscapes and topographical tropes through which she resisted the Nazis by reconfiguring a politically controlled social space into her own poetically organized domain. As Amir Eshel writes, 'Jewish writers across the generations of exile were not so much obsessed with the urge to return to Zion – a notion many of them regarded as messianic – but were motivated by the desire to inhabit their dwelling place poetically, at least, and thus, by doing so, ontologically *to be*.'[15] Kolmar's imaginary Orient has been interpreted as an escapist place and substitute homeland, and indeed this hope for an ancient Asia had been a central theme in German-Jewish attempts to redefine Judaism and Jewish nationalism.

Gertrud Kolmar did not survive the Nazis, and neither did the less widely recognized writer, Albrecht Haushofer. As a policy advisor at the Foreign Office, he became involved with people from the Kreisau Circle, who took part in the failed 1944 plot to assassinate Hitler. Haushofer was an academic and had never written poetry, but he started writing the *Moabiter Sonette* (Moabit Sonnets (published posthumously in 1946)) after he was incarcerated in Berlin's Moabit prison. He was carrying one of his sonnets, 'Schuld' (Guilt), at the time of his execution on the night of 22 April 1945:

Doch schuldig bin ich. Anders als Ihr denkt!
Ich musste früher meine Pflicht erkennen,
Ich musste schärfer Unheil Unheil nennen,
Mein Urteil hab ich viel zu lang gelenkt ... [16]
...
Ich hab gewarnt – nicht hart genug und klar!
Und heute weiß ich, was ich schuldig war.[17]

(But I am guilty. Not in the way you think!
I should have recognized my duty earlier,
I should have called evil evil more sharply;
I steered my judgement much too long ...

. . .
I did warn – not hard enough and clear!
And today I know what I was guilty of.)[18]

Of the Jewish survivor stories in Berlin, Inge Deutschkron's *Ich trug den gelben Stern* (I Wore the Yellow Star; translated as *Outcast: A Jewish Girl in Wartime Berlin* (1978)) is one of the best known. Deutschkron starts her reminiscences with the first episode that marred her happy childhood, when her parents inform her that she is Jewish and can no longer play with other children. To support his family, Inge's father learns new occupations, and Inge is driven from one Jewish school to another, until the last has closed. The family moves from lodging to lodging until they end up in the cramped quarters of a *Judenhaus* in Schöneberg. A major part of their lives consists of following ordinances designed to marginalize Jews, such as women having to adopt Sara as their middle name, submitting a list of everything they owned to city authorities, relinquishing their telephone and radio, and not straying into urban areas forbidden to them. One month after the wearing of the yellow star became law, in September 1941, the deportations started, affecting most of Inge's family. For a considerable period, she was able to continue her secretarial work for Otto Weidt's workshop in the Rosenthaler Straße, where he employed blind Jews. In the last months of the war, Inge and her mother even lived more openly in Berlin, for they succeeded in passing themselves off as refugees who had lost their papers in their last-minute flight from the advancing Russians.

Marie Jalowicz's *Untergetaucht* (Gone Underground), published in 2014, tells her story of a survivor who operated completely on her own by cutting all ties with her extended family. This was easier for her than for many Berlin Jews because both of her parents died before the Holocaust, and as the daughter of a Jewish lawyer, Marie realized that she had to adjust her behaviour to her working-class environment quickly if she was to survive. One of her mentors explained that she should not act normally in abnormal conditions. *Untergetaucht* relates in detail how middle-class Jews were often unprepared for their changed situation and chose death rather than go into hiding. In 1941 Marie slipped out of the official city records when she told the postman who had come to deliver a letter from the employment office that her 'neighbour' Marie Jalowicz had been deported. The postman noted that she had moved to an 'unknown destination in the East', and the young woman vanished from the records. Marie's friends recognized her determination, and, when she told them that she would write her story down one day, they predicted she would be the only one to survive. By assuming a false identity, Marie realized how merging with Berlin's working class and using its dialect was the key to survival. As the Jewish middle class perished, she writes, the educated German bourgeoisie failed in a similar way when asked to help Jews. However, when she meets another survivor after the war who uses standard German and not dialect, she can hardly control her emotions and feels she is back home. Marie Jalowicz Simon died in Berlin in 1998 after a long and successful career as a professor of ancient literature and culture at Berlin's Humboldt University.

Ruth Andreas-Friedrich was one of the Germans who built up a network to find hiding-places for Jewish Berliners. In her Berlin diary, *Der Schattenmann* (The Shadowman; translated as *Berlin Underground* (1948)), Andreas-Friedrich showed the Jewish survival from the non-Jewish German perspective. As her diary reveals, Andreas-Friedrich, the conductor Leo Borchard, the doctor Walter Seitz and approximately eight of their friends helped by creating an underground organization, 'Onkel Emil', that saved countless Jews from deportation, hid war deserters and helped many others with illegal papers. Her extensive diary is one of the best sources about the difficult life during the Third Reich.

Anja Lundholm's *Das Höllentor* (The Gate of Hell (1988)) gives a disturbing account of the atrocities that took place in the infamous camps near to Berlin, Sachsenhausen and Ravensbrück. Lundholm was a political prisoner in the Ravensbrück women's concentration camp, and despite its fictionalized character, *Das Höllentor* is a highly personal book. When Lundholm is on a work assignment, she asks herself whether the people outside the camp are not bothered by the smell of burning flesh that covers the entire town of Fürstenberg: 'Burning bones have a different smell than burning wood. Does nobody question the origin of the smoke that blackens their houses?'[19] At night, Lundholm ponders the fate of the prisoners being killed:

> First the Jews and Gypsies, then the sick and those unfit to work. It will be everybody's turn. Everybody. I will die, you will die, he, she, it will die. Words that our brain recites without letting the meaning enter our brain cells. Tomorrow or the day after tomorrow I will be dead as well. What will I look like then? Like Wanda, chewed up by rats?[20]

The author includes in her book a copy of the SS's financial calculations about the profit the prisoners generate, an average of 1631 marks. When Lundholm was liberated in 1945, she was twenty-seven years old and reduced to a skeleton. When a woman who helped her asked for her name, she could not remember it; the only thing she recalled was 'Youthere' ('Duda'), as the camp guards had addressed her.[21]

Downfall

Surprisingly, a number of foreign authors and journalists stayed in Berlin until the very end and provided some of the more objective accounts of Berlin's increasingly disturbing atmosphere. The Danish author Karen Blixen observes restaurant guests at the fin-de-siècle Adlon Hotel that contrasts with Berlin's wartime greyness. The Swedish journalist Gösta Block witnesses a scene on the underground when a Nazi official grabs a seat from an old Jewish woman but is resisted by the entire train car. The Polish journalist Jacob Kronika describes the increasing scenes of destruction in the bombed-out city, among them a dead American fighter pilot sitting with his plane on top of a flower shop, or scenes of teenagers engaging in public sexual acts in a bomb shelter.[22] As a result of the carpet-bombing, Berlin ceased to exist as such. What had been a ten-minute walk could take hours through areas of rubble and blocked streets. Increasingly Berlin took on the look of the uninhabited landscapes of the Eastern steppes. Berlin had lost its pride; its atmosphere was marked by tension, poverty, anger, prostitution and despair. Marie (Missy) Illarionovna Vassiltchikov's volume *Berliner Tagebücher* (Berlin Diaries (1988)) is considered the best account of the carpet bombings. Vassiltchikov was a Russian émigré writer who spent the war years working with Adam von Trott in the German Foreign Office, where she was involved in the plot to assassinate Hitler in July 1944. Her diaries take on an air of the surreal as she writes about days with lunches at the Adlon and nights spent in ruined apartments gossiping about her noble friends planning the intended killing of Hitler.

Among the accounts of Berlin's downfall, Marta Hiller's and Traudl Junge's are the best known. *Eine Frau in Berlin* (A Woman in Berlin) is the autobiographical account of Berlin women as rape victims of the Soviet Army, which was first published anonymously in 1954, and republished as a bestseller in 2003. The author has since been revealed as the journalist Marta Hiller. Traudl Junge's *Bis zur letzten Stunde* (Until the Final Hour (2002)), about her work as Hitler's secretary, began as a documentary film, *Im toten Winkel* (translated as *Blindspot* (2002)). Junge was taught to believe in Germany and was oblivious to the morbid implications of the Nazi ideology. She had access to Hitler's inner circle and provides many vignettes on Hitler and the people around him. Moving within and outside Hitler's bunker, Junge notes the vast differences between the unreal, suspended life on the inside and the raging, unstoppable destruction outside. She barely sees anything in Berlin other than what she perceives as the frightening labyrinth of the huge complex of the Reich Chancellery.

Meanwhile, by 1945, Hans Fallada knew that he had compromised everything, his existence as a writer, his personal morals and his life, and as a result he had a nervous breakdown and ended up in an institution. After returning from Moscow in 1945 the Expressionist poet and later Cultural Secretary of the GDR, Johannes R. Becher, persuaded Fallada to write a grand novel about the final days of the Nazis with a focus on resistance. As a member of the provisional Soviet government in Germany, Becher had access to Gestapo files, where he found the case of Elise and Otto Hampel, a couple who had been executed for distributing anti-Nazi material. As Becher relates, Fallada began writing Germany's first resistance novel in 1945, based on the Hampel file.[23] The resulting work, *Jeder stirbt für sich allein* (translated as *Every Man Dies Alone*, or *Alone in Berlin* (1947)), arguably Fallada's most powerful, begins with the postwoman Eva Kluge delivering the mail door-to-door in a tenement building, starting with the family of the staunch Nazi Persicke, who used to own a Berlin pub, but has risen to prominence in the Nazi hierarchy. Kluge, who has kind words for all her letter recipients, then rings the Quangels' doorbell, aware of the fateful content of the letter she bears – their son's official death notice. Otto Quangel, who had been a middle-class craftsman, is now working for a company manufacturing mortar shell boxes and coffins. Other tenants are introduced, among them the retired state prosecutor Fromm and the Jewish widow Rosenthal. And along with the main characters in this apartment building, we encounter Eva Kluge's husband, Enno, an occasional petty criminal who is connected to wartime Berlin's underworld. The social mix of the tenement building setup allows the reader a glimpse into the secretive goings-on in the closed-off world of a country at war.

Fallada's kaleidoscopic narrative, with its focus on petty fortune seekers, underscores Otto Quangel's noble character, which is gradually developed throughout the story. The simple Berliner Otto Quangel sees his principles of fairness and justice violated by the Nazis and undergoes a major change in a key scene. Quangel and his son's girlfriend, Trudel Baumann, meet in the former's workplace in front of a Gestapo poster that displays resistance fighters who had been executed:

> And a vision appears before him of how one day a poster with his own name and Anna's and Trudel's might be put up on the wall ... He shakes his head unhappily. He is a simple worker, he just wants peace and quiet, nothing to do with politics, and Anna just attends to the household and a lovely girl like Trudel will surely have found herself a new boyfriend before long ... But the vision won't go away. Our names on the walls, he thinks, completely confused now. And why not? Hanging on the gallows is no worse than being ripped apart by a shell, or dying from a bullet in the guts. All that doesn't matter.

The only thing that matter is this: I must find out what it is with Hitler. Suddenly all I see is oppression and hate and suffering, so much suffering ... 'Papa', she says, 'I will never forget that when I stood crying over Otto, it was in front of a poster like this. Perhaps – I don't want it to be – but perhaps it'll be my name on a poster like that one day'.[24]

The gruesome posters in the background represent the brutal Nazi reality Quangel had blocked out for so long, but which he is now forced to confront. As he quickly finds out, the girl has already gone much further in her resistance to the Nazis and joined an underground group. In this single scene, Fallada shows how the unremarkable character Quangel is transformed into a political being and resistance fighter. An encounter with Mrs Rosenthal, whom his wife has been hiding in their apartment, hardens his resolve to act against the Nazis. He decides to act alone: 'I don't want to be dragged into other people's funny business. If it is to be my head on the block, I want to know what it's doing there, and not that it's some stupid things that other people have done.'[25] He is a loner who wants to take on the Nazis, and ultimately ready to die 'alone in Berlin', as the title of the British translation suggests. *Jeder stirbt für sich allein* follows Fallada's fundamental artistic principle, whereby the environment – specifically that of National Socialist Berlin – triggers a reaction and transformation in the character, leading to life-and-death consequences. Since Quangel is a loner, he does not understand the destructive nature of the Nazis until the bitter end, and, when it is almost too late, he finally comes to his senses. Although he is not able to rebuild the destroyed city, he can give it back some dignity, at the price of his life.

Berlin's destruction resulted in new forms both of common cause and of isolation, of being together and of being alone in Berlin. Not unlike the Communists, the Nazis based their ideology on solidarity but embarked on a colossal distortion of how to build a society. The Communist resistance in Berlin provided strong examples of their ideology in their street novels, especially in the barricade novel, which would become the prime genre of resistance during the Nazi period. There is no such genre of Berlin literature written by Nazis during the Third Reich; *Hitlerjunge Quex* was published before 1933. Rather, most books written during the Nazi period were escapist and conceived either by authors of the Inner Emigration or by blood and soil authors. Escapism included escape from the realities of Berlin, as in *Barb, Roman einer deutschen Frau* (Barb, Novel of a German Woman (1933)) by Nazi writer Kuni Tremel-Eggert, who traces the trajectory of a woman from unhappy city life to a romantic country existence. In contrast to such kitschy popular writing, the majority of works of serious literature during the Nazi period pay tribute to the victims of the Nazis, including Jews and resistance fighters, and the city of Berlin is a particular arena for that tribute. At the same time, there has hardly been a period in German literature where literary experimentation has played such a small role, under the pressure – for more progressive writers – of the demand for sober testimony. The recent publication of Marie Jalowicz's *Untergetaucht* indicates that more narratives in this testimonial mode may well appear in years to come.

NOTES

1. Victor Klemperer, *I Will Bear Witness: A Diary of the Nazi Years, 1933–1941* (New York: Modern Library, 1999), pp. 6–10.
2. Jost Hermand, *Kultur in finsteren Zeiten: Nazifaschismus, Innere Emigration, Exil* (Cologne: Böhlau, 2010), p. 126.
3. Joachim C. Fest, *Hitler* (London: Harvest Books, 1974), pp. 139–40.
4. Quoted in Sebastian Graeb-Könneker, *Autochthone Modernität: Eine Untersuchung der vom Nationalsozialismus geförderten Literatur* (Opladen: Westdeutscher Verlag, 1996), p. 79.
5. Konrad Merz, *Ein Mensch fällt aus Deutschland* (Berlin: Aufbau, 1998), p. 6.
6. Thomas Wolfe, 'I Have a Thing to Tell You', *The Short Novels of Thomas Wolfe* (New York: Charles Scribner's Sons, 1961), p. 242.
7. Martha Dodd, 'Hitler Needs a Woman', quoted in Oliver Lubrich, *Travels in the Reich, 1933–1945: Foreign Authors Report from Germany* (Chicago: University of Chicago Press, 2010), p. 50.
8. Ibid.
9. Ibid.
10. Heinrich Spoerl, *Der Gasmann* (Reinbek: Rowohlt, 1957), pp. 92–3.
11. Erich Kästner, *Kästner für Erwachsene: Ausgewählte Schriften*, vol. 1 (Zürich: Atrium, 1983), p. 336 (my translation).
12. Erich Kästner, *Notabene 45: Ein Tagebuch* (Munich: dtv, 1989), p. 8.
13. Monika Shafi, 'Turning the Gaze Inward: Gertrud Kolmars Brief an die Schwester Hilde 1938-43', in *Facing Fascism and Confronting the Past: German Women Writers from Weimar to the Present*, ed. Elke P. Frederikson (Albany: SUNY Press, 2000), pp. 108–9.
14. German and English versions in *Dark Soliloquy: The Selected Poems of Gertrud Kolmar*, trans. Henry A. Smith (New York: The Seabury Press, 1975), pp. 122–5.
15. Amir Eshel, 'Cosmopolitanism and Searching for the Sacred Space in Jewish Literature', *Jewish Social Studies*, 9.3 (2003), pp. 121–38 (p. 125).
16. Ellipsis in original.
17. Albrecht Haushofer, *Moabiter Sonette* (Berlin: Lothar Blanvalet, 1946), p. 48.
18. My translation.
19. Anja Lundholm, *Das Höllentor: Bericht einer Überlebenden* (Reinbek: Rowohlt, 2000), p. 27.
20. Ibid., p. 176.
21. Quoted from an interview with Raimund Hoghe: 'Mehr als ein Leben', *Die Zeit*, 3 June 1994.

22. Lubrich, *Travels in the Reich*, p. 321.
23. Johannes R. Becher, 'Was nun? Zu Hans Falladas Tod', *Aufbau* 2.3 (1947), pp. 97–101.
24. Hans Fallada, *Every Man Dies Alone* (New York: Melville House), pp. 31–2.
25. Ibid., p. 89.

7

ALISON LEWIS

Writing in the Cold War

Barely had Berlin begun the enormous task of rebuilding at the end of the Second World War than the troubled metropolis found itself at the centre of a new war. Positioned precariously along the frontier between NATO and the Warsaw Pact, Germany was soon plunged into a major international crisis that turned into the forty-year-long conflict of the Cold War. Like the rest of Germany at war's end, Berlin was occupied and divided into four sectors. With the formation of two rival German states in 1949, Berlin was carved up, this time into an Eastern sector, which became the capital of the German Democratic Republic, and a Western 'other'. As a capitalist enclave, West Berlin was stranded in the heartlands of the new socialist republic, and with its special status and subsidies, quickly became a thorn in the side of the East Germans and the Soviets. In a further cruel twist of fate, in 1961 the division of Berlin was rendered semi-permanent by the erection of a fortified concrete and barbed-wire fence zigzagging down the middle of the city. The border running through the centre of Berlin was not merely an external frontier: it was an internal border dividing what was once one nation.

The period of the Cold War saw a faltering in representations of Berlin as a modern metropolis that embodied everything that was both exciting and frightening about modernity. This was not only due to the odd kind of largely invisible warfare that was the Cold War; it was also the result of the bankruptcy of Nazi visions of the city, which had pandered to notions of Berlin as a city of grand designs and mass spectacles. If Berlin became a more modest city in the postwar period, it certainly did not lose any of its appeal. On the contrary, its unique political situation ensured it remained for writers on both sides of the Cold War divide a site of projections of longing and desire, as well as an intense battleground for dreams of a better Germany and Europe. For international writers, Berlin, along with the cities of Prague and London, formed the dramatic backdrop to many postwar espionage novels, the most notable of which was John le Carré's *The Spy Who Came in from the Cold* (1963). But it has been in German literature from this turbulent period that Berlin's special status has been most notably memorialized, not merely as a politically and geographically divided city but as a partially enclosed, capitalist-socialist island in a Communist-dominated landscape. In many ways Berlin became a liminal space in the Cold War, an unstable territory wedged in between the superpowers, perpetually in transition and under threat. At the same time, however, writers discovered that the multiple flows that characterized Berlin in this period – the movement of goods, raw materials, labour, intelligence and people as well as the flows of desire and attraction – meant that the entire city was transformed into a type of borderland, a contact zone in which fixed, prescribed Cold War identities and politics could be challenged and reinscribed in less oppositional terms.

Cold War Berlin in the East and West German Literary Imagination

Despite the extraordinary nature of the East-West partition of Germany on the one hand and the division of its former capital on the other, neither of these two peculiarities of the postwar geopolitical landscape proved popular topics for literature in this period. Writers in each of the German nation-states had very different reasons for this omission. West Berlin was no longer the capital of the Federal Republic, which had moved to Bonn, although East Berlin, or simply Berlin, as the East German regime referred to it, was unequivocally the capital city of the GDR. West German writers were content to focus on regions and regional urban centres, and eschewed all nostalgia for the lost capital of Berlin and, for instance, the heady heydays of the Weimar Republic. Martin Walser's works frequently have rural or small town settings from the region around Lake Constance. Siegfried Lenz's works are either set in his adopted hometown of Hamburg and the coastal landscapes of Schleswig-Holstein, such as in his most famous work *Deutschstunde* (German Lesson (1968)), or return to the town of his birth in East Prussia, now Poland. Like Lenz, Günter Grass, also a refugee from Germany's former territories in the East, chose the 'Free City of Danzig', now Gdansk, as the setting for *Katz und Maus* (Cat and Mouse (1961)) and *Die Blechtrommel* (The Tin Drum (1959)). Similarly, the works of Heinrich Böll are deeply rooted in the Catholicism of the Rhine region around Bonn and Cologne, whereas other writers such as Alfred Andersch were drawn to natural borderlands such as the Eifel Mountains around Aachen.

While West German writers appeared to steer a wide berth around the beleaguered former capital, East German authors were less perturbed by Berlin's anomalous status during the Cold War. Since the eastern half of the city was at least still the designated capital of the fledgling socialist republic, there was no need to avoid East Berlin as the setting for dramatic and literary works, even if tackling it meant negotiating a veritable minefield of ideological and linguistic obstacles. These impediments were never fully and openly articulated, remaining constantly in flux and, moreover, impossible to predict. Questions of representation as well as politics confronting many GDR writers were therefore rather different from their counterparts in the West. In the East, aesthetic decisions concerning genre and setting of works, for instance, were always inherently political. Complicating East German writers' choices in style, genre and topic were the abrupt about-faces, shifts in direction and backlashes that could affect cultural politics seemingly overnight. Many works were commissioned by publishers and the Writers Guild only to find that by the time of their completion and publication, the political climate had transformed from a thaw to a frost or vice-versa.

As the Cold War intensified towards the end of the 1950s, it become clear to many that writing about the nation's divided capital city was going to require the exercise of extreme diplomacy. East German writers responded to the uncertainties around political correctness in relation to Berlin by choosing topographies in the city which were less likely to challenge Politburo sensibilities or overtly critique socialist policies or practices. Many sites in the city were considered to be ideologically neutral, such as Berlin's grand boulevards, featuring for instance in the title of Christa Wolf's short story 'Unter den Linden' (Under the Linden Trees (1969)). Others, such as the Fernsehturm, or Television Tower, built in 1968, were positively connoted, and references to this unforgettable landmark on Berlin's skyline were unlikely to raise a critical eyebrow with the censors or authorities. This was certainly not the case with political landmarks such as Friedrichstraße Station, which was once a central hub on the main S-Bahn (urban railway) route crossing the city from East to West. Referred to popularly as the *Tränenpalast*, or Palace of Tears, it was the site at which the border between East and West converged with a major traffic route and, hence, the place where Berliners bid farewell to their loved ones on the other side of the Iron Curtain.

One of the most curious aspects of German literature written during the Cold War is that the division of Germany was rarely ever a dominant theme of literary works. In the first two decades of the postwar era, only three works were published that tackled the topic in some detail: Arno Schmidt's short novel *Das steinerne Herz* (The Stone Heart (1956)), Hans Erich Nossack's novel *Der jüngere Bruder* (The Younger Brother (1958)) and Alfred Andersch's *Ein Liebhaber des Halbschattens* (A Lover of

Half-Shade (1962)). West German writers were certainly not indifferent to the plight of Germans behind the Iron Curtain, and a number, such as Günter Grass, registered their protest at the building of the Berlin Wall. However, the historical event never managed to find its way into major works of West German literature during the twenty-eight years of its existence. To be sure, Grass and other leading writers were themselves frequent visitors to East Berlin and nurtured several close friendships with East German writers, but most never penned literary works about the city.

One of the few German writers to tackle the East-West divide was Uwe Johnson. A refugee from Pomerania, Johnson settled with his family in Mecklenburg after the war and attended university in Rostock and Leipzig. After his first literary work was published in the West, he moved to West Berlin in 1959, where he quickly acquired the status of a pan-German writer with an especial interest in the division of Germany. His 1961 novel *Das dritte Buch über Achim* (The Third Book about Achim) is about the largely unspectacular events surrounding a three-month visit of Karsch, a journalist from Hamburg, to East Berlin around 1960, when the Wall had not yet been built but the state borders had already been fortified. While in Berlin, Karsch, who initially only intended to pay an old girlfriend a visit, decides to stay and write the biography of Achim, an East German elite cycling athlete. Achim epitomizes for him the potential of socialist Germany, its 'Kraft' ('power') and 'Zukünftigkeit' ('futurity'),[1] which he hopes to capture in his transnational project of writing the story of an East German representative of Germany through the eyes of a West German. His biography is thus an attempt to remember 'die gemeinsame Vorgeschichte', the shared prehistory,[2] of the country now drifting apart, and to overcome the unsettling foreignness of the city and country – the terrible feeling of 'fremde[n] Staatlichkeit' ('alien statehood')[3] – that greeted him upon crossing the border. But Karsch struggles to come to grips with the differences between the two Germanys, which are not just territorial but linguistic, cultural and ideological as well. Not even the common language can assuage his sense of alienation in Berlin, since it only exacerbated the 'Täuschung von Zusammengehörigkeit',[4] the illusion that the two cities and countries belonged together. Johnson's ethnographical approach to inner-German cultural difference remained a rarity in German literature over the following decades, which was dominated in the East, in particular, by substantially partisan portrayals of the division, such as Brigitte Reimann's *Die Geschwister* (The Siblings (1963)), Anna Seghers's *Die Entscheidung* (The Decision (1959)), Hermann Kant's *Die Aula* (The Auditorium (1965)) and Christa Wolf's *Der geteilte Himmel* (Divided Heavens (1963)).

East German Perspectives on Berlin: Love, Politics and Divided Heavens

Possibly the most iconic text from the Cold War period is Christa Wolf's *Der geteilte Himmel*. Twenty-five years after the division of Germany was overcome, Wolf's metaphor of divided skies and heavens is as fresh as ever, and it is still being invoked to reference the extraordinary events of twentieth-century world history. For the budding young writer, the novel, which was her first longer work, helped establish her reputation in the GDR and abroad as a major new literary talent. Its appeal lies in the clever pairing of an 'ordinary' theme like love with the extraordinary circumstances of a country poised on the verge of closing off all its major connections – from its streets, utility grids and telephone systems – to its estranged other half. At the time no treatment captured the essence of the Cold War better than Wolf's story of Rita and Manfred, lovers who are separated by the building of the Berlin Wall on 13 August 1961. The novel was seen as affirming Wolf's commitment to the GDR, but on closer analysis, her account of the impact of the Cold War reveals itself to be far more nuanced and ambivalent. Wolf has added an ideological twist to the archetypal tale of lovers divided by war, revolution or plain happenstance, and one that is ingenious.

Towards the end of the novel, Rita is living apart from Manfred, a chemist who has temporarily moved to West Berlin in search of better work opportunities. The couple's separation coincides with the months leading up to the building of the Wall. It is around this time that Rita's love is put to its first real test, and she begins to express resentment at Manfred's neglect of her and to question his cynical outlook on life. Finally, Manfred entreats Rita to join him in West Berlin on a longer-term basis, and with this in mind, she pays him a visit. At the end of the trip, Rita returns home to her village, confused by the entire experience. Through this particular plot construction, Wolf has taken care to play down the role of politics and to show that Rita is not caught out by the unexpected closing of the borders; she has, by all intents and purposes, fallen out of love *before* the Wall goes up. Moreover, she has had an opportunity to join Manfred, has travelled to the West and decided to return home. Thus, on the face of things, the lovers are not torn apart by the erection of barbed wire through the middle of Berlin. It is not politics that drives them apart but love itself.

Wolf's other main invention is to split her narrative into two time segments and to alternate between them. In the framing narrative, which covers only a few months and stretches from the last days of August to November 1961, Rita is convalescing in hospital after collapsing in the train carriage factory where she has been gaining work experience as a trainee. The accident is more likely to have been a suicide attempt, and the doctors suspect love is the most probable reason. The second narrative begins a few years earlier, spans two summers and winters and sees Rita meet the stiff and rather distant, older Manfred and fall in love. This narrative, in which she commences studying at a teaching institute, is structured like a female *Entwicklungsroman*, or novel of personal development, which traces Rita's coming-of-age in the context of the work brigade she joins during her summer internship. The environment in which Rita must assert herself is a tough man's world dominated by physical hardship and constant setbacks. Each narrative segment has an overarching upward trajectory: the coming-of-age narrative sees her grow in confidence and mature both in her relationship to Manfred and her associations with friends, brigadiers and colleagues. The convalescence narrative, which begins with Rita withdrawn and crying in hospital, unable to articulate the reason for her sorrows, gradually sees her begin to take an interest in the outside world and return to her previous life. Notwithstanding the happy end to the plot, Rita's breakdown or collapse at work, which is narrated at the very outset, casts a melancholic pall over the entire story. The reader knows that the lovers are doomed and that their parting has caused huge, unspeakable suffering to Rita. Most importantly for the construction of the novel, though, is the manner in which Wolf chooses to merge the two time frames and the twin tragedies of the story, thus linking the building of the Wall to Rita's attempted suicide.

Wolf could have brought the two narratives together in a description or narration of those ill-fated weeks in the middle of August 1961 but chooses not to. Curiously, after Rita's disappointing visit to West Berlin, there are no further scenes set in August in the novel. The reader is not privy to Rita's emotional distress upon her return nor to her state of mind leading up to the accident, which are both referred to only fragmentarily in the framing narrative in Rita's conversations with others. Even more significant than this is the glaring omission of a chapter or narrative segment dealing with the construction of the Wall itself. This event occurs off-stage in the blanks or gaps between the two narrative segments; it is never named and only referred to as 'die ersten Nachrichten', the first news,[5] in Rita's recollections of events. As history, it falls between the cracks of Wolf's story, although it is a glaringly 'present absence'.[6]

One of the last scenes in the novel is the account of Rita's visit to Manfred in West Berlin. It is a pivotal scene, serving as a turning point in the romance narrative as well as the denouement of the *Entwicklungsroman*, which has watched her blossom into a confident young woman with firm opinions and social responsibilities. It is also the scene in which the imagery in the novel's title is elaborated in detail. One of the influences on *Der geteilte Himmel* was Seghers's novel *Die Entscheidung*, in which Seghers was keen to illustrate how Cold War politics affected the most intimate aspects of people's lives.[7] Like Seghers, Wolf sets out to explore the immense toll of world events on human lives, especially on women's lives. At the start of the journey Rita is undecided whether she will leave Manfred or stay behind in West Berlin. The description of her trip and her crossing over the border prepares the reader for the complex interplay of political and personal factors behind Rita's dilemma: however Rita decides, we can be assured it will be the result of a combination of reasons to do with both love and politics. In her telling of the journey, Wolf mobilizes popular East German perceptions of the Western city as a 'Diversions- und Agentenzentrale' ('centre of diversion and espionage').[8] Rita's palpable sense of apprehension on the train 'that does not ease up' cannot be fully explained by the daunting decision that awaits her and is heightened by a diffuse feeling of doing something illicit or clandestine (*DgH*, p. 231). Adding to the scene's tension is Rita's fear that her trip could be misinterpreted as 'Republikflucht' (defection), and she could be seen as having joined the exodus of the thousand disloyal Easterners leaving daily for the West. She has not told anyone about her plans, and as if to underscore the scene's air of subterfuge, we are told that Rita is irritated by the inquisitive gaze of a stranger in the train carriage, even as she tries to reassure herself that her trip is the 'most natural and right thing in the world' (*DgH*, p. 231). The only direct references to the superpower standoff around the status of Berlin in the summer of 1961 are when her travelling companion quizzes her about where her fiancé lives. Rita is scared and lies, unsure whether to interpret this remark as a test or a warning. Although Rita is resolved to return and travels lightly with little luggage, just in case she might stay in West Berlin, she says her goodbyes to the East.

Through her use of the semantics of space Wolf creates pairs of oppositions between the friendly, often idealized socialist landscapes in the East, such as Rita's romanticized home village, and the cold foreign spaces associated with the West. Her first impression of Berlin is that it is 'not a pretty city', exuding an air of 'cold' (*DgH*, p. 236)). West Berlin is what Barclay calls an 'Ort der Abschreckung und der Sehnsucht' ('site of deterrence and longing'),[9] and a forbidden object of desire. So as not to get lost on arrival Rita memorizes a straight line from the train station to Manfred's apartment from a map and tries valiantly to walk it to his place. Her plan is of course an attempt to inoculate herself against temptation, which beckons from every corner of the Kurfürstendamm and its side streets: 'In dieser riesigen, unheimlichen Stadt war ihr eine feine dünne Linie vorgezeichnet. An die mußte sie sich halten. Wich sie von ihr ab, würde es Verwicklungen geben, deren Ende sie sich gar nicht ausdenken konnte' ('In this huge unnerving city a fine thin line lay in front of her. She had to stick to it. If she deviated from it there would be implications whose outcomes she could not even imagine' (*DgH*, p. 238)). In internalizing a Cold War map she has also reproduced the impasses and blockages of the era and effectively curtailed her curiosity for the other half of Berlin, prematurely closing off all new openings for an alternative life story it might offer. West Berlin holds no surprises for Rita, if only because it lives up to her preconceived, stereotyped notions of a capitalist city where material goods are in abundance. She allows herself to take a peek at kiosk windows on the train station and see the oranges and chocolate, cigarettes and cheap books, but having no map she dares not deviate from the straight and narrow. A few months later she admits all the glass and cellophane in the shop windows and the consumer goods on display were enticing but hastens to add that she 'knew that beforehand' (*DgH*, p. 244). In another passage set in West Berlin she concedes to Manfred that she found the city attractive but that it still seemed so totally 'other' to her. It awakened a feeling of alienation that was 'worse than being abroad' (*DgH*, p. 246), because of the common language.

Rita's initial impressions of West Berlin's inhospitality are reinforced when she and Manfred seek out a park which is not a 'park' but, in Manfred's words, a 'Grünanlage' ('green space'), and Rita is quick to point out its lack of redeeming features: 'Das wird hier nie ein Park. Die paar Bäume und Sträucher – Birken, Linden, Schneeball und Flieder – hatten ihre beste Zeit in diesem Jahr hinter sich. Sie waren grau von Staub, und ihre Blätter rollten sich in der Hitze wie dünnes Pergament' ('This will never be a park. The few trees and shrubs – birch, linden, viburnum and lilac – had passed their best time in this year. They were grey from the dust, and their leaves rolled in the heat like thin parchment' (*DgH*, p. 250)). Later in her recollections of this visit, Rita identifies the enduring foreignness of the city as her main reason for leaving Manfred. Reading between the lines, of course, it is not all that surprising that Rita, an immigrant who had lost her homeland once already when she and her mother fled from Germany's former provinces in the East at war's end, cannot face the upheaval of another permanent migration. However, Wolf cites instead another more ideological reason for staying in the East when she has Rita explain to her mentor Schwarzenbach that the West's attractions of travel and shopping were not compelling enough grounds for her to abandon her life in the East. She missed a greater purpose in life, she tells him, something more than 'eating and drinking' and 'gorgeous apartments' (*DgH*, p. 244), something like the 'Sog einer großen geschichtlichen Bewegung' ('pull of a great historical movement' (*DgH*, p. 254)). Since Manfred does not share her faith in socialism's future, in West Berlin her misgivings about his belief system come to a head, and she realizes she is already estranged from him, emotionally, socially and politically.

The estrangement of the lovers finds expression in a much-cited scene in West Berlin in which Manfred and Rita discuss how before parting, lovers sometimes choose a star in the sky to remind them of each other. Manfred remarks cynically that at least 'they' could not divide the heavens. Rita disagrees and debunks the pathos of the moment with the most famous sentences of the novel: 'Den Himmel? Dieses ganze Gewölbe von Hoffnung und Sehnsucht, von Liebe und Trauer? "Doch," sagte sie leise. "Der Himmel teilt sich zuallererst."' ('The heavens? This entire edifice of hope and desire, of love and sorrow? "Yes they can," she said softly. "The heavens are the very first thing that gets divided".' (*DgH*, p. 261)). Love cannot triumph over politics, Rita seems to be suggesting to him, and private lives are the first casualty of war.

Rita's sobering remark, spoken in the heat of the moment, proves prophetic. It is important to note that it is uttered before the escape route to the West has been sealed off with barbed wire in Operation 'Rose' in the night of 12 to 13 August.[10] Her comment about dividing the heavens initially serves to capture the resignation both Manfred and Rita feel that their relationship may have run its course. The mood of the scene, we are told, is devoid of hope but not yet 'von Verzweiflung gefärbt' ('tinged with desperation' (*DgH*, p. 261)). The lovers part unhappily and without any inkling that this meeting will be their last. Indeed, the overwhelming sense of despair at losing Manfred comes later, although this is more implicit than explicit, after history has intervened and ensured that the lover's separation is permanent. In the absence of guidance from the narrator, we are forced to infer that Rita's breakdown was triggered by the shock announcement of the building of the Wall. When Rita recalls that lovers often pledged to follow the one they love over 'forests and seas' (*DgH*, p. 250), Wolf leaves the reader in no doubt that romantic promises such as these are futile in the face of an impenetrable militarized Wall. While the novel is unable to name the most devastating cause of human suffering of this era, in its omissions and suggestive silences it still manages to convey the immense human cost caused by the division of Germany.

Der geteilte Himmel reflects Wolf's pragmatism early in her career and her willingness to sacrifice truth for partisanship to the regime at a time of national crisis. In the sections of the story dealing with the dire situation in factories and other work places – of shortages in materials and labour, disputes over norms and quotas – Wolf alludes to the most commonly peddled rationale for the erection of the Wall. Wolf's construction has less in common with the ideological 'antifaschistischer Schutzwall' (anti-fascist protective wall) designed to ward off the threat of Western agents and saboteurs than with another frequently cited justification for its erection. In the novel, the building of the Wall is portrayed as a stabilizing measure in the interests of world peace, a desperate but necessary act of force to stop the debilitating flows of skilled labour. As an unwanted 'Schlupfloch', or escape hole,[11] for the regime and a 'shop window' for capitalism,[12] West Berlin was a thorn in the side of the Eastern bloc, a symbol of Communism's failure to thrive and to win out over the political freedoms and economic prosperity of the West. It is Manfred's friend Martin who expresses the most extreme view that the building of the Wall in fact comes too late. If a valuable worker like Manfred had been made to stay behind 'even through force' (*DgH*, p. 197), he would have had to persevere and commit to the socialist cause.

Especially after the *Wende*, the 'turn' of reunification, Wolf's topos of divided love in a divided city was taken up again by many writers who used the trope of the couple once divided and now hoping to be united, or its opposite, the couple whose marriage falls apart not despite unification but because of it. In Brigitte Burmeister's *Unter dem Namen Norma* (Under the Name of Norma (1994)), the marriage of the protagonist falls victim to the stresses of unification when Marianne, like Wolf's figure Rita, refuses to join her husband Johannes in the West. In Ingo Schramm's novel *Entzweigesperrt* (Locked Apart (1998)), Wolf's story finds a melancholic sequel in which an East German couple, previously separated by the Cold War, tries but fails to be reunited. In both cases politics intervenes in individuals' private lives, only now it is the politics and circumstances of German unification that drive a wedge between couples. In both of these cases, the West, once a repressed object of desire as we see in *Der geteilte Himmel*, becomes the subject of disavowal and repression, an unattainable, estranged object of desire for the spouse left behind in the East.

West German Perspectives on Berlin: Island City, Political Refugees and Border-Crossers

Although published shortly after German reunification in 1991, Martin Walser commenced writing his novel *Die Verteidigung der Kindheit* (The Defence of Childhood (1991)) prior to the historical events of November 1989. The work is set entirely during the Cold War and spans virtually its entire duration, starting in February 1953 and ending in 1982 with the death of its protagonist. It tells the story of Alfred Dorn, an eccentric but likeable character, an unashamed 'mother's boy', who, like many of Walser's male figures, is a 'weak individual faced with powerful exterior forces'.[13] Dorn finds himself at the outset of the novel an illegal refugee in West Berlin when he is dispatched to the Western sector of Berlin by his estranged parents to complete his legal studies. In Berlin, his parents tell him, he will have a greater chance of passing his final examinations, which he has failed twice already in Leipzig. Berlin beckons as the last bastion of hope for their son, who had failed not due to any fault of his own – and most certainly not because of 'Verweichlichung' ('turning soft') as his father believes – but because of 'politische Schwierigkeiten' ('political difficulties').[14] Dorn divides his time as a student and later as a legal clerk between Berlin and his sorely missed hometown of Dresden, which he visits at every opportunity. Dorn is reluctant to apply for political refugee status in West Germany because this would cut him off once and for all from Dresden. While the inner-German borders had been sealed off by 1952, free movement between East and West Berlin, and between the Western part of the city and East Germany more broadly, continued as thousands of East Berliners commuted daily to work in the Western sectors, and West Berlin attracted more and more refugees from the East in transit to West Germany.

Some critics have been puzzled by the novel's decided lack of interest in contemporary historical events, which seems especially odd, given Walser's outspoken comments about his longing for Germany to be reunified.[15] Walser's novel furnishes few temporal references to dates of the postwar period to guide the reader, offering instead a wealth of spatial or geographical detail that references the cities of Berlin and Dresden. There are many allusions to Berlin's topography, which are precise and almost documentary in style. Walser includes passing descriptions of street names, house addresses, and train and S-Bahn stations, as well as references to various government offices. These serve as realistic historical effects to anchor what is otherwise a narrative dominated by internal psychodramas, Oedipal conflicts and Dorn's increasingly apparent neuroses and idiosyncrasies.

The spaces and places of Berlin form part of Dorn's own personal geography of the city. His sense of direction is skewed from the moment he arrives at Bahnhof Zoo, when north seems to him south, and east and west appear reversed: 'Solange er in Berlin war, lag er, was den Verlauf des Kurfürstendamms angeht, verkehrt. Der erste Eindruck war bei ihm immer unkorrigierbar' ('Whenever he was in Berlin, the Kurfürstendamm seemed to him to run in the opposite direction. He could never correct first impressions').[16] Both Berlin and Dresden function as highly charged symbolic sites in Dorn's psychic household, representing in many ways twin poles that, much like his parents, demand different things of him and pull him in opposite directions. His father wants nothing more than for Dorn to become a successful lawyer and a 'real man', and if he has to turn his back on Dresden, this is not too high a price to pay. For his mother, however, the separation from her son is hard to endure, as it is for Dorn, especially when the East German regime threatens to bar him from re-entering the country again.

In Walser's novel Berlin has a peculiar 'psycho-geography' whereby the divided city could be seen as representing the 'reality principle' in Dorn's life, the demands of study and a life beyond the family. Walser's Berlin is rather like a post-Oedipal playground for adults, a cutthroat city in which Dorn has to fend for himself and build the practical, independent future his parents have envisaged for him. If West Berlin was the 'thorn' in the Soviets' side in the 1950s, then Dorn (literally, thorn) is in many ways the thorn in his parent's side, or at least a source of his parents' constant quibbles. Berlin promises an escape from the family's imperatives, an escape which could constitute a 'line of flight' away from the 'despotism' of the Oedipalized family in the terms of the 'schizo-analysis', or critique, of capitalism as developed by Gilles Deleuze and Félix Guattari.[17] Oedipus is the myth, according to them, that turns desire centripetally back towards the family and contains it, preventing it from experimenting with new possibilities.[18] Hence, for Dorn Berlin promises much but fails to deliver a new beginning or a resolution to old problems. Its liminality is, like Homi Bhabha's experience of the migrant, a 'living in the interstices', being caught inbetween the positions of the nativist and the assimilated newcomer.[19] It is the scene of his repeated failures, not only of his failed legal exams but also his personal failure to form intimate relationships with either gender. Dresden, by the same token, increasingly comes to represent the past in his imagination, the idyll of his childhood, his untrammelled dreams and a happy time when the family was still intact. In many ways Dresden becomes linked to Freud's 'pleasure principle', the city which offers the illusory prospect of uncensored fulfilment of desire, which he is denied, although Dorn's actual experience of the city was anything but pleasurable. Closely entwined with the maternal, Dresden is not only associated with his own past, it is also the scene of unmastered trauma and violence since Dorn and his family are survivors of the Allied bombing of Dresden in the Second World War. Whether it started before his relocation to Berlin or earlier is unclear, but Dorn develops a fixation on the past, which, like an obsessional neurosis, begins to impact his every movement and decision.

While his sojourn in Berlin provides a refuge from the authoritarian Communist regime of his childhood, Dorn cannot truly enjoy his newfound freedom. In Dresden he had suffered from the effects of Communist policies which discriminated against those from 'non-progressive' backgrounds. And yet West Berlin offers him a circumscribed freedom, a freedom in chains, a temporary respite made less pleasurable because of his constant and well-founded fears that he might be cut off from Dresden. His fellow refugees from the East studying in Berlin are glad to be in the Western sector of Berlin, but for Dorn it remains a partially blocked escape route that does not free him from the tyranny of dictatorial rule, nor allow him to escape from an overbearing father. West Berlin is foreign and disorientating, less 'herzlich' ('genial') than the East, 'überfüllt, aber menschenleer' ('overcrowded, but devoid of humans'),[20] albeit with select comforts and guilty pleasures such as the cinemas and the shopping strip on the Kurfürstendamm.

Most importantly for the context of the Cold War is the fact that Walser's Berlin is a city hamstrung by time-consuming and stultifying bureaucracy in all of its four sectors. When Dorn sends his father a cortisone skin cream from the West concealed inside a packet of coffee and camouflaged by soap, much to his distress it is confiscated by East German customs. Dorn's mother's almost daily express-post parcels of cake and sausage to her son usually arrive in disarray after having been vetted at the border. Dorn finds the interference in his life to be a 'German vice' 'pure and unadulterated'.[21] Hence, in Walser's account Berlin is less a city divided by Cold War ideologies than an island city with fortified, heavily policed borders. It is a city under siege.

As Heike Doane writes, Dorn is always in transit, 'both physically and emotionally shuffling between Dresden and Berlin, between East and West, between mother and school and job, between the past and the present – and never comes to the end of his journeying'.[22] Berlin's beleaguered status leads to two sorts of frenetic movements on the part of Walser's protagonist. On the one hand, there is Dorn's constant scuttling back and forth across the city in search of either cheaper rent, food or transit visas, and on the other his constant desire to cross over the state border, to return home to Dresden, for birthdays, Easter, Whitsuntide and Christmas. For Dorn, like so many citizens in the Cold War, crossing borders has become part of the new normality of life, even though in heading eastwards he is going in the opposite direction to most other political refugees of the time. Dorn is no stranger to swimming against the tide, whether it be in his excessive longing for Dresden or in his unfashionable support for the Christian Democrats in the 1960s. In this respect, Dorn echoes the views of his author who was one of the few public intellectuals in the 1980s to voice his opposition to the partition of Germany. Walser spoke unashamedly about his 'Leipzig-Stuttgart-Gefühl' ('Leipzig-Stuttgart-feeling'),[23] and of how he suffered deeply from the loss of the other half of Germany, much as one would from a 'phantom pain'.[24]

Dorn's interest in preserving the past becomes an all-consuming passion, and represents another attempt at what Deleuze and Guattari would call a 'line of flight' away from the family, which of course, proves to be anything but an escape from Oedipal pressures to conform; it is instead a return to the past, to a maternal pre-Oedipal space in which he can be alone with his mother. After three years of living in the divided city he is no longer content to document the stages of his life with photographs, so he devises a new outlet for his frustrations in a series of hobbyhorse history projects. One of these is to collect documents and photographs and evidence more generally of his past.[25] Driving his collecting mania is a keen sense of loss that has stayed with him since 13 February 1945, when his family lost all the family photo albums and films of him as a child in the firebombing of Dresden. He expends considerable energy rescuing fragments of the past from photographs, family china, furniture and even his mother's underwear. In his spare time he immerses himself in a history project about famous figures from eighteenth-century Saxon history. He is drawn to the royal court of Dresden and its flamboyant, decadent figures, which seem to offer a counterweight to Prussian militarism, which he sees epitomized in the East German regime and in its desolate capital of Berlin. His family's possessions and the history of the Saxon royals are, moreover, signs of a past presence that contemporary society has sought to obliterate.

If Dorn's unconventional hobbies offer some protection from the harsh realities of the Cold War before the building of the Berlin Wall, after 1961 his efforts only intensify. When his mother grows frail and sick, Dorn's collecting mania borders on the fetishistic, and when she dies, he wants to erect an elaborate memorial for her to mark his loss. The lavish tombstone that he designs has to be built in a Berlin cemetery because the borders have now been sealed off. As the realities of Berlin's exceptional status encroach more on his life and his freedom to move around the country to attend to sick family members and celebrate their birthdays back home in the East is curtailed, Dorn's image of Dresden alters. As if requiring the mobilization of ever-stronger defences against loss, he elevates his 'inner' Dresden, his internalized imago of the city, to ever more fantastical and grandiose proportions. In a similar way to Wolf's memorized map of West Berlin, Dorn's inner map of Dresden represents a defensive position, a retreat from the world, and reproduces existing geopolitical and libidinal blockages.

Walser's character Dorn embodies a far more radical psychological response to the ineluctable dilemma of the divided heavens once invoked by Christa Wolf. While Wolf's Rita is permitted a brief period to mourn the loss of love before taking up her old life again, Dorn's entire adult life is dedicated to mourning and monumentalizing loss. He devises increasingly elaborate psychological coping mechanisms to offset his losses and to neutralize the impact of the Cold War on his life. His multiple 'lines of flight', although prolific and frenetic, offer him no relief from the rigid dichotomy of a country divided along strict ideological lines and perched on the front lines of two warring superpowers. Hence, his projects are ineffectual, even regressive, leading to the restoration of the old rather than the emergence of something new, culminating in what Deleuze calls a reterritorialization rather than a deterritorialization.[26] Hence, Walser's Dorn and his highly idiosyncratic, almost perverse responses to the historical and political realities of the Cold War take the reader into territory that was taboo for Wolf but which Walser explores in order to expose the hidden and largely repressed psychopathology of postwar Germany and its split metropolis Berlin.

The Last Decade of the Cold War: Berlin's Madness, Wall Jumpers and the Wall in the Head

In *Der geteilte Himmel* Wolf's deserter Manfred confesses to Rita that some of the hysterical and insane features of Berlin had rubbed off onto him: 'Ich bin selbst schon verrückt' ('I am already mad myself' (*DgH*, p. 251)). Peter Schneider picks up on this trope in his essay 'Berliner Geschichten' (Berlin Stories) when he recalls how, like the concept of postmodernism in New York, the word 'Wahnsinn', madness, had found a natural home in Berlin.[27] A central part of this everyday madness was, says Schneider, the fact that the Wall itself, 'like the God of the Old Testament', was invisible in the lives of its citizens.[28] The 'schizophrenic situation',[29] which afflicted the 'Siamese city',[30] had led to two German cultures and languages, which Schneider summed up in the famous phrase of the 'Wall in the head'. In his 1982 novel about East-West friendships and various border-crossers, *Der Mauerspringer* (The Wall Jumper), Schneider reflects on the deep rifts that Cold War divisions had inflicted on German culture and would continue to exert in future: 'Die Mauer im Kopf einzureißen wird länger dauern, als irgendein Abrißunternehmen für die sichtbare Mauer braucht' ('It will take us longer to tear down the Wall in our heads than some wrecking company will need for the Wall we can see').[31] Like Walser, who could not desist from 'picking' at the 'wound' that the division of Germany had inflicted, Schneider too continued to highlight the curious effects of living in such close geographical proximity to antagonistic world systems. He argues that twenty years of living in a walled-in city had not led to the city growing apart, as Christa Wolf had predicted. Instead, we are to infer that it produced its own siege-like mentality in which, as Schneider claims, Berliners had learnt to accept the other political system just like they were accustomed to watching both East and West German television news. The price for sharing this knowledge of how the other half of the city lives and thinks was, he argued, ultimately a loss of self.[32] Schneider's most enduring image for the Cold War is his literary construct of the 'Mauerspringer'. The wall jumper is based on the true story of a refugee who turns his original act of jumping over the Wall into a regular sport by illegally jumping back and forth over the fortification in both directions. Rather like Schneider's post-unification figures of twins and doubles, the wall jumper is a liminal figure, as much born of desperation as of liberation, one that is perpetually in motion between Western and Eastern halves of the city and opposing systems and unable to arrive fully in one or the other.

Berlin's unique geopolitical topography during the Cold War frequently found indirect expression in its last decade in many works of East Berlin's burgeoning bohemia. For the Prenzlauer Berg poets, who lived in the dilapidated housing at the rear of the inner city blocks of the area, the cityscape with its borders, walls, concrete and stone had become part of a stifling, claustrophobic landscape, which its fringe-dwellers neither wanted to escape from nor fully embrace. Durs Grünbein captures the group's sense of being the 'object of a cynical historical joke', as Karen Leeder puts it, in his poem 'O Heimat, zynischer Euphon' (Oh Homeland, Cynical Euphony) from March 1989, when he describes his generation as follows: 'Der kranken Väter Brut sind wir, der Mauern / Sturzgeburt . . . ' ('We are the sick fathers' offspring, the walls' / precipitous birth . . . ').[33]

Towards the end of the Cold War, the Wall lost its materiality, colonizing the very consciousness of the generation of 'Hineingeborenen', those 'born into' the divided city who had no experience of pre-Wall reality. As Sascha Anderson writes,

> ich bau mir meine mauer selbst durch den leib,
> die eine hälfte fault sofort
> die andere mit der zeit
>
> ('I build my own wall through my flesh,
> one half's rotting straight away
> the other's rotting over time'.)[34]

It is therefore perhaps not surprising that the divided city and the emblematic structure of the Berlin Wall, which was either one of the uncomfortable truths of the metropolis or an outright taboo, had a more active presence in its afterlife in the post-unification era than it did during its lifetime.

NOTES

1. Uwe Johnson, *Das dritte Buch Buch über Achim* (Frankfurt am Main: Suhrkamp, 1961), p. 40.
2. Ibid., p. 23.
3. Ibid., p. 7.
4. Ibid., p. 23.
5. Christa Wolf, *Der geteilte Himmel*, ed. Agnes Cardinal (London: Methuen & Co., 1987), p. 254 (henceforth *DgH*).
6. The same can be said for West Berlin, see David E. Barclay, 'Westberlin', *Erinnerungsorte der DDR*, ed. Martin Sabrow (Munich: C. H. Beck, 2009), p. 431.
7. Katharina von Ankum, *Die Rezeption von Christa Wolf in Ost und West: Von Moskauer Novelle bis 'Selbstversuch'* (Amsterdam: Rodopi, 1992), p. 62.
8. Barclay, 'Westberlin', p. 432.
9. Barclay, 'Westberlin', p. 432.
10. Hope M. Harrison, 'Berlin and the Cold War Struggle over Germany', in *The Routledge Handbook of the Cold War*, eds Artemy M. Kalinovsky and Craig Daigle (Abingdon and New York: Routledge, 2014), p. 65.
11. Barclay, 'Westberlin', p. 432.
12. Harrison, 'Berlin and the Cold War', p. 62.
13. Stuart Parkes, 'Not Top of the Pops?: Martin Walser's Writing Since 1990', *German Literature in the Age of Globalisation*, ed. Stuart Taberner (Birmingham: University of Birmingham Press, 2004), p. 136.
14. Martin Walser, *Die Verteidigung der Kindheit* (Frankfurt am Main: Suhrkamp, 1991), p. 30.
15. See Michael Braun, 'Die Suche nach Vergangenheit', *Nürnberger Nachrichten*, 10 August 1991.
16. Walser, *Die Verteidigung der Kindheit*, p. 15.
17. See Gilles Deleuze and Félix Guattari, *Anti-Oedipus: Capitalism and Schizophrenia* (Minneapolis: Minnesota Press, 1983), p. 54.
18. Todd May, *Gilles Deleuze: An Introduction* (Cambridge: Cambridge University Press, 2005), p. 146.
19. Homi K. Bhabha, *The Location of Culture* (Abingdon: Routledge, 1994), p. 321.
20. Walser, *Die Verteidigung der Kindheit*, p. 53.
21. Ibid., p. 398.
22. Heike A. Doane, 'The Cultivation of Personal and Political Loss: Walser's *Die Verteidigung der Kindheit*', in *New Critical Perspectives on Martin Walser*, ed. Frank Pilipp (Columbia: Camden House, 1994), p. 143.
23. Martin Walser, 'Ich hab' so ein Stuttgart-Leipzig-Gefühl: *Stern*-Gespräch mit Martin Walser', *Martin Walser: Auskunft: 22 Gespräche aus 28 Jahren*, ed. Klaus Siblewski, Frankfurt am Main: Suhrkamp, 1991), p. 249.
24. Ibid., p. 249.
25. Walser, *Die Verteidigung der Kindheit*, p. 195.
26. See Adrian Parr, *The Deleuze Dictionary* (Edinburgh: Edinburgh University Press, 2010), p. 148.
27. Peter Schneider, 'Berliner Geschichten', in *Deutsche Ängste: Sieben Essays* (Darmstadt: Luchterhand, 1988), pp. 7–8.

28. Ibid., p. 8.
29. Ibid.
30. Peter Schneider, *Der Mauerspringer* (Darmstadt: Luchterhand, 1982), p. 7.
31. Ibid., p. 117.
32. Ibid., p. 16.
33. Karen Leeder, '"ich fühle mich in grenzen wohl": Metaphors of Boundaries and Boundaries of Metaphor in Prenzlauer Berg', in *Prenzlauer Berg: Bohemia in East Berlin?*, eds Philip Brady and Ian Wallace (Amsterdam: Rodopi, 1995), pp. 19–44 (p. 24).
34. Sascha Anderson, *Jeder Satellit hat einen Killersatelliten* (Berlin: Rotbuch, 1982), p. 26.

8

KATHARINA GERSTENBERGER

Writing after the Wall

According to a 2010 article in the cultural magazine *Literaturen*, the majority of German writers live in Berlin.[1] Living in Berlin does not, of course, mean that these authors necessarily also write about their place of residence, but their presence, together with an array of institutions such as the Literary Colloquium Berlin, the Literature Forum in the Brecht-House or the Literature House Berlin, underscores the importance of united Germany's capital for the production and the reception of contemporary literature. Contemporary literature, according to one broad, yet useful definition by literary scholar Michael Braun, is about issues that the majority of readers have witnessed or lived through in one form or another.[2] In the case of Berlin literature since the fall of the Wall on 9 November 1989, this involves the experiences of unification and the physical, social and economic changes visible in the city in the years following this event. Peaking around 1999, newness, transition and rupture are the predominant themes and subjects of this post-unification Berlin literature, told from a variety of perspectives and in a range of literary styles. Beginning around 2005, we can observe a shift away from the concerns and stories of the immediate present towards narratives that examine aspects of Berlin's past, exploring contexts and continuities, but also historical differences. In particular, the years of division have come into focus in a range of retrospective renderings of the former East and West Berlin and the cultures they harboured.

The physical and political reconstruction of the 1990s was accompanied by a highly publicized 'search' for a novel that could capture Berlin's transformation from divided city to capital of united Germany. Several factors contributed to this phenomenon. Most importantly, there is the expectation in German society that writers should and will weigh in on important social but also political questions. There is, still, the notion that literature as an expression of high culture is an appropriate medium for capturing and interpreting for the reader large-scale developments such as the fall of the Wall and its consequences. And, there is the abiding idea of a representative

Berlinroman or Berlin novel, which has its historical model in Alfred Döblin's canonical city novel, *Berlin Alexanderplatz* (1929). Such assumptions, together with a concerted marketing campaign promoting Berlin as Germany's new political, cultural and architectural capital, led publishers, critics and the directors of literary institutions to raise the prospect of a novel that would capture the essence of the post-unification period. Throughout the 1990s, newspaper feuilletons called for a novel capable of representing the atmosphere of the times and doing for the 1990s what Döblin's modernist masterpiece had done for the late 1920s. The significant number of 300 or so prose texts about Berlin published in the first post-unification decade must be understood in the context of the search for the definitive Berlin narrative and the fertile environment it provided for writers.

No one novel, at least to this day, has been able to approximate the canonical status of Alfred Döblin's exceptional example of city literature. The journalist Holm Friebe observed as early as 1999 that 'the fate of the Berlin novel is not to exist'.[3] Yet, given the literary scene's preoccupation with the topic, it should come as no surprise that the search for a *Berlinroman* itself has become a topic of literature. Robert Gernhard's delightful 'Couplet vom Hauptstadtroman' (Couplet of the Capital Novel), published ten years after the fall of the Wall, pokes gentle fun at the phenomenon: 'Die Sonne zieht Tag für Tag ihre Bahn—/Was sie nicht bescheint, ist ein Hauptstadtroman' ('The sun shines daily long and hot –/But on the capital novel it shines not').[4] And, to give another example, the main protagonist in Joachim Lottmann's satirical 1999 novel *Deutsche Einheit* (German Unity (1999)) finds it much easier to attract women once they learn that he is a writer-in-residence at the prestigious Literary Colloquium on the Wannsee who is working on a Berlin novel. Inspired by the need to reinvent the city of Berlin after forty years of division, the search for the Berlin novel must be understood as a phenomenon representative of 1990s culture at large, rather than a purely literary pursuit.

Berlin literature of the 1990s is rich in imagery and often highly creative in its adaptation of literary traditions. For instance, several texts translate the city's division and subsequent unification into stories of physical and psychological violation, presented through images of wounded bodies, scars and trauma. The tradition of describing a city as body goes back to the nineteenth century and underscores the idea of a city as a living organism, its streets often likened to arteries and its parks to lungs. Conversely, the city's impact on the human body is often described as negative because overcrowded urban quarters prevent it from getting the air and sun it needs. Berlin literature after 1989 continues in this tradition when it describes the Wall as a scar that runs through the body of the city and the rebuilding activities as a process of surgery. Images of illness and health, and, in some cases, healing, offer up interpretations of German history as a disease that manifests itself in the urban spaces of Berlin.

Such texts include Thomas Hettche's *Nox* (Night (1995)), a nightmarish story set in the course of 9 November 1989, which likens the opening of the Wall to scar tissue breaking open after years of dormancy and involves violent sexual practices as well as allusions to Nazi torture. Meanwhile, Inka Parei's *Die Schattenboxerin* (The Shadow-Boxing Woman (1999)), a story about a rape, creates connections between an urban space marred by destruction and neglect and the abused body of the female protagonist (see Chapter 9). Set less than a year after the fall of the Wall, the novel takes place in areas on both the East and the West Berlin sides of the former Wall. The possibility of healing comes as the protagonist begins to rebuild her life by moving into a temporarily empty building in East Berlin's Mitte that offers her shelter and the opportunity of a new beginning during the transition period of the early 1990s. And Christa Wolf's novel *Leibhaftig* (In the Flesh (2002)) blends descriptions of physical illness with images of the city diseased by war and destruction in a story about a gravely ill female protagonist whose feverish dreams lead her down into the air raid bunkers and construction pits of Berlin, where she encounters the remnants of the city's Nazi past. The opening of the Wall, in these texts, inspires images of the disease that afflicts the city as well the bodies of the protagonists.

While some seek to understand and represent a city through body imagery, others conceive of the city as a text that can be read and interpreted. To the skilled observer, buildings and streets reveal information about the city's history and preserve the memory of events that took place there. Closely linked to the idea that the city's physical appearance is also a repository of its history is the figure of the flâneur, the person who walks through the city at a leisurely pace and observes the people and sites that surround him. In the case of Berlin, this tradition begins with works like the Berlin stories of E. T. A. Hoffmann. Hoffmann's 1822 'Des Vetters Eckfenster' (My Cousin's Corner Window), a short prose text in which a housebound man watches the crowds on the city's centrally located Gendarmenmarkt from his window, letting his eyes wander among those in the market place below and inventing stories for them, is a telling variation: observation from a fixed position instead of while walking emphasizes the importance of processing and interpreting what is seen (see Chapter 2). The practice of observing and decoding the city then finds its most prominent expression in the 1920s in the canonical essays and feuilleton pieces of Walter Benjamin, Franz Hessel, Joseph Roth and Siegfried Kracauer, among others, with their astutely observed descriptions of Weimar Berlin's modernist architecture and its traffic, but also its parks and its diverse population.

Chronicling Change at the Potsdamer Platz

The practice of reading the city as a text and of using specific sites for the purpose of describing and interpreting Berlin's past, present and future continues into the 1990s. The Potsdamer Platz plays a prevalent role in this context because nowhere is change over time more visible than here. A major urban site since the late nineteenth century, the Potsdamer Platz has a long tradition of being depicted in literature and art. Examples include Paul Boldt's poem, 'Auf der Terrasse des Café Josty' (On the Terrace of Café Josty (1912)), his Expressionist tribute to one of Berlin's most famous cafés, but also Ernst Ludwig Kirchner's 1914 painting *Potsdamer Platz*, with two prostitutes referencing the link between such focal sites of the city and transgression. Less stark is Erich Kästner's humorous poem 'Besuch vom Lande' (Visitors from the Countryside (1930)) about provincial tourists intimidated by the speed and the sounds at the Potsdamer Platz; yet it, too, describes the city as a threatening place. Badly bombed during the Second World War and then bisected by the Berlin Wall, the Potsdamer Platz neighbourhood was cleared almost entirely of physical structures. Sarah Kirsch's 1982 poem 'Naturschutzgebiet' (Nature Preserve) puts into words the stark contrast between the bustling 1920s and the area's emptiness in the 1980s, daring the reader to visualize the site's vastly differing incarnations. Beginning in 1994 and aided by a heavy marketing campaign, construction of unprecedented dimensions began at the Potsdamer Platz, transforming the fallow urban space in the centre of the newly united Berlin once again into an arena of commerce and entertainment.

The Potsdamer Platz, more than any other site in the city, captured the experience of transformation and change in 1990s Berlin. The Infobox, a temporary structure erected at the Potsdamer Platz, afforded visitors a prime spot to observe the construction projects, and bookstores stocked coffee table books with colourful illustrations of the site's spectacular transformation. For writers as well, the Potsdamer Platz was a symbol of change and thus an opportunity to reflect on the developments unfolding before everyone's eyes. Social and economic critique tends to prevail in these texts focusing on reconstruction, but few could resist the fascination emanating from the mass of machinery at work. Much of this critical probing involved the Nazi past and the uncertainty as to how united Germany would integrate this aspect of its history into its emerging identity as a leading democratic nation. Peter Schneider, for instance, in his 1999 novel *Eduards Heimkehr* (Eduard's Homecoming), writes about the need to remove hidden tumours 'before the new heart could be implanted'.[5] Similarly, Dutch writer Cees Nooteboom has his protagonist in *Allerseelen* (All Souls' Day (1999)) observe the construction workers digging up the ground as if they were searching for the 'Vergangenheit persönlich' ('the past in person').[6] Excavation work at the Potsdamer Platz construction site translates into images of unearthing the past and reflections about the challenges of integrating this past into the united Germany's new self-confidence as a nation. The fear that the past might become inaccessible finds expression in Christian Försch's *Unter der Stadt* (Underneath the City (2001)), a detective novel of sorts in which the Potsdamer Platz serves as a crime scene. The protagonist's comment that 'Alle Spuren waren verdeckt' ('all traces had been covered'),[7] uttered in response to the finished buildings, is also a remark about German history.

Other writers look to the Potsdamer Platz not so much to express anguish over the changing status of history for German identity but to put into words confusion about the present. Ulrike Draesner, in her short prose text 'Atmer' (Breather), captures the sense of disorientation that befell many when she writes, 'Potsdamer Platz, sofort dreht das Taxi im Kreis' ('Potsdamer Platz, immediately the cab spins in a circle').[8] The spinning motion is emphasized by the ambiguous grammar ('drehen' should be a reflexive verb if it is the cab itself that is spinning, but it is left here with a vertiginously open predicate). Bodo Morshäuser's observation that the only thing one recognizes at the Potsdamer Platz is the fact that one cannot recognize any of its old features is another way of expressing that loss of familiar points of reference.[9] Yet the Potsdamer Platz also embodies the present. For Kathrin Röggla, an Austrian writer based in Berlin, it becomes an erotic site for the 1990s, captured in a stream of non-standard orthography: 'ganz sony-trunken das gelände da draußen, sieht sie, ganz sony-frisch auch seine hände' ('completely sony-drunken the site outside, she sees, completely sony-fresh also his hands'),[10] she writes in one of her short stories in *Irres Wetter* (Crazy Weather (2000)), referring to the Sony building going up on the Potsdamer Platz to render a sexual encounter in the New Berlin. And finally, Lukas Hammerstein's *Die 120 Tage von Berlin* (The 120 Days of Berlin), a 2003 novel about a group of social outsiders who take up residence in the new buildings at the Potsdamer Platz for the period indicated in the title and before the corporate tenants move in, suggests that the completion of the Potsdamer Platz marks the end of an era. Hammerstein's work chronicles events during a limited and exceptional period of time but without the depictions of violent sexual practices depicted in the Marquis de Sade's 1785 *The 120 Days of Sodom*. What comes after is the new normalcy of a united Germany, hoped for by many but experienced as the end of a period of openness and promise by others. The literary responses to the Potsdamer Platz as illustrated in these select examples reflect important aims of 1990s Berlin literature in general: to capture in literature the atmosphere of a city in transition; to comment and to critique; and, in some cases, to develop new ways of 'writing the city' by rendering the changes in Berlin's urban landscape in an innovative fashion.

Ownership and Belonging

Schneider's *Eduards Heimkehr* counts among the most prominent examples of literary works seeking to assess the realities of 1990s Berlin and will therefore be discussed here in somewhat more detail. Born in 1940 and an active participant in West Berlin's student movement, Schneider has written extensively about Berlin in both fiction and nonfiction. The famous phrase about the 'Wall in the Head' persisting long after the real Wall has been dismantled stems from his 1982 novel *Der Mauerspringer* (The Wall Jumper). For Schneider, as for many others on the West German Left, the fall of the Wall raised fears of the return of nationalism in a united Germany, with Günter Grass's 1990 article against unification in *Die Zeit* as perhaps the most high-profile case in point.[11] In *Eduards Heimkehr*, Schneider revisits the political positions of the student movement and its now middle-aged participants. Set in the mid-1990s, the 400-page novel captures the process of unification during the height of construction and thus in its most physical manifestation. Schneider's protagonist, the bio-chemist Eduard Hoffmann, returns after eight successful years at Stanford University to take a job at a research institute in Berlin. The novel's basic premise of a return to a changed Berlin mirrors that of Döblin's *Berlin Alexanderplatz*, whose protagonist must find his way around Berlin after having served a four-year prison term. When he arrives, Eduard learns that he has inherited a house in Berlin's eastern district of Friedrichshain, which, however, is occupied by squatters unwilling to acknowledge Eduard's ownership rights. To complicate matters further, his American-Jewish wife, fearing a revival of German nationalism, is reluctant to relocate to Berlin with their three children.

After eight years abroad, no longer an insider but also not a complete outsider, Eduard is an ideal observer of the changing city. 'The Wall had vanished without a trace',[12] he notes with bewilderment about that ultimate marker of Berlin's division. Eduard's own identity, by contrast, is very much entangled in various layers of the past and anything but 'vanished'. His new colleagues in eastern Berlin think of him as a 'Wessi' (Westy) and 'American' whose presumed airs of superiority they reject; for his Jewish-American wife he is German and thus implicitly responsible for the nation's problems; for the squatters who occupy his house he is a capitalist and, when it becomes clear that the property once belonged to

Jews, a Nazi. These legacies and complications, which form a stark contrast to the rapid changes and the fascination with newness that pervades the city, are the topic of the novel.

Eduard's inherited house is occupied in more than one sense. Here, too, the Nazi legacy is central. As Eduard battles his unwanted tenants with the help of an indifferent lawyer and a shady potential buyer, he becomes enmeshed in the financial as well as human intricacies of unification, and the moral and legal struggle over property rights. When a newspaper article accuses him of being the grandson of a Nazi who appropriated the house from its Jewish owner, Eduard delves into the history of the building as well as his family. In a significant departure from regular German history, his grandfather, an employee of the Jewish owner, had bought the property above market price, enabling the family to flee Nazi Germany. In the end, Eduard sells his house to the squatters for less than a million marks, well shy of the four million he had anticipated and, more importantly, gains a family record untainted by Nazism. Eduard's Jewish wife decides to join him in Berlin after all, giving credence to the vision of a multicultural Germany as an answer to the Nazi legacy.

Multicultural Germany is a theme present in much of Berlin literature in the decade after unification, presenting a vision for the united Berlin as poised to assume its place among other cosmopolitan cities of the worlds. The presence of non-German characters in texts of the time serves to gauge the success of German society as open, tolerant and mindful of its history. Marcia Zuckermann's *Das vereinigte Paradies* (The United Paradise (1999)) describes a milieu of Russian Jews in West Berlin's Charlottenburg district, a neighbourhood that also had a sizable Russian-Jewish community in the 1920s. Telling a story about organized crime, mixed with memories of the Holocaust, Zuckermann's novel features Jewish protagonists who cleverly use German guilt about the Nazi past to their advantage. The openness of post-Wall Berlin and the Germans' preoccupation with themselves provides the perfect setting for criminal pursuits that are also a way of getting even. Other texts along similar lines include the works of Wladimir Kaminer, a Russian Jew who immigrated to Berlin immediately after unification. In one of his many short pieces involving different ethnic groups now present in the city, included in the 2000 collection *Russendisko* (Russian Disco), Kaminer suggests that Berlin is more multicultural than most Germans suspect, when, for instance, they do not realize that the employees posing as Turks in a döner snack bar are in fact Bulgarian.

Not all texts display this kind of optimism or humour, however. Anja Tuckermann's novel *Die Haut retten* (To Save the Skin (2000)), set in Berlin's Kreuzberg district with its significant Turkish population and invoking the religious and culinary culture these immigrants brought with them, tells the story of a woman who has a son by a Turkish father but struggles to establish a long-term relationship with an American-Jewish man. Whereas the presence of Turks provides a multicultural setting, German–Jewish relationships continue to prove problematic in Berlin at the very end of the twentieth century. And Yadé Kara's *Selam Berlin* (Hello Berlin (2003)), as a final example, is told from the perspective of a young Turkish man raised in West Berlin who must find out what unification means to him as the Germans around him are celebrating the fall of the Wall. The historical upheaval brings to light his father's extramarital affair with an East Berlin woman, complicating the meanings of East-West-relationships. Multiculturalism in Berlin literature of the 1990s explores the changes in German identity by expanding the topic to characters of non-German background and, importantly, to Jewish protagonists. They represent test cases for the united Berlin's ability to provide a home for them and to accommodate their differences. Like the reflections about the Potsdamer Platz, the topic of multiculturalism is a significant part of the reconfiguration of German identity after 1989.

Eastern Blocks

East Berlin is one of the most important domains of 1990s Berlin literature, both in terms of chronicling change in the urban landscape and regarding the social issues that arose as the city's eastern neighbourhoods saw a significant influx of West Berliners and West Germans at large. Unlike the Potsdamer Platz, East Berlin, especially the residential Prenzlauer Berg and Mitte areas, was no *Stadtbrache* (urban fallow space). The population consisted mainly of workers but also artists and others who refused compliance with the rules of East German society. The neighbourhood's historic housing stock was run down by decades of neglect, a feature captured powerfully in Heiner Carow's iconic 1973 film *Die Legende von Paul und Paula* (The Legend of Paul and Paula). In the decade after 1989, as real estate was being transferred to private ownership and large-scale renovation began, about 80 per cent of the original population left and was replaced by younger West Berliners and West Germans, among them a disproportionately high number of *Akademiker* or university graduates.

Literature about East Berlin can be divided into two general categories that coincide with the lines of the city's division. Writers of West German or West Berlin origin, especially those born in the later 1960s and early 1970s, tended to celebrate the discovery of the Eastern parts of Berlin as new and uncharted urban territory that promised liberation from their parents' well-intentioned but at times stifling anti-authoritarian political attitudes. Writers with an East German background, by contrast, were more likely to put into words the confusion and the economic insecurities many citizens of the former GDR experienced as a result of unification. As a rule, writers with East German backgrounds tended to choose settings in Eastern Berlin while West Germans drew on the entire city. A pertinent example of the latter, to be discussed below, is Tanja Dückers's 1999 novel *Spielzone* (Play Zone), the title of which alludes to the attitude many non-East Germans had towards the Eastern parts of town. Examples of works by East German writers are Jens Sparschuh's humorous novel *Der Zimmerspringbrunnen* (The Indoor Fountain (1995)) about an East Berliner who has trouble adapting to a capitalist economic system and finally finds work as a traveling salesman for a West German purveyor of apartment fountains, as well as Ingo Schramm's rather more serious *Fitchers Blau* (Fitcher's Blue (1996)), a novel about two siblings who grow up separated by the Berlin Wall. A story of profound disorientation, it abounds in bleak descriptions of the changing city whose streets and subway system have turned into an inescapable labyrinth. Or there is Peter Wawerzinek's *Café Komplott* (Coffee Complot (1998)), a whimsical novel set in 1999 that sheds an ironic light on the nostalgia for East Berlin, including the West German preoccupation with Prenzlauer Berg's dissidents, and exposes the post-Wall event culture as shallow and media-driven. Or, finally, Christoph Hein's *Willenbrock* (2000), set in the new suburbs that sprang up at the outskirts of Berlin during the 1990s, and thus somewhat different from the previous examples, combines a story of globalization and international crime with memories of the restrictions on movement and travel across borders in East Germany. All of these texts, from different perspectives, explore the end of East Berlin and the often difficult adjustment process East Germans had to undergo as a result. Instead of the euphoria of the fall of the Wall, we find in these narratives protagonists who struggle with loss, fear and the challenges of new beginnings.

Born in West Berlin in 1968, Tanja Dückers counts among the writers who came of age before the opening of the Wall and began their literary career right after this decisive event. Her work includes poetry as well as critical essays on questions of German identity, especially regarding the united Germany's changing attitudes towards the Nazi past. Published in 1999, *Spielzone* is her first novel. The time of the narrative is the early 1990s; her protagonists are young inhabitants of Berlin for whom political ideologies, including the conflicts between East and West, are peripheral. Looking for a place unencumbered by either nostalgic memories of alternative lifestyles in West Berlin's Kreuzberg neighbourhood or remnants of GDR-culture, Berlin's 'new' districts, Mitte and Prenzlauer Berg, are their playgrounds.

Prenzlauer Berg, according to one character, is a 'wunderbare Grauzone, nicht mehr Osten, noch nicht Westen, genau richtig, um sich selber auszu-testen' ('wonderful grey area, no longer East, not yet West, just right to put oneself to the test').[13] Eager to reach the 'zone' before it vanishes, Dückers's protagonists congregate in sections of Berlin whose in-between status provides them the space to pursue their own desires, which include escaping from the parents' political concerns; and they find expression in the pursuit of sex beyond the heterosexual paradigm yet without the feminist politics of the previous generation.

Spielzone consists of loosely connected segments. The first part of the 200-page novel is titled 'Die Thomasstrasse' and takes place in Neukölln near the Hermannplatz, in a milieu of clerks, small government employees, students and the unemployed. The second part, titled 'Die Sonnenburger Straße', is named after a small street in Prenzlauer Berg near the former Wall. Each of the novel's twenty short chapters is dedicated to a different character, most of whom know one another. In the Neukölln section we meet, for instance, Laura, a fifteen-year-old secondary school student who feels misunderstood by her parents of the 1968 generation. The novel's 'Thomasstrasse' section ends as Katharina, a twenty-seven-year-old university student, leaves Neukölln for Sonnenburger Strasse in Prenzlauer Berg, leading the way into the play zone. Geographically, Katharina moves north, socio-politically, she goes from the old West to the new Centre. While Katharina enjoys the unfinished state of her Prenzlauer Berg existence, one of the novel's few East German characters aptly identifies Prenzlauer Berg as a figment of the West German imagination when he wonders why some 'unbelehrbare Wessis' ('unteachable Westies') think of the area as their 'neue Abenteuerspielplätze' ('new adventure playgrounds').[14] The New Berlin provides relief from the ordinary without the dangers of truly wild territories.

As I have argued elsewhere, *Spielzone* shows sympathy for the young inhabitants of Prenzlauer Berg and their efforts to assert independence from the political projects of their parents.[15] Unlike the 1968 generation, Dückers's protagonists experience sexual exploration as set apart from politics, and while the unsettled political and topographic environment of post-*Wende* Berlin provides an apt space for such exploration, the freedoms of this play zone are not without ambivalence. Fifteen-year-old Laura is almost raped by a rock star on whom she has a teenage crush, and a dissatisfied Katharina leaves the play zone for Italy at the end of the novel, in the hope of finding romantic love. A novel that captures the transitional atmosphere of the early 1990s, *Spielzone* is about breaking away from the social and political ideologies of West Berlin and a lot less about understanding East Berlin.

Very different in tone and intent is Klaus Schlesinger's *Die Sache mit Randow* (That Thing with Randow (1996)), even though the novel depicts some of the same areas of Berlin. Schlesinger (1937–2001) lived in Prenzlauer Berg for extended periods of time before and after unification and must be counted among the area's dissident artists. Set in 1991, *Die Sache mit Randow* moves back and forth between May 1945 and March 1990. Based on historical facts, Schlesinger's novel fictionalizes the story of Werner Gladow, the eighteen-year-old leader of a criminal organization who was executed in 1951 by the GDR authorities according to a Nazi-era law. Schlesinger turns these events into an exploration of the early years of the GDR and the enduring oppressive practices that link the Nazi era to the GDR while at the same time reflecting on East Germany's end.

Die Sache mit Randow is about a group of adolescent boys who grow up in an East Berlin destroyed by war in the early 1950s. It follows Tommie Thomale, a professional photographer, as he tries to find out who betrayed Randow, a young criminal on the run, to the police after he had sought refuge in his group's hideout in a war-damaged building. Repeatedly shifting perspective from the early 1950s back to the final days of the Second World War and into the late 1980s and early 1990s, the novel reveals that Tommie Thomale himself, at the time of the events a twelve-year-old school boy, unintentionally gave away the fugitive's hideout during a police interrogation and is thus guilty of cooperation with an oppressive police backed by Soviet military power. *Die Sache mit Randow* complicates the question of how to remember the GDR by exploring the use of history and memory both in the GDR itself and after its end. Tommie Thomale grows up to become a professional photographer. As a hobby he takes pictures of Prenzlauer Berg's Dunckerstrasse and its adjoining streets from the same perspective every few years. After the fall of the Wall, when a friend suggests to him that he should publish his photographs of East Berlin's rundown houses, Thomale doubts that anyone could be interested in the 'Sujet einer verfallenden Stadt' ('subject of a decaying city').[16] Decrepit façades have, of course, in fact become an icon of East Germany after the Wall and picture books like the one suggested to Thomale have sold exceedingly well. *Die Sache mit Randow* ends in the early 1990s when West Berliners and West Germans began to discover Prenzlauer Berg as the 'New Berlin' described in works like Dückers's *Spielzone*. Schlesinger's novel preserves the memory of East Berlin without idealizing it, rejecting notions of *Ostalgie* (nostalgia for the East) as much as West German fantasies of new beginnings. Instead, he tells a story of those who lived in East Berlin from its beginnings to its end, raising questions of memory as well as complicity. East and West German writers offer decidedly different perspectives on the experience of unification, yet their texts all recognize that the period of transition following the fall of the Wall had a unique and fleeting quality to it.

Perspectives for the Twenty-First Century

The first phase of post-Wall Berlin literature with its focus on rapid change and the fascination with large-scale construction ended in the early 2000s. Susanne Ledanff, in her wide-ranging book on Berlin literature, observes that the worship of Berlin has cooled down, a development she dates to about 2001.[17] The title story of Ralf Bönt's collection *Berliner Stille* (Berlin Silence) of 2006 echoes this sentiment when a protagonist describes the opening of the Wall and his decision to live in united Berlin as a moment of quiet and arrival, rather than anticipation and newness.[18] The relocation of the German government to Berlin in 1999 into the newly renovated Reichstag, the inauguration of the Holocaust Memorial in 2005 and also the restoration and reopening of the museums on the Museums Island in Berlin's traditional centre, together with the completion of the spectacular construction projects at the Potsdamer Platz, are outward manifestations of a process commonly referred to as normalization. Germany is seen as having moved out from underneath the shadow of its Nazi past and asserted its position as a united democratic nation among its peers in Europe and beyond. Germany's forty-year division, along with the post-unification decade of transition, are the exceptions to the new normalcy of democratic and united Germany. It is a normalcy that cannot, of course, be taken for granted. The many monuments, plaques and works of art in the city of Berlin that reference and commemorate the crimes of the Third Reich are also a response to the fears expressed in 1990s Berlin literature that these might be forgotten.

Beginning in the mid-2000s, there is a noticeable shift in Berlin literature away from the concerns of the present towards stories set predominantly or entirely in the past. If the fall of the Wall is included, it is no longer a rupture followed by a quest for newness or a period of confusion; instead, it figures as an unexpected event whose impact on the protagonist's life is not immediately assessable and, in the end, of limited importance. Normalization, in other words, can also be found in literary works. An example of Berlin's new normalcy is a book like Helene Hegemann's debut novel *Axolotl Roadkill*, a contemporary story full of drug use and teenage confusion, the celebration of which was quickly followed by a scandal over accusations of plagiarism. For Hegemann's young protagonists, the fall of the Wall is already a thing of the past. The united Berlin is just another contemporary metropolis breeding the decadence that has been associated with metropolitan literature since its inception in the nineteenth century.

At the end of the post-unification period, with the focus on newness and transition having run its course, interest in larger historical contexts began to reemerge. The fall of the Wall, writers and others realized, not only meant the end of East Berlin and the GDR but also of West Berlin. An early example of this is Sven Regener's *Herr Lehmann* of 2001, an ironic story about a young West German who realizes that the opening of the Wall means the end of his comfortably unambitious Kreuzberg lifestyle, free from social and economic pressures. Motivated by the concern that memories of West Berlin are fading, the 2009 essay collection, *War jewesen: West-Berlin 1961–1989* (Had Been: West-Berlin 1961–1989), develops the retrospective focus on West Berlin further.[19] And Annett Gröschner's *Heimatkunde Berlin* (Local Studies Berlin (2010)), a short volume of essays about the city's history as well as its present, narrated from the biographical perspective of the GDR-born writer, also reflects the trend towards more encompassing perspectives in terms of both time period and geography. The volume's self-ironic emphasis on the local, captured in the somewhat antiquated term *Heimatkunde*, is a departure from the focus on national identity and globalization that many Berlin texts of the 1990s sought to address. This, too, might be considered an aspect of normalization.

Continuity rather than rupture is the underlying theme in many works after 2005. Ralf Rothmann's *Feuer brennt nicht* (Fire Does Not Burn (2009)), a *Künstlerroman*, or artist's novel, about a middle-aged writer and his relationship with two women, is largely set in West Berlin before 1989, and the fall of the Wall is mentioned only indirectly. Life, with all of its private pursuits and worries goes on, the text suggests, even as an era comes to an end and a new one begins. Instead of reflecting on the profound character of the changes that followed the fall of the Wall, Rothmann's protagonist offers recollections about the underground rides that led West Berliners past the 'ghost stations' underneath the territory of East Berlin.[20] A move from overcrowded Kreuzberg to the leafy East Berlin suburb of Friedrichshagen leads to confrontations with neighbours suspicious of the newcomers and the discovery that toxic building materials from GDR stock have been used in the apartment's renovation.[21] The novel ends with one woman's suicide after a diagnosis of cancer. It is a departure from Berlin literature of the 1990s in the sense that it does not focus centrally on the city's unification either as a catalyst for change in the characters' lives or as a foil for social commentary. Instead, it uses the changing city as the setting for a story about private lives and the tragedies that can disrupt them, no matter on which side of the former Wall the protagonist may dwell.

Another example of a novel that emphasizes continuity rather than rupture is Hans-Ulrich Treichel's *Grunewaldsee* (Grunewald Lake (2010)).

The novel spans the 1980s in West Berlin through the fall of the Wall into the 1990s and follows a protagonist who moved from West Germany to the enclave of West Berlin to pursue his studies. Like Rothmann's novel, *Grunewaldsee* does not present the fall of the Wall as a major caesura, suggesting that the changes brought about by unification are perhaps not as fundamental as much of the literature of the 1990s implied, at least not for the individuals portrayed in these more recent texts; or, put differently, that what is needed is a more nuanced and perhaps less sensationalized understanding of what unfolded after 1989. Treichel's protagonist experiences the changes which do occur after 9 November 1989 as gradual and not in entirely predictable ways.

Grunewaldsee, whose title signals 'Berlin' to everyone even vaguely familiar with the city, chronicles the story of Paul, a gifted but not overly assertive young man from Braunschweig who studies history at Berlin's Free University in the 1980s. His rundown apartment in Kreuzberg, near the Landwehr Canal, is representative of the experience of many who arrived in West Berlin during that decade. Nothing very dramatic happens to Paul: he makes good progress in his studies but then spends years on hold as he is waiting for his internship slot as trainee teacher and tries unsuccessfully to land a clerical job in the State Library or as a tour guide. The most exciting episode in his life takes place in southern Spain, where he has a passionate sexual relationship with the somewhat older and married María. In the end – we are now in the early 1990s – María does travel to Germany as she had promised but confesses to Paul that she has fallen in love with another man. She also has no interest in seeing his Berlin.

Grunewaldsee revisits the 1980s in West Berlin and conjures up once more the longing for freedom that many young West Germans harboured when they left their provincial hometowns for West Berlin, preferably Kreuzberg. With his understated humour and a protagonist who tends to get outmanoeuvred by those around him despite his intellectual capacities and perhaps because of his friendly demeanour, Treichel calls into question the idea of self-realization in the big city, a project that already failed for the title figure of Irmgard Keun's *Das kunstseidene Mädchen* (The Artificial Silk Girl (1932)) in the 1920s. The eponymous Grunewaldsee is one of Paul's favorite places. The novel shows him accompanied by various women, turning the lake in Western Berlin into one of the city's less described erotic sites. Even more important is the Pfaueninsel, or Peacock Island, in the southwestern part of the Wannsee Lake, close to the former border with East Germany. Initially used as an industrial site, the Pfaueninsel in the early nineteenth century housed foreign animals and plants in a park designed by the landscape architect Peter Lenné and dotted with idiosyncratic buildings by Karl

Friedrich Schinkel. By centring on a somewhat remote location, not typically the site of Berlin literature yet steeped in Berlin history, Treichel broadens the frame of what 'Berlin' means both historically and for the contemporary period. Pfaueninsel's artificial exoticism, which can be read as a rural counterpart to Kreuzberg's socioeconomic exceptionalism, its proximity to the Berlin Wall and the fact that the island itself did not change in 1989 make it uniquely suited for Treichel's project of understanding change and continuity as historical processes.

The fall of the Wall comes as a surprise and, for Paul, is as unexpected as the phone call from María he receives a few days later.[22] What is more, Paul does not join the ranks of those who seek urbanity and cosmopolitanism in Eastern Berlin, preferring instead to walk around the Grunewaldsee.[23] *Grunewaldsee* explores the geographical and historical margins of Berlin. With its short and precise sentences and its ordinary story, Treichel's novel is a departure from some of the extravagant plots and the linguistic exuberance we find in many of the works of the 1990s. It is no coincidence that Treichel's and Rothmann's stories about private lives and character development take place far away from Berlin's new centres.

With growing historical distance from the events of 1989, the focus on the fall of the Wall gives way to retrospective reflections on periods of Berlin's history when German unification seemed entirely inconceivable. One such example is Tanja Dückers's 2011 novel *Hausers Zimmer* (Hauser's Room). Set in 1982, the year of the Falklands War, it tells the story of a childhood and adolescence in West Berlin. The novel chronicles a year in the life of a young teenage girl who lives with her politically progressive parents and her older brother in a large rented apartment, crammed with books and works of art, close to the Kurfürstendamm. *Hausers Zimmer* recreates the 1970s and early 1980s in West Berlin, and thus a time when no one expected the city's insular status to change. Detailed descriptions of the areas around Kurfürstendamm, including houses still pockmarked with gunshot holes from the war, trash-strewn empty lots, sex shops and an endless supply of graffiti – 'All you need is LSD' – capture the urban atmosphere of the time.[24] Advertising slogans, brand names, song titles and references to events like the death of German movie star Romy Schneider round out the re-creation of the 1980s. True to the spirit of West Berlin as a city welcoming of alternative lifestyles, the characters that populate this novel are involved in a range of artistic projects, mostly of questionable quality. The narrator's obsession with the goings-on in the apartment across the courtyard that is inhabited by the eponymous Mr Hauser, an unemployed would-be artist in his thirties, together with her desire to emigrate to a place as far away as Patagonia, hint at the limitations of West Berlin's self-absorbed environment for the generation that will come of age with the fall of the Wall.[25] Yet, unlike *Spielzone*, published twelve years earlier, *Hausers Zimmer* offers alternatives only as an adolescent fantasy.

Another example of recent retrospective Berlin literature is Julia Franck's *Rücken an Rücken* (Back to Back), also of 2011. An East German counterpart of sorts to Dückers's West Berlin novel, it tells the tragic story of a brother and a sister, Thomas and Ella, who grow up at the outskirts of East Berlin in the 1950s. The relative privilege of a large house close to the Müggelsee lake is undercut by episodes of sexual violation and the brother's suicide a few months after the construction of the Berlin Wall. Unlike *Hausers Zimmer*, the novel makes only sparse references to the city. It almost entirely avoids allusions to the war devastation that was still very prevalent at the time, shifting the focus to the creation of a new society and the effect of these efforts on those coming of age in the 1950s. The city of Berlin is exemplified by the Charité, East Berlin's main hospital, where Thomas works as an intern and where he meets the woman with whom he will commit suicide by overdosing on the opium she steals from the hospital. The Charité's severe lack of staff, medical supplies and empathy for the sick and dying is also an indictment of the East German economy and culture.

A critical assessment of the beginnings of the GDR and of those who supported it, *Rücken an Rücken* assumes the perspective of those who experienced the emerging GDR as a system that severely restricted personal and professional choices. Among the new state's most ardent supporters is the siblings' mother, an artist and Holocaust survivor hardened by her own life experience who is unable to empathize with her children's desire for individual freedom and is blind to the various types of abuse they suffer over the course of the novel. The young protagonist's suicide a few weeks after the construction of the Berlin Wall is his response to the realization that he will not be able to fulfil any of his aspirations under the current system. In Franck's novel, whose systemic violence some critics have rejected as contrived, Berlin's division goes beyond the span of a human lifetime.

At the same time, literary violence of other, more generic kinds abounds. The display tables with 'Berlinliteratur' that could be found in many of the city's bookstores in the 1990s disappeared at about the time when Berlin's supersized and hyper-promoted construction projects at the Potsdamer Platz and elsewhere neared completion. In their place one now finds shelves dedicated specifically to crime fiction set in Berlin. While there are examples of Berlin crime fiction also in the 1990s, prominently among them the works by Pieke Biermann, Thea Dorn and Horst Bosetzky, Berlin 'Krimis' today command a life and presence of their own. The rise of detective stories set in Berlin is a response to the international phenomenon of crime fiction in which the location is an important aspect of the plot, even though the

Berlin crime novels are not yet reaching an international audience. As a rule, these works combine gripping plots set against historically accurate backgrounds with social and political commentary. They include Volker Kutscher's series of historical crime stories set in 1920s and 1930s against the background of a vibrant and cosmopolitan city about to fall into the hands of the Nazis, as well as Susanne Goga's works set during the same period and also intent on recreating the 1920s as a time characterized by rapid modernization and impending political disaster. While an example set in the contemporary period is Herbert Beckmann's *Verrohung* (Brutalization (2014)). Here, not coincidentally, the crimes under investigation take place at the Potsdamer Platz, whose crowds and places of entertainment underscore the site's suitability as a crime scene in a Berlin characterized by growing poverty, traffic jams and bureaucratic ineptness. The novel's male protagonist, demoralized by his female superior's unwillingness to entertain his suggestions as to how to solve the crime, together with a perpetrator unhinged by PTSD as a consequence of his military service in Afghanistan, underscore contemporaneity through reversed gender hierarchies and the consequences of 9/11.

Twenty-five years after the fall of the Wall the preoccupation with newness and change that dominated Berlin literature of the 1990s has given way to explorations of larger contexts and retrospective reflections on the city's past. The focus has shifted from differences between the East and the West German experiences of the fall of the Wall and the question of whether or not multiculturalism can succeed to rewritings of the past and depictions of the present as new reality rather than a phase of transition. Whether or not there will be another novel like Döblin's *Berlin Alexanderplatz* remains to be seen. Canonical works cannot be willed into existence. Nevertheless, the plentiful and often excellent literary output of post-unification Berlin captures a variety of experiences and speaks to the many cultural elements present in Germany and its capital. The more recent retrospective texts suggest that history continues to be important and that new perspectives on Berlin's rich past are not only possible, but that their time has come.

NOTES

1. 'Literaturhauptstadt Berlin', *Literaturen* 1 (2010), p. 29.
2. Michael Braun, *Die deutsche Gegenwartsliteratur: Eine Einführung* (Cologne: Böhlau, 2010), p. 20.
3. Holm Friebe, 'Wende-Romans Bruder', *Jungle World* 30 (1999), http://jungle -world.com/artikel/1999/29/33652.html (accessed 2 January 2015).
4. Robert Gernhardt, 'Couplet vom Hauptstadtroman', in *Berlin Zehner: Hauptstadtgedichte* (Zurich: Haffmans Verlag, 2001), pp. 12–16.

5. Peter Schneider, *Eduard's Homecoming*, trans. John Brownjohn (New York: Farrar, Straus and Giroux, 2010), p. 203.

6. Cees Nooteboom, *Allerseelen* (Frankfurt am Main: Suhrkamp, 1999), pp. 75–6.

7. Christian Försch, *Unter der Stadt* (Berlin: Aufbau, 2001), p. 158.

8. Ulrike Draesner, 'Atmer', in *Park: Zeitschrift für neue Literatur*, 51/52 (1998), pp. 28–32 (p. 32).

9. Bodo Morshäuser, *Liebeserklärung an eine hässliche Stadt* (Frankfurt am Main: Suhrkamp, 1998), p. 117.

10. Kathrin Röggla, 'bettgeschichte (platz für geschichten)', in *Irres Wetter* (Salzburg: Residenz Verlag, 2000), pp. 63–9 (p. 65).

11. Günter Grass, 'Kurze Rede eines vaterlandslosen Gesellen', *Die Zeit*, 9 February 1990.

12. Schneider, *Eduard's Homecoming*, p. 16.

13. Tanja Dückers, *Spielzone* (Berlin: Aufbau, 1999), pp. 108–9.

14. Ibid., p. 165.

15. Katharina Gerstenberger, *Writing the New Berlin: The German Capital in Post-Wall Literature* (Rochester, NY: Camden House: 2008), p. 35.

16. Klaus Schlesinger, *Die Sache mit Randow* (Berlin: Aufbau Verlag, 1996), p. 20.

17. Susanne Ledanff, *Hauptstadtphantasien. Berliner Stadtlektüren in der Gegenwartsliteratur 1989–2008* (Bielefeld: Aisthesis, 2008), p. 379.

18. Ralf Bönt, *Berliner Stille* (Göttingen: Wallstein, 2006), p. 97.

19. D. Holland-Moritz and Gabriela Wachter, eds. *War jewesen: West-Berlin 1961–1989* (Berlin: Parthas, 2009).

20. Ralf Rothmann, *Feuer brennt nicht* (Frankfurt am Main: Suhrkamp, 2009), p. 35.

21. Ibid., p. 71.

22. Hans Ulrich Treichel, *Grunewaldsee* (Frankfurt am Main: Suhrkamp, 2010), p. 165.

23. Ibid., p. 232.

24. Tanja Dückers, *Hausers Zimmer* (Frankfurt am Main: Schöffling & Co., 2011), p. 15.

25. Ibid., p. 34.

9

LYN MARVEN

Women Writers and Gender

From Berolina to Germania, to 'Goldene Else'[1] or Viktoria riding the Quadriga on the Brandenburg Gate, from Christopher Isherwood's Sally Bowles through Wolf Biermann's 'deutsch deutsche Frau' ('German German woman') to Tom Tykwer's Lola, Berlin's image at home and abroad has frequently been embodied in feminine form. In contrast to this visibility of (notably male-authored or -designed) female figures in the contexts of architecture, culture, mythology and literature, women writers are frequently underrepresented in accounts of Berlin writers and Berlin writing. The current chapter intends to counter this relative literary-historical invisibility by analyzing some of the most prominent Berlin texts by women. Although the focus here is exclusively on women, the chapter does not endorse views of women's writing as an aesthetically distinct form, even as some writers featured here do attempt to define or create a feminine subjectivity or aesthetic through their representation of women's experiences of the city.

Berlin has been a significant location for women writers since at least the late nineteenth century, as Petra Budke and Jutta Schulze explain in the introduction to their ground-breaking directory *Schriftstellerinnen in Berlin 1871–1945* (Women Writers in Berlin 1871–1945 (1995)). Despite the increasing productivity and visibility of women writers in the city through the last century, female authors have tended to be featured only infrequently in anthologies and literary guides focusing on Berlin writing in or before the early twentieth century, notwithstanding the fact that many bestsellers of their day were written by women, such as Margarete Böhme or Mascha Kaléko. Berlin women are more often represented as the object of male writing: in *Hier schreibt Berlin* (This is Berlin Writing (1929)), one of the earliest anthologies of writing from and about the city, a female presence is found only in an affectionately satirical paean to 'Die Berlinerin' (the female Berliner) by Carl Zuckmayer.[2]

Accounts of authors living and working in Berlin offer an alternative way to gauge women's involvement in literary production. Although these volumes take a biographical approach to Berlin literature, there is substantial overlap between authors living in the city and thematizing it in their work. Budke and Schulze list some 200 authors for the period 1871–1945, whilst also asserting that some 1,000 women were active as writers in Berlin during those years, noting with considerable understatement that few of these are known today.[3] Fred Oberhauser's and Nicole Henneberg's *Literarischer Führer Berlin* (Literary Guidebook to Berlin (2003)) by contrast lists a total of just eighteen women – compared with ten times as many men – for a similar time period. As these divergent figures suggest, the lack of representation of women as Berlin authors or as writers of Berlin literature indicates at best their low profile amongst literary-critical or editorial compilers and, at worst, a selection process that excludes women, whether intentionally or not.

This chapter focuses particularly on the depiction of women in two key periods of redefinition for Berlin: the Weimar period and the era after the *Wende*, or 'turn' of unification in 1990. I analyze in detail three novels which highlight the relationship between gendered self and the city: Irmgard Keun's late-Weimar novel *Das kunstseidene Mädchen* (The Artificial Silk Girl (1932)), and two contemporary texts, Inka Parei's *Die Schattenboxerin* (The Shadow-Boxing Woman (1999)) and Annett Gröschner's *Walpurgistag* (Walpurgis Day (2011)). Keun and Parei foreground their gendered perspective by referencing their female protagonists in the titles of their novels; Gröschner's text takes its title from German abbess Saint Walpurga and evokes the witches associated with Walpurgis Night. All three interrogate the literary forms open to women writers and female protagonists engaging with the city.

Irmgard Keun, *Das kunstseidene Mädchen*: a Weimar Woman

The significance of the Weimar era for women writers was and is twofold: first, it saw substantial numbers of women writing in public forms – whether newspapers or literary bestsellers – and second, the image of Berlin in the 1920s and 1930s remains a touchstone for female characters through the literature of the twentieth and twenty-first century. Indeed, the late twentieth century has if anything seen increased interest in Berlin novels by women from the Weimar period: journalist Gabriele Tergit's Weimar novel *Käsebier erobert den Kurfürstendamm* (Käsebier Conquers the Kurfürstendamm (1931)) was republished in a new version in 1976; the Berlin-based Aviva Verlag, founded in 1997, has championed women writers from the Weimar period; and novels from Dinah Nelken's *Das angstvolle*

Heldenleben einer gewissen Fleur Lafontaine (The Fearful Heroic Life of a Certain Fleur Lafontaine (1971)) through to *Pola* (2014), Daniela Dröscher's fictionalized account of screen actress Pola Negri in the 1920s and 1930s, are also concerned with Weimar femininity and the experience of the city.

Irmgard Keun's *Das kunstseidene Mädchen* is a portrait of the late-Weimar city through the eyes of a young girl who runs off to Berlin from Cologne. It not only explores the boundaries of the opportunities offered by the city and the reality behind its image, but also interrogates the availability of gendered metropolitan figures as frames of reference to a young woman of the time. A bestseller on its release in 1932, *Das kunstseidene Mädchen* was banned by the Nazis in 1933. Doris, the sassy first-person narrator, is attracted to the image of glittering Berlin, picturing herself as a film star in her stolen fur coat, but the reality proves very different. Her initial impressions of Berlin are external views of the streets and the transport systems, the cafés and shops, and particularly the people; as her fortunes wane she withdraws from the city into domestic space and takes to the street only to be mistaken for – or act as – a prostitute.

Alongside the views of contemporary Berlin, the novel is notable for the informal, colloquial style in which Doris narrates her adventures: her guileless stream-of-consciousness prose reflects the overwhelming nature of the metropolis in the cinematic style espoused by Döblin. Keun's relaying of Doris's casual style also relates to the anecdotal prose of the lifestyle-oriented, often city-focused feuilleton sections popular in the local Berlin press, such as in Mascha Kaléko's *Das lyrische Stenogrammheft* (The Book of Lyrical Shorthand (1933)). This collection, touted on its back cover as the most successful German book of poetry of the twentieth century, contains vignettes of city life, setting relationships and encounters against a backdrop of urban noise, transport and office life. Kaléko writes in the first person from a female perspective, universalized as the experience of the metropolis. By contrast, Keun's protagonist remains constrained by her gender: as a woman she is unable to take the role of the flâneur as detached observer that is available to male characters within the city.

The attraction of Berlin to Doris is escape, not just from poverty, but fleeing her crime of stealing a fur coat; the city offers anonymity and the means of making a living unofficially: 'da taucht man unter' ('you can go underground there').[4] Although this is perfectly unremarkable colloquial phrasing in German, the ostensibly neutral 'man' conceals gender distinctions in experience of the city. Berlin is frequently portrayed in literature as a location for (internal or international) migration or social improvement; the success protagonists have is refracted through expectations of masculinity and femininity, and the historical forms of employment available to either sex. In Clara Viebig's *Das tägliche Brot* (Our Daily Bread (1900)), for example, two young girls from the provinces come to Berlin at the turn of the twentieth century to work as servants, one of the few positions open to women; their individual and collective fates are decided by the extent to which they conform to expectations of feminine behaviour. By the Weimar period more and new jobs were open to women – chiefly white-collar secretarial work – but with no papers and few employable skills, Doris is unable to make her way in the city through formal employment; rather, she is reliant on men and the custom of 'treating' (exchanging sex or attention for favours and material goods). She does in fact go underground by leaving the public space of the streets, where she is frequently propositioned (although this is occasionally her intention, even if she denies it), for internal, domestic spaces and the life of a housewife looking after Grüner Moos ('Green Moss', her nickname for one of the men who take her in).

On arriving in the city, Doris confirms the staple Weimar images of Berlin's modernity and consumerism, noting the city's lights and adverts, the underground system and omnibuses (*kM*, pp. 68–9), but her observations quickly turn to gender: she sees 'schicke Männer wie Mädchenhändler, ohne daß sie gerade mit Mädchen handeln' (*kM*, p. 67) ('elegant men like white-slave traders without exactly trafficking in women at the moment' (*ASG*, p. 55)), and remarks, 'Auf dem Kurfürstendamm sind viele Frauen. Die gehen nur. Sie haben gleiche Gesichter und viel Maulwurfpelze – also nicht ganz erste Klasse – aber doch schick – so mit hochmütigen Beinen und viel Hauch um sich' (*kM*, p. 67) ('There are many women on the *Kurfürstendamm*. They simply walk. They have the same faces and a lot of moleskin fur – not exactly first class, in other words, but still chic – with arrogant legs and a great waft of perfume about them' (*ASG*, p. 56)). Unable to see beyond surface appearances at this stage, Doris does not recognize them as prostitutes.

When she later describes the city for blind war veteran Brenner, her vision of the Kurfürstendamm is a more acute and less romanticized one, born of her subsequent experiences of the city; she mentions the colourful adverts but notes that no one is looking at them, and precisely renders the poverty of beggars and street-sellers underneath the bright lights. Although she brings him 'Berlin, das in meinem Schoß liegt' (*kM*, p. 100) ('Berlin, which is resting in my lap' (*ASG*, p. 87)) – a sexually suggestive phrase for Berlin as she sees it – she is conversely enabled to act as detached flâneur because she is appropriating a male view here. She later accompanies Brenner on a night out when the city appears dark and unwelcoming despite her attempts to convince him of its attractions. Brenner's negative impression of the city supersedes her own and proves more realistic as the narrative goes on:

> 'Die Stadt ist nicht gut, und die Stadt ist nicht froh, und die Stadt ist krank', sagt er – 'du bist aber gut, und ich danke dir.'
> Er soll mir nicht danken – er soll nur mein Berlin schön finden. Und jetzt sieht mir alles ganz anders aus. (*kM*, p. 118).

> ('The city isn't good and the city isn't happy and the city is sick,' he says – 'but you are good and I thank you for that.'
> I don't want him to thank me. I just want him to like my Berlin. And now everything looks so different to me. (*ASG*, p. 103)).

Compared with her home city of Cologne, Doris experiences Berlin as mass of streets with no connection: 'Zu Hause waren auch viele Straßen, aber die waren wie verwandt zusammen. Hier sind noch viel mehr Straßen und so viele, daß sie sich gegenseitig nicht kennen. Es ist eine fabelhafte Stadt' (*kM*, p. 68) ('At home, we had lots of streets too, but they were more familiar with each other. Here, there are so many more streets that they can't possibly all know each other. It's a fabulous city' (*ASG*, pp. 56–7)). The anonymity of the metropolis appears positive here, but the lack of connections extends to Doris herself. She wants to belong to the city or more prosaically, given her theft of the fur coat, to disappear amongst the crowd, and appears to do so on arrival: 'Das war mein Ankommen in Berlin. Und ich gehörte gleich zu den Berlinern so mitten rein' (*kM*, p. 72) ('That was my arrival in Berlin. And so I was immediately one of the Berliners, being right in the middle of it – that pleased me enormously' (*ASG*, p. 61, translation modified)). But later she admits her exclusion: 'Und Berlin ist sehr großartig, aber es bietet einem keine Heimatlichkeit, weil es verschlossen ist' (*kM*, p. 88) ('And Berlin is fabulous but it doesn't feel like home because it closes itself off' (*ASG*, p. 75, translation modified)). To her own cost, she remains invested in the city – 'Mein Leben ist Berlin und ich bin Berlin' (*kM*, p. 92) ('My life is Berlin and I'm Berlin' (*ASG*, p. 78)). The text does not overtly allegorize the city through Doris, but from the undertones of right-wing politics and anti-Semitism visible through her ventriloquism of some of the men she meets, it is clear that the city in 1931 is as much on its uppers as she is.

After her initial impressions, it is striking that Doris refers to relatively few streets and places within the city by name: it is the idea of Berlin, rather than the reality of any particular locality, which attracts her. Her streets are generic locations which she treats as cinematic backdrops: 'Ich gehe und gehe durch Friedrichstraßen und gehe und sehe und glänzende Autos und Menschen, und mein Herz blüht schwer' (*kM*, p. 93) ('I walk and walk through *Friedrichstrasse* and walk and look and shiny cars and people, and my heart is a heavy blossom' (*ASG*, p. 80, translation modified)). The internal rhyme of 'gehe und sehe' (walk and look) stresses the connection between walking and viewing, the perspective of the flâneur. However, her presence on the street, that archetypal city location, does not constitute the detached, disinterested role of the male flâneur: as a woman, she remains the object rather than the subject of observation. On one of the few journeys she makes alone in the city, treating herself to a taxi ride, she does so in order not to view the city but to be seen like the film star she dreams of becoming. Women walking alone are taken to be streetwalkers, not just the object of the male gaze but entirely objectified as part of the male-oriented cityscape. After the end of yet another affair, homeless and wandering the streets, Doris copies (consciously or not) the distinctive gait of the prostitutes:

> überall abends stehen Huren – am Alex so viele, so viele – auf dem Kurfürstendamm und Joachimstaler und am Friedrichbahnhof und überall. Und sehn gar nicht aus wie welche, sie machen so einen unentschlossenen Gang – das ist gar nicht immer das Gesicht, was eine Hure so ausmacht – ich sehe in meinen Spiegel – das ist eine Art von Gehen, wie wenn einem das Herz eingeschlafen ist.
>
> Ging ich langsam an der Gedächtniskirche vorbei, Tauentzien runter, immer so weiter und mit Gleichgültigkeit in meinen Kniekehlen, und da war somit mein Gehen ein Stehenbleiben zwischen einem Weitergehnwollen und einem Zurückgehnwollen, indem ich zu keinem von beiden Lust hatte. Und dann machte an Ecken mein Körper einen Aufenthalt, denn Ecken machen dem Rücken so eine Sehnsucht nach einer Anlehnung. (*kM*, pp. 144–5).

(But there are whores standing around everywhere at night – so many of then around the *Alex*, so many, along the *Kurfürstendamm* and *Joachimstaler Strasse* and at the *Friedrichstrasse* Station and everywhere. And they don't always look the part at all either, they walk in such a hesitant way. It's not always the face that makes a whore – I am looking in my mirror – it's the way they walk, as if their heart had gone to sleep.

So I was slowly walking past the Memorial Church, down the *Tauentzien*, walking farther and farther with an attitude of indifference in the backs of my knees and thus my walking was a kind of staying in place between wanting to walk further and a desire to walk back again, in that I really didn't want to do either. And then my body came to a stop at the corner, because corners create in one's back such a longing for contact. (*ASG*, p. 125)).

Doris's intimate relationship with Berlin, her knowledge of the streets and the material form of the city (street corners, streetlamps), all appear to conspire with her body to cast her as prostitute. Rather than the casual wandering of the detached flâneur, a slow walk signalling indifference has different connotations for a woman. Here the internal rhyme of Gehen and Stehen (walking and standing) emphasizes the gendered nature of bodily presence on the streets of the metropolis. And this is a recurring motif in women's texts set in Berlin: Keun's contemporary Vicki Baum also portrays women as part of the Berlin cityscape, attributing this clearly to a male view. In *Menschen im Hotel* (People in the Hotel, translated as Grand Hotel (1929)) provincial incomer Kringelein eyes up women's legs while Zinnowitz signals that he is off-duty in the same fashion, by squinting after silk stockings. And decades later, when the protagonist of Herta Müller's *Reisende auf einem Bein* (Traveling on One Leg (1989)) arrives in West Berlin from an unnamed country (clearly Müller's native Romania) in the summer preceding the fall of the Wall, she experiences the city as an extension of her body through a sexualized, traumatic lack of boundaries. Her views of women walking the Berlin streets recall Keun and Baum through striking synecdoche, reducing women to their legs and stockings: 'Mit leicht verrutschten Nähten gingen Frauenstrümpfe den Rinnstein entlang, auf Straßenenden zu, als hätten die Frauen nur Beine. Beine für Männer. Beine mit Schlingen. Sie fingen Blicke ein' ('Women's stockings with seams slightly out of place walked along the gutter toward the ends of streets as if women were legs only. Legs for men. Legs with snares. They would catch eyes').[5]

Beyond these recurring motifs, indicating the broader sexualization and objectification of women, Keun's novel is one of a number of Berlin-based texts which touch on the subject of prostitution, from Margarete Böhme's controversial bestseller set in imperial Berlin, *Tagebuch einer Verlorenen* (The Diary of a Lost Girl, 1905), through to Ulrike Draesner's internet-age sperm-collector in the story 'Gina Regina' from *Hot Dogs* (2004), or Sonia Rossi's notorious autobiographical novel with the self-explanatory title *Fucking Berlin* (2008). Like Keun's Doris, both Böhme's and Rossi's protagonists also arrive in Berlin as outsiders and seek to exploit the anonymity of the metropolis. Tracing the representation of this theme raises issues of gendered agency and power through history, as well as creating alternative topographies of the city through the particular spatial practices of prostitution.

Inka Parei, *Die Schattenboxerin*: a *Wende* Woman

Women writers are increasingly prominent in contemporary Berlin literature. Judith Hermann, whose text 'Sommerhaus, später' (Summerhouse, Later (1997)), in the collection of the same name, captured early 1990s Berlin and spearheaded the burgeoning of German-language writing and particularly the growth of short story writing which have accompanied the *Wende* and the return of the reunified Berlin as literary capital of Germany. Nonetheless, the early 1990s search for *the* new Berlin novel or *Wenderoman* (novel of reunification; often synonymous with Berlin for obvious reasons) initially revolved around the 'norm' of male protagonists, typically from the former GDR, in male-authored novels. Thomas Brussig's Berlin-based *Helden wie wir* (Heroes Like Us, 1995) was the first to be acclaimed, satirically associating masculinity with the opening of the border. Less attention has been given to Berlin *Wende* novels by established women writers such as Monika Maron's *Stille Zeile Sechs* (Silent Close No. 6 (1991)) or *Animal triste* (1996), Brigitte Burmeister's *Unter dem Namen Norma* (Under the Name of Norma (1994)), or Helga Königsdorf's *Im Schatten der Regenbogen* (In the Shadow of the Rainbow (1993)). However, increasing distance from the historical caesura has led to increased openness to other stories told by women, migrants and foreigners, or those from the former West.

Inka Parei's debut novel *Die Schattenboxerin* presents a female perspective on the city that spans the *Wende* and reunification, linking the protagonist to Berlin in a way that counters the easy, stereotypical equating of East to female, West to male and *Wende* to rape that underpinned much of the popular characterization of the two states at the time.[6] Protagonist and first-person narrator Hell moves from West Berlin to the (now former) East shortly after the fall of the Wall, traumatized by an attack (presumably rape, though not depicted in detail) during the May Day riots around Görlitzer Bahnhof and Lausitzer Platz, which she had intended to watch but not participate in. She takes refuge in learning Chinese shadow-boxing as self-defence, and like Keun's *Das kunstseidene Mädchen*, the novel revolves in part around Hell's perceptions of the changing, unfamiliar city as she re-learns how to 'see' after her ordeal. Her (female) gaze becomes the subject of seeing rather than an object of the (male) gaze, through the transformation of her traumatized, heightened perception into the martial awareness of the 'shadow boxer'. The unusual feminization of the title suggests that, like Doris's attempts to act as flâneur, the protagonist's adoption of masculine traits does not sit entirely easily, and her relationship to the city and its history remains mediated by her gender. As well as writing a Berlin-based *Wenderoman* that does not focus on a male, Eastern protagonist, Parei also constructs a *Krimi* (detective story) from a dual female perspective, with Hell (her name means 'Light') as both victim and detective trying to find her missing neighbour and double, Dunkel (or 'Dark').

Parei contends that her novel is about the effects of violence rather than the city of Berlin, but the rape is nonetheless intrinsic to Hell's relationship with

Berlin. The lack of representation of the rape itself, plus the details of its location and timing – it takes place in West Berlin on 1 May 1989, months before the Wall falls – means it does not function as an easy metaphor for the *Wende*. However, the attack is anchored in the topography of the city: Hell's flashback leading up to the elided rape depicts the approaches to Görlitzer Bahnhof with cartographical accuracy. This is later translated into a visual metaphor that further associates the rape with the city, when Hell describes a map (a distinctive Falkplan) of Berlin as if she is within it:

> Ich selbst befinde mich im Zentrum, ungefähr zwischen N12 und T7, und diese Zentrum löst sich langsam auf. Am Tiergarten, abgegriffen vom vielen Blättern, kleben Krümel einstigen Grüns. Siegessäule und Brandenburger Tor sind völlig in Knickfurchen verschwunden.
>
> Am schlimmsten aber ist es um die Gegend rund um das nördliche Neukölln bestellt, denn dort ist ein Loch.
>
> Ich weiß, daß ich auf das Loch zurutsche, es jeden Augenblick mit einem durch mein Gewicht verursachten Riß vergrößern und in die dahinterliegende Dunkelheit stürzen werde.

> (I'm in the centre, somewhere between N12 and T7, and this centre is gradually disintegrating. Crumbs of former green are stuck to the Tiergarten, shabby with use. The Victory Column and the Brandenburg Gate have disappeared entirely into the creases.
>
> But the worst is the area around the north of Neukölln – all that's there is a hole.
>
> I know I'm slipping towards the hole, about to enlarge it with a rip caused by my weight at any moment, only to tumble into the darkness behind it.)[7]

The map thus reflects the traumatic gap surrounding the rape, though in contrast to the heightened details of Hell's flashbacks, which are symptomatic of traumatic effect, here the area is only described elliptically, as 'the area around north Neukölln', so relying on the reader's knowledge of the city to make the connection with the attack.

After the influx of GDR citizens into the West in November 1989, Hell flees into the East, where she squats in a tenement house in Lehninerstraße: this invented street is described in such detail that it can be identified as the real Zehdenickerstraße, but as a fictional location, it too remains a gap on the map of Berlin.[8] The tenement house is nearly empty as the building is readied for redevelopment: Mitte is one of several previously working-class districts in the former East to have undergone gentrification since reunification. Hell's neighbour, the last official resident of the house, is the woman called Dunkel who has apparently disappeared without anyone noticing; Hell comments, 'Vielleicht liegt es daran, daß es Frauen wie sie und mich haufenweise gibt in dieser Stadt' (*S*, p. 12) ('Perhaps it's because women like her and me are ten a penny in this city' (*SW*, p. 8)). This statement both relates the women to each other and suggests a link between the city and the anonymity of the women who disappear or live invisibly (by squatting). As their paired names suggest, the two women are *Doppelgänger*, living in opposing flats which are mirror images of each other; they even look interchangeable. As Gilson notes, female *Doppelgänger* are unusual in literature, and their symbolic and narrative doubling suggests an allegorical representation of Berlin's two halves, recalling also the many instances of split or paired female characters in Irmtraud Morgner's novels set in divided Berlin. However, Parei's characters do not map directly onto East and West respectively: both women have in fact moved from the West (Germany and Berlin) to East Berlin. Hell sets out to find Dunkel, with the result that their two stories are narratively intertwined, converging upon each other when the two women are reunited in what Katharina Gerstenberger reads as an allegorical reunification.[9] If this does represent the reunited city – and I would contend that the detail of the texts disrupts, though does not completely undermine, this allegorical possibility – then it is notable that reunification takes place within the East which has become the centre of gravity for the city since the *Wende*.

The rape changes Hell's perception of Berlin, making it incomprehensible to her; Hell's diminished ability to process and interpret visual information leads her to experience the arrival of GDR citizens in the West as a form of zombie attack, symptomatic of her skewed perception as well as the novel's cinematic touches. Thus, she describes wandering through Friedrichstraße station as an experience of dislocation:

> An manchen Tagen laufe ich durch die Stadt, in der ich geboren bin, wie eine Fremde, zum Beispiel neulich, da gerate ich in den Bahnhof Friedrichstraße. [...] Ich bin gefangen in einem Dschungel aus Symbolen und Beschriftungen, deren Botschaften verfrüht oder veraltet sind. (*S*, pp. 77–8).

> (Some days I walk through the city where I was born like a stranger in town; I ended up in Friedrichstrasse station recently. [...] I was caught in a jungle of symbols and labels, all their meanings premature or outdated. (*SW*, p. 71)).

She has lost her ability to read the city as a result of trauma, but here her confusion is specifically due to the transitional state of the station, a key border crossing during the time of division. In the early 1990s – the narrative present – signs point to GDR-era parts of the building, such as the Intershop, which have disappeared, and to renovations and additions that have not yet been completed. It is the eponymous shadow-boxing training Hell takes up after moving to the East which finally allows her to interpret the city around her; she turns her heightened perception into a state of ever-ready martial awareness: 'Mit dem Sehen und Hören muß ich ganz von vorn anfangen. Ich muß es neu lernen' (S, p. 117) ('I have to start over from the beginning with seeing and hearing. I have to learn it all over again' (SW, p. 110)). The descriptions of the city narrated from Hell's perspective teeter between careful observation and overwhelming information, signalling either hyper-awareness or trauma, rather than mere realist detail.

In addition to changing her view of the city, Hell also adopts male attri-butes as she reconstructs her life. In particular, she takes on the traditionally masculine attribute of smoking a pipe: Dunkel's old childhood friend März, who is also looking for her, recognizes Hell as 'die Frau mit der Pfeife' (S, p. 28) ('the woman with the pipe' (S, p. 24)). Hell steals the pipes and a tobacco pouch from her rapist (S, p. 64), thereby transforming herself in some manner from victim into attacker. Aside from the obvious phallic symbolism, the pipe is also a gender-crossing nod to fictional detective Sherlock Holmes. The pipes are associated with Hell facing the outside world – that is, the city – again after her attack as she takes up smoking on her balcony, as well as giving her a kind of physical meditation that precedes her kung fu training. More significant, and more unsettling within the text, is the gendered reversal which sees violence adopted by the victim as Hell becomes a perpetrator, albeit defensively. This counters her experience of male space within the city at the demonstration: the 1989 May Day riots were later condemned in accounts of the events as simply 'Männergewalt' ('male violence'). On her way through the streets before she is raped, Hell notices a poster that depicts 'Ein kleines Mädchen mit geschwärzten Vorderzähnen' (S, p. 14) ('A little girl with blackened front teeth' (SW, p. 11)), in a paramilitary pose, an image that to an extent Hell replicates through her subsequent kung fu training.

In *Writing New Berlin*, Katharina Gerstenberger suggests that 'sexual identity is connected to the emergence of New Berlin' in three texts by women writers: Tanja Dückers' *Spielzone* (Play Zone (1999)), Christa Schmidt's *Eselsfest* (Donkey's Feast (1999)) and *Die Schattenboxerin*.[10] However, only Parei's text focuses on a single female protagonist (as opposed to multiple protagonists and a male perspective respectively), and it is markedly less upbeat about the sexual opportunities in the post-*Wende* city. More positive depictions of contemporary metropolitan female sexuality (up to a point, at least) can be found in the depiction of Berlin's nightlife in Helene Hegemann's *Axolotl Roadkill* (2010) and Anna Blumbach's *Kurze Nächte* (Short Nights (2009)), which 'does for Kaffee Burger what *Axolotl Roadkill* does for Berghain',[11] or Olga Grjasnowa's structurally complex *Die juristische Unschärfe einer Ehe* (The Legal Haziness of a Marriage (2014)) about equally complex sexualities in

Berlin and Baku. And Annett Gröschner's *Walpurgistag*, which I analyze below, is frank about female sexuality, showing women as well as men seeking out no-strings sex in the anonymity of the city.

Gerstenberger posits that in Parei's text, 'the city is no longer viewed as a female body that simultaneously allures and threatens the male subject. Instead, the female body is the surface on which the contradictions and tensions of the New Berlin become visible.'[12] As I have suggested, the detail (or lack of this) within the text resists straightforward allegorization of Berlin and its recent history through the female body. However, the shift of agency and subjectivity that Gerstenberger identifies is also apparent in the choice of a female narrator and protagonist in what is not only a Berlin novel and *Wenderoman* but also an urban detective story. Parei's text is one of a number of post-1989 publications using tropes of the crime or detective novel, from Pieke Biermann's feminist *Krimis* to Gröschner's *Moskauer Eis* (Moscow Ice-cream (2000)), where Annja Kobe attempts to figure out the apparent suicide of her father by freezing himself. These writers and texts offer an experience of the city that shifts women's agency away from victim status towards perpetrator or investigator, in co-opting a genre that is often highly masculine-coded.

Annett Gröschner, *Walpurgistag*: Berlin in the Foreground

Beth Linklater's 2004 article about Germany as background in post-*Wende* women's writing focuses on the contrast between global settings and Berlin in texts by Hermann, Dückers, Jenny Erpenbeck, Katrin Dorn and Julia Franck.[13] This relegation of the city to a mere backdrop is certainly the case for many texts (not only by women), with the city simply acting as realist(ic) setting for short stories and novels that otherwise have little to say about the contemporary or historical metropolis. Texts such as Keun's or Parei's employ the city as a more meaningful location, with the historic or symbolic significance of Berlin playing a crucial role in the lives of the characters who nonetheless are the main focus of the texts. A number of contemporary (women) writers go even further: their texts not only foreground the city, but their œuvres demonstrate a substantial engagement with Berlin through a range of literary and artistic forms. The work of Monika Maron, Emine Sevgi Özdamar, Katja Lange-Müller, and particularly Irina Liebmann, repeatedly features the city and reflects upon it. These authors share a commitment to history and locality, and integrate women fully into the fabric of Berlin's narratives. While prominence is given to female characters in their texts, this is deliberately unremarkable; they form part of a spectrum of characters ranging in age, class and/or background amongst other positionalities.

Perhaps the most prolific Berlin author across a range of genres, Annett Gröschner engages with the city through a variety of literary forms, with a particular focus on the area of Prenzlauer Berg – like Parei's and Irina Liebmann's Mitte, a district that has undergone substantial regeneration and gentrification since reunification. Her fictional publications – the two novels, *Moskauer Eis* and *Walpurgistag*, along with a number of short stories – are outnumbered by reportage texts, such as *Jeder hat sein Stück Berlin gekriegt* (Everyone Got Their Piece of Berlin (1998)), essays and opinion pieces such as *Parzelle Paradies* (A Parcel of Paradise (2008)) and *Heimatkunde Berlin* (Berlin Local History (2010)). And she has also (co-)edited several Berlin documentary or historical texts committed to preserving the disappearing history of the city.

Gröschner's writing is deeply embedded in Berlin's landscape: she has undertaken frequent writer-in-residence projects around Berlin, most recently in July 2014 when she spent a month in a former border watchtower in Treptow. Describing this residency, Gröschner states, 'Mein Beobachten ist reine Schreibübung. Flanieren auf Papier' ('My observation is purely an exercise in writing. I'm a flâneur on paper').[14] Her style, in both factual and fictional work, is detailed and detached, but this is not the stance of the disinterested flâneur; rather it constitutes an ethical commitment to representing the city. Her observation is knowledgeable and engaged. In particular, her work often highlights women's experience of the historical city, such as during the Second World War while many men were at the front in *Backfisch im Bombenkrieg* (Teenage Girl in the Bomb War (2013)), or contemporary Berlin, not least the women disproportionately represented amongst the older generation as a result of war losses, such as the fictional characters who first appear in *Parzelle Paradies* before taking a key role in *Walpurgistag*.

Walpurgistag is a day in the life of Berlin in the carnival mode, presenting the multiple facets of the twenty-first-century city with humour, occasional fantasy and telling detail. It is set on 30 April 2002, that is, the day leading up to the infamous Walpurgisnacht, a night of mayhem and witchery preceding the charged 1 May and the male-dominated riots which feature in Parei. The text charts twenty-four hours in Berlin; chapters are structured by time, and the paths of the characters cross in various ways before converging at midnight on the Mauerpark, where the Berlin Wall was first dismantled by citizens of the GDR after 9 November 1989. Events in the novel are inspired by real occurrences sent in to Gröschner after she broadcast a call to find out what people did on 30 April – something referenced within the novel in a form of montage effect when an amnesiac character practices writing by copying down every piece of signage and lettering she sees while travelling on the U5 underground line to Alexanderplatz, including the author's advertisement. The novel creates a portrait of the city at both micro and macro levels by relating individual characters' life stories within the city and through the cumulative patchwork effect of the narrative.

Gröschner's œuvre is concerned with the multiple layers of history present as a palimpsest at once in Berlin's material form (such as streets and houses) and as preserved within personal memory or through individual life stories. Berlin is always in the foreground of the novel, which focuses particularly on micro-locations (the famed *Kiez* or neighbourhood); each chapter starts with reference to a (real) street, and the older characters from the GDR, especially, also map the city through named schools or workplaces. The first chapter, set at midnight, sees an older woman on the eve of moving house, as her tenement building is sold for redevelopment, a recurring theme in the novel. Like Parei's Dunkel, she is the last remaining resident in her house. Gerda Schweickert's reminiscences reach back to the war and the years of the GDR, as well as encompassing the other inhabitants of her block; each memory is anchored in a specific street in a highly localized area around her current residence in Danzigerstraße; and even the street names are a form of history, having changed since the times she recalls. Together with Frau Köhnke (Ilse) and Frau Menzinger (Trude), two other residents of the sheltered housing that she moves into on Kollwitzplatz, and recalling some of the interviewees in Gröschner's reportage texts, Gerda preserves in her memory the history of her area, her house and its inhabitants. The fictional trio are the vehicles for local knowledge, evoking Prenzlauer Berg in the pre-war years, during the conflict – not least the wave of rapes carried out by the incoming Soviet army – and the GDR.

Gerda blames the *Wende* for her change in circumstances, although to an outside view it might look like an improvement. Dreadlocked itinerant Alex later suggests a similarly reversed, satirical perspective on post-*Wende* gentrification through its effect on rats: 'Diese Ratte kann froh sein, dass sie mitten auf dem Alexanderplatz wohnt. Ein attraktiver Ort, besser als Marzahn oder Reinickendorf, möchte man meinen ... Die Ratten hatten ihren Zeit, die ist vorbei. Ihre Schlupflöcher – Trümmergrundstücke und verlassene Häuser – sind abgeräumt und renoviert.' ('This rat ought to be glad it is living right in the middle of Alexanderplatz. An attractive location, better than Marzahn or Reinickendorf ... The rats had their time, and it has passed. Their bolt-holes – ruins left after the war and derelict houses – have been cleared and renovated.).[15] The anthropomorphized rats suggest a conflicted view of the *Wende* as bringing both loss of 'Heimat' ('homeland'

(*Wt*, p. 126)) and material improvement; here, this is not specifically related to the heritage of the GDR (though it is clear that this is most affected) but to the whole city. At the same time, the changing housing stock offers opportunity for those happy to live on the margins of society (again, like Parei's Hell), such as Annja Kobe who has gone underground (literally, at the beginning of the novel, living in a GDR-era bunker) after being wrongly suspected of her father's murder, a story developed in Gröschner's first novel *Moskauer Eis*.

Gröschner plays with such common urban novel tropes as the notion of the city being written on the body. This is taken quasi-literally when Alex attempts to ascertain the origins of a woman he finds on Alexanderplatz with amnesia, first by testing her accent and knowledge of Berlin dialect – 'Leute, die den Konjunktiv benutzen und berlinern, sind immer aus Ostberlin' ('People who use the subjunctive and talk in Berlin dialect are always from East Berlin' (*Wt*, p. 129)) – and then by examining her arm for GDR-specific immunisation scars. The novel is also self-aware about its forebears in city literature, setting up a reference to *Berlin Alexanderplatz*, perhaps the Berlin novel par excellence, in the prologue, set on the Alexanderplatz. Here Alex (also the nickname of the square) asks the policemen about to arrest him to list the trams that crossed the square in 1929, and the cryptic-descriptive chapter titles are also reminiscent of Döblin's style. Frequent references to 'der Himmel über Berlin' (the original German title of the Wenders film *Wings of Desire* (1987), literally 'the sky above Berlin') are a further nod to one of the most famous depictions of the city in a magical realist style that matches Gröschner's fantastic touches.

Fittingly for a novel named after Saint Walpurga, whose feast day (or rather, night) has become associated with witches, it is female characters who are most prominent in the novel. Of the twenty characters named in chapter titles, thirteen are women (as well as 'die Unbekannte', the amnesiac woman), compared with six men (plus Stalin the dog). In addition to the sheer number of female characters, women also provide some of the most memorable characters in *Walpurgistag*, namely the two trios: the older women, Frau Köhnke, Frau Menzinger and Frau Sieckert, and the young Turkish/Kurdish-German gang consisting of Sugar, Cakes and Candy (a.k.a. Hatice, Emine and Ayşe). Both sets belong to groups who are arguably marginalized within the city, and they are carefully sketched through their metropolitan dialects, ranging from broadest Berliner to deliberately exaggerated pidgin Turkish-German. Furthermore, the trios – who mirror each other in causing mayhem within their local area by vandalizing open-top cars belonging to men – are linked specifically to Goethe's witches in the 'Walpurgisnacht' scenes from *Faust*. The older women cause trouble on Walpurgis Night, and their conversations are reported in dramatic notation, while Sugar, Cakes and Candy recite *Faust* and Mendelssohn's cantata *Die erste Walpurgisnacht* (The First Walpurgis Night). Several of the other female characters are also united through their association with witches: at 22.55 Viola and Heike (two of another trio of similarly-aged women) dicuss the heathen, matriarchal origins of *Walpurgisnacht* in the Celtic festival of Beltane and recall taking part in the ancient custom of leaping over fire on the eve of 1 May in previous years, before men took over the Mauerpark. Citing Berlin's reputation as a city that offers shelter for marginalized groups and alternative lifestyles, and satirizing identity politics, Viola defends the women to a disapproving policeman:

> Jeder hat in der Stadt seinen Tag. Die stark dezimierten Arbeiter den 1. Mai, die Schwulen den Christopher Street Day, die Migranten den Karneval der Kulturen, die Exilkölner ihren Hilfs-Fasching, die Techno-Freaks die Love-Parade, die Kiffer die Hanf-Parade, die Nationalisten den Tag der Deutschen Einheit und nur wir Hexen, wir sollen nicht feiern dürfen?

> (Everyone has their own day in the city. The severely depleted workers have May Day, gay people have Christopher Street Day, migrants have the Carnival of Cultures, expatriates from Cologne have their spin-off carnival, the techno-fans have the Love Parade, tokers have the Cannabis Parade, the nationalists have the Day of German Unity, and we witches are the only ones who are not allowed to celebrate? (*Wt*, p. 416))

As this theme suggests, Gröschner's novel belongs to an often overlooked seam of fantastic literature set in the city which lends itself to feminist interpretation. Else Lasker-Schüler's *Mein Herz* (My Heart (1912)), a one-sided epistolary novel, is full of flights of fantasy from the bohemian Café des Westens. Lasker-Schüler's first-person correspondent assumes a series of male alter ego characters and treats the city as a gender-fluid lover; the relationship between self and city swings between identifying with and objectifying the city – the latter a position often associated with a masculine mastery of the metropolis. Christa Wolf's sex-change novella, *Selbstversuch* (Self-Experiment (1975)) is also set in Berlin, and her *Leibhaftig* (In the Flesh (2002)) evokes the still-divided city in 1988 as the feverish protagonist explores in her hallucinations a Berlin tenement house. Gröschner's novel particularly evokes Irmtraud Morgner's 'feminist Bible', *Das Leben und Abenteuer der Trobadora Beatriz nach Zeugnissen ihrer Spielfrau Laura* (The Life and Adventures of Trobadora Beatrice as Chronicled by Her Minstrel Laura (1974)) and its sequel, *Amanda: Ein Hexenroman* (Amanda: A Witch Novel (1983)), which are both set largely against the backdrop of East

Berlin. The function of the city in Morgner's texts is to provide a familiar, real but incongruous setting for mythical characters, such as the spectacle of witch Amanda flying around the Platz der Akademie (now the Gendarmenmarkt square). And the magical elements in *Walpurgistag* – Annja's permanently frozen father or Alex putting other characters in his bag, and the meta-level of their interaction with the narrator – are similarly jarring in an otherwise seemingly accurate representation of Berlin.

Walpurgistag's structuring device of the twenty-four hour portrait of Berlin allows the characters to represent a multiplicity of positionalities, as well as emphasizing the serendipity and/or randomness of city life. Similar effects are seen in novels set in specific buildings – from Baum's *Menschen im Hotel*, a multi-character novel set in a hotel in 1920s Berlin, or her *Pariser Platz 13*, through to Irina Liebmann's reportage *Berliner Mietshaus* (Berlin Tenement (1982)) – or novels set in streets such as Inge Heym's *Die Leute aus meiner Straße* (The People on my Street (2000, though also written in 1982)) and Dücker's *Spielzone*, set in two streets in the districts of Neukölln and Prenzlauer Berg. These are common city tropes which enable a range of characters to encounter each other and assume the narrative focus. These multi-character novels also move away from the authenticity of the experience of a first-person narrative focalizer and into detached observation and overt fictionalization. They thus represent a shift from the personal mode that women's writing has tended to be associated with, a mode that both Keun's and Parei's work falls into, albeit with fictional characters rather than autobiographical texts. Gröschner's fictional work, in contrast to her nonfictional work, which is authentic (historical accounts) and often subjective (reportage), combines the telling detail of realist Berlin texts with devices – plot and structure derived from the form of the city – which emphasize fictionality. Her commitment to the city, its material history as well as its varied inhabitants, crosses genres to create a multi-layered, multimedia image of Berlin.

The three novels examined in depth in this chapter reflect changes in women's relationship to Berlin through the archetypal city motif of the streets. In *Das kunstseidene Mädchen* women on the street are identified as streetwalkers, their bodily presence in public subject to the gaze of others and objectified as part of the city's sights; Doris retreats into private spaces until she becomes homeless and is forced into prostitution on the streets. For Parei's *Hell*, Berlin's streets represent the vulnerability of women in public as male rioters take over on May Day, but she reclaims a place in the city through adopting masculine traits and training in self-defence. Finally, Gröschner's *Walpurgistag* stages the encounters between her multiple characters largely on the streets: her twenty-first-century city is a carnivalesque site, in which women are agents of chaos and possibility, at least for one exceptional day and night.

Women writers have contributed to the literary image of Berlin throughout the twentieth century, and in the twenty-first are increasingly central to Berlin literature. Since the turn of the millennium, early Berlin women writers have been acclaimed belatedly in critical works or rediscovered by a wider public through republication of their works: see for example the aforementioned Clara Viebig, Margarete Böhme and Mascha Kaléko, or Alice Berend, known as 'little Fontane', the author of realist Berlin texts such as *Spreeman & Co* (1916). These contribute to an increasingly feminized (or, one might say more pointedly, balanced) literary view of the city; though, of course, it must be remembered that women writers do not only write about women's experiences (Berend's texts, for instance, tend to focus on male figures), nor is the depiction of female protagonists the sole purview of female authors. The changing literary landscape of Berlin is finally being reflected in many late twentieth- and twenty-first-century anthologies, particularly those devoted solely to contemporary literature, which approach parity in their choice of authors, with some even registering a majority of women writers. The 2005 volume *Kanzlerinnen, schwindelfrei über Berlin* (Female Chancellors with a Head for Heights above/about Berlin (2005)) features exclusively women writers (including Gröschner, whose text forms the basis of a chapter in *Walpurgistag*) who were installed in a 'Verkehrskanzel' (traffic tower, and hence the play on Kanzlerinnen), their texts both embedded within the city and detached from it. The editor, Corinna Waffender, feels no need to justify her single-sex selection beyond the implicit reference to Chancellor Angela Merkel who took office in Berlin in the same year, stating programmatically in her introduction 'Schriftstellerinnen können über alles schreiben' ('Women writers can write about everything').

NOTES

1. The nickname given to the statue on the top of the Siegessäule (Victory Column).
2. Herbert Günther, ed., *Hier schreibt Berlin: Eine Anthologie* (1929) (Nachdruck, Berlin: Fannei & Waltz, 1989).
3. Petra Budke and Jutta Schulze, *Schriftstellerinnen in Berlin 1871 bis 1945: Ein Lexikon zu Leben und Werk* (Berlin: Orlanda Frauenverlag, 1995), p. 7.
4. Irmgard Keun, *Das kunstseidene Mädchen* (Berlin: List, 2004), p. 58 (henceforth *kM*). Irmgard Keun, *The Artificial Silk Girl*, trans. Kathie von Ankum (New York: Other Press, 2002), p. 49 (henceforth *ASG*).
5. Herta Müller, *Reisende auf einem Bein* (Berlin: Rotbuch, 1989), p. 75. Translation from *Traveling on One Leg*, trans. Valentina Glajar and André Lefevere (Evanston: Northwestern University Press, 1998), p. 64, translation modified.

6. See particularly Ingrid Sharp, 'Male Privilege and Female Virtue: Gendered Representations of the Two Germanies', *New German Studies*, 1.18 (1995), pp. 87–106.

7. Inka Parei, *Die Schattenboxerin* (Munich: btb, 2006), pp. 109–10 (henceforth *S*). Inka Parei *The Shadow-Boxing Woman*, trans. Katy Derbyshire (Calcutta: Seagull Books, 2011), pp. 102–3 (henceforth *SW*).

8. Gilson suggests that the street-name evokes the historical Lehninerstraße, formerly in Kreuzberg/Neukölln (now Lilienthalstraße, renamed 1929) which is not far from the location of the rape, but transported to the East, merging both history and political geography of the city. Elke Gilson, 'Selbstbegegnungen in der Stadt: Zu den postromantischen Wahrnehmungsweisen in Inka Pareis Berlinroman *Die Schattenboxerin*', *Orbis Litterarum* 65.4 (2010), pp. 318–46.

9. Katharina Gerstenberger, 'Play Zones: The Erotics of the New Berlin', *German Quarterly* 76.3 (2003), pp. 259–72 (p. 260).

10. Katharina Gerstenberger, *Writing the New Berlin: The German Capital in Post-Wall Literature* (Rochester, New York: Camden House, 2008), p. 25.

11. As described by Berlin-based blogger and translator Katy Derbyshire, http://love germanbooks.blogspot.co.uk/2011/04/anna-blumbach-kurze-nachte.html (accessed 15 January 2015). Kaffee Burger is the club which hosts the well-known Russendisko (Russians' disco); Berghain is a famously wild, and exclusive, nightclub.

12. Gerstenberger, 'Play Zones', p. 260.

13. Beth Linklater, 'Germany as Background: Global Concerns in Recent Women's Writing in German', in *German Literature in the Age of Globalisation*, ed. Stuart Taberner (Birmingham: Birmingham University Press, 2004), pp. 67–88.

14. Annett Gröschner, 'Abends riecht es nach Hasch und Fleisch', *Der Tagesspiegel*, 26 July 2014 http://www.tagesspiegel.de/kultur/berliner-tuerme-4-grenzwach turm-schlesischer-busch-abends-riecht-es-nach-hasch-und-fleisch/10254680.html (accessed 15 January 2015).

15. Annett Gröschner, *Walpurgistag* (Munich: Deutsche Verlags-Anstalt, 2011), p. 126 (henceforth *Wt*). Translations are my own.

10

ANDREAS KRASS
AND
BENEDIKT WOLF

Queer Writing

'Welcome to Berlin!' This salutation, uttered by Emcee, the Master of Ceremonies in the musical *Cabaret*, inverts the title of the novel on which the musical is based: *Goodbye to Berlin*, published by Christopher Isherwood in 1939 as Nazi Germany unleashed the Second World War. Although the novel has strong homoerotic overtones, it refrains from openly addressing the topic of homosexuality. In his autobiography, *Christopher and His Kind* (1976), Isherwood made it clear, though, why he was attracted to Berlin – because of its flourishing queer scene during the Weimar Republic.

This chapter offers a brief history of queer literature in Berlin from the late nineteenth to the early twenty-first centuries. The first section reconstructs the effect of the German sodomy law on queer writing and publishing in Berlin, and the subsequent parts outline the history of queer literature in Berlin according to the main eras of modern German history: German Empire, Weimar Republic, Nazi Germany, postwar Germany and Germany after the fall of the Wall. Each period of queer writing in Berlin is first portrayed in general and then illustrated through an exemplary text. While the close readings focus on gay male literature, the general picture attempts to cover the broad range of queer literature, including lesbian and transgender writing.

The 'One Hundred and Seventy-Fivers'

The *Schwarzbuch Deutsch* (Black Book German (2009)), a dictionary of obsolete German words, lists the word *Hunderfünfundsiebziger* (One Hundred and Seventy-Fiver) and comments: 'homosexual, named after the former § 175 of the Penal Code'.[1] Although the word is rather awkward to pronounce, it was apparently more awkward still to refer directly to 'the love that dare not speak its name' (Lord Alfred Douglas). The lifespan of the word is more or less congruent with the existence of the law to which it alludes. Replacing Paragraph 143 of the former Prussian penal code, the law was introduced in the German Empire (1872), then adopted by the Weimar Republic, tightened by the Nazis (1935), taken over in postwar Germany (1949), moderated in the late 1960s (1968 in the GDR, 1969 in the FRG) and abolished first in 1987 in East Germany and finally in 1994 in Germany as a whole – four years after reunification. The word was widely used by the German postwar generation, since the fascist version of the law was still in operation during the Adenauer era. Even homosexual men who had survived the concentration camps still had a criminal record; for them, fascism did not end in 1945.

Paragraph 175 is closely linked to Berlin. Berlin was the German capital when the law was introduced to the penal code; and it was the political arena where it was controversially debated until the Nazis put an end to the discussion. From 1897 to 1933, the Scientific-Humanitarian Committee, a group of sexual rights activists, led by the physician and sexologist Magnus Hirschfeld, adamantly campaigned against § 175. They collected more than 5,000 signatures from prominent Germans, including the writers Hermann Hesse, Thomas Mann, Heinrich Mann, Rainer Maria Rilke, Max Brod, Stefan Zweig and Gerhart Hauptmann, for a petition to overturn the Paragraph. In 1898 the petition was proposed by a socialist politician but rejected by the majority of the parliament. In 1919 the film *Anders als die Andern (§ 175)* (Different from the Others (§ 175)), a melodrama pleading against the Paragraph, was released. Magnus Hirschfeld advised playwright and director Richard Oswald on the project and even appeared in the film himself. Following the repeal of Paragraph 175 seventy-five years later, civil unions were legalized in 2001, and for the first time an anti-discrimination law was passed. Homophobia is now widely considered as, at least, politically inopportune. In 2011, the federal Magnus Hirschfeld Foundation was established in order to promote equal rights for gay, lesbian, bisexual, transgender and intersexual people and to financially support their social, cultural and political projects.

The word 'One Hundred Seventy-Fivers' was only attributed to men, with the law in question exclusively referring to 'unnatural fornication performed by persons of the *male sex*'.[2] This does not, however, mean that lesbians were not criminalized. In fact, the more general subordination of women resulted in the elision of female homosexuals from the penal code. Lesbians were already subject to discrimination *as women*, and there were other ways to persecute them, in particular under the National Socialist regime. This is the reason why the Memorial to Homosexuals Persecuted under Nazism, erected in 2008 in central

Berlin, close to the Memorial to the Murdered Jews of Europe, refers to both the male and the female victims of Nazi homophobia.

While the German sodomy law was gendered, the anti-pornography (§ 184) law was not. The latter was introduced in 1900 and generally called *Lex Heinze* after a heterosexual pimp of that name who lived in Berlin. The anti-pornography law has often been used as an instrument of censorship against gay, lesbian and transgender literature. For this reason its enactment in the first year of the twentieth century is also a significant milestone in the German history of queer writing.

Queer Writing in Berlin?

What exactly does 'queer writing in Berlin' signify? The question has three aspects:

First, what is *queer* writing? From a historical point of view the word 'queer' can be applied to early as well as more recent literature written by gay, lesbian, transgender and intersexual authors. For a long time the word 'queer' was used in its pejorative meaning in order to discriminate against people who did not conform to heteronormativity. The German equivalents mostly addressed gay men, as in the case of the aforementioned 'One Hundred and Seventy-Fivers'. In the 1990s, however, the English word was appropriated by queer activists and turned into an affirmative self-designation; in this new sense the word has also been adopted into the German language.

Second, does queer writing refer to queer authors, queer characters, queer topics or queer readers? From a theoretical point of view it makes sense to focus on the socio-historical conditions of the production, distribution and reception of queer literature. In his study *The Rules of Art*, French sociologist Pierre Bourdieu introduced the notion of the 'literary field', meaning a specialized, relatively autonomous area in the wider realm of cultural production. The literary field is organized first by distributors such as publishing houses, journals and bookshops; second by the producers such as authors, editors and translators; and third by the recipients of literature, the community of readers. Furthermore, it is structured by patterns such as literary genres and traditional narratives. In the German context, the subfield of queer literature originated in the German Empire and the Weimar Republic along with the emerging homosexual civil rights movement; it collapsed when National Socialism came to power but gradually redeveloped after the Second World War.

Third, what is queer writing *in Berlin*? Berlin can be considered a centre of queer writing in Germany, since it has been the German capital since

1871 – with the exception of West Germany from 1949 to 1990. Even during the years of division, however, West Berlin continued to be a centre of queer writing, since it offered a space for non-conformity that was lacking in the conservative and religious city of Bonn that served as the provisional capital of West Germany.

On 3 March 1896 Adolf Brand published the inaugural issue of *Der Eigene* (The Particular One), the first homosexual journal worldwide, and this date may be considered the birthday of queer writing in the German Empire. The journal continued to appear – with some interruptions – until 1932. As the subtitle (from 1903), 'A Journal for Masculine Culture', indicates, the journal placed emphasis on the notion of 'true' masculinity. It covered a broad range of erotic stories, poems and pictures, as well as political and scholarly essays. In the same year, Max Spohr, a publisher in Leipzig who had already printed several books on homosexual topics, began systematically to publish books and brochures about homosexuality, soon becoming the most important German publishing house for queer writing. And in 1901 Magnus Hirschfeld's Scientific-Humanitarian Committee founded the *Jahrbuch für sexuelle Zwischenstufen* (Yearbook for Sexual Intermediates). The second important homosexual journal next to *Der Eigene*, it ceased publication in 1923. In these early years of the queer literary movement, the repressive situation often resulted in self-censorship. In 1902, Otto Kiefer, a classical scholar sympathizing with the first homosexual civil rights movement, published a pamphlet called *The Significance of the Love for Young Men in Our Time* under the pseudonym Dr Reiffegg. In this text he points out that fiction on love between men should 'convince a wide circle of laypersons of the fact that the homosexual's feelings are also noble, pure and good and that his thoughts are not at all constantly directed towards raw sensual delights'.[3]

In 1919, the change from monarchy to democracy in the aftermath of the First World War made possible a range of new homosexual journals, among them *Die Freundin* (The Girlfriend), one of the first lesbian journals, which was published from 1924 to 1933. The diversification of the queer literary field responded to the emergence of a 'consumer sub-culture, a market whose target audience was the middle-class homosexual'.[4] One of the most dynamic publishers of the Weimar Republic was Friedrich Radszuweit, leader of the Bund für Menschenrecht (Association for Human Rights), which championed homosexual and other civil rights from 1922 to 1934. Establishing two publishing houses, Orplid-Verlag and Friedrich Radszuweit-Verlag, and distributing widely read journals such as *Blätter für Menschenrecht* (Papers for Human Rights (1923–33)), its literary supplement, *Die Insel* (The Island), and the aforementioned lesbian journal, *The Girlfriend*, Radszuweit deeply influenced homosexual popular culture in Berlin until the year 1933.

In National Socialist Germany the institutional and commercial conditions for queer literature collapsed. At the same time, as Sabine Rohlf has noted, the antifascist and socialist exile communities in Europe and the USA characterized the Nazi as non-masculine and, in consequence, sexually deviant.[5] The phantasm of the homosexual Nazi frustrated almost every effort at writing in an affirmative way about queer identities. The only attempt to continue the flourishing queer literary consumer culture of the Weimar Republic was the Swiss journal *Der Kreis* (The Circle (1943–67)), co-founded by Berlin émigré Karl Meier, a former collaborator of Adolf Brand's, under the pseudonym of Rolf.

When Germany was liberated from National Socialism and occupied by the Allied Forces, all publications were controlled by the occupation powers. Only in the 1950s did a few new queer journals appear in the newly founded Federal Republic of Germany. Berlin lost its leading position in the publication of queer writing. Nearly all homosexual journals of the 1950s appeared in Hamburg, among them *Die Insel der* (from 1952: *Der Weg zu*) *Freundschaft und Toleranz* (The Island of (The Path towards) Friendship and Tolerance (1951–70)), a journal addressed only to gay men. In 1969 the liberalization of § 175 made possible the publication of new and more explicit gay journals such as *Du & Ich* (You & I (since 1969)). At the same time, in parallel with the Homosexual Liberation Movement of the 1970s, several gay bookshops were founded in West Germany. The first one opened in West Berlin in 1978 and was named Prinz Eisenherz (Prince Ironheart) after the German version of the comic strip *Prince Valiant*. The gay and lesbian bookshops became highly important for the distribution of queer literature in West Germany, as did the newly founded gay publishing houses such as Rosa Winkel (Pink Triangle, Berlin, 1975–2001), Bruno Gmünder (Berlin, founded 1981), Männerschwarm (Men's Crush, Hamburg, founded 1992), and the Querverlag, founded in Berlin in 1995, which covers the whole range of queer literature. In 1987 the Research Centre for Homosexuality and Literature was established at the University of Siegen and, until its closure in 2008, did much research work on the history of German homosexual literature, publishing the findings in the journal *Forum Homosexualität und Literatur*.

German Empire and Weimar Republic: The Third Gender

The first phase of queer Berlin literature includes the German Empire (1871–1918) and the Weimar Republic (1918–33). As repressive as this period was at its beginning, it culminated in the permissive 'Golden Twenties', when Berlin was the European capital not only of sexology but also of sexual libertinage. When Isherwood first travelled to Berlin in 1929 he moved into a guesthouse run by Magnus Hirschfeld's sister, Recha Tobias, and part of the villa also housed Hirschfeld's famous Institute for Sexual Research – the centre of the first German gay liberation movement as well as an international magnet for writers and artists. In the beginning Isherwood was not aware of this since he was more interested in the boys he could meet in the numerous gay bars of Berlin.

Hirschfeld's influence on the literary life of the German Empire and Weimar Republic is well documented. In 1909, Otto Reutter, a popular singer in Berlin, wrote the so-called *Hirschfeld-Song*, making fun of how innocent behaviour suddenly assumes sexual significance in the presence of Hirschfeld. Hirschfeld is also mentioned in gay novels such as *Liebchen* (Sweetheart (1908)) by an anonymous author, *Seelenwanderung* (Metempsychosis (1913/14)) by Jules Siber and *Alf* (1929) by Bruno Vogel. And he appears in canonical literature such as Alfred Döblin's Berlin novels *Die beiden Freundinnen und ihr Giftmord* (The Two Girlfriends and Their Murder by Poisoning (1924)) – a semi-documentary report on a lesbian couple killing the violent husband of one of the partners – and *Berlin Alexanderplatz* (1929). Many gay-related novels were reviewed in a journal published by Hirschfeld's Scientific-Humanitarian Committee, including Thomas Mann's *Tod in Venedig* (Death in Venice (1911)), Klaus Mann's *Der fromme Tanz* (The Pious Dance (1926)) and Stefan Zweig's *Verwirrung der Gefühle* (Confusion of the Emotions ((1927)). Hirschfeld wrote a review of the novel *Der Puppenjunge* (The Pansy (1926)) by Sagitta (i.e. John Henry Mackay) and – in keeping with his comment that literature was his 'first love' – contributed to literary history himself. He wrote the poem 'Drei Gräber in fremdem Land' (Three Graves in a Foreign Country (1909)), remembering his thoughts and feelings while visiting the graves of three famous gay Germans during a trip to Italy: archaeologist Johann Joachim Winckelmann (1717–68) in Trieste, poet August Graf von Platen (1796–1835) in Syracuse and lawyer and sexologist Karl Heinrich Ulrichs (1825–95) in Aquila. He was also the author of a documentary book on *Berlins Drittes Geschlecht* (Berlin's Third Sex) in 1904 (Figure 10.1). Here, he describes the homosexual subculture of Berlin in detail, with the title referring to the notion of homosexuality as a third gender: a female soul trapped in a male body and vice versa. One chapter of his voluminous study, *Die Homosexualität des Mannes und des Weibes* (The Homosexuality of Men and Women (1914)), provides a brief history of homosexual literature from antiquity to modernity, and the film script that he co-wrote for *Anders als die Andern* was loosely based on a 1904 novel of the same title by Bill Forster.

Figure 10.1: Cover of Magnus Hirschfeld's *Berlins Drittes Geschlecht*
(Berlin's Third Sex), 1904

In the late nineteenth and early twentieth centuries, the emancipatory discourse on same-sex love was shaped by two competing concepts: 'homosexuality' on the one hand and 'friendship' on the other. Thus, in 1900 Adolf Brand published Elisar von Kupffer's famous anthology of homoerotic world poetry titled *Lieblingminne und Freundesliebe* (Courting Favourites and the Love of Friends). The rival notions of same-sex love – mostly referring to love between men only – are also mirrored in the first dissertation on the literary history of homosexuality, written by Hans Dietrich Hallbach and published in Leipzig in 1931. As the title – *Die Freundesliebe in der deutschen Literatur* (Love of Friends in

German Literature) – indicates, Hallbach takes sides with Brand rather than Hirschfeld, although he discusses the latter's concept of homosexuality. In Hallbach's view, Stefan George represents the climax of German poetry on male friendship and love.

There are also examples of lesbian and transgender literature during the German Empire and the Weimar Republic. In 1931 the film *Mädchen in Uniform* (Girls in Uniform), a tragic love story between a student and a teacher at a residential school for girls in Potsdam, was released. It was based on a theatre play written by the German-Hungarian author Christa Winsloe and subsequently adapted as a novel by the same author (*The Girl Manuela* (1933)). And Walter Homann's novel, *Tagebuch einer männlichen Braut* (Diary of a Male Bride (1907)), which is based on a true story, presents the biography of a transvestite. The main character narrates how he spent his childhood in a provincial town and then moved to Berlin, where he attracted the interest of a sexologist (Hirschfeld), was introduced to the homosexual subculture and eventually became a travesty star in the theatre. A love affair with a bourgeois man and the fear of being discovered drives him to commit suicide. Indeed, travesty served more generally as a framework for the subversion of gender and sexual norms. One striking example is the silent film *Hamlet* (1921), shot in Berlin, with Asta Nielsen in the main role. It is based on the assumption that Hamlet was a girl brought up as a boy in order to guarantee the succession to the throne, which leads to considerable gender trouble, in particular concerning Hamlet's intimate relationships with Ophelia and Horatio.

Anonymous, *Sweetheart: A Romance between Men*

The novel *Liebchen: Ein Roman unter Männern* (Sweetheart: A Romance between Men), anonymously published in 1908, is one of the first German narratives situated in an explicitly homosexual milieu. It tells the story of a well-off bourgeois homosexual protagonist blackmailed by a male sex worker. The story refers to the first homosexual scandal of the German Empire, the so-called Harden-Eulenburg affair, which was set off in 1907 by the journalist Maximilian Harden who denounced high-ranking members of the government for their alleged homosexuality. As Norman Domeier has noted, the affair introduced the discourse on homosexuality, which had previously been conducted mainly in scientific and civil rights circles, into the public sphere, and further fuelled public homophobia, which was already rife.[6] The trial of Eulenburg is frequently referred to during a soiree at the protagonist's house in the third chapter of the novel.

The story is located in a secret homosexual milieu. The members use nicknames in order to protect themselves from prosecution, since the sodomy law encouraged sex workers to blackmail their clients. The main character is Paul Muxberg, a rich, married industrialist. He is captivated by the beauty of the heterosexual sex worker, Eduard Kieseke, a proletarian boy speaking the dialect of Berlin. Eduard's nickname, 'Tantenede', hints at the homosexual men he serves ('Tante' means 'aunt'). When Muxberg is blackmailed by Kieseke and the newspapers begin to allude to his homosexuality, he eventually commits suicide. Following the concept of the third gender, the narrator calls Muxberg an 'effeminate' man (L, p. 18),[7] whose moustache looks 'like a lie' (L, p. 9), whereas he ascribes a 'masterly nature' to Kieske (L, p. 18). Thus, the class hierarchy between the bourgeois and the proletarian is crossed with the gender hierarchy between the manly Kieseke and the womanish Muxberg. The gender stereotypes also reflect the sexological discourse about 'true' and 'false' homosexuality. While Muxberg represents a homosexual by nature (born with an entirely 'inverted' constitution), Kieseke stands for a homosexual by behaviour (a heterosexual man temporarily committing homosexual acts).

The conversation that takes place during the soiree revolves around the Harden-Eulenburg affair. A lady remarks that 'a trial like this one would corrupt the morals of the nation and one would be ashamed when opening the newspaper' (L, p. 36). A psychiatrist, on the other hand, claims that a huge part of the population is 'pathological' and that homosexuals should be subjected to medication in a sanatorium (L, p. 39). A more liberal opinion is expressed by sexologist Doctor Billing, who refers to authorities like Krafft-Ebing, Ivan Bloch, Magnus Hirschfeld and Albert Moll: 'It is spiteful to punish an innocent person for something that is not his fault' (L, p. 63). These different stances on homosexuality, all taken up by heterosexuals, reflect the scope of wider public discourse on the topic.

There are also lesbian overtones. During the evening party two women, Muxberg's wife Marga and the unmarried Fräulein Doctor Senftlach, with-draw to the privacy of a boudoir. They use the language of passionate friendship and romantic love: '"Marga, you have me – me and my friendship ... and my love",[8] she whispered, kissing her ear. Quietly she said: "My lover, my one and only lover, you are mine and you shall not belong to anyone else"' (L, p. 46). The heightened homosocial relationship is marked by both gender and social difference. The housewife's 'soft curves' are contrasted with the academic's 'hard-boned body' (L, p. 47). At the end of the boudoir scene their physical intimacy comes to a climax: 'The two women's bodies almost flowed into each another, trembling ' (L, p. 51).

Though the novel is not at all pornographic, it goes some distance in describing sex between men. When Kieseke and Muxberg have sexual intercourse in a disreputable hotel, the act itself is marked by three asterisks (*L*, p. 22). However, afterwards the narrator allows for a glimpse into what has actually happened: 'The lad lay on the bed, the pillows rumpled. The room smelt of sweat. The water pot stood on the floor, crumpled towels lay scattered on the floor, the door of the bedside locker was half open and a few charred cigarette butts swam in the dirty water of the pitcher' (*L*, p. 23). The scene evokes the image of a past orgy, with the dirty objects in the bedroom hinting at the tabooed practice of anal intercourse. The scene may be meant to be an accusation against the repression of homosexuality forcing gay men into the underground. At the same time, however, it illustrates the tendency of bourgeois homosexuals to pass their bad reputation on to the proletarian sex workers.

Liebchen provoked numerous imitations, among them *Die Süßen* (The Sweet Ones (1910)) by Karl von Linden, *Zwischen den Geschlechtern* (Between the Sexes (1919)) by Homunkulus (a pseudonym) and *Men for Sale* (Männer zu verkaufen (1931)) by Friedrich Radszuweit. The last of these, which grants the protagonist a happy ending, is also testament to sexual freedoms – however imperfect – that would soon come to an end.

Nazi Germany: The Pink Triangle

Paragraph 175 has always been criticized for criminalizing same-sex love and making homosexual men susceptible to the threat of blackmail and slander. Nevertheless, the gay and lesbian subculture flourished in Berlin during the Weimar Republic, until the situation dramatically changed when the Nazis came into power on the 30 January 1933. Less than four weeks later, the interior ministry issued a decree that gay bars and bookshops offering erotica were to be shut down. The plundering of Magnus Hirschfeld's Institute for Sexual Research on 6 May was a prelude to the book burning on 10 May 1933 (as witnessed and described by Isherwood). The police raided Adolf Brand's publishing house several times, confiscating thousands of books and journals and thus ruining him economically. Ernst Röhm, the openly homosexual commander of the Sturmabteilung (SA) and member of Hitler's cabinet, was executed in July 1934 in the course of the so-called Night of the Long Knives. In June 1935, Paragraph 175 was revised and the scope of fornication extended. The Gestapo compiled lists of homosexual men, hunted them down and arrested them. During the Berlin Summer Olympics of 1936, the persecution of homosexuals was temporarily suspended, but in October 1936

Heinrich Himmler, commander of the SS, created the Reich Central Office for the Combating of Homosexuality and Abortion, the main instrument for the systematic and relentless persecution of homosexuals. Between 1933 and 1944, more than 50,000 men were convicted for homosexuality and sent to the concentration camps, where they had to wear a specific badge: the pink triangle. Many of them were castrated, tortured and killed. Horrible medical experiments were conducted on them in order to 'cure' them of homosexuality.

While homosexual women were not directly subject to the homophobic decrees, there were other means to persecute them. The tragic story of Lily Wust and her Jewish lover Felice Schragenheim – who was sent to a concentration camp in 1944 and died in 1945, probably during a death march – was made into the 1999 feature film *Aimée and Jaguar*, set in Berlin during World War Two. The film is based on the documentary book published by Erica Fischer in 1994, fifty years after the deportation of Felice Schragenheim.

In this time of wholesale suppression and persecution of homosexual men and women, the gay and lesbian literary scene in Berlin (and Germany as a whole) collapsed. Homosexual authors who managed to leave Germany early enough continued writing in exile. While fascist literature celebrating the 'Aryan' body, with its manifold homoerotic overtones, continued the political and military tradition of male bonding that had already existed long before, this is, of course, not to be confused with the writing of queer authors persecuted by the fascists.

Hirschfeld survived Nazi Germany because he had started a worldwide reading tour in 1931. He never returned to Germany and died in 1935 in Nice. Four years after his death, the English novelist Robert Hichens wrote a novel alluding to the relationship between Hirschfeld and his Chinese lover and assistant Tao Li (his actual name was Li Shiu Tong), with the emblematic title, *That Which Is Hidden* (1939).

Klaus Mann, *The Volcano*

Klaus Mann's novel *Der Vulkan* (The Volcano), printed in 1939 in Amsterdam, deals with the experience of *not* living in Berlin. The main characters, nearly a dozen in number, share the experience of Nazi terror, flight and exile. They flee from Berlin, the former centre of their lives, to Paris, Zurich, Prague, Amsterdam and other metropolises. The novel begins with a letter written by Dieter, a young man still living in Berlin, to his friend Karl, who has fled to Paris. Dieter tries to persuade Karl, whom he considers an 'Aryan', to come home (*V*, p. 8).[9] Using racist language, Dieter accuses Karl of living 'like the gypsies' (*V*, p. 10), praising Germany's turn to National Socialism as a 'national awakening' and the beginning of 'something beautiful, productive, and positive' (*V*, pp. 8–9). The implicit message of the letter is that Karl is betraying his nation by not being part of the 'awakening'. This scene alludes to the opening of the author's debut novel *Der fromme Tanz* (The Pious Dance (1926)), one of the most important gay novels of the Weimar years, which also shows a young man writing a letter to his friend. While *Der fromme Tanz* colourfully depicts queer life in Berlin during the Golden Twenties, *Der Vulkan* traces what was lost after the Nazis had come to power.

The first chapter introduces several German emigrants arriving in Paris. Most of them did not have anything in common while they were still living in Germany: some of them had to flee because they were – or were thought to be – Jews or Communist or Social Democratic activists; some of them despise fascist ideology on principle. Berlin is omnipresent in their thoughts and conversations. Marcel Poiret, a French poet, sums up the radical displacement when he exclaims: '"Poor Berlin!"' (*V*, p. 28). The loss of the queer spaces of Berlin is illustrated through the character of Schwalbe, the former owner of a bar near the Kurfürstendamm where young leftist intellectuals and queers, now dispersed all over the world, used to meet. Her physiognomy and behaviour hints at a certain type of butch lesbian of the Weimar years. She is depicted as an elderly woman with 'short, bristly, grey hair and a reddish tanned skipper's face' (*V*, p. 14), with 'a thick cigar in her mouth' (*V*, p. 18).

Although the novel was published in 1939, the extensive threat posed by the National Socialists to queer culture and life is not explicitly dealt with. One reason for this reluctance may be the enormous pressure put on homosexuals by the socialist antifascists who linked homosexuality with fascism. In an article published in 1934 Klaus Mann argued against this connection by pointing out that it does not make sense to fight against racism on the one hand and to promote homophobic prejudices on the other.[10] Against the backdrop of such debates, *Der Vulkan* prefers a subversive strategy for dealing with homosexuality. The novel shows homosexual emigrants who are highly aware of the political situation in Germany without dwelling on their homosexuality. When Martin, a German emigrant, meets Kikjou, a young French man, their exchange of glances and their first night together in a hotel room is depicted in the same way as incipient heterosexual love affairs. Homosexual desire here appears to be so ordinary that it is not even necessary to address it in specific terms.

Nevertheless, the novel ends tragically for Martin. He becomes a morphine addict, is ruined by his drug abuse and eventually dies of pneumonia. *Der*

Vulkan does not go so far as to create an antifascist homosexual hero. The novel clings to traditional narratives of morbid homosexual characters, not least Gustav von Aschenbach in *Death in Venice* by Klaus's father, Thomas Mann. However, it hauntingly demonstrates how life becomes unbearable for queer people deprived of their own spaces. For Martin, the goodbye to Berlin eventually means a farewell to life.

Postwar Germany: 'It Is Not the Homosexual Who Is Perverse . . . '

The year of the liberation from National Socialism, 1945, was not a 'zero hour' for homosexual Germans. The Nazi version of Paragraph 175 remained in operation, and gay men were still imprisoned by the authorities. Like other victim groups – such as Romany people – homosexuals persecuted before 1945 were never rehabilitated, either in the Federal Republic or in the GDR. The highly repressive situation made it extremely difficult to form a civil rights movement for homosexuals, and the so-called Homophile Movement that emerged in the 1950s in West Germany was not able to staunch public homophobia.

When the Wall was erected in 1961, East Berlin remained the capital of the GDR, while the small city of Bonn, located in the Catholic and conservative Rhineland, became the provisional capital of the Federal Republic. West German postwar literature was first preoccupied with looking back at the catastrophic past. In 1947, Hans Siemsen – who had already written several homoerotic stories in the 1920s – published the semi-documentary *Geschichte des Hitlerjungen Adolf Goers* (The Story of Hitler Youth Adolf Goers), an English version of which, with the title *Hitler Youth*, had already been published in 1940. The narrative is to a large extent an account of the protagonist's homosexual experiences in the Hitler Youth, thereby reinforcing the antifascists' stereotype of the fascist homosexual. Berlin is only mentioned as the site of the concentration camp where Adolf is imprisoned until he manages to flee from Germany.

In 1957 the film *Anders als du und ich (§ 175)* (Different from Me and You (§ 175)) was released, and it was the first German postwar film to thematize homosexuality, with its title alluding to *Anders als die Andern (§ 175)*, discussed above. The film was directed by Veit Harlan, who had produced several fascist propaganda movies in the National Socialist years, such as the maliciously anti-Semitic film, *Jud Süß* (Süss the Jew (1940)). *Anders als du und ich* is a homophobic pamphlet that aims to 'inform' parents about the threat homosexual men pose to their sons. In the following year, a remake of *Mädchen in Uniform*, with Romy Schneider and Lilly Palmer in the leading roles, was released, though with its queer potential largely contained. While homophobic books and films were easily published during this time, queer-friendly authors and directors faced immense problems. Thus, Hans Henny Jahnn, a West German author writing rather openly about sexual practices between men, had to consider subscription-based editions in order to avoid legal consequences.

In the late 1960s, however, the socio-political and cultural climate in West Germany significantly changed. The leftist German student move-ment of 1968, with many sympathizing with Marxist positions and fem-inist theories, asked questions about the fascist past of their parent's generation. In 1969, Paragraph 175 was reformed: male homosexuality was no longer forbidden in general but 'only' in certain specified cases. In 1971 the film *Nicht der Homosexuelle ist pervers, sondern die Situation, in der er lebt* (It Is Not the Homosexual Who Is Perverse, But the Situation in Which He Lives) premiered at the Berlin Film Festival, and this event turned out to be the starting point of the new Gay Liberation Movement that began fighting for equal rights of homosexuals as well as for sexual liberation in general. The makers of the film, director Rosa von Praunheim and screenwriters Martin Dannecker and Sigurd Wurl, toured all over West Germany, screening the film and discussing it with audiences. In consequence, many local gay activist groups were founded; and together they formed West Germany's Gay Liberation Movement. Since then Rosa von Praunheim has directed many films militating for equal rights, includ-ing *Schwuler Mut: 100 Jahre Schwulenbewegung* (Gay Courage: 100 Years of the Gay Rights Movement (1997)) and *Der Einstein des Sex: Leben und Werk des Dr. Magnus Hirschfeld* (The Einstein of Sex: Life and Work of Dr Magnus Hirschfeld (1999)). The film *Nicht der Homosexuelle* tells the story of a young homosexual man immersing himself in the gay subculture of Berlin. His experiences reach from a monogamous relationship to encounters in gay bars, in the hyper-masculine leather scene and in public toilets. By implementing distancing effects such as incongruity between images and audio track and imitating the language of instructional films, the film challenges the recipients to deliberate on their social and sexual behaviour as well as its socio-political dimension. Many gays felt offended or even insulted when they first saw the film because of its uncompro-mising view of homosexual life.

In the 1970s, so-called Second Wave Feminism questioned the androcentric literary canon and called for new ways of expressing women's, and not least lesbians', lifestyles, feelings and sexualities. Verena Stefan's book *Häutungen* (translated as *Shedding and Literally*

Dreaming (1975)) proved to be a cult text of the feminist movement. Set in the urban space of Berlin, the book explores the scope of what French second wave feminists called *écriture feminine*, contemplating what it means to be and to write as a woman, to be oppressed by patriarchy and to fight against that oppression. Lesbian desire is celebrated as a way of experiencing love and lust beyond male sexist approaches to women's sexuality. Similarly, Johanna Moosdorf's novel, *Die Freundinnen* (The Girlfriends (1977)), depicts the relationship between two women in the early 1970s in West Berlin that is repeatedly challenged by the male characters' claims on one or both of the women. The book, originally titled *Sappho*, was rejected by the author's regular publisher, before appearing seven years later with a different publishing house. And Christa Reinig's novel *Die ewige Schule* (The Everlasting School (1981)) borrows from Christa Winsloe's *Das Mädchen Manuela* but doubles the love story of a female boarding school student who falls in love with her female teacher, mirroring Winsloe's original constellation in a similar version set in the 1970s.

In 1989, the year when the Berlin Wall fell, Heiner Carow's film *Coming Out* premiered in East Berlin. The film tells the story of the teacher Philipp who starts a heterosexual relationship with Tanja but is unable to control his homosexual desires. In an East Berlin gay bar he gets to know a boy named Matthias and falls in love with him. While Philipp tries to hide his homosexual affair from Tanja, when she and Matthias eventually encounter each other, he has to make a decision. He accepts his homosexuality and comes out in his workplace. *Coming Out* was first screened on 9 November 1989, and immediately after the screening, the audience was informed that the border between East and West Berlin had just been opened. Thus, it is a document at once of the increasing acceptance of homosexuality in the GDR and of the last throes of the Communist German state.

Ronald M. Schernikau, *And When the Prince ...*

The way young gay men – students, workers, clerks, artists – lived and loved in the early 1980s in West Berlin is depicted in an artful novel written by Ronald M. Schernikau. The ironic title, *Und als der prinz mit dem kutscher tanzte, waren sie so schön, daß der ganze hof in ohnmacht fiel* (And When the Prince Was Dancing with the Coachman, They Were So Beautiful That the Whole Court Fainted (1982)), mimics the heteronormative stereotypes of a fairy-tale plot, while replacing the princess with the coachman. The substitution of characters is significant in terms of gender (a woman replaced by a man), class (aristocracy replaced by the working class) and sexuality (heterosexuality replaced by male homosexuality). The overly long title – more in the character of an abstract – evokes a genre that is not affirmed by the story (in the subtitle the novel identifies itself as a 'utopian film'). However, there are several fairy-tale-like elements, such as frequently interspersed lines from German pop songs, expressing naive romantic hopes and fantasies.

The form the author chooses for his novel is an artistic blend of realistic narration and film script. The reader is invited to use his or her mind's eye in order to *see* the laconic text and project it into an imaginary movie. Paradoxically, the reader is placed very close to the four protagonists – the banker Tonio, the singer Franz, the student Paul and the decorator Bruno – but at the same time kept at distance. The film that he or she is supposed to envision is documentary rather than melodramatic. Over the course of the story the reader witnesses the changing constellation of love relationships. In the way the male couples – Tonio and Franz, Paul and Bruno – are gradually rearranged, the novel is to a certain extent reminiscent of Goethe's *Die Wahlverwandtschaften* (Elective Affinities (1809)). Paul and Franz share an apartment; their respective lovers are Bruno and Tonio. While Paul and Franz have ordinary monosyllabic forenames in common, the names of Bruno and Tonio are similar with respect to the sound (polysyllabic with nasals and dark vowels, both ending with an 'o'). Tonio's name is an obvious allusion to Thomas Mann's novella *Tonio Kröger* (1903) – the more so as the narrator remarks that he should rather have the name Hans Hansen, who is Tonio's beloved friend in Mann's homoerotically coloured novella. With respect to their gender, the singer Franz and the decorator Bruno coincide, since they are both presented as effeminate men (Franz wears his hair 'like a woman'; Bruno should rather be called 'Erika').

The notion of unstable symmetries is also evident in the structure of the novel. The text comprises forty-eight chapters that are organized in two competing ways. On the one hand, they are divided in five groups of ten chapters, marked by the striking brevity of the tenth, twentieth, thirtieth and fortieth chapters, and with two chapters lacking at the end of the novel. On the other hand, the number of chapters is divisible by two, three and four, which might be read as a signal for changing attraction between the protagonists – a set of four characters consisting of two couples and being threatened by the triangular dynamic of erotic rivalry. Eventually, the couples split up and two new couples form. While Tonio and Bruno favour a monogamous love relationship, Paul and Franz are rather polyamorous. At the end of the novel, Schernikau introduces a series of motifs illustrating the uncontrollable dynamic of desire: a spinning chairoplane, a labyrinth of mirrors and a swimming pool in the rain. The dissolving effect includes the heterosexual characters of the story. Thus, the novel can be seen as an attempt at questioning romantic love in general and opening a space of queer desire that indeed deserves to be labelled utopian.

Ronald M. Schernikau wrote the novel in 1982 when he was twenty-two years old. He died at the age of thirty-one from the consequences of AIDS. His 'dreamlike life', as Matthias Frings puts it in the title of his touching biography,[11] is oddly interlaced with the history of West and East Germany. He was born in Magdeburg (GDR), grew up in a small town near Hannover (FRG), studied in West Berlin (1980–6) and moved to Leipzig (GDR) in order to continue his studies at the Johannes R. Becher-Institute for creative writing (1986–9). In 1989 he acquired East German citizenship and spent his last years in East Berlin (1989–91). *Und als der prinz . . .* was written in 1982, first printed as a part of his novel *Legende* (Legend (1991)) in 1999 and finally published separately in 2012.

After the Wall: 'Poor but Sexy'

When the Wall fell, Berlin of course changed fundamentally: suddenly the city was twice as big as before, and the clash between the capitalist and the socialist system ceased to exist. The situation changed for gay, lesbian and transgender activism, too. In political terms, the shift from socialism to capitalism affected both the eastern and the western sides of the Gay Movement. The Gay Movement of East Berlin lost the ideology it had been based upon; while its counterpart in West Berlin, Marxist for the most part, had to face the epochal victory of capitalism, too. In cultural terms, however, the reunified city of Berlin experienced an explosion of subcultural activities. Rents were very cheap, especially in the former East Berlin districts of Prenzlauer Berg, Friedrichshain and Mitte, and many of the numerous abandoned buildings were used for subcultural events and parties. In the early 1990s, the mixture of gay parties, sex culture and techno music became very popular, with its focal point in the legendary nightclub Ostgut, located at the border between Kreuzberg and Friedrichshain. The nightclub reopened in 2004 under the name of Berghain – today one of the most famous clubs in the world, and one that even initiated a distinctive literary genre, including Airen's *Strobo* (2009) – a diary-like account of a young man's experiences with club culture, excessive drug use and promiscuous sex with both men and women, Helene Hegemanns's *Axolotl Roadkill* (2010) and Oscar Coop-Phane's *Bonjour Berlin* (2013).

In the 1990s, the gay and lesbian cultures of Berlin became explicitly queer in orientation. After a short period of cooperation, the gay and lesbian movements had mostly gone their separate ways, but things changed after Judith Butler's ground-breaking book *Gender Trouble* was published in German (1991) and queer theory was introduced to German academia and to culture at large. The heteronormative binaries of gender and sexuality were increasingly contested politically and culturally, and transgender as well as intersexual issues came more and more to the fore. However, the traditional gay and lesbian movements still persisted – often feeling uneasy about the deconstruction of sexual identity after a long period of identitarian struggle for acceptance and equal rights.

From 2001 to 2014, Klaus Wowereit, the first openly gay politician in Germany, was the Mayor of Berlin. His dictum about Berlin – 'poor but sexy' (2003) – became common currency. It alludes to Berlin's reputation as a city of low rents and high permissiveness, a metropolitan image that is mirrored in many novels, serving to attract forms of queer migration. Christoph Geiser, in his novel *Das Gefängnis der Wünsche* (The Prison of Wishes (1992)), presents Berlin as a queer space where two famous time-travellers meet: Johann Wolfgang von Goethe and the Marquis de Sade. In this novel, the classical becomes perverse and, conversely, the perverse classical.

Many queer people have escaped the oppression of the German provinces in order to find freedom and happiness in Berlin. Markus Orth's novel, *Corpus* (2002), tells the story of two childhood friends losing sight of each other and meeting again in Berlin after many years, where they refresh their memories of painful events from their youth. The encounter opens new opportunities for Christoph, one of the friends, a Catholic priest-to-be who has a triangular affair with a heterosexual couple. Falk Richter's theatrical 'project' *Small Town Boy*, created for the Maxim Gorki Theatre in 2014, its title a homage to Bronski Beat's 1984 pop song of the same name, also deals with the flight of queers from the provinces to Berlin.

On the occasion of the Berlin Queer Pride in June 2010, Judith Butler gave a lecture at the Volksbühne theatre in Berlin, calling for the development of queer alliances and anti-war politics. The following day she publicly rejected the Civil Courage Award offered to her by the Berlin Queer Pride Committee on the grounds that some established queer institutions showed racist tendencies. This incident marked the increasing awareness amongst queer activists of the intersections of gender, class, race and sexuality and, as a result, different grades of discrimination. The connection of homophobia and racism had already been the topic of a play performed in 2008 at Ballhaus Naunynstraße, a small stage in Kreuzberg devoted to post-migrant theatre. The work, written by gay playwright Nurkan Erpulat, has the title *Jenseits – Bist du schwul oder bist du Türke?* (Beyond – Are You Gay Or Are You a Turk?). It illuminates the ambiguous position of gays with Turkish origins: on the one hand, Turkish men are often considered to be inherently homophobic; on the other, they are often constructed as objects of desire by gay men of German origin. Thus, contemporary queer culture in Berlin has become complicated by transcultural trends.

Joachim Helfer, *What Makes a Man?*

In 2006, Joachim Helfer, a German novelist living in Berlin, published *Die Verschwulung der Welt* (The Queering of the World, translated as *What Makes a Man?*).[12] The book, which caused lively controversy in German newspapers and magazines, is a response to a text in Arabic published in Beirut, *Awdatu l'almani 'ila rushdihi* (How the German Came to His Senses (2005)) by the Lebanese author Rashid al-Daif (which also accompanies Helfer's text, in German translation). Both Helfer and al-Daif drew inspiration from the renowned Wissenschaftskolleg institute for advanced studies in Berlin. Helfer met his Lebanese colleague in the German 'West-Eastern Divan' – an exchange programme that was co-sponsored by the Wissenschaftskolleg in order to promote cultural dialogue between Germany and the Middle East. The two complementary texts allow for illuminating insights into Eastern and Western discourses on male same-sex sexuality. It seems that to a certain extent the situation of homosexuals in Lebanon in the 2000s corresponds to that which prevailed in postwar Germany.

Al-Daif had visited Helfer for several weeks in Berlin, and the latter repaid the visit and spent several weeks with his Lebanese colleague in Beirut. While in Beirut, Helfer became acquainted with a German journalist working for an Anglophone newspaper published there. They became friends and talked about their respective wish for a child, finally deciding to have a child together. While Helfer was not willing to give up his long-term relationship with his partner, neither did the journalist want to give up her career. Al-Daif interprets this event as an unexpected turning point, like a device in a novel. He transforms Helfer's life story into an oriental fairy tale about the miraculous conversion of a gay European to heterosexuality. Helfer, on the contrary, vividly pleads for the warmth and security of a queer family that consists of a single straight mother, a partnered gay father, the gay father's partner in the role of the child's grandfather, the gay father's younger lover as the nanny and a most welcome, tenderly loved and happy daughter. According to Helfer, this family may be considered non-traditional but it is nevertheless functional and intact.

After the exchange, al-Daif wrote a report on his encounter with a gay man and published it in Arabic. The title of his book, *How the German Came to His Senses*, is a pun, since the Arabic word for 'senses' or 'reason' is homonymous with the author's name, Rashid. The ironic subtext of the title is not so difficult to grasp: Helfer came to his senses by visiting Rashid al-Daif. With tongue-in-cheek humour, al-Daif suggests that a man living in a same-sex relationship is insane, but his condition has a cure: 'knowing' a woman and fathering a child. Helfer, rather than flatly disallowing the publication in German of this book-length reportage on his private life, chose to respond to al-Daif's text by interspersing it, dialogically, with commentary. As he demonstrates, al-Daif reinterprets the actual events according to traditional Eastern prejudices about the character, desire and lifestyle of Western homosexual men. Sometimes, it is hard to tell whether or not the stereotypes presented by the narrator reflect the author's own beliefs. Many reviewers thought that the story told by al-Daif is self-deprecating and that he invented the role of the naïve narrator in order to ridicule homophobic anxiety in Arab societies and to prompt critical reflection. Yet Helfer not only comments on the text, but gives his own account of the actual encounter with the real person al-Daif. It was the man al-Daif, not an ironic literary mask, who did and said what Helfer reports.

Instead, Helfer chose to scrutinize the heteronormative stereotypes in both al-Daif's account and discourse, and to prove how absurd they are. He repeatedly states that such homophobic fantasies indicate a cultural anachronism rather than a fundamental gap dividing the West and the East. He interprets the level of homophobia in a culture as simply reflecting the degree to which societies have become democratic and liberal. It may be understandable if al-Daif plays the heteronormative fool in order to challenge and even expose Arab stereotypes on homosexuality. But while al-Daif performs a carnivalesque ritual of male heterosexuality, Helfer is not willing to subscribe to heteronormativity, not even tongue-in-cheek. In a sense, al-Daif is right in suggesting that Helfer came to his senses when he visited him in Lebanon. The cultural exchange program he participated in, as well as his host's account of it, inspired Helfer to write a commentary that relentlessly deconstructs all the heteronormative biases that al-Daif mocks. Helfer stirs up traditional opinions about gender and sexuality. He juggles with the distinctions of sex and gender, men and women, homosexuality and heterosexuality until not one stone is left standing.

After the vicissitudes of one hundred and fifty years of Berlin literature – from the beginnings of the German Empire to the first decades after the fall of the Wall – Helfer's book may be considered as something of a herald. It takes the narrative of 'difference from the others', which has been outlined here in its variety of forms, into a new chapter. And so it looks forward to genuinely queer writing in and of Berlin in its contemporary, transculturally complicated condition.

NOTES

1. *Schwarzbuch Deutsch: Die Liste der untergegangenen Wörter*, ed. Johannes Thiele (Wiesbaden: Matrixverlag, 2006), p. 20.
2. *Strafgesetzbuch für das Deutsche Reich vom 15. Mai 1871*; http://lexetius.com/ StGB/175,7 (accessed 20 July 2015, emphasis added).
3. Reiffegg (i.e. Otto Kiefer), *Die Bedeutung der Jünglings-Liebe für unsere Zeit* (Leipzig: Max Spohr, 1902), p. 23; Reiffegg refers here to Hanns Fuchs-Stadthagen, 'Die dichterische Verwertung der Homosexualität', *Der Literat: Monats-Schrift für öffentliches Leben, Kunst und Literatur*, 2.1 (1901), 98–102 (101).
4. David J. Prickett, 'Defining Identity via Homosexual Spaces: Locating the Male Homosexual in Weimar Berlin', *Women in German Yearbook*, 21 (2005), 134–62 (140).
5. Sabine Rohlf, 'Antifaschismus und die Differenz der Geschlechter in *Der große Mann* von Heinrich Mann', in *Gender – Exil – Schreiben*, ed. J. Schöll (Würzburg: Königshausen & Neumann, 2002), pp. 147–62.
6. Norman Domeier, *Der Eulenburg-Skandal: Eine politische Kulturgeschichte des Kaiserreichs* (Frankfurt am Main and New York: Campus, 2010).
7. Anonymous, *Liebchen: Ein Roman unter Männern* (Vienna/Leipzig: Wiener Verlag, 1908), p. 18 (henceforth *L*). The text of the reprint (Berlin: Janssen, 1995) is not quite reliable.
8. Ellipsis in original.
9. Klaus Mann, *Der Vulkan: Roman unter Emigranten*, 3rd edn (Reinbek bei Hamburg: Rowohlt, 2004), p. 8 (henceforth *V*).
10. Klaus Mann, 'Homosexualität und Faschismus', *Zahnärzte und Künstler: Aufsätze, Reden, Kritiken 1933-1936*, ed. Uwe Naumann and Michael Töteberg (Reinbek bei Hamburg: Rowohlt, 1993), pp. 235–41 (p. 237).
11. Matthias Frings, *Der letzte Kommunist: Das traumhafte Leben des Ronald M. Schernikau* (Berlin: Aufbau, 2009).
12. The volume appeared in English under the title *What Makes a Man? Sex Talk in Beirut and Berlin*, trans. Ken Seigneurie and Gary Schmidt (Austin: Texas University Press, 2015).

II

YASEMIN YILDIZ

Berlin as a Migratory Setting

In his 1943 novel *Kürk Mantolu Madonna* (Madonna in a Fur Coat), Sabahattin Ali presents the story of the extremely introverted and peculiar Turkish man named Raif who spends a few years in 1920s Berlin.[1] Aimlessly wandering the streets and the parks of the city, minimally pursuing the ostensible purpose of his stay in educating himself in modern industrial technologies to adapt in his family's business back in Turkey, he is an observer who remains a foreigner not just to others but also to himself. Nevertheless, Berlin is also the place where he encounters a great love that almost leads him to finally find happiness. His complex relationship with the German-Jewish painter and singer Maria, a radical 'new woman', takes him to diverse, identifiable corners of the city and its surroundings. Based on the author's own stay in the city in the late 1920s, the Berlin cityscape is an integral part of this Modernist novel. Written in Turkish in 1930s Turkey and translated into German only in 2008, this novel reminds us that 'Berlin literature' need not be coterminous with 'German literature'. For 'Berlin' is written in many languages, in many different places, and circulates at times far from the city itself.

Thinking of the literature of Berlin as multilingual and transnational gives us an expanded view of what could belong to this corpus. At the same time, the distinction between 'literature of Berlin' and 'German literature' invites us to think of the former as a particular analytical lens, rather than just a thematic focus. This lens foregrounds the local while not taking the national dimension for granted. It can thereby draw attention to the production and interplay of local, national and transnational dimensions in a given work. Through this lens, even works written in Berlin and published in German can be revisited for the way in which they negotiate multiple locales, histories and memories. In this chapter, I thus propose to use this category as an opening to understand transnational dynamics precisely through the very local.

The interplay of the local, national and transnational can of course be found in the literatures of other urban centres as well. But the specifics of Berlin's history and demographics ensure the distinctive nature of literary encounters with this city. Its late but rapid growth and modernization, its status as the centre of a genocidal and then defeated state, its division into two and its path in reunification – a capital city marketed as 'poor but sexy' – all mark a unique set of circumstances that literary works engage with but also help to shape. The postwar condition of Berlin as a city divided between two Germanys, for instance, has had a particular resonance for Korean and Korean-German authors. As critic Yun-Yong Choi argues, Berlin has lent itself to thinking through the postwar Korean experience of division into two states.[2] For much of postwar history, Choi further notes, it was easier for South Koreans to meet North Koreans in Berlin than elsewhere, since it was the only city in the world with both a South and a North Korean embassy. Korean literature on Berlin thus treats the German city as a space of possibility for working through Korean concerns and is just one illustration of how the uses and imaginations of 'Berlin' differ widely across contexts.

The transnational literary circulation of Berlin owes much to individuals whose paths led them to and through the city. Like Sabahattin Ali, numerous individuals who stayed in Berlin temporarily – as visitors, as students or on professional assignment – have produced literary works deeply entwined with the city. Christopher Isherwood is the most prominent of these. His *Goodbye to Berlin* (1939; adapted as the film *Cabaret* (1972)), has shaped the image of interwar Berlin on the verge of Nazi takeover as a sexually permissive and politically tense arena. While Isherwood's writing and its subsequent adaptations have been received and incorporated into the self-image of the city, the writings of other temporary Berlin residents have had their impact primarily elsewhere. Maybe the best example of such a case is that of Japanese author Mori Ogai, who studied in Berlin in the 1880s. His Berlin-based story 'Maihime: The Dancing Girl' (1890) is widely considered a breakthrough text of modern Japanese literature for the novel way in which it renders subjectivity. As critic Ai Maeda demonstrates, the protagonist's subjectivity in turn is crucially intertwined with the depiction of the Berlin cityscape.[3] The plot of Ogai's story unfolds around a Japanese student's affair with a poor German girl in Berlin. A classic trope of city literature, a (male) foreign visitor's sexual relationship with a local resident is a frequent motif of this type of transnational writing. Likewise, wandering around the city in the style of a flâneur and sexual exploration often go hand in hand. And in another commonality, these temporary residents tend to write in their original languages rather than in German and publish their works elsewhere, thus producing the aforementioned versions of Berlin in many languages.

Keeping this diverse archive in mind, this chapter will focus, however, on the literary production of those who have migrated to and *settled* in the city. In contrast to passing observers, these authors negotiate a complex, multilocal relationship to the city as a *home* rather than as a curious spectacle or site of adventure. As such, they also offer a different challenge to the conception of what Berlin is and of who counts as a Berliner than do authors who see themselves and are seen by others as mere transient guests.

For a long time, migrations have been seen as marking the arrival of outsiders who had to adapt to the new place, while the place itself was thought of as defined solely by the 'natives'. Newer conceptions of migration, however, challenge such a view. The Dutch cultural studies scholars Murat Aydemir and Alex Rotas adapt the term 'migratory settings' to capture the fact that migrations thoroughly affect places.[4] Rather than understanding migration as merely 'movement from place to place', they invite us to think of migration as 'installing movement *within* place'.[5] In this conception, migration becomes a deeply local affair, shaping the place in multifarious ways instead of just being external or incidental to it. Aydemir and Rotas draw attention particularly to a range of intangible effects. For them migration leads to place being 'thickened' as 'it becomes the setting of the variegated memories, imaginations, dreams, fantasies, nightmares, anticipations and idealizations that experiences of migration, of both migrants and native inhabitants, bring into contact with each other'.[6] This conception applies particularly well to urban sites, which, as Andreas Huyssen has argued, are always densely palimpsestic in the layers and cross-connections of histories, memories and desires.[7] At times 'thickened' in this manner and at times stripped down, migratory settings reveal the negotiation of multiple spaces and imaginations not necessarily contained by national borders or horizons.

Although migrations have been integral to the making and shaping of Berlin, they are not always integrated into general narratives about the city's history and present. To give a sense of their nature and extent throughout the city's history, the next section provides an overview of significant migrations to Berlin. As we will see, different waves of French and Eastern European arrivals, in particular, have shaped the character of the city. The remainder of the chapter then focuses on the settlement and literary works of Turkish-Germans, the city's largest immigrant community since the 1970s. Texts by Turkish-German authors of different generations engaging in depth with local history and memory (Aras Ören), the division of Berlin into East and West (Emine Sevgi Özdamar), and the fall of the Wall (Yadé Kara) are the springboard to investigate the different ways Berlin is constructed as a migratory setting in contemporary literature.

Migrations and the Making of Berlin

Although Berlin seems self-evidently a German capital now, the earliest German settlers were themselves new arrivals compared to the local Slavic population that initially established itself in the area. The first rise of Berlin from a rather small and backwards town to a slowly, but steadily growing city resulted in part from the immigration policy of its early modern Hohenzollern rulers. As part of their development plan, they invited particular groups of religious refugees and immigrants into the city. Thus, French Huguenots arrived in the late seventeenth century, followed by other Protestant refugees such as the Bohemians. Remnants of the 'Bohemian village' where most of the latter lived are still visible in today's Neukölln district, while the French Cathedral on the Gendarmenmarkt square built by the Huguenots is among the most well-known architectural monuments of the city centre. Smaller groups at this time included Flemish, Dutch, Danish and Jewish immigrants. As was the case with subsequent newcomers, each of these groups brought diverse languages, cultural habits and professional skills to the city and thereby shaped it significantly. This change in turn drew further arrivals of German speakers from elsewhere, and the city grew. In the eighteenth century, Berlin thus had a rather mixed population, with a strong French presence constituting about 20 per cent of the inhabitants at one point. Well-known German writers of Huguenot background include the Romantic author Friedrich de la Motte Fouqué (1777–1843), famous for his mermaid novella *Undine* (1811), and novelist Theodor Fontane (1819–98), one of the most significant Berlin authors of the late nineteenth century. The literary impact of communal migrations may accordingly continue to be felt generations later, as descendants stake out their place in the city's culture.

After the Huguenots, two other distinct French groups contributed to the shaping of late eighteenth and early nineteenth century Berlin. Numerous political refugees from the French Revolution sought safety in the city. Among them was the young aristocrat Louis Charles Adélaïde de Chamissot de Boncourt who would go on to learn German and become a well-known German Romantic writer under the name Adelbert von Chamisso (1781–1838). His most famous work is *Peter Schlemihl's wundersame Geschichte* (Peter Schlemihl's Wondrous Story (1814)), whose protagonist sells his shadow and ends up crisscrossing the world in his seven-mile boots without ever finding a home. Today, the most important literary prize for non-German authors is named after him, and some critics speak of 'Chamisso authors' when referring to writers who adopt German as a literary language later in life.[8] In fact, all three Turkish-German authors to be discussed later in this chapter have won the Chamisso Prize: Ören in 1985, Özdamar in 1998 and Kara in 2004. While the French language and culture had been highly admired until then, Napoleon's occupation of Berlin in the early 1800s led to a major reorientation and to politically anti-French attitudes. Although short-lived, the occupation forced a series of bureaucratic, educational and military reforms that altered both the city and the Prussian state substantially. Today's Humboldt University was founded in this context, for example (see Chapter 2).

Despite earlier diversity and growth, it took a true mass migration of unprecedented scale to make Berlin into a modern metropolis. Particularly after becoming the capital of the newly formed German Reich in 1871, the city nearly quadrupled its population from about one million around 1870 to close to four million by 1914. Most of the new arrivals came from the East; a substantial number of them were Polish. They worked in the rapidly growing manufacturing industries of the city. Writers such as Clara Viebig (1860–1952) chronicled the difficult experiences of these newcomers from Eastern, rural areas.

Though much smaller in number than the French communities and much more radically circumscribed in their movements and their rights, Jewish immigrants and their descendants also played a significant role in the cultural life of the city from the late eighteenth century onwards. The great Enlightenment philosopher Moses Mendelssohn (1729–86) arrived there from Dessau and became a key figure and facilitator of modern German-Jewish culture. The most exciting salons of the late eighteenth and early nineteenth centuries were run by Jewish women such as Henriette Herz (1764–1847) and Rahel Varnhagen von Ense (1771–1833), whose families had established themselves in Germany a few generations earlier. A new wave of Jewish migration to Berlin came in the early twentieth century as many Eastern European Jews moved to the city to escape pogroms and persecution in Czarist Russia. While some of the more affluent families established themselves in the bourgeois neighbourhood of Charlottenburg, then nicknamed 'Charlottengrad', most of the poor lived in an area near Alexanderplatz called the 'Scheunenviertel', which itself has become subject to mythologizing accounts in German literature. As a result of this migration, Berlin in the interwar years housed the largest number of Yiddish-language presses in the world, and significant Yiddish writers such as Modernist author David Bergelson (1884–1952) worked there, underscoring the multi-lingualizing effects of migration on urban spaces.

The 1917 October revolution also brought an influx of non-Jewish Russian refugees to Berlin. One of the initial destinations of aristocratic, anti-Communist Russian exiles, Berlin sheltered thousands of them until the mid-1920s. Among these was Vladimir Nabokov (1899–1977), who lived in the city from 1922 to 1937 and wrote many of his major Russian works there. In contrast to someone like Isherwood, who was drawn to the city and lived there by choice, Nabokov was an unwilling exile from his homeland and thus had an ambivalent relationship to Berlin, a place where his father was killed by a fellow Russian émigré. Despite the extended period of his stay, he never embraced the city and claimed not to have learned the language or met its people. Yet Weimar Berlin is a backdrop or setting of novels such as *Mashen'ka* (1926; translated as *Mary* (1970)) and stories such as 'A Guide to Berlin' (1925). The gloomily represented city often functions as a key contrast to the vivid depictions of Russia found in these works. Nabokov's case highlights the significance of the type of mobility that takes individuals and communities to a new place and that leaves its mark on the writing produced about it. Exile provides a potentially much more conflicted lens on a place than voluntary travel and temporary residence do.

This distinction between types of mobility and their literary manifestation also comes to bear on the entirely different migration from the Soviet Union that occurred decades later. The end of the Cold War enabled new migration patterns from Eastern Europe, which have in turn had a major impact on post-unification German literature. Many of the most critically and/or commercially successful authors of the last two decades have been Eastern and Southeastern European immigrants and refugees who have begun to publish in German. The most popular among these is Russian-Jewish author Wladimir Kaminer, whose first book, *Russendisko* (Russians' Disco (2000)), consists of highly entertaining short tales, which describe the lives of Russian arrivals in the city in 1989 as wild and bizarre adventures. The title of the book is taken from the club night featuring current Russian music that Kaminer co-initiated as a DJ at the East Berlin Kaffee Burger, which has become a cultural phenomenon in its own right. In Kaminer's writing, specific aspects and places in the city, particularly the Eastern part where the author lives, appear in a new light as mysterious places of possibility and cross-ethnic interaction. While stories set in the Soviet Union also appear in his writing, they are not rendered in any nostalgic or longing way, but rather, in Kaminer's typical comic mode, they provide a broader context and a sense of mobility and fluidity for his Russian immigrant figures in Berlin.

Berlin, as this short account indicates, has never been an ethnically homogenous place. Instead, its demographic has changed over time in relationship to larger geopolitical developments. The various French and Eastern European migrations have added crucial layers to the palimpsest that is the city. Some of these layers are still visible in the urban architecture (such as the

Gendarmenmarkt), while others exist primarily as cultural memory (such as the destroyed Scheunenviertel). The literature to which these migrations have given rise in the short or long term is first and foremost characterized by its belonging to its literary historical context, whether that is Romanticism, Realism, Modernism or contemporary Pop Literature. It is also further refracted through the particular type of displacement that brought its authors to the city. The themes of belonging, alienation and difference that appear in these texts are negotiated through these different modes. In the following, the focus will be on writers of Turkish background who have settled in Berlin, published in German and engaged with the city as a complicated home.

Berlin in Turkish-German Perspective

When the protagonist of the 2011 big-budget action film *Unknown*, played by Liam Neeson, arrives in Berlin, one of the first locals he encounters is a Turkish cab driver. The viewer enters the city accompanied by the sounds of the cabbie's Turkish conversation on his cell phone. In this manner, the film establishes the Turkish presence as characteristic of the Berlin scene: you know you are in Berlin when you hear someone speak Turkish. The Turkish presence, in other words, has become part of the imagination of contemporary Berlin in global popular culture. How did this presence come about? Although individual Turkish residents – such as Sabahattin Ali – can be documented as far back as the seventeenth century, the current communities are the result of more recent developments. In fact, the history of Turkish mass migration to Germany is intimately tied to Berlin history and especially the historical edifice of the Berlin Wall.

While West Germany had begun recruiting guest workers from Italy (1955), Spain and Greece (1960) for its booming economy, the need for labour grew further with the building of the Wall in the summer of 1961. At that time, divided Berlin was a point of emigration for GDR citizens, who could and did leave their country in significant numbers via the subway and other crossings. Some East Germans also worked in the Western part of town and commuted home each day. This supply of labour was suddenly cut off with the building of the Wall. To satisfy the need for new workers, West Germany turned to another country: Turkey. The labour recruitment agreement with Turkey was signed less than three months after the construction of the Wall, in the autumn of 1961, and began to bring a new group of nationals to the city. In contrast to some countries, such as then still-fascist Spain, that were reluctant to send their citizens to the most critical border region of the Cold War for fear of Communist agitation, the Turkish state willingly provided workers to West Berlin. As a result of these policies, the Turkish population there grew throughout the 1960s and particularly in the 1970s, when the workers' family members began to arrive in greater numbers. Later waves of immigration from Turkey added leftist political refugees who fled the 1980 military coup and ethnic Kurds who escaped massive repression in the 1980s and 1990s. As these latter cases also begin to indicate, immigrants from Turkey comprise a highly diverse group in many regards. Besides ethnic Turks and Kurds, the population includes smaller communities such as Armenians and Assyrians, with groups subscribing to a wide variety of religious and political beliefs. Today estimated at 200,000 or about 6 per cent of the total population of the city, Berliners whose families hail from Turkey constitute the city's largest minority.

Paradoxically, this Turkish presence has been both highly visible and discounted at the same time. The visibility of the Turkish communities in Berlin has registered particularly in a variety of popular formats over the last decades. When David Bowie lived in the city during the late 1970s, the Turkish music he encountered there inspired songs such as 'Neukoln' and 'Yassassin' (whose title means 'live long' in Turkish), which draw on Turkish musical features. Contemporary travel guides to Berlin regularly incorporate the Turkish presence as an exotic feature of the city, directing visitors for example to the immensely popular Turkish open-air market along the Maybachufer Canal between Kreuzberg and Neukölln. Mainstream German discourse, meanwhile, has treated the Turkish presence in more ambivalent ways. Even though clustering with fellow immigrants and persisting as communities is a characteristic feature of migration both historically in Berlin (recall the 'Bohemian village') and internationally (think of 'Little Italy' and 'Chinatown'), German media and political discourse has frequently seen the settled Turkish community as problematic and worrisome, with the notion of unruly 'ghettos' and 'parallel worlds' dominating representations.

As in the popular imagination, the Turkish presence in the literature of Berlin has most often been of a superficial type. Heidrun Suhr observed in 1990 that Turkish immigrants '[a]s an integral part of the city's local color ... are present, as backdrop, in all forms of [contemporary] fiction'.[9] Yet as this description confirms, the Turkish presence has more often served as a background rather than occupying the foreground for most non-Turkish German authors, reflecting a hesitation to integrate it into city narratives. Even a case such as Uwe Timm's Berlin novel *Rot* (Red (2001)), where a Turkish-German character, Nilgün, appears as a secondary but outspoken figure in the narrative, is not yet commonplace.

Sten Nadolny's 1990 novel *Selim oder die Gabe der Rede* (Selim or the Gift of Speech) is not only one of the major exceptions in this regard but also provides a powerful image for this uneven presence. In Nadolny's novel, labour migration is an integral part of the story of postwar West Germany. Alongside the primary narrator Alexander, Selim and a number of other Turkish guest workers play a pivotal role. In the late 1960s, Selim and his coworkers build a bridge over the Teltow Canal in Berlin.[10] Managed by dubious subcontractors, the work proceeds under exploitative conditions in sub-zero temperatures, which leave workers sick and exhausted. Years later, the novel's narrator Alexander visits 'Selim's bridge' on a summer's day. 'You can't tell the anguish of those days by looking at it',[11] he notes, as he gazes at the idyllic scene of hobby fishermen dozing by the canal. Instead of carrying any visible trace of the Turkish immigrant workers who built it, the bridge now features multiple graffiti that read: 'Türken raus' ('Turks out').[12] The bridge, itself a highly symbolic spatial construct connecting two opposite sides, becomes a place where the impact of migration is both materially present and invisible at the same time. Migrants contribute directly to the urban landscape and the infrastructure that makes it the particular place it is. However, their contribution remains invisible as long as it is not narrated. In the absence of such narration, it becomes the writing surface for anti-immigrant sentiments. By staging both the original contribution and its forgetting, and subsequent radical reversal, Nadolny's novel makes this landscape legible as a conflictual migratory setting.

In contrast to prevalent discourses that see the Turkish presence either as colourful and exotic or as disturbing and alien, but in any case at most as backdrop, Turkish-German literature of Berlin demonstrates a marked entanglement with local sites, histories, and cultural memories that signals complex belonging. In fact, Turkish-German literature of Berlin is itself a literary archive that captures perspectives on and histories of the city that have frequently not achieved entry to non-migrant literary texts. These perspectives themselves are time and again informed by transnational vantage points that raise the question of how exactly to delimit the borders of the 'local'. As the following examples reveal, instead of simply putting migration in the foreground, this literature constellates multiple histories that do not usually get told together. In each of these examples, Berlin is described in identifiable ways that refer to the city map and make the steps of these protagonists and the gazes of the narrators locatable in a realist space. Yet they also add to and rearrange the layers of the palimpsest that make up these spaces already.

A Berlin Street Transformed by Migration: Aras Ören

As is so often the case with new immigrants, Turkish arrivals in Berlin were pushed into less desirable corners of town, particularly rundown working-class areas close to the Wall. In this manner, 1970s Kreuzberg became home to a large enough number of Turkish immigrants to be referred to as 'Little Istanbul', adding a new spatial configuration to the Berlin map. Although by no means the sole Berlin neighbourhood to feature in Turkish-German literature, Kreuzberg has since become an iconic and frequent reference point there. Aras Ören's 1973 book-length epic poem *Was will Niyazi in der Naunynstraße* (What Does Niyazi Want in Naunyn Street), which is generally considered a quintessential text of so-called 'guest worker literature' and is the first Turkish-German literary text to garner attention in Germany, zeroes in on a specific street within the neighbourhood to trace the transformations brought about by migration in an innovative form.

A Turkish theatre actor and poet, author Ören (b. 1939 in Istanbul) first came to Berlin in the 1960s before marrying a German designer and settling in the city for good in 1969. Not a guest worker himself, he has nevertheless long been fascinated by the changes brought about by migration. Much of his work touches on this process in different genres and styles, from poems and short stories to novels and essays, over the years moving from leftist engaged literature to postmodern self-reflexivity. With many of his works set in different parts of the city, Ören has been recognized as a Berlin author and was inducted into the Berlin-based German Academy of Arts in 2012, where his literary archive is also held.

Written in free verse, *Was will Niyazi in der Naunynstraße* follows the thoughts and reminiscences of a cross-section of the inhabitants of the street. Although his name appears in the title, Niyazi Gümüskilic is only one of several figures we encounter in the poem. From the pensive German widow Frau Kutzer to the entrepreneurial Turkish guest worker Ali, from the troubled German working-class man Klaus Feck to the promiscuous Turkish female guest worker Halime, the text moves across nationalities and genders to give a multi-perspective view of the evolving neighbourhood. In this mixture, neither the Turkish nor the German neighbours function as mere 'backdrop' for each other but rather together constitute Naunynstraße as a migratory setting.

As the title indicates, the poem's exploration of migration's effects takes place not on the national or even transnational scale, but rather in the engagement with the very local. The present of the poem stays anchored in the specific location of Naunynstraße and its immediate vicinity throughout. This 'local' scale, meanwhile, is itself open to resituating and 'thickening' (in the sense of Aydemir and Rotas). After introducing the street in anthropomorphizing ways, as ready to 'awaken' in the snow, the poem begins with Niyazi on his way to work in the early morning hours:

> Niyazi Gümüskilic aus der Naunynstraße
> Geht mit schnellen Schritten,
> Wie Mitte September,
> zum Blaufischfang in der Bucht von Bebek
> geht er spät, mit schnellen Schritten,
> den Kopf tief zwischen den Schultern,
> zur Nachtschicht.
>
> (Niyazi Gümüskilic from Naunyn Street
> Walks with fast steps,
> As if in the middle of September,
> To catch blue fish in the bay of Bebek
> He goes late, with fast steps,
> Head set deep between his shoulders,
> To the night shift.)[13]

While Niyazi is located in and even identified as 'from' Naunynstraße in the present of the poem, his own steps simultaneously call up a different time and place, namely a past September in the Istanbul district of Bebek (to whose history of gentrification the poem later returns more fully). Through Niyazi's bodily movement Naunynstraße becomes the site in which the reader briefly glimpses an Istanbul neighbourhood, and thus the poem becomes multilocal. The poem, then, figures migration not through a retracing of the movements of individuals from one national place to another as in a classic migration story with departure, arrival, and adjustment, but rather through an emphasis on the resonance of multiple spaces in the place of settlement. The local site of Naunynstraße is in the foreground, yet through the movements of a figure it is already shot through with the presence of other localities ('Bebek') in a new transnational imaginary.

The poem's preoccupation with the local and its resituating of what 'local' means can also be observed in its next move. As Niyazi leaves the street, the poem remains there and shifts its focus to Frau Kutzer, who is lying in her bed, rubbing her cold feet and calling up her working-class Berlin life. The poem's extended sections on Frau Kutzer tell her personal and family story: from life in the late stages of the Kaiserreich and during World War I, through the upheavals of the Weimar Republic, the near-arrest of Frau Kutzer's Communist husband by the Nazis and his quick political resignation, the black market economy of the early postwar years, and up to her own present situation as an impoverished and lonely widow observing life in a consumption-oriented world from a distance. Through this vantage point, the reader encounters a succinct but broad view of twentieth-century German, and more specifically Berlin, history, with insights into individual dreams and disappointments attached to specific locations in the city.

This seemingly very 'German' memory of Berlin in the twentieth century, however, is written by its Turkish-German author in Turkish. Like almost all of his other works, Ören wrote the text first in Turkish but with an eye towards immediate translation into German. It was in fact published in a German translation in which Ören collaborated in 1973, long before the Turkish 'original', *Niyazi'nin Naunyn Sokağı'nda İşi Ne?*, appeared in 1980. Content, language and publication history of this text thus do not neatly follow national lines. Instead, the poem turns Turkish into a local language, in which diverse Berlin histories and memories can be imagined and put into transnational, translational circulation. Likewise, the form of the poem itself is indebted to the great Turkish modernist poet Nazim Hikmet, whose 'epic novel in verse',[14] *Memleketimden İnsan Manzaraları* (Human Landscapes from my Homeland (first published in 1967)), paints a multiperspectival, panoramic view of the new Turkish nation. Ören adapts this form, yet not for the purpose of narrating nation but of exploring the settings of migration. With its emphasis on the internal monologues of both migrant and non-migrant Berlin figures, highlighting their memories, dreams, fears, disappointments and hopes, together with its translational form, Ören's poem thus performs poetically how 'migration installs movement in place' decades before the theoretical formulations of Aydemir and Rotas.

1970s Naunynstraße was only one block over from the Berlin Wall, yet the poem barely mentions it or the division of the city. Even as this literary work expands backwards in time and indexes local specificity, the topic of German division remains outside its purview. In this manner, we are reminded that this poem, like all literary works, produces an imaginative geography, not an actual map of the city. Other Turkish-German writers, however, have incorporated the divided nature of Berlin in their works and built a different imagined geography around it, and none more so than Emine Sevgi Özdamar.

Moving across the East-West Divide: Emine Sevgi Özdamar

Within the German-language literature of Berlin, the division of the city has primarily been seen as a German-German issue, in which Turkish-German immigrants, despite their status as the largest resident minority during much of the Wall's existence, do not feature significantly. Yet, as we will see in this section and in the next, for a number of Turkish-German authors, division is an inextricable part of the migratory setting that they explore. Divided Berlin is a setting in many of the texts of Emine Sevgi Özdamar (b. 1946 in Malatya/Turkey), one of the critically most acclaimed Turkish-German authors. In fact, from her first collection, *Mutterzunge* (Mother Tongue (1990)), to the two later parts of her Istanbul-Berlin trilogy and numerous shorter stories and essays, Özdamar's literary Berlin topography encompasses both parts of the city to an unusual degree. Drawing heavily on her own life story, her second novel *Brücke vom Goldenen Horn* (Bridge of the Golden Horn (1999)) follows an eighteen-year-old Turkish girl who arrives in West Berlin in 1965 as a guest worker. Wanting to earn money for acting school in Istanbul, the young woman begins to observe her German environment and becomes a witness to the historical moment leading up to the 1968 upheavals. She herself becomes politicized during her time in the city while working in a radio lamp factory and living near the ruins of the Anhalter Bahnhof train station. Told with much humour, irony, and wordplay, the novel paints a picture of the late 1960s that precedes the West Berlin of Ören's *Niyazi*, even though it was written decades later. The second part moves to Istanbul and observes the Turkish version of 1968.

Although Berlin's division is already present in *Brücke vom Goldenen Horn*, it comes fully to the foreground in Özdamar's third novel, *Seltsame Sterne starren zur Erde: Wedding–Pankow 1976/77* (Strange Stars Stare to Earth: Wedding–Pankow 1976/77 (2003)). Without explicitly referring back to the earlier book, *Seltsame Sterne* continues the story of a Turkish theatre actress who now returns from Istanbul to Berlin. In Turkey, she had been banned from artistic work as a result of political repression after the 1971 military coup. Leaving behind both the political situation and a failed marriage in Istanbul, she comes to Berlin for an unofficial internship at the Volksbühne in East Berlin, one of the GDR's foremost theatres. Due to visa regulations, however, she also has to spend considerable time in West Berlin, where she ends up living in a student commune. Written in 2003, the novel does not return to the moment of unification like so many *Wenderomane* (novels of unification) do, but rather unfolds a cultural memory of late-1970s 'German-German' history, when the effects of division were particularly pronounced.

Through a Turkish protagonist who repeatedly moves back and forth between the two parts of the city, *Seltsame Sterne* develops a migratory gaze that renders the division of Berlin as a state both of separation and of connection. A repeated sentiment when crossing the border is the surprise of the narrator at the weather 'Hier regnet es ja wie im Osten' ('Oh, here it is also raining like in the East').[15] This surprise indicates that what is difficult to grasp about Cold War Berlin is not the division but rather the simultaneity of the co-existence of the two parts. Absolute separateness is so ingrained in the experience of the divided city that the true challenge lies in recovering its existence in the same plane of reality, even as social, political and cultural differences persist. One of the major feats of Özdamar's *Seltsame Sterne* is to accomplish this volatile dance between disjuncture and continuity. Both parts of the divided city become lived-in places and reference points via the criss-crossing protagonist and first-person narrator who renders the peculiarities of the cultural objects, habits and urban landscape of East and West via the curious gaze of a semi-outsider/semi-insider in both places.

The form of the novel further underscores the representational problematics posed by a divided city and experiments with a solution for it. Like the city, the autobiographical novel is divided into two distinct parts. The first is a retrospective narrative told by the first-person narrator of the period 1976–7 and takes place predominantly in West Berlin. The commune in which the protagonist lives is a site through which the novel depicts the shift in the leftist student movement's emphasis from political to individual transformation. The narrator observes her German roommates' search for alternative paths in therapy, sexual experimentation and the reorganization of everyday life. The large, freestanding tub in the bathroom without a door, in which all roommates bathe together, encapsulates this desire for unconventional practices. Political events such as the pursuit of the terrorists of the Red Army Faction in the 'German autumn' of 1977 likewise come close to the protagonist who is without papers for a significant part of the time.

The second part of *Seltsame Sterne* switches to the form of contemporaneous diary entries of the actress from that period, primarily recording her stay in East Berlin. In contrast to the everyday figures the novel introduces in the Western part – their everydayness marked by the fact that they only have first names – numerous identifiable cultural figures of the GDR appear in the later pages of the book, such as the well-known actress Gabriele Gysi; her father, the GDR culture minister Klaus Gysi; and her brother, the lawyer and politician Gregor Gysi. Revisiting a decisive moment in GDR history, the novel closely observes the repression of dissidents such as Rudolf Bahro and Wolf Biermann and the subsequent cultural turmoil. It also records the moments when seminal theatrical works such as Heiner Müller's *Hamletmaschine* (Hamlet Machine (1977)) start to take shape. The present tense used in the diary format produces a sense of immediacy and proximity to these East German events, even as they are marked as the historical past through the date notation. East and West Berlin histories, the novel thus suggests, continue to operate along different temporal registers of memory in the early 2000s.

As Ela Gezen notes, these observations of East and West Berlin are crucially triangulated with Turkish political history and repeated invocations of Istanbul locations.[16] In a diary entry from May 1976, the narrator relates sitting in the Volksbühne canteen and thinking 'Ach, schöne Jahre, in Berlin auf der Bühne stehen, Josef, ach, Wald in Istanbul, ach, die Toten, die Getöteten. Ich bin nicht rückwärts gegangen, ich bin nach vorne geflüchtet, alles in Ordnung' (Oh, beautiful years, being on the stage in Berlin, Josef, oh, the forest in Istanbul, oh, the dead, the murdered. I did not go backwards, I escaped forwards, everything is ok).[17] Moving from the present in (East) Berlin to the past in Istanbul in an associative manner, the protagonist remains haunted by the memory of the victims of the military regime in Turkey. Her perspective on both sides of Berlin is 'thickenened' by this memory. That is, the construction of a cultural memory of 'German-German history', holding both sides together, is enabled by a transnational migrant whose movements in turn are propelled by personal and political dynamics in multiple places.

While Özdamar's criss-crossing narrative constructs division as a migratory setting via the movements of a singular figure and focalizer, other Turkish-German literary engagements with division at once stress and produce communal memories. Hakan Savas Mican's 2009 play *Die Schwäne vom Schlachthof* (The Swans of the Slaughterhouse) retells stories of Turkish-Germans who were entangled in the East-West divide in some form. At the centre of the play is the real-life case of Çetin Mert, who drowned in the river Spree on his fifth birthday in 1975 because the GDR forces, who had jurisdiction, refused to let Western rescuers enter the water in time. Mert was just one of a number of guest worker children who suffered this fate. Anthropologist Jeff Jurgens describes these children as the 'Wall victims from the West' and analyzes how the various publics – East, West, immigrant – responded to the deaths and how they have been commemorated since.[18] As Jurgens shows, they have been only minimally present in the memory of the city even though their cases made headlines at the time and led to large protests. It is in recent cultural work such as Mican's play that their memory has been revived. Turkish-German literature of Berlin thus at times tells deeply local stories that are neglected by the mainstream German public, which continues to have difficulty registering immigrants as residents and participants in the landscape and history of the city. Migratory settings are sometimes preserved only in the writings of minorities.

Dis/Unity after Unification: Yadé Kara

The most famous chant of East German demonstrators against their government in autumn 1989 was 'Wir sind das Volk' (We are the people). With it, they challenged the GDR government's claim to represent them and their political will and called for radical democratic changes. Yet already by late fall of the same year, this chant changed in a subtle but far-reaching way. Now protestors exclaimed 'We are one people', 'ein Volk', moving the discourse from the civic to the national register. The demand for unification with West Germany, which this altered slogan expressed, thus immediately foregrounded the issue of belonging. Who, indeed, did belong to this 'people', this 'we'? In the mainstream discourse of the time and in much literature of the so-called *Wende*, or 'turn' of unification, this event has been perceived and represented as a purely German-German affair, often cast in kinship terms. Unification, in this view, brought together long separated 'brothers and sisters', or else constituted a complicated 'marriage' between East and West.

Yadé Kara's 2003 debut novel *Selam Berlin* draws on and reworks such dominant and potentially exclusionary tropes of the period from the perspective of a minority subject.[19] Kara was born in 1965 in Turkey but grew up in Berlin from the age of six. Belonging to a younger generation than Ören and Özdamar, she is thus the only one of the three to have spent her childhood and youth in the city. The story she tells stages this kind of deep familiarity with one's hometown, only to gravitate into a sense of alienation. Set between the historically charged dates of 9 November 1989 and 3 October 1990 – that is, between the fall of the Berlin Wall and the official unification of East and West Germany – *Selam Berlin* follows nineteen-year old protagonist and first-person narrator Hasan Kazan as he tries to participate in this historic moment. Written in an initially humorous and irreverent but then increasingly serious tone, the novel charts how the unification of the city ultimately causes the breakup and reconfiguration of Hasan's family. His father, it is revealed, has had a long-term affair with an East German woman. The Wall enabled him to have two separate families in the two parts of the city without being exposed. The opening of the Wall therefore leads to a moment of familial crisis rather than celebration precisely because it can 'unify' families that had been kept apart.

Even as it is written in a breezy, colloquial style that might lead the reader to overlook the seriousness of its thrust, Kara's novel contributes to making visible the minority experience of post-unification Berlin, which diverges from that of white Germans from both East and West. Like so much contemporary minority and immigrant youth, the protagonist of *Selam Berlin* defines his identity primarily through his attachment to a city rather than a nation. Although Hasan's biography is marked by commuting between Berlin and Istanbul, he articulates a strong identification with Berlin. Whenever asked about his background in Istanbul, he responds unequivocally with 'Berlin, Berlinli ... Und dabei betonte ich Berlin so, als wäre es ein Staat für sich. Der Berliner Bär muss irgendwie durch meine Pupillen hindurchgefunkelt haben, so dass viele mir den Stolz anmerkten, ein Berliner zu sein' ('Berlin, Berlinli ... And I stressed Berlin as if it were a state unto itself. The Berlin bear must have somehow shone through my pupils so that many sensed my pride in being a Berliner'.)[20] Berlin explicitly functions as an alternative scale of belonging. The appearance of one of the few Turkish words in the German text, 'Berlinli' (Berliner), further highlights a visible, and joyful, hybrid Turkish-German identity tied to the city.

The events of the fall of the Wall are consequently recounted from the angle of this personal identification with the city rather than as a national event. Seeing the images of the newly opened Wall on Turkish television in Istanbul, Hasan exclaims: 'Massen an der Mauer; auf der Mauer; auf meiner Graffitimauer ... Plötzlich standen Straßen, Plätze, Orte meiner Kindheit im Interesse des Weltgeschehens' ('Masses at the Wall; on the Wall; on my graffiti Wall ... Suddenly streets, squares, places of my childhood were in the focus of world affairs'.)[21] What is broadcast as a historic event of global significance is highly personal for this Turkish-German subject. Instead of constituting a barrier or political symbol, the Wall appears as a deeply familiar point of orientation, tied to childhood. As a child, Hasan recalls, he found his way to school by following the Wall and on his way contributing small graffiti to it.[22] Having inscribed himself there, the disappearance of the Wall also takes traces of his childhood with it.

Through the path that Hasan subsequently takes in post-unification Berlin, the novel stages the particular experience of minority subjects of this period. As Damani Partridge has argued, rather than expanding the city, the removal of the Wall led to a paradoxical situation for many residents who did not look stereotypically 'German': their ability to move safely around the city and the larger region became unexpectedly and radically limited.[23] The writing of Afro-German poet and activist May Ayim from the period attests to this changing of the map and the urban environment. Whereas previously she had found it easier to be a Black German in Berlin than elsewhere in the country, the immediate post-Wall period brought a new sense of exclusion and dislocation: 'For the first time since I had been living in Berlin I now had to protect myself almost daily against undisguised insults, hostile looks, and/or openly racist offenses.'[24]

Although Turkish-German Berliners were clearly not the only racialized group to suffer from such experiences, the combined economic, social and spatial effects of the post-unification period led many to the frequently repeated statement 'When the Wall fell, it fell on the Turks.'[25]

Selam Berlin charts this change through the encounters of its protagonist and the cumulative effects they have on him. Hasan's sense of being a proud Berliner is deeply undercut once he leaves Istanbul and returns to Berlin. Upon arriving in the city, Hasan takes his usual underground line to go home. There, he sees East Berliners in their exploration of the Western part of the city. He views them via their clothing as other and creates a 'Western' subject position for himself. Yet he also notices them looking at him in a strange way: 'War mein Hosenschlitz auf? ... War ich von einem anderen Planeten? Ich fühlte mich begutachtet wie ein Kamel im Berliner Zoo ... Ich kam mir plötzlich so fremd vor in der Berliner U-Bahn, mit der ich praktisch aufgewachsen war' (Were my trousers unzipped? ... Was I from another planet? I felt assessed like a camel in the Berlin zoo ... I suddenly felt so foreign in the Berlin underground with which I had practically grown up.)[26] It is in this way that he begins to register a sense of displacement from the most familiar surroundings via an othering gaze directed at him. The novel does not attribute this displacement solely to East Germans. West German figures are just as active contributors to this dislocation from home. His later West German roommates, three young women from the provinces, also treat him as an exotic object of anthropological interest and constantly confront him with their stereotypes about Turks. Here, too, the very home becomes the site where an identity that to him is unproblematic ('Berlinli') is continuously questioned. He is the only native Berliner in the apartment, yet the newly arrived West German roommates continually displace him from this urban space. Situations such as these gradually increase in the course of the novel and culminate in racist attacks on him and his friends that lead them to contemplate leaving the city.[27]

Selam Berlin details the process by which the home becomes increasingly alien and uninviting as a result of the unification process. Yet the close structural parallels between the 'divided' and 'reunited' Turkish-German family and the city, on the one hand, and the coming-of-age process of the protagonist and the process of national unification, on the other, reveal a dynamic in which German national history frames the individual Turkish-German histories, even as these histories do not have a home in the telling of this national history and its celebratory accounts of 'brothers and sisters' reuniting. Despite this lack of recognition, the novel illustrates how national history becomes a migratory setting.

As the poems, novels and plays discussed here demonstrate, Turkish-German literature of Berlin is written both in Turkish and in German and evidences a strong connection to the city as a complicated home. It constitutes a cultural memory of the city from the vantage point of migration. Yet, that does not mean that only one story is told. Just as the literary forms differ, the stories that emerge, and with them the imaginary maps of the city that are constructed, vary from text to text. In other words, Turkish-German literature of Berlin is itself a historically changing, diverse body of works that produces migratory settings, combining intensely local topographies with transnational angles. Berlin, in these literary works, is never only contained or containable in an exclusively German national narrative.

Coda: Returning to Naunyn Street

In 2008, the Naunynstrasse witnessed the opening of the theatre Ballhaus Naunynstrasse, which set for itself the goal of telling diverse stories of migration and settlement in Berlin. One of the early shows at the theatre, which has since become a celebrated and influential cultural site in town and beyond, was presented as a 'performance parcour'. The series of dramatic, artistic and musical performances in quotidian Turkish-German locations such as coffee houses and sports clubs around the neighbourhood was called *Was will N. in der Naunynstrasse?* (What Does N. Want in Naunyn Street?). It also included Turkish composer Alper Maral's adaptation of *Niyazi* as a short opera. The theatre even hung a large banner across the street with a quotation from Ören's poem: 'Ein verrückter Wind eines Tages/ Wirbelte den Schnurrbart eines Türken,/ Und der Türke rannte hinter seinem Schnurrbart/ Her und fand sich in der Naunynstraße ('A crazy wind one day/ Twirled the moustache of a Turk/ And the Turk chased after his moustache/ And found himself in Naunyn Street').[28] Thus the epic poem that in recent years had been primarily known to specialists returned in this mediated form to its setting and to a larger public.

The redefinition of Naunyn Street as a site of migratory cultural memory involved a new generation of writers, performers, artists and activists who have inscribed themselves into this space in novel ways. Among them is author and curator Deniz Utlu (b. 1983 in Hannover), who served as a research assistant for the parcour and in this context learned much about the history of the street. This research, in turn, inspired his own Berlin novel *Die Ungehaltenen* (The Indignant (2014)), which continues to tell post-unification Turkish-German stories that are both locally specific and transnationally mobile.

NOTES

1. Sabahattin Ali, *Kürk Mantolu Madonna* (Istanbul: Remzi Kitabevi, 1943). *Madonna in a Fur Coat*, trans. Maureen Freely and Alexander Dawe (London: Penguin, 2016).
2. Yun-Yong Choi, 'National? Transnational oder transterritorial? Berlinbilder in koreanischen Romanen', *Deutschsprachige Literatur und Kultur*, 20 (2011), pp. 295–319.
3. Ai Maeda, 'Berlin 1888: Mori Ogai's 'Dancing Girl', trans. Leslie Pincus, *Text and the City: Essays on Japanese Modernity* (Durham: Duke University Press, 2004), pp. 295–328.
4. Murat Aydemir and Alex Rotas, 'Introduction: Migratory Settings', *Thamyris/ Intersecting*, 19 (2008), pp. 7–32.
5. Ibid., p. 7.
6. Ibid., p. 7.
7. Andreas Huyssen, *Present Pasts: Urban Palimpsests and the Politics of Memory*, (Stanford: Stanford University Press, 2003).
8. Weinrich, H. 'Chamisso, Chamisso Authors, and Globalization', trans. M. Brown and J.K. Brown, *PMLA*, 119.5 (2004), 1336–46.
9. Heidrun Suhr, '*Fremde* in Berlin: The Outsiders' View from the Inside', *Berlin: Culture and Metropolis*, ed. Charles Haxthausen and Heidrun Suhr (Minneapolis: University of Minnesota Press, 1990), 219–42, (p. 235).
10. Sten Nadolny, *Selim oder die Gabe der Rede* (Munich: Piper, 1990), 254–5.
11. Ibid., p. 258.
12. Ibid.
13. Aras Ören, *Was will Niyazi in der Naunynstraße* (Berlin: Rotbuch, 1973), p. 5.
14. Thus the subtitle of the English translation: Nazim Hikmet, *Human Landscapes from My Country: An Epic Novel in Verse*, trans. Randy Blasing and Mutlu Konuk (New York: Persea Books, 2002).
15. Emine Sevgi Özdamar, *Seltsame Sterne starren zur Erde: Wedding – Pankow 1976/77* (Cologne: Kiepenheuer & Witsch, 2003), p. 40.
16. Ela Gezen, 'Staging Berlin: Emine Sevgi Özdamar's *Seltsame Sterne starren zur Erde*', *German Studies Review*, 38.1 (2015), 83–96.
17. Özdamar, *Seltsame Sterne*, p. 104.
18. Jeff Jurgens, '"A Wall Victim from the West": Migration, German Division, and Multidirectional Memory in Kreuzberg', *TRANSIT*, 8.2 (2013), 1–23.
19. The first chapter is available in English translation: *Selam Berlin*, trans. Tim Mohr, www.wordswithoutborders.com 2009 (accessed 28 December 2014). A simple rendition of the title as 'Hello Berlin' would miss its bilingual nature.
20. Yadé Kara, *Selam Berlin* (Zurich: Diogenes, 2002), p. 18.
21. Ibid., p. 8.
22. Ibid., p. 34.
23. Damani Partridge, *Hypersexuality and Headscarves: Race, Sex, and Citizenship in the New Germany* (Bloomington, Indiana University Press, 2012).
24. May Ayim, '1990, Home/land and Unity from an Afro-German Perspective', *Blues in Black and White*, trans. Anne Adams (Trenton: Africa World Press, 2003), pp. 45–59 (p. 48).

25. Nevim Çil, 'Türkische Migranten und der Mauerfall', *Aus Politik und Zeitgeschichte*, 21–2 (2009), pp. 40–6.
26. Kara, *Selam Berlin*, p. 21.
27. In the sequel, *Café Cyprus* (2008), Hasan and his best friend have in fact moved to London.
28. Ören, *Was Will Niyazi*, p. 21.

12

DAVID BARNETT

Modern Drama and Theatre

Drama has never been terribly good at representing place. While the novel can evoke location with descriptive passages and poetry can distil it in epic or lyrical modes, drama is better at suggesting what it is like to live in particular places and times. There may be something rotten in the state of Denmark, but *Hamlet* gives the audience precious little sense of setting. Developments in scenography, since the early twentieth century, have also pushed theatre design away from naturalistic representations of place that might once have competed with the novel's evocative power. This chapter is thus not so much concerned with depictions of Berlin on stage as with the influence that the city has had on the writing and producing of drama.

The performing arts in Germany benefit from the country's late unification in 1871. Before this date, Germany was a vast patchwork of over three hundred states, dukedoms and principalities, each with their own social infrastructure, including theatres. These had been on the increase since the late eighteenth century and flourished in the nineteenth with the expansion of the urban middle class. While the British bourgeoisie valued the accumulation of capital as a way of differentiating and liberating itself from the aristocracy, its German equivalent set much stock by its investment in culture in general and the theatre in particular (as opposed to the French predilection for the novel). As a result of these historical and sociological factors, the German theatre was and is remarkably decentralized. Unified Germany retained its theatres and nationalized them shortly after the foundation of the Weimar Republic in 1918. The value it placed on theatre endures today: despite funding cuts and theatre closures that began in the wake of reunification in 1990, the German theatre system is still the most highly subsidized in Europe. High levels of subsidy have effects on both the way theatre is made and how it is received. Put rather crudely, theatres are under less pressure to fill their houses because they do not singly rely on ticket sales. Consequently, they can afford to take greater risks in terms of their repertoire and approaches to staging. In turn, audiences are exposed to more radical plays and production styles, and rather than these standing out as being exceptional, over time, they become the norm.

It may, then, seem odd to single out one city in a country that has many important theatres within its borders. Munich, Frankfurt, Leipzig, Hamburg and Dresden all boast major theatres and have contributed to the richness of German theatre culture over the years, together with theatres in more minor municipalities, like Bremen, Bochum or even little-known Anklam. Berlin, however, benefits from a number of factors that make it the most significant of Germany's theatre cities. Politically, it was the heart of Prussia, the most powerful state in pre-unification Germany, and it was the obvious choice for the capital of the new Reich in 1871. Even during the division of Germany between 1945 and 1990, when the Federal Republic made Bonn its capital, Berlin became a cultural focus of the Cold War, with the governments in the East and West pumping in money to enhance their own prestige. Also Berlin was and is Germany's most populous city, with the largest potential audience; it has correspondingly hosted the greatest number of theatres. So, while it is fair to say that the German theatre system is decentred and does not have a 'theatre capital' like London in the UK or New York in the USA, it does have a more select set of creative hubs, and Berlin is the most important of these.

Berlin offers itself as both a site of abundance, in terms of its infrastructure, and diversity, in terms of its variegated social strata. Such factors have marked the city as a particularly fertile space for the production of theatre and as a magnet for those who want to take advantages of the city's well-funded capacity to rise to aesthetic challenges and to supply audiences who may seek to engage with them. Its political centrality also puts it at the heart of debates not as present in other cities or in the provinces. However, as Bertolt Brecht noted in 1929, 'Theater "theatert" alles "ein"' ('theatre "theatres" everything into theatre').[1] That is, the institution of the theatre can have a remarkably conservative effect in that it has the propensity to transform potentially subversive or challenging work into consumable product by dint of its own production processes. The question thus arises as to how a theatre system as rich as Berlin's is able to respond to textual challenge in performance and whether its virtues can offer audiences productions that do not simply reduce innovative dramaturgies to harmless, saleable goods.

The Arrival of German Naturalism

Today, Naturalism, the accurate reproduction of everyday life without stylization, is standard fare on television and in cinemas. To an extent, it still survives in more conservative theatres as a default aesthetic, yet in the last decades of the nineteenth century, such an approach was radical and daring. Audiences, accustomed to either light, entertaining diversion or the more serious high art of Shakespeare, Goethe or Racine, were confronted with gritty depictions of social problems, often delivered in the vernacular. Berlin had hosted a production of Henrik Ibsen's *A Doll's House* in 1880, although the management sweetened the bitter pill of the final scene, in which Nora leaves her husband and children, by casting a favourite of the audience in the lead role. By 1887, Ibsen's *Ghosts*, a play that confronted the taboo topic of familial reputation and congenital syphilis, finally made its appearance on the Berlin stage and delivered a production that did not pull its punches. The full force of Naturalism with its uncompromising stance on representing reality in the raw had arrived to an audience that was both enthusiastic and hostile.

It is not surprising that the frisson of excitement drew the man who would become Germany's most important Naturalist playwright to the city. Gerhart Hauptmann was born in Silesia, a region now mostly in Poland but which was then a province of Prussia that remained German until the end of the Second World War. Hauptmann's move to Prussia's and Germany's capital in 1889 was logical: in the wake of *Ghosts*, it offered him the theatrical means to realize his ambitions of bringing German Naturalist writing to the stage. While he did not stay long, returning to Silesia two years later, he continued to have many of his plays premiered in Berlin theatres.

Over the years, Hauptmann, like Ibsen, wrote in a variety of styles, and *Die versunkene Glocke* (The Sunken Bell (1896)), a mystical, fairy-tale-like drama was his most performed play during his lifetime. However, it is as a Naturalist that he is remembered, and his play *Die Weber* (The Weavers (1892)) is perhaps the most radical example of his work in this style because of its refusal to follow the conventions of other Naturalist dramas. Based on an uprising of weavers in Silesia in 1844, the drama has no single hero as such, unlike Hauptmann's other Naturalist plays, but, rather, makes the working class itself the driver of the action. And although factory owner Dreißiger could be singled out as 'the villain', he is more a representative of forces acting upon the weavers in the form of technological modernization and its effects on artisan labour.

While the five-act structure might suggest that the play was conventional, the acts themselves shift perspective and never let the audience settle in one place. The play opens in a room in Dreißiger's house in which the weavers deliver their wares, shifts to one of the weaver's dilapidated shacks, then moves on to a pub frequented by the weavers, stops at Dreißiger's villa, and finally, in contrast, arrives at the home of the Hilse family, weavers who initially do not take part in the uprising. Each act is prefaced by and suffused with extensive stage directions that aim to confer authenticity on the action. Hauptmann also refrains from offering commentary or value judgements, preferring to let the events unfold and allowing the spectators to make up their own minds. The climactic action, for example, concerns the killing of Old Hilse, who refuses to join the uprising and continues to weave. As the military starts to shoot down the protesters, Hilse is hit by a stray bullet. The play offers no opinion on Hilse's decision: he is portrayed as neither a hero nor a fool. He finds himself in the wrong place at the wrong time, and it is the situation itself that raises the questions.

Not everyone, however, read Hauptmann's open dramaturgy like this. In a city with both a growing urban proletariat and an increasingly nervous Junker class of landed gentry and industrial bourgeoisie, forces of revolution and reaction found a social crucible in the drama. The Berlin police authority banned the play from public performance on 3 March 1892 for fear of public disturbance arising from the political implications of representing strikers on stage. *The Weavers* was consequently premiered in private for members of the Freie Bühne (free stage) theatre club on 26 February 1893. The organization had been set up in Berlin by proponents of Naturalism, and critic and director Otto Brahm was its chair. Brahm, who was a close friend of Hauptmann's, also directed the production when it was finally performed publicly on 25 September 1894, yet he, too, deviated from the presentational approach the playwright had taken. Tapping into an apparent metropolitan theatrical radicalism, the director engaged with the social tensions of the time in ways that collapse Naturalism's apparent claims to objectivity. He sought to accentuate the weavers' suffering and privations while underplaying the more positive aspects of Dreißiger and his allies. In addition, reviews of the time also suggest a perhaps surprising closeness between the actors and the audience, something one would not expect in a dramatic style famed for its attempts at impartiality. The production had thus somewhat skewed Hauptmann's aims and turned the text into something altogether more militant and emotive. The struggle for social justice in Berlin, exemplified by debates in the Reichstag, became the production's implicit co-director.

Over time, Naturalism's star began to wane. Reformers such as the Russian Vsevolod Meyerhold criticized it for its inartistic cluttering of the stage with irrelevant details, and he demanded a more stylized theatre. In France, symbolist theatre was emerging with the aim of representing only the hidden aspects of human existence through symbols, myth and mood in a deliberately poetic manner. In Germany, however, a different movement was starting to gain dominance in the early decades of the twentieth century.

The Transfiguration of an Expressionist

Today, German drama may not be that well known for its experiments with Naturalism – the Norwegian Ibsen, the Swede Strindberg and the Russian Chekhov have all endured rather better than Hauptmann – but Germany's playwrights and theatres were busy developing forms for a type of theatre that was rarely aped successfully beyond its borders. Expressionism is typified by its desire to externalize characters' interior thoughts and feelings in speeches and action that no longer resemble the everyday fare of Naturalism. Characters spew monologues that give voice to inner passions and turmoil, and settings are no longer faithful reproductions of familiar scenes, but rather dreamlike or nightmarish. Philosophically, Expressionism was associated with the realization of 'the new human being', born of urban modernity. The two leading exponents of this style were Georg Kaiser and Ernst Toller. Kaiser's plays mostly premiered in Frankfurt, Toller's in Berlin. Kaiser worked through the moral rebirth of his characters; Toller was the more overtly political writer, experimenting with the development of new people for a new politics in a city that saw burgeoning numbers of workers theatre groups. He was a convinced socialist and had actively taken part in the failed revolution in Munich in 1918–19 in which he was briefly chair of the Soviet. At this time he wrote his first major play, *Die Wandlung* (Transfiguration (1919)), and completed it in prison. Having been charged with high treason in the wake of his revolutionary activity, he spent five years behind bars and, having been banished from Bavaria, moved to Berlin as a centre of revolutionary innovation in the theatre upon his release in July 1924.

His time in the capital brought him into contact with one of the most important theatre-makers of the Weimar Republic, the director Erwin Piscator. Piscator had taken advantage of the capital's theatre infrastructure and pushed it as far as possible to develop a multimedia stage onto which films were projected and challenging new sets and structures were erected. Toller began work on a play that was designed to survey Weimar society and its political interconnections. *Hoppla, wir leben!* (Hoppla, We're Alive! (1927)) is a product of a not altogether easy collaboration between playwright and director, although the final production rewarded both with plaudits.

The prologue follows an uprising in 1919, an autobiographical nod from Toller, and is set in a prison cell. The six revolutionaries await news of their fate. The death sentence is handed down to all defendants, but the president of the new republic simultaneously issues a pardon. Four of the revolutionaries are sent to an internment camp before release; Karl Thomas, for whom the experience is too much, spends the next eight years in an asylum and is released in 1927. It is through his eyes that the rest of the play unfolds, in five acts. He is thus able to see the characters and situations afresh, having missed out on the birth and development of the new republic. Unlike Toller's earlier Expressionist work, *Hoppla* avoids the dominance of Thomas's subjective experience and takes in wider aspects of the urban political milieu: the *dramatis personae* runs to forty-nine named figures as well as additional supernumeraries. The action follows Thomas as he seeks out his old comrades and discovers, to his astonishment, how much they have changed. One has become the minister of the interior, embroiled in corruption, while two more, despite sticking with a leftist party, seem to have lost their former idealism in the name of day-to-day political pragmatism. Thomas becomes increasingly desperate and disaffected, and hatches a plan to assassinate the minister in the hotel in which he works as a relief waiter. Just as he reaches for his revolver, a nationalistic student guns down his target, yet Thomas is left with the weapon. The final scenes echo the prologue, with all the former revolutionaries, save for the dead minister, in gaol. Thomas hangs himself before evidence is brought that clears him of the crime.

The drama doubtless has its heart in the right place, but the outline of the plot reveals some of its weaknesses. The improbable plot twists and the self-pity of the main character undermine Toller's good intentions, yet what liberated the play from its literary shortcomings was the collaboration with Piscator. The director had been at the cutting edge of political theatre, tapping into a tendency of active directorial intervention to divine new meanings. Leopold Jessner, who held senior positions in major state-run theatres in Berlin from 1919–30, had, for example, developed a special kind of scenography with his designer Emil Pirchan, in which a dynamic system of levels and steps replaced more customary representational sets. He caused a riot when he applied such ideas to Schiller's *Wilhelm Tell* in 1919, but was praised for their deployment in Shakespeare's *Richard III* the following year. The Berlin audience thus became one of the first in Germany to be exposed to a radical rewriting of play texts in performance and, over time, came to expect such practices as the rule rather than the exception. Jessner thus pioneered the practices of *Regietheater* (directorial theatre) in which the director, rather than the writer, assumed a greater amount of creative control in performance.

Piscator developed similar strategies of direction that sought to subject the text to his political perspectives, but while Jessner was working with dead authors, Toller was very much alive. The director wanted the characters to be drawn with clearer social backgrounds, suggesting figures typical of their class. In an urban, industrial society, spectators could actively engage with an interrogation of the nineteenth century's sovereign individual and explore the meaning of membership of particular social groupings. Piscator's main imposition, however, concerned the central character. Toller wanted Thomas to persevere through adversity, but Piscator believed that he was too weak for that. He prevailed upon his writer and forced the suicide, yet there is an interesting discrepancy between the standard printed version of the text and the one Piscator used for his production. In performance, a series of film projections noted that this was not the way that a real revolutionary dies and that the choice at hand was between hanging oneself or changing the world.

Originally, Piscator's production was supposed to form a joint world premiere with one in Hamburg on 1 September 1927, yet technical difficulties prevented Piscator from going ahead with the plan, and the public had to wait a further two days. It is Piscator's production that is remembered today due to its innovative use of projections and staging. Under Piscator's influence, Toller's published text notes both the integration of film material and the use of a large scaffold, divided into different rooms, in order to suggest simultaneity of action on stage, the non-linear blur of modern urban life. Piscator had just opened a new theatre in Berlin that was specially configured to allow large-scale projection and had the facilities for a revolving stage. The inclusion of a scene in a radio station at the top of the hotel betrays the team's desire to show that the implicit Berlin of the play was also connected to other parts of the world as stock market prices and the satirical jazzy title song, 'Hoppla, wir leben!' resounded around the auditorium. This multimedia production represented an ultimately productive collaboration between two left-wing artists, and a new world of technical possibilities enabled by Berlin's centrality for both playwright and director.

Theory and Practice in Action: Brecht and the Berliner Ensemble

Bertolt Brecht, one of the most important playwrights, theatre theorists and directors of the twentieth century was also involved in Piscator's theatre for about a year between 1927–8 where he joined the director's left-wing dramaturgical collective. He pursued various other projects in Berlin until his fifteen-year exile from Germany after the Nazis came to power in 1933.

Brecht's route back to the city was hardly the most direct, and he attempted to find permanent employment in Salzburg and Munich before finally settling in what was to become the capital of the German Democratic Republic, East Berlin. His plan to set up a theatre company, which would become the world-famous Berliner Ensemble, opened wth a statement that one of its aims was to 'help re-establish Berlin as the cultural centre of Germany'.[2]

Most of the plays commonly associated with Brecht, such as *Mother Courage and her Children*, *The Caucasian Chalk Circle* or *Life of Galileo*, were written in exile and thus cannot be considered in any straightforward sense as 'literature of Berlin'. Although his work with the Ensemble mostly involved direction, he did not stop writing plays after founding the company with his wife, Helene Weigel, in the ruined city in 1949. While attempting to continue original dramatic composition, a task which was only partially successful, Brecht worked on a series of adaptations of both well- and lesser-known plays. The adaptation process allowed Brecht and his collaborators to engage with existing dramas and to rework them to suit his own politicized ends. Together with his assistants, he mostly went on to stage the plays using methods he had theorized in exile, but could not work through, because he had little access to theatres.

Brecht's most ambitious adaptation and the one that he did not complete before his death in 1956 was Shakespeare's *Coriolanus*. Erstwhile school-friend and collaborator Caspar Neher suggested Brecht read the play in April 1951. He was immediately enthused by it and started adapting the play with his assistants at the Berliner Ensemble. The main work had been completed by 1953. Only the battle scenes at the end of the first act were left untouched, awaiting development in rehearsals that were not to take place in Brecht's lifetime.

The adaptation, known today as *Coriolan* as a way of distinguishing it from Shakespeare's original, includes a range of interventions that reshape the material and shift the emphasis from the individual to society. Brecht's review of the play affected many of its constituent parts. The way that Coriolanus speaks, for example, changes with the person being addressed: he uses more earthy language when talking to the plebeians and becomes more elegant with the patricians. The general is thus carefully re-formed to acknowledge that he, too, is a part of society in his choice of register. This intervention into the protagonist's linguistic *Gestus* reflects the integration of modern society into the very fabric of the play. Such deliberate anachronism is clearly signalled in the very opening scene when a plebeian talks of Rome's 'third district', an administrative division unknown to the ancients. The historical setting openly exposes itself as a construction, and the audience can be in little doubt that it is the addressee of a play that is engaging with issues of Roman polity to serve more contemporary ends. The shift betrays Brecht's experience of Berlin in the 1920s and the centrality of the city in his conceptualization of his drama.

The changes Brecht made that pervade the text all have the purpose of refocusing the action away from Coriolanus onto the structures of society, which is more reminiscent of industrial class division than the feudalism and agro-based society of the play's times. For example, Brecht added two scenes, IV i and V vii. The former is a replacement of Shakespeare's short IV iii in which a Roman spy recounts the uprising against Coriolanus, its dispersal, and, more importantly, the general's banishment. This gives his Volscian interlocutor courage to tell Aufidius, their leader, that an attack will almost certainly succeed without the great general to defend Rome. Brecht's similarly short scene sees a Roman and a Volsican exchange experiences rather than vital information. While the Volsican asks after Corioli, which is now in Roman hands and whose conquest gave Coriolanus his honorary name, the two agree that their lives are essentially the same: regardless of who is in government, they 'eat, sleep and pay taxes'.[3] The banishment is mentioned more as an afterthought and elicits a sense of relief from both men. The figures on stage present life as lived by its citizens under capitalism as a sham of democracy: whichever party rules, it imposes the same burdens on its working people. Adapting Shakespeare for East Berlin, Brecht was able to contrast his audience's imputed experience of socialism with those of their neighbours in the West.

Brecht's new final scene, which has no equivalent in Shakespeare, is deliberately low-key. It follows Coriolanus's murder at the hands of Aufidius and his confederates, and is thus something of a planned anti-climax, set as it is in the peaceful chamber of the Senate. We see the restitution of captured Corioli to the Volscians as the news arrives of Coriolanus's death. There is a short silence before Menenius, Coriolanus's noble friend, proposes that his name be inscribed in the Capitol, but Menenius is interrupted by Brutus, one of the people's tribunes, who proposes they carry on with the business of state. A consul asks whether mourning clothes will be worn for the next ten moons; he receives the answer 'rejected', which serves as the single word conclusion to the play.[4] The contrast between this scene and its highly charged predecessor in Shakespeare is stark. Yet it is worth noting that the Senate is not the seat of plebeian power: Menenius is still there, but its work shows how matters can be treated without the malign influence of the dead general and in concert with the plebeians.

The overall effect of the adaptation is to redefine the tragedy. It is no longer the individual quality of pride that arouses interest, but the ways in which Roman society engages with a general who is dialectically an asset and a liability. It is his individualism that is tragic: while Coriolanus views it positively, society takes a far more pragmatic approach. When he tries to take revenge on Rome, the populace unites against him. It is Coriolanus who has miscalculated his own social worth and he dies for his failure to understand his place in the society of the day. The calm nature of the final scene amply demonstrates the shift from individual glory to collective security. In a way, this is also a 'reader for city dwellers', the name of a poetry cycle Brecht wrote under the influence of Berlin in the Weimar Republic.

The adaptation reduced Shakespeare's play to roughly 60 per cent of its original size, and in the new version, Brecht added roughly 17 per cent. Overall, then, only a half of *Coriolanus* survived in *Coriolan*. The revised text, written in the early years of the GDR, was criticized by the ruling Socialist Unity Party in 1951. The Party had problems with adapting the *Erbe*, the nation's untouchable 'cultural heritage' and almost certainly suspected a critique of Stalin in the treatment of Coriolanus himself. The project was also prevented from entering production because Brecht was unable to find a suitable actor for the lead role. Nonetheless, he adapted Shakespeare for his new audience in Berlin as an example of how innovative dramaturgy could interact with a new kind of audience. He wanted to show just how Shakespeare could be reworked for a socialist society and for performance in a socialist theatre in which the social concerns of an urban working class were to be addressed, not those of an arrogant member of the ruling class.

'Constructive Defeatism' as a Response to Brecht

Heiner Müller is regarded by many as Brecht's most adept successor. He was born in 1929 and, after a brief, early dalliance with Berlin, finally moved to the capital of the GDR in 1952. Initially, he tried unsuccessfully to gain a position as an assistant at the Berliner Ensemble, and then went on to pursue a writing career. Official censure in the 1960s of plays set in the GDR turned Müller's gaze away from more immediate problems, and he sought wider historical contexts for the nation's difficulties.

Germania Tod in Berlin (Germania Death in Berlin (1977)) is a montage of thirteen scenes that mostly follow the pattern of a scene taken from German history and one from the GDR. The pairs offer associative points of contact, and are only interrupted by the eleventh scene, which is a dumb show. The play takes up figures from history, myth, fiction and theatre, including Hilse from Hauptmann's *Die Weber*. Here Müller tries to connect the contradictions of the past with those of the present. The mention of Berlin in the title locates its centrality in the play's dramaturgy. Six of the scenes explicitly take place there, and the second half of Georg Heym's poem of 1910, 'Berlin III', provides the sole content for the penultimate scene, 'Death in Berlin I', in which death and the revolutionary 'Marseillaise' both feature. The dialectic of past and present plays out as a series of fragments against the backdrop of Germany's capital. The shifts in scene and context echo the city's diverse landscapes: the street contrasts with the bar, a castle now used by the workers state's president with the prison that holds them after the uprising of 17 June 1953.

The play, which won the prestigious West German Mülheim prize for best new play in 1979, was barred from being staged in the GDR for its association of socialist martyr Rosa Luxemburg with a prostitute and the scene titles 'Hommage à Stalin I and II'. It finally graced the Berliner Ensemble in January 1989 in a production that consciously forewent the revue format of the play in favour of a dry presentation of the material that disappointed many reviewers. Director Fritz Marquardt staged a sober reckoning with the city in which the play was finally performed at a period in the GDR's history when East Berlin no longer held the potential Brecht ascribed to it in the 1950s, but was limping its way through the economic, political and cultural stagnation of the 1980s.

However, earlier that decade, Müller detected the changes that were to blow in from the Soviet Union with the appointment of the reformer Mikhail Gorbachev as General Secretary of the Communist Party in 1985. He took up a form developed by Brecht in the late 1920s and early 1930s, the *Lehrstück*, or learning play. Brecht understood the form as one for which there was no need for an audience, as the main learners were the performers themselves. Often, such plays reflected on an event from the past in the present, as in the most (in)famous example, *Die Maßnahme* (translated as *The Measures Taken* or *The Decision*) in which four socialist revolutionaries justify killing a fifth as a necessary action during their successful political work to a massed chorus. Nowadays, *Lehrstücke* tend to be performed for an audience, yet Müller nonetheless allows for an amount of learning by the performers through his radically open dramaturgical form.

Wolokolamsker Chaussee (translated as *The Road of Tanks*) is a five-play cycle, written, published and performed in pieces from 1983–7 and only produced together in 1989. It is made up of 'Russian Opening', 'Forest Near Moscow', 'The Duel', 'Centaurs' and 'The Foundling'. Each part deals with a traumatic experience in the history of European socialism. The first two draw on motifs from Alexander Bek's novel *Volokolamsk Highway*, which is set during World War Two. 'The Duel' is set during the GDR workers' uprising in the East Berlin of 17 June 1953 when a subordinate stands up to a boss, exploiting the moment of potential freedom. When the uprising is put down, the subordinate writes an inevitable self-criticism, as order is restored by Soviet tanks. 'Centaurs' and 'The Foundling' are also set in the GDR. The former is a grotesque, a nightmare, set in an anonymous official building in which all offences against the state have ceased. One of the officers sends an underling to cross the traffic lights when the pedestrian signal is on red to create work for the office again. The underling dies carrying out the order. Then, before the officer realizes, s/he has become one with the desk. Just as Bek served as source for the first two parts, Kafka's *Metamorphosis*, the grotesque narrative of a man who inexplicably turns into an insect, informs this one.

These descriptions of the playlets may suggest that there are clear characters and actions running through them, but this is not the case. Each part is written in verse, covers six to nine pages, and includes no character attribution, that is, there is no indication as to who is speaking. Each narrative takes place in the past, with the 'I' reflecting on a painful event. The lack of named speaker leaves his or her identity open; indeed, Müller suggests that there is no need to match actor with a character at all. Instead, the texts go beyond the experience of the individuals in the five parts and extend into antithetical mindsets that cover different ways of approaching historical wounds.

This unusual dramaturgy has some notable implications. What Müller offers theatres is deliberately unfinished, and the texts suggest no obvious solutions to the problems he sets: how many people are to speak them and who speaks when? Even though the texts are not divided by more conventional markers of character, there is certainly more than one voice that can be detected in each of them. The playlets are a provocation to the creative team that wants to stage them. The customary questions as to how actors deliver lines are made all the more probing and require a far more fundamental engagement with the texts and their contexts. In this way, Müller re-activates the *Lehrstück* form for problems that, by dint of their historical intransigence, resist simple solutions. Actors in the present confront the contradictions of the past, but have the freedom to construct these in a manner agreed by the team as a whole. In production, the Münchner Kammerspiele staging of April 1989 chose to have pairs of actors perform the scenes, whereas a production in Leipzig later that year deployed large choruses to give the sense that there is more at stake than just the plight of the individual.

Here it is possible to discern a further development of Piscator's (and later Brecht's) preference for staging the individual as a representative of a class. Müller goes further to suggest greater fluidity in the human personality and actively encourages multiple actors playing different roles or, indeed, the same one. Yet even the presence of a disruptive playlet alone could engender a livelier interpretation of a production as a whole. 'Russian Opening' was premiered as a preface to Johannes R. Becher's *Winterschlacht* (Battle in Winter (1942)) at the Deutsches Theater, Berlin, in May 1985. Müller's open invitation to the production team contrasted with Becher's conventional use of character markers in his play. By placing Müller first, the production made the tacit melding of actor and character in the evening's main show problematic. That such a formally challenging playlet as this was first staged in East Berlin marks Müller's role as playwright in a theatre capital capable of realizing plays that actively provoke more experimental approaches to stagecraft.

The dramaturgy of the playlet cycle is an example of what Müller called 'constructive defeatism',[5] an oxymoronic formulation that combines hope and despair. The texts are bleak and uncompromising – they offer nothing but a series of historical defeats. Yet their form encourages participation and input, something that resists the sense that the defeats are eternal and unchangeable. It is also worth noting that the text from which Müller's paradoxical phrase is taken marks his disavowal of the *Lehrstück* in 1977, a form he believes is no longer of any value 'until the next earthquake'.[6] This seismic shift arrived with Gorbachev and allowed Müller to develop a series of works that offered theatre-makers and audiences alike the opportunity to tackle the problems of socialism, with a view to rethinking them in public. As a citizen of Berlin, the playwright was able to make a direct response to the changes in the East, even though his own government resisted them until it was too late to ignore them, in 1989.

Pluralism after the Wall

The fall of the Berlin Wall in November 1989 led to the collapse of the GDR, and Germany was reunified in September 1990. The parliamentary decision to move the Federal Republic's capital city from Bonn to Berlin was taken in June 1991, and the transfer of power was completed in 1999. During this period, Berlin's theatres faced a funding crisis: the divided city of the Cold War, into which two governments plunged large subsidies to enhance their own standing, was now one and found itself with more major theatres than it could afford to run. The Schiller-Theater, rebuilt in 1951 after it was destroyed in World War Two, was closed by the Berlin Senate in 1993, a decision that suggested that even a theatre with a great and illustrious reputation could not withstand the ravages of financial stringency.

Some theatres flourished in this period and used the uncertain political times to their advantage. The Volksbühne, a theatre into which renewed life had been breathed by its *enfant terrible* leader, Frank Castorf, benefitted the most. The very idea of this 'people's stage' took hold in the late nineteenth century when social dynamics were in such flux that the bastions of middle-class culture started to face a challenge from a new, interested constituency of spectators. At the end of the twentieth century, when class boundaries were already becoming more porous, Castorf gathered innovative theatre-makers to offer a diverse and dynamic programme that connected itself to the new political landscape of the 1990s. His success was such that he opened a second venue, in an old Berlin beer garden known as the Prater, and by the 2001–2 season, he had appointed a dedicated director for the space, René Pollesch. Unlike Castorf, who directs plays and adapts novels for performance in the *Regietheater* tradition that can be traced back to Jessner and Piscator in Weimar Berlin, Pollesch writes and directs his own unique brand of texts.

Pollesch is a prodigious playwright and in his first season at the Prater, he penned three new works for the venue: *Stadt als Beute* (City as Spoils), *Insourcing des Zuhause: Menschen in Scheiß-Hotels* (Insourcing at Home: People in Crap Hotels) and *SEX*. His writing at this stage of his career was marked by several key features that can be seen in a representative quotation from *Insourcing des Zuhause*:

> C: Und die Einrichtung sieht echt scheisse aus, aber alle Angebote sonst sind attraktiv. Alles das, was man nicht sieht. Diese Fabrik, die eine Vorstellung von Zuhause produziert.
>
> T: Alle Dienstleistungen hier sind irgendwie attraktiv. Und echt. Die sind alle so ECHT, DIE GEFÜHLE, DIE MIR ENTGEGENGEBRACHT WERDEN UND DIE PERSÖNLICHE ANTEILNAHME! SCHEISSE!
>
> N: Ich bin in diesem Hotel, und da gibt es diese fliessenden Übergänge zwischen Wohnen und Arbeiten.

> [C: The furniture looks really crap, but everything else [the hotel] offers is really attractive. Everything you can't see. This factory which manufactures a sense of being at home.
>
> T: All the services here are somehow attractive. And real. They're all so REAL, THE FEELINGS I'M CONFRONTED WITH AND THE EMPATHY! FUCK!
>
> N: I'm in this hotel and life and work keep dissolving into each other!][7]

The play is nominally set in a new type of hotel that was springing up all over Germany, and not least in Berlin, the 'boarding house', in which space is rented out, but made to feel like home. The intellectual substance of the piece is informed by a scholarly article.[8] In the quotation, the figures touch on the complex relationship between cognition and feelings: while they know that their environment is artificial and deliberate, they are unable to inhibit the warm, homely feelings it engenders. There is also an obvious collapse of the distinction between high and low culture in the play as rarefied theoretical concepts mix with earthy vernacular and expletives.

There are also no characters to speak of: the letters designating a change of speaker merely indicate the first names of the three female actors who performed in the premiere. They are there to present, rather than to represent, their lines. This complex task is made easier to execute by Pollesch's approach to staging such strange speeches. As a director, he has his actors deliver the words in lower case as quickly and as neutrally as possible. The words in upper case are screamed out. This bifurcation of performance modes creates a striking effect in performance. On the one hand, the actors tear through increasingly contradictory speeches without necessarily registering the contradictions through facial expression or physical action. On the other, the enforced shouting acts like an emotional break, a moment of utter despair. Yet this moment is transitory and does not prevent the actors from continuing headlong through the texts. In addition, the speed at which the actors have to deliver the lowercase texts means that they frequently get lost in the complex lines they have been assigned, and the house prompter plays a visible and active part in orientating the actors in live performance.

So, what are the actors representing, if they are not representing characters? The texts are impersonal: there is nothing to connect C, T or N to their lines explicitly. It is as if they are only conduits for ideas and responses, and this connects with Pollesch's political agenda: in an age of globalization, in which the individual is increasingly overshadowed and reduced by multinational corporations and international political unions, the actors reflect their own precarious existences. Individuality is not, however, completely erased by Pollesch's process. Each actor registers the cost of such systems through the anguish and misery of the capitalized lines, and, in addition, each actor brings their own unique voice to the production, however canalized it is by the incessant text it has to speak. The experience of such plays in performance is also a challenge to the audience: the sheer speed of delivery makes the positions and arguments all but impossible to assimilate, and so spectators are also confronted with the vagaries of globalization and cannot simply sit back and absorb them. This profoundly urban experience of anonymity, subjugation to structures seemingly beyond one's control, and personal despair crystallize in Pollesch's texts for the Prater, including *Stadt als Beute*, which thematizes the ways in which Berlin itself has become a plaything for global capital and neoliberal deregulation.

Pollesch's theatre helped to herald a series of innovations in Berlin theatre in the first years of the twenty-first century. Elsewhere, a new theatre complex arose out of three existing ones: the Theater am Halleschen Ufer, the Hebbel Theater and the Theater am Ufer, all in Berlin's Kreuzberg district, combined to become the Hebbel am Ufer or HAU. It opened in the 2003–4 season as a new kind of theatre. The UK's theatre system is made up of producing houses, such as the National in London or the Citizens in Glasgow, that primarily make their own work, and receiving houses that either commission groups from outside or host touring companies. The German system almost exclusively comprises producing houses with regular ensembles of actors. The HAU became Germany's first major receiving house and promoted all manner of innovative work, including performance theatre, dance and a host of international collaborations. It had and has little commitment to staging plays – something that the other major houses in Berlin do and have done for centuries – yet part of its self-developed brief was to engage with Berlin and its diverse populace.

Rapid immigration in the 1960s and 1970s made Berlin the city with the largest Turkish community outside Turkey. It is also the most cosmopolitan city in Germany and the most recent census of 2011 puts the number of foreign nationals at roughly 14 per cent. Ignored by much of the drama already discussed, migrants have started to figure more strongly in theatres since the turn of the last century. The play *Schwarze Jungfrauen* (Black Virgins) by Feridun Zaimoglu and Günter Senkel was premiered at the HAU in March 2006 as a part of the 'Beyond Belonging – Migration Hoch Zwei [Migration to the Power of Two]' festival, which was curated by Shermin Langhoff. It is comprised of ten monologues, dense heightened distillations of authentic interviews with young Moslem women. The play itself challenges stereotypes and was produced in a stylized manner, complementing the HAU's reputation for experiment. Five of the ten monologues were staged by five women, all dressed in similar grey shapeless outfits and wearing bald caps. It is, however, the festival's curator who is of greater interest: Langhoff went from the HAU to lead the then somewhat little-known Ballhaus Naunynstraße after it was reopened in 2008.

Langhoff pioneered what has been termed a 'post-migrant' theatre culture at the old dance hall, one in which the theatre is not so much concerned with migration as a theme, but with the lives of people who are now settled parts of the city's social fabric. The Ballhaus under Langhoff balanced plays with dance and performance work. The best-known play to emerge from her tenure is *Verrücktes Blut* (Mad Blood) of 2010, by Nurkan Erpulat and Jens Hillje, a free adaptation of the French film *La Journeé de la jupe* (Skirt Day (2008)). The action follows a white, German teacher in a class of predominantly Turkish-German pupils. She is trying to teach them Schiller's *Die Räuber* (The Robbers) and is greeted by indifference, until she happens upon a pistol that falls out of one of the pupil's bags and forces the class to learn about Schiller's concept of humanism by performing scenes from his *Kabale und Liebe* (Intrigue and Love) at gunpoint. The play exploits its metatheatrical mode by calling stale stereotypes into question as the pupils and their teacher performatively defy expectations under the pressure of events. Like *Schwarze Jungfrauen* before it, it has been performed widely all over Germany.

Langhoff remained at the Ballhaus until the 2013–14 season, when she became the general manager of Berlin's smallest major theatre, the Maxim Gorki, off the Unter den Linden thoroughfare. There she continues to develop new ways of engaging with the city's communities, with radically transcultural and queer programming, challenging received opinions. Named 'Theatre of the Year' by the magazine *Theater heute* in 2014, the theatre points to widening its audience ever further by introducing English surtitles to its performances. The theatre is actively helping to engineer Berlin's place as a global theatre capital. In an age where major British theatre-people, like the playwright Simon Stephens and the director Katie Mitchell, are increasingly finding interest for their work in Germany in general and in Berlin in particular, Langhoff is building bridges not only between Berlin's different communities, but between those of Europe, too.

The writing of playwrights in Berlin, of which only a survey has been offered here, attests to the unique constellation of bustling metropolis and high-quality theatres. Since the unification of Germany in 1871, Berlin has drawn talented writers, directors, actors, set designers and others, and they have collaborated to produce lively, engaging texts and productions over the decades. While it is true that other theatre centres in Germany have also had an important effect on the German stage, none has been so consistent and diverse. Berlin's critical mass allowed it to endure, due to its capacity and its diversity of styles and approaches. Playwrights have found opportunities in the city to engage with a wide-ranging understanding of the political, well beyond the narrowness of party politics, and a theatrical apparatus capable of discovering and developing fitting performance modes. Berlin has accompanied the major movements, such as Naturalism and Expressionism, but more importantly, has driven its own agenda over time. Brecht's Berliner Ensemble and Heiner Müller had a worldwide profile; the work of the Volksbühne has inspired experiment, and the developments in post-migrant theatre have finally brought Germany's largest ethnic minority onto the stage in a serious, concerted and non-tokenistic way. With robust infrastructure and a reputation for theatrical innovation, it is unlikely that Berlin will lose any of its lustre for future generations of theatre practitioners.

NOTES

1. Bertolt Brecht, 'Anmerkungen zur *Dreigroschenoper*', in Brecht, *Schriften 4, Berliner und Frankfurter Ausgabe*, vol. 24, eds Werner Hecht, Klaus et al (Berlin and Frankfurt am Main: Aufbau and Suhrkamp, 1991), pp. 57–68 (p. 58). Translations from the German are mine unless otherwise acknowledged.
2. The anonymous document, almost certainly written by Brecht, 'Theaterprojekt B.' is available in German, in Werner Hecht, *Brecht und die DDR: Die Mühen der Ebenen* (Berlin: Aufbau, 2013), pp. 20–1 (p. 20).
3. Bertolt Brecht, *Coriolanus*, trans. Ralph Manheim, in Brecht, *Berliner Ensemble Adaptations*, ed. David Barnett (London: Bloomsbury, 2014), pp. 67–172 (p. 137).
4. Ibid., p. 172.
5. Heiner Müller, 'Isolated Texts Waiting for History', in Müller, *Germania*, ed. Sylvère Lotringer (New York: Semiotext(e), 1990), pp. 239–40 (p. 240).
6. Ibid., p. 239
7. René Pollesch, *Insourcing des Zuhause: Menschen in Scheiss-Hotels*, in Bettina Masuch, *Wohnfront 2001–2002: Volksbühne im Prater* (Berlin: Alexander, 2002), pp. 43–80 (pp. 50–1). Translation: René Pollesch, *Insourcing at Home: People in Crap Hotels*, trans. David Tushingham, unpublished translation, 2003, made available through the Goethe Institut and the Rowohlt Verlag, p. 9.
8. Brigitte Lorenz, Renate Kuster and Pauline Boudry, 'Das Insourcing des Zuhause', *Widersprüche*, 20: 78 (2000), 13–26.

13

GERRIT-JAN BERENDSE

Twentieth-Century Poetry

> Twenty thousand people
> Cross Bösebrücke
> Fingers are crossed
> Just in case
> Walking the dead
> David Bowie, 'Where Are We Now?'

While, politically, 'Berlin' will be forever associated with the city's locus as the epicentre of the momentous and far-reaching events of the twentieth century, culturally, and with equally extensive consequences, Berlin is the cradle of Modernism, a movement that has, from the beginning of the last century, transformed European art and literature. As a cultural hub, Berlin has, in its various manifestations, been a centre for artists and writers from the late nineteenth century, following in the steps of Paris, London and Rome. Those writers who have been associated with Berlin have always enjoyed reputations extending far beyond the metropolitan and, indeed, national boundaries.

Following reunification, however, and on into the early years of the twenty-first century, the poetry of Berlin has returned home, moving away from its scholarly, international audience and finding, instead, a more localized readership among the city's ordinary people, caught up in a period of sustained urban pandemonium. Some of the new Berlin poetic voices speak of direct, first-hand experience and achieve their circulation via blogs and other social media, a long way from the conventional traditions of modern European culture which are seen as too abstract and, ultimately, as irrelevant to the point of extinction.

That being said, contemporary poetry of Berlin as *Weltstadt*, or 'city of the world', owes much to, and is infused by, the ground-breaking energy which has been evident throughout the period of Modernism. In *Das große Berlin-Gedicht* (The Great Berlin Poem (2011)), for example, amateur poets from different areas of the city, writing about their particular neighbourhood, or *Kiez*, are assisted by professional poets with established reputations in the field of European literature.[1] This collaboration bestows upon the new work acceptable literary credentials and provides evidence of its rightful place within the canon of modern poetry. The work stands in the tradition of dynamic cultural innovation which has so reinvigorated Western literary culture. The huge number of published anthologies of Berlin poetry bears witness to the success and power of this cultural cross-fertilization, which is investigated and classified in Hans-Michael Speier's study *Poesie der Metropole* (Poetry of the Metropolis, (1990)).[2] Further, Berlin's most prominent poetic genre, *Großstadtlyrik* (Lyric Poetry of the City), has been reinvigorated. The attraction of this genre is that throughout the twentieth century, the poems in question have displayed new forms and unfamiliar ways of seeing. Berlin became a much-visited theme, with the city portrayed in all its multifaceted qualities: as a centre of prosperity, as the birthplace of Modernism, as the home of a knowledge society and, at the same time, as a dark location in the political history of Europe.

Through the lens of poetic writing, this chapter will investigate ways of approaching the complex history of the city by focusing on some of the most significant issues faced by Berlin and Berliners in the twentieth century. It will address the bleakest aspects of that turbulent period. War, death and destruction are key ingredients in the history and identity of Berlin, and its poetry is testament to this. Consequently, the artistic profiles presented here do not dwell on the city's magnificence. Instead, they challenge notions of glamour and beauty by emphasizing that the wellspring of Berlin's poetry is death. The chapter will also consider the juxtaposition of the official triumphalist rhetoric of the various regimes which presided during the periods of Berlin's prosperity and the poetic themes of fragmentation, isolation and emptiness represented here by four major lyrical voices: Gottfried Benn, Bertolt Brecht, Volker Braun and Heiner Müller. While none of them was actually born and brought up in Berlin, they have nevertheless each managed, in writing Berlin poetry, to express the city's fortunes, misfortunes and atmospheres in different historical times and contexts by concentrating on a central theme.

Death Dances in Berlin

The struggle to sustain a creative existence while facing the often brutal reality of everyday urban living has a long history in the art of Berlin. As a matter of fact, the earliest known verse, written in the settlement of Berlin-Cölln in 1469, was a *danse macabre*, depicting the scourges of war, hunger and disease, in particular The Black Death, which ravaged Europe in the Middle Ages. Most of the verses and images, expressing the indiscriminate, universal potency of death, have survived, and are now displayed on the walls of Berlin's Marienkirche as the *Berliner Totentanz* (Berlin Dance of Death). Centuries later, and with Berlin as the capital city of a succession of German states, the forces of destruction have not diminished. In fact, principally as the result of ideological disputes and conflicts, they increased in the course of the twentieth century and presented themselves in new and varied guises.

For obvious reasons, the twentieth century has been called the 'century of war',[3] and Berlin became a traumatic centre of terror and destruction in this time. In *Death in Berlin* (2010), Monica Black describes the all-pervading presence of death in the city in the century during which it became the centre of the so-called 'Nazi Revolution', the seat of Axis power in the Second World War, the target of relentless Allied bombing raids, the divided city of the Cold War, and finally, the capital of a – for some, at least, ill-considered – reunified country. Today, the most visible evidence of the violence forced upon a group of Berliners are the so-called *Stolpersteine* or stumbling stones, small metal plaques set in the pavement indicating the sites of door-to-door razzias which preceded the deportation of Jewish families to the Third Reich's death camps. But there also remain physical signs of the devastation wrought upon the city during the various Battles of Berlin, of which the ruined tower of the Kaiser Wilhelm Memorial Church is the most potent example. Until November 1943 most Berliners had remained relatively untroubled by the deadly violence of the war elsewhere in Europe because, for the first four years, only a few confronted death in the city at first hand. The Allied bombing raids on Berlin which began that month, however, would present citizens with an unprecedented challenge to traditional views of the dead: 'Corpses suddenly became a material fact of everyday life; they appeared in the streets or had to be recovered beneath piles of rubble.'[4]

As Black observes, '[d]eath is a classic topic in the history of mentalities precisely because it can help to show us the role of human imagination, collective structures and patterns of emotion in history'.[5] Her *Death in Berlin* is of great historiographical interest, relying on both archival resources and oral accounts. In their representation of human beings and their life stories in all their diversity, other devices of cultural memory such as poetry have also proved to be a valuable means of both archiving and commenting on urban affairs. These Berlin poems not only embody the varied and often extremely violent events in the city, they also offer us new ways of seeing. The cataclysmic episodes in the capital, as captured in poetry, provide us with alternative histories of Berlin. Poetic texts also explore the various possibilities of linking political extremism and private lives in the sphere of death, with which Berlin appears to have a particularly intimate relationship. One of the first poets to embrace this apparently morbid topic in his work as early as the second decade of the twentieth century – not least, in his famous *Morgue* poems – was Gottfried Benn.

Gottfried Benn: Dissecting Berlin

Benn was a central figure of the innovative Berlin art scene, which we now know as Modernism, in the early years of the last century. He was associated with a group of artists committed to Modernism in its Expressionist form. It has been argued that the disadvantages of breakneck technological progress in modern times became both the source of, and the crucial inspiration for, the ground-breaking energies of intellectual and cultural renewal in the movement of Expressionism. The group's poetry and paintings reflect the impact on the poet's voice and the painter's eye of the increase in Berlin's population and the speed of its technological and architectural changes.

With a print run of just 500 copies, the publication of nine poems under the title *Morgue und andere Gedichte* (Morgue and Other Poems (1912)) illustrates the novel cultural significance of Benn's writing. The innovation consisted of a strange juxtaposition of realistic – even almost photographic – reproductions of the body and grotesque textual forms. The book generated shock waves on the Berlin scene by bringing a scientifically detached gaze to bear upon the individual body, with no concern for the corpse's humanity. This kind of focus on the physical body was an entirely new approach and originates, as Lethen notes, from Benn's Berlin poems.[6] Indeed, the conventional view of Benn is that his verses lack any personally or socially motivated compassion, and that his preoccupation is only with aesthetics.

With the exception of his later creation, Dr Rönne, for Benn the complexity of the individual soul is absent. He is attracted to the human body only as the inspiration for an aesthetic of ugliness. In later years, his interest in human beings is reduced to an anthropological quest, the analysis of what he called the 'phenotype' of people,[7] an artificial being beyond time and space. The city interests him merely as a laboratory in which minutely to observe and study these bodies. Poems such as 'Schöne Jugend' (Fine Youth), 'Kleine Aster' (Little Aster) and 'Mann und Frau gehen durch die Krebsbaracke' (Man and Woman Go through the Cancer Barrack) – all written during the time Benn worked as a young medical student in the so-called 'Berliner Leichenschauhaus', or morgue, in Moabit – portray realistic scenes which become suddenly transformed into surreal phantasmagoria. The analytical gaze of these macabre poems, written during the peak of Berlin's economic and technological prosperity, exposes the darker reality beneath the city's glamour and ornament. What was once full of vitality, temperament and soul is now regarded as nothing more than an inert vessel.

This is also the way that Benn approaches Berlin – as a lifeless urban body. In his late poem, 'Berlin' (originally published with the subtitle 'Die versteppte Stadt' (The City Become Steppe)) of 1948, an abandoned city is displayed in a way similar to the dissected corpse after the work of the anatomist. 'Berlin' addresses a typical apocalyptic theme and represents the widespread fear of a third World War in the style of the then fashionable *Trümmerromantik* (Romanticism of the Ruins).[8] At a time when Benn had to reinvent himself (and justify his multiple existences as Expressionist, Nazi fanatic, surgeon and essayist), and with the Federal Republic of Germany about to come into being, the poem is very much an expression of Cold War and anti-Soviet angst. It anticipates the possibility of a nuclear strike, while raising, in the first stanza, the fearful spectre of being 'swallowed by the steppe'. In this line, the implication of those vast, isolated territories in the reviled Soviet Union becomes obvious. The second stanza highlights the only remaining weapon against forces perceived as culturally inferior:

> Eines kann man nicht vertreiben:
> dieser Steine Male bleiben
> Löwen noch im Wüstensand,
> wenn die Mauern niederbrechen,
> werden noch die Trümmer sprechen
> von dem grossen Abendland.
>
> (not to be erased forever,
> stones as remnants of endeavour:
> lions from a monument,
> though the noble walls are falling,
> fragments eloquently calling:
> behold the mighty Occident.)[9]

More than simply an expression of fear, the poem is a Cold War propaganda document. In 1948 Berlin had been downgraded from the capital city of a sovereign nation to a divided city embedded in the Soviet zone of occupation – already, so to speak, located in the centre of the 'Steppe'. Berlin, or rather the 'island' of West Berlin where Benn lived and worked after the Second World War, felt the need to uphold the accomplishments and values of the 'free' world. In Benn's 1933 essay, 'Confession of Faith in Expressionism', the then fanatical Nazi warned against the 'red danger'.[10] After the war, not much seemed to have changed for him, particularly in his assessment of Marxism. As J. M. Ritchie observes, 'in the last few years politics meant [for Benn] Marxism, meant Russia, assassination of all bourgeois and intellectual levels of society'.[11] One of those 'levels of society' is art; and the annihilation of Western culture is Benn's greatest fear, as it was when he was involved in National Socialist cultural politics. Hence, for Benn, art is the only means to withstand 'barbarism'.

Gottfried Benn dissects Berlin and identifies the only precious artefact that survives an anticipated apocalypse, a piece of art: the 'Löwen' as 'Male', 'lions' as 'monuments'. In 1948 Benn scrutinized Berlin in the same way as he had previously done with human cadavers, in the sense that the corpses could be better presented when moulded into an artwork. The 'deceased' Berlin is given a similar status since all nouns in the poem 'Berlin' relate to stone or sand – the materials for creating sculptures. Benn's prediction of the aftermath of destruction is not a bare wasteland but the representation of what is for him the greatest gift of humanity, art. The noun 'Löwen' destabilizes the reading of the poem and should be related to Roland Barthes's category of 'pictum',[12] that is, it forces the reader to follow its iconography – here both related to Berlin's history as a powerful empire, and alluded to by the noun 'Burg' or fortified castle in the first stanza. Images of lions can indeed be found all over European capital cities, including Berlin, where they recall the city's 'glorious' days as the centre of an empire.

Benn's imagined wasteland Berlin (a prevailing image which he must have observed on his return to the city in 1945) is the result of human destruction by the Asiatic 'hordes' and 'armies'. What remains are lifeless 'houses', as if on the mortuary table. It is a poem without hope and affording no form of human life. The body of the city is artificial, constructed out of words, and what remains is art as monumental fragment. There is a striking similarity here to the *Morgue* poems. As with the dismembered body of the drowned truck-driver in 'Kleine Aster', the Berlin body shows no signs of redemptive potential. It is cut open and dissevered, literally and metaphorically, without respect: like his *Morgue* corpses, surviving only morbidly as an artefact.

Bertolt Brecht: Berlin Requiem

In his excellent biography of Brecht, Stephen Parker argues that the writer and Berlin were 'near-synonymous, defining not just Brecht's own career but also the prevailing image of 1920s Berlin as a site of restless innovation and change, of violence, audacious brinkmanship and unscrupulous dealings'.[13] Andrew Webber, too, emphasizes Brecht's – albeit not unconditional – love at first sight for Berlin, as revealed in his correspondence as a newcomer to the capital city from Bavaria.[14] However, in most instances, Brecht, perhaps the best-known playwright and poet of Berlin, avoids mentioning it in his writing and, instead, substitutes sites such as London, Chicago or a fictitious city like Mahagonny.

Indeed, it is striking that in the early poems, where he demonstrates survival skills in Berlin, the city is not named as such. In this new metropolitan, ideological battleground – a time of advanced modernization and political turmoil – 'cool conduct' is a strategy for survival.[15] But 'cool conduct' is not restricted to a specific location (say Berlin) but has become, for Brecht and many other leading intellectuals in those days, second nature to all city dwellers. In the volume *Hauspostille* (Manual of Piety (1927)), for example, the residents of Berlin are not identified, but are referred to only by their role and function, 'der Kerl in Violett' (the bloke in violet), 'altes Weib' (old wife) and 'der tote Soldat' (the dead soldier). At the same time, the centre of action in many of the poems on Berlin is removed to the suburbs and to the countryside. This is apparent not only in the *Hauspostille* but also in his final collection of urban poetry, *Buckower Elegien* (Buckow Elegies), written in 1953 but published posthumously in one volume in 1986. In both collections of, albeit very varied, Berlin poetry, one central aspect can be observed: Brecht's treatment of the self – which can be seen as related to the concept of the abject as defined by Julia Kristeva in 1982.[16] The abject body contradicts the image of a clean and proper social entity and, for this reason, must have shocked readers. As with Benn, in Brecht's, early nihilistic phase, a morbid poetics becomes evident when in most of the poems it seems impossible to discriminate between object and subject, as the two are subsumed by the abject. What Kristeva would call the 'power of horror', as encapsulated in the abject, fascinated Brecht, at least in his earlier poems.

Like Benn's drowned drayman in the poem 'Kleine Aster', Brecht's drowned girl in 'Vom ertrunkenen Mädchen' (The Drowned Girl) in *Hauspostille* thus becomes an abject, aesthetic object. In contrast to Benn's *Morgue* poems, however, the girl's corpse here is fragmenting of its own accord, not being fragmented by human intervention. Instead, her decomposing body – based on Rimbaud's image from the 'Ophélia' poem of 1870 – blends into her environment. Brecht's drowned girl decays and is forgotten piecemeal in the *Flusslandschaft*, the wider inter-connected river and canal system in and around the city. The final stanza, which indicates that 'die Leiche' (the corpse) gradually becomes one with nature, that it is in a final state of decomposition (*Auflösung*), is almost presented as redemption, or *Erlösung*, relating to the ironic appropriation of a religious framework in the *Hauspostille* volume.

Als ihr bleicher Leib im Wasser verfault war
Geschah es (sehr langsam), daß Gott sie allmählich vergaß
Erst ihr Gesicht, dann die Hände und ganz zuletzt erst ihr Haar.
Dann ward sie Aas in Flüssen mit vielem Aas.

(When her pale body had rotted in the water
God's slow and gradual forgetting of her began:
First her face, then her hands and last of all her hair.
Then she became carrion in rivers with much carrion.)[17]

The absence of the human being, the process of dehumanization, in this Ophelia motif is in stark contrast to the crowded urban setting of the majority of Brecht's other *Hauspostille* poems. Life in the capital city is characterized as 'cold', much like the girl's corpse, both of them seeming to be detached from an inner core. Neither the name of the girl nor that of the city is revealed in the poem. The girl seems to be liberated, even as she is aesthetically objectified. In modern times, individuals are displaced by cold apparatuses. Helmut Lethen argues in his monograph *Cool Conduct* that the modern world of commodities embraces, but eventually also crushes human life. The only means of survival from this 'warm' embrace is a radical 'cold' break – voluntary or involuntary.[18] Indeed, the ultimate detachment from the world of commodities, as shown in Brecht's poem, contains a paradox: the drowned girl who left modernity appears even more human and alive now that she is liberated from inhuman objectification and no longer enmeshed in modern city life.

This particular poem indicates a transitional phase in Brecht's early aesthetics. Poems such as 'Liturgie vom Hauch' (Liturgy of Breath) and 'Legende vom toten Soldaten' (Legend of the Dead Soldier) obviously comment on social and political maladministration in the Berlin of the late 1920s. Berlin experiences another dehumanizing encounter in Brecht's verses in his *Hauspostille* due to the ideological battles of the interbellum, where fighting was relocated from modern global warfare to the civic battles fought on the streets of Berlin. Brecht's poems show that Berlin was already starting to evolve into a 'topography of terror', even before the SS began directing terror operations from their headquarters and tens of thousands of prisoners were brutalized in the nearby Sachsenhausen concentration camp. The individual experiences a downgrading of humanity and, eventually, concludes in death. 'Vom ertrunkenen Mädchen', however, is more than that: it is an excellent example of Brecht's shift from his anarchist-nihilist phase to a Marxist focus in the interwar period in Germany. The poem was written in 1919, and originally entitled 'Vom erschlagenen Mädchen' (The Murdered Girl). It is also sung in the play

Baal (1918/19) by the protagonist while he tramps in the forest in the scene, 'Landstraße, Weiden' (Country Road, Poplars). Originally, Brecht's poem refers to the killing of a girl Baal had seduced, and the lyric is an eerie tribute to her. The poem did not find its way into the manuscript for earlier versions of the *Hauspostille*, but was only later included in the 1926 *Taschenpostille* (Pocket Manuel of Piety) version, and then in the full 1927 edition published by Propyläen Verlag. In the following year it was set to music by Kurt Weill as 'Ballade vom ertrunkenen Mädchen' (Ballad of the Drowned Girl) for the *Berliner Requiem* (1928), a cantata for chorus and orchestra, written for the Frankfurter Sender radio station. Its aim was to express what 'the urban man of our era has to say about the phenomenon of death'.[19] The text was meant as an epitaph, a *Gedenktafel* or memorial plaque, for the revolutionary socialist and co-founder of the anti-war Spartacus League, Rosa Luxemburg, killed in January 1919 and found in the Landwehr Canal four and a half months later. As was widely reported in the German press, she had been clubbed and shot by Freikorps soldiers. Through his portrait of the drowned woman, the Berlin Brecht combines a 'Baal-esque' way of dealing with women together with his own genuine political anxiety.

In many of the Brecht poems of this period featuring Berlin, the city resembles a ghost town, a cold and lifeless place, with few traces of real people. And this absence of Berliners in Berlin was also expressed by Brecht decades later, in a different form, after his return to what was about to become the capital of the GDR. The lines 'Wäre es da / Nicht doch einfacher, die Regierung/Löste das Volk auf und/Wählte ein anderes?' (Would it not be easier/In that case for the government/ To dissolve the people/And elect another?), from the iconic poem 'Die Lösung' (The Solution), are an example of the paradox of an absent presence of people.[20]

The elimination of human existence or the threat of elimination of what stands for humanity is also a recurrent theme in the elegies written in Buckow, a lakeside community outside Berlin. From his rural retreat, he detaches himself from people in the centre of the city. The setting of the *Buckower Elegien* is far away from the centre of power and the events in the heat of the city, most notably from the workers' uprising on 17 June 1953. Werner Hecht has documented Brecht's engagement as the Party's critical friend, but he also emphasizes the magnitude of Brecht's marginalization.[21] Brecht still seemed to be living in exile after he returned to his beloved Berlin in the late 1940s. This is a way to read the *Buckower Elegien*: he directs the gaze of anybody concerned with Europe's future in those days away from the centre of action in the power house Berlin to his secluded garden in its outskirts. It displays the writer's own disruption, the internal separation he had to undertake in order to survive in this city and to maintain his sanity.

Volker Braun: Combat Zone Berlin

The absence of Berliners in Brecht's *Buckow* poems mirrors the fact that in the early years of the German Democratic Republic many East Berliners moved to the western part of the city. Brecht did not live to see the construction of the Berlin Wall, which was supposed to prevent the haemorrhaging of the population. One, albeit hardly visible, piece of evidence for the link between the end of the war and the beginning of the GDR's demonstrable hegemony was the fact that much of the bombed wasteland of the mid-1940s in Berlin became the foundation for stretches of the Berlin Wall in the city centre. On 13 August 1961 large zones of what became known as the death strip, or 'Todesstreifen', on the east side of the Berlin Wall, were located on a no-man's land, which used to be the drained Luisenstädtische Kanal and was used as a landfill site for the rubble after the Battle of Berlin in 1944.[22] The Wall became the ultimate site of 'Death in Berlin' in the second half of the twentieth century. Marc Silberman argues, in his introduction to the volume *The German Wall*, that the 155-kilometre barrier surrounding West Berlin not only represented the architectural incarnation of the Iron Curtain but also became a source on which many historians and scholars feed, inviting 'approaches and objects of inquiry, modulated by methodological diversity'.[23] This diversity is also present in the many cultural representations of the Wall, and not least in poetry.

Some scholars have characterized the Cold War as a series of rhetorical battles.[24] In Volker Braun's 'Die Mauer' (The Wall), which he had tentatively entitled 'Die Grenze' (The Border), the linguistic war is apparent. Berlin is here – metaphorically – a battlefield, and at the same time a virtual oasis, in which the border – and therefore the opposing ideological dogmas – can be crossed. Braun goes beyond the common Cold War dichotomy, as he focuses on Berlin's fate after the summer of 1961 from different viewpoints and in different versions, published in both East and West Germany. At the same time, however, as a Marxist and also as a critical GDR writer, Braun was constrained by the directives of the East German authorities because he wanted to avoid being labelled as a dissident, as one who could thus be straightforwardly marginalized and subsequently ignored by the state. Instead, Braun wanted to be heard on both sides of Berlin. In that sense, his poem 'Die Mauer' is unheard of, because it expresses and shatters a taboo at the same time. Braun enters the taboo zone when he talks about the inner German border and manoeuvres his way through a terrain of ideological pitfalls. The poet displays an antipodal way of writing, a style that was to become his signature.[25] A few years after the building of what he calls 'Dreck aus Beton' (filth made of cement), in the two versions of the poem, published in both East and West Germany, he signifies oppositional points of view regarding the Wall, by questioning the official accounts of its purpose. By constantly alternating between an Eastern and a Western perspective, he assists the reader to cross the Wall virtually, in spite of the difficulties faced by East Germans trying to get hold of books from the West. These different perspectives respond to geopolitical divisions. Originally, 'Die Mauer' was published in 1966 as one of 'Fünf Gedichte auf Deutschland' (Five Poems on Germany) in the fairly new West German journal, *Kursbuch*. Only ten years later, in the second edition of the volume *Wir und nicht sie* (We and not They (1970)), published in the GDR, was a radically amended version of the poem approved by the East German cultural authorities. And in 1979 the same version was included in the Suhrkamp edition of Braun's poems.[26] The two different versions shed light on the many different ideological attitudes towards the Berlin Wall. What follows here is only the first half of the third stanza of the first, early Western version, as published in *Kursbuch*.

> Aber
> Ich sag: es bleibt Dreck, es steht
> Da durch die Stadt, Unstattlich
> Es stinkt zum offenen Himmel, der Baukunst
> Langer Unbau, streicht ihn schwarz
> Die Brandmauer, nehmt die Fahnen ab
> Ich sage: es ist ein
> Schundbau, scheißt drauf[27]

> (But
> I say: it remains filth, there stands
> Throughout the city, unimposing
> It stinks to high heaven, architecture's
> Long non-construction, paint it black
> The firewall, take the flags down
> I say: it is
> Jerry-built, shit on it)

Braun seems to imitate Western hostility towards the Wall by referring to Cold War rhetoric in such words such 'Schundbau', resonating with the

Western phrase 'Mauer der Schande' (Wall of shame), whereas the official name the GDR authorities gave the Wall was 'antifaschistischer Schutzwall' (Antifascist Protective Wall).

In 1976, in the volume *Gedichte*, edited by Christel and Walfried Hartinger and published by Reclam Leipzig, the poem was entitled 'Die Grenze'. What is noticeable in the East German version is that Braun highlights the short period of euphoria among the GDR *intelligentsia* in the early 1960s. In this way it illustrates another side of the impact of the Wall, although only for a minority of Berliners. He avoids barefaced ideological vocabulary, and seems, instead, to write from a non-political perspective, reflecting the short period of support for the construction of the Wall and the accompanying euphoria which many of his colleagues, writers and intellectuals, experienced when sharing the GDR government's myth of anti-fascism. For them the building of the Wall was a simple and positive statement. The title of the volume, *Wir und nicht sie*, refers to Friedrich Gottlieb Klopstock's poem 'Sie, und nicht wir' (They, and not We (1790)), which cast an envious look at the French and American processes of emancipation and liberation. By echoing Klopstock, Braun highlights current ideological differences. The title and the poem itself express a utopian concept. For the young poets in the GDR, the real revolution, heralding a freeing of intellectual discourse, was about to be realized.

'Die Mauer' conveys a nervous impatience. Braun's friend and fellow poet Adolf Endler admitted in an interview in 2009: 'All of us – including Wolf Biermann and Bernd Jentzsch – thought this would initiate the big debates, and that the liberation of literature from dogma and ideologies would start from now. From today's perspective this sounds paradoxical but most of us had this belief. Soon, however, it became obvious that no great debate had started, that instead the wall was used to destroy and crush everything.'[28] In the poem, however, Braun's embeds within his utopian faith a sub-textual vocabulary associated with death and despair, established in the chain of nouns such as 'Beton / Eisen Draht Rauch' (concrete/iron wire smoke) and 'Schüsse' (shots), later 'Krieg' (war), 'Massengräber' (mass graves), 'Panzer' (tanks) and 'Minen' (mines). These features are linked to the so-called 'Zone des Todes' (the zone of death), or the 'Symbol für Ein- und Ausgesperrtsein' (symbol of being locked in and locked out).[29] The Wall is directly linked to traumatic portrayals of war when referring to the painting black of the firewall. The line 'Es stinkt zum offenen Himmel' denotes both the particular stench of the dead, and to death in both secular and theological terms, with 'Himmel' referring to both sky and heaven.

Braun surprises us by sending us into the combat zone and inviting us to cross the violent schism through his presentation of contradictory versions.

The poem visualizes the open wound in Berlin's centre. For this reason, as the second part of the poem reveals, the Berlin Wall is a permanent reminder of the violent oppression and aggression of the Cold War. At the same time Braun warns us not to become complacent and to resist the notion that the Berlin Wall is nothing more than a memorial. Through the constant shifting of perspectives the reader should be in a position to resist any kind of 'fencing off' of a space and try instead to establish a stable territory or identity without becoming encircled by it. Braun's 'Die Mauer' represents a significant projection of a construction-site of identity for Berliners. Spaces and social structures are constantly forged, just as they are negotiated and challenged by both East and West Berliners. The final two stanzas of the poem create a 'between' by directly addressing people on either side of the Wall, without parroting the political jargon of the respective authorities. For that reason it does not matter whether the shameful character of building the Wall is related to 'unsre' (our) or 'eure Schande' (your shame) – it is to be found on both sides.

Heiner Müller: Doomed Berlin

During the *Wende*, the 'turn' which followed the fall of the Berlin Wall, Heiner Müller published 'Mommsens Block' in the first issue of *Drucksache*, the publication forum of the Berliner Ensemble of which he was one of the artistic directors from 1992 until his death in 1995.[30] The poem had two sources. The first was the placing of the statue of the historian Theodor Mommsen in the front courtyard of the Humboldt University in 1993. The second was the misinformation Müller received about the reuse of the pedestal of the Mommsen statue. Müller was told that this block of marble, which had been in the University since 1907, had been used to support the statue of Karl Marx. Indeed, Marx's statue had replaced the Mommsen statue by authority of the SED – the ruling Socialist Unity Party of the GDR – in 1953. The new Marx statue was situated prominently in front of the university council chamber, but the 'Block' was never recycled. This was mere hearsay.[31]

Theodor Mommsen had been a professor of Ancient History at the Friedrich-Wilhelms-Universität in the second half of the nineteenth century. In 1902 he became the first German to receive the Nobel Prize for Literature for his monumental work *A History of Rome*. At the same time, he persistently criticized Otto von Bismarck for his eccentric and dangerous political manoeuvres. There is a mystery surrounding Mommsen: he failed to write the final volume of his masterpiece, which was to have been a study of the Roman Emperors. Müller does not write a documentary but, instead, links Mommsen's assumed writer's block, with his own difficulties in writing about the so-called 'red Caesars' in the GDR (and elsewhere in former Communist Europe) and in evaluating the new mechanisms of power in the reunified Germany. In the poem Müller asks for advice from the 'Comrade Professor', and with his help, investigates the causes of his failure when trying to write about his own collapsed 'empire'. In this respect, Heiner Müller and Theodor Mommsen share similar backgrounds, both living through newly established political entities with disastrous endings. They also faced the complex task of writing about previously failed 'empires', whether Rome or the Soviet Union. Further, it was in Berlin that they both wrote about the downfall of these apparent strongholds.

Müller's text is a poem and performance text, broadcast as a play for voices in 1993 for Deutschlandradio. The textual 'block' (the pun is operative in the text) is held together by a multiplicity of different texts and allusions. Owing to the intertextual nature of the collage, the text induces circular movements that can be registered as the continuous process of the writer's consciousness. The collage facilitates Müller's project of contrasting and comparing different times and geopolitical events and to synchronize Mommsen's failure with his own, and those of politicians past and present. Müller does not seek closure; he does not want to answer the question of why Mommsen did not finish his magnum opus. Rather, the text is imperfect and, consequently makes us aware that incompletion or fragmentation is in itself a valuable artistic quality.

> Er mochte sie nicht die Cäsaren der Spätzeit
> Nicht ihre Müdigkeit nicht ihre Laster
> Er hatte genug an dem einzigen Julius
> Der ihm wert war wie der eigene Grabstein
> Schon CÄSARS TOD ZU SCHILDERN hatte er
> Wenn er gefragt wurde nach dem ausstehenden
> Vierten Band NICHT MEHR DIE LEIDENSCHAFT
> Und DIE FAULENDEN JAHRHUNDERTE nach ihm
> GRAU IN GRAU SCHWARZ AUF SCHWARZ Für wen
> Die Grabschrift Daß der Geburtshelfer Bismarck
> Zugleich der Totengräber des Reiches war
> Der Nachgeburt einer falschen Depesche
> Konnte geschlossen werden aus dem dritten Band
> Mürbe geworden war in Charlottenburg
> Zweimal täglich die Fahrt mit der Pferdebahn
> Im Staub der Bücher und Handschriften vierzig
> Tausend im Haus Mommsen Machstraße acht
>
> (He didn't like those Caesars of the later empire
> Not their languor not their vices

He'd had enough of the peerless Julius
Whom he liked as much as his own tombstone
Even TO WRITE ABOUT CAESAR'S DEATH he had
When he was asked about the still missing
Fourth volume NOT ENOUGH PASSION LEFT
And THE PUTRESCENT CENTURIES after him
GRAY IN GRAY BLACK UPON BLACK   For whom
The epitaph   That the midwife Bismarck
Was as well the gravedigger of the empire
That afterbirth of a counterfeit dispatch
Could be concluded from the third volume
Jaded had become in Charlottenburg –
Twice daily the trip with the horse-drawn trolley
In the dust of books and manuscripts forty
Thousand in the Mommsen house Number Eight Mach Street)[32]

This passage is evidence of the persistent role that death plays in 'Mommsens Block', a theme that runs through most of Müller's later work, as for example in his last play: *Germania 3 – Gespenster am Toten Mann* (Germania 3 – Ghosts at Dead Man (1995/6)). In the 'reborn' Berlin in the newly reunified Germany, Müller cannot conceal his disgust with developments in social, political and cultural life, particularly the disrespect shown by the *nouveaux riches* to the dead and to the past. What Müller calls the 'rubbish of the new' is for him associated with decadence and ultimately with downfall.[33] The past, represented by the dead, is projected as the future. This is not a cry for *Ostalgie*, or nostalgia for the East: respect for death and the dead is necessary because they become the building blocks of the future and enable us to mould the present. In other words, Müller absorbs a past that was either glorified or repressed by the GDR. In his view, the writer's task is to treat the dead with respect, also in intertextual terms. Therefore, his *Totengespräche* (Conversations with the Dead), as acts of walking and talking with the departed, celebrate failure in contrast to the new Berlin's emphasis on success. In an interview for *Lettre International* in 1994, Müller told the critic Frank M. Raddatz: 'The level of a culture depends on how it deals with the dead.'[34] What used to be a collective custom in ancient cultures seems to be a potent clarion call from the heart of the present Berlin as the centre of this neo-liberal and money-orientated empire.

It is not a matter of not being able to write in the face of a new era (leaving the debris of the past behind – as Walter Benjamin's angel of history does) but more of the impediment of the deadly present. The poet investigates the best way to write poetry in a city on the threshold of a new historical era after a century of war and global devastation. He offers a new literary approach in regard to a presumably doomed Berlin at the end of the twentieth century. Berlin, as proposed by 'Mommsens Block', is sick with decadence as Rome once was. As Müller sees it, the capital no longer speaks with a unified voice, and he situates Berlin within a new doomed future. Paradoxically, the only resolution to this nihilistic position is for the writer to preserve the dead in his work.

Conclusion: 'Walking the Dead'

Throughout the final decades of the twentieth century and the beginning of the twenty-first, the poetry of Berlin has become increasingly complex, not least in response to the political context. Poems demand more of their readers – not only by virtue of a more refined set of poetics, but also because national and international affairs have dragged Berlin into the condition of progressive entanglement. Berlin has become a centre of world politics and has paid the price.

Of course, many more poets have represented death in Berlin in their poetry than the four discussed here. Speier's study, *Poesie der Metropole*, is a useful and very specific resource, pointing out differences in themes, historical contexts and the functions and reception of poems in the period 1925–87.[35] Speier discusses and evaluates relevant anthologies from the interwar period and the 'Third Reich', as well as pointing out the similarities and differences between the poetry of East and West Berlin. All are related, as Monica Black argues, to the theme that moulded the psyche of Berliners: death. Because '[i]n the end, Berlin was the final European battleground of that cataclysmic war [and] Berlin was the site of the first major crisis of the Cold War ... which seemed to anticipate World War III'.[36] In the 'century of war', death was a constant.

In this chapter, as well as in Speier's investigation, many striking voices which have participated in the discourse of Berlin have not been heard: the poets who wrote during the resistance against Hitler; Turkish-German poets; and, not least, women poets. The distinctive lyrical voices of, for example, Else Lasker-Schüler, Nelly Sachs, Karin Kiwus and Kerstin Hensel have made significant contributions to Berlin's cultural profile. Needless to say, all of these other voices would help to complete the picture drawn here. Another omission is a glimpse into the future of Berlin poetry now that the 'century of war' has been succeeded by the 'war on terror'. And more generally, an account and assessment of the anthologies published in the new Berlin are still overdue.

The late twentieth and early twenty-first centuries have already shown what new challenges are in store for poet and reader in what is now a world city rather than the centre of a national empire. The theme of this chapter, however, remains relevant in the twenty-first century and is not restricted by national affiliation. In 2011, for example, the English singer and songwriter David Bowie, who lived in, and helped shape the cultural image of, the West Berlin of the 1970s, released his single 'Where Are We Now?', accompanied by a video by the artist Tony Oursler. Shot in black and white, it presents a Berlin of memory and dream. The video mimics a *danse macabre*, as Bowie journeys through stations in Berlin's landscape and history. His lyrics explore themes of freedom, loss, ageing and death:

> Sitting in the Dschungel
> On Nürnberger Straße
> A man lost in time
> Near KaDeWe
> Just walking the dead[37]

Bowie manoeuvres between his own ecstatic Berlin experience of the 1970s and the city's gloomy recent past. He lived in Schöneberg in the centre of West Berlin's nightlife while hanging out with fellow pop stars Iggy Pop and Lou Reed in the Dschungel (Jungle) discotheque on Nürnberger Straße, close to the KaDeWe department store. At the same time, this street has the infamous reputation of being associated with the frequent razzias by the Nazis. The repetition of the words 'walking the dead' and the opening shot of the video, a skull, makes this product of popular culture a respectable reflection and memory document of contemporary Berlin, where death indeed casts a ubiquitous shadow. Between what has been described as Bowie's twentieth-century Berlin elegy and the first known poem in Berlin, the fifteenth-century *Berliner Totentanz*, multiple examples of poetic depictions, both high cultural and more popular, have focused on this quintessential subject that has helped to define contemporary Berlin.

NOTES

1. Matthias Kniep and Thomas Wohlfahrt (eds.), *Das große Berlin-Gedicht* (Berlin: be.bra verlag, 2011).
2. Hans-Michael Speier, *Poesie der Metropole: Die Berlin-Lyrik von der Gründerzeit bis zur Gegenwart im Spiegel ihrer Anthologien*, Wissenschaft und Stadt 10 (Berlin: Colloquium Verlag, 1990).
3. Gabriel Kolko, *Century of War: Politics, Conflicts, and Society since 1914* (New York: New Press, 1994).
4. Monica Black, *Death in Berlin: From Weimar to Divided Germany* (Cambridge: Cambridge University Press, 2010), p. 111.
5. Ibid., p. 5.
6. Helmut Lethen, *Der Sound der Väter: Gottfried Benn und seine Zeit* (Berlin: Rowohlt Berlin, 2006), p. 73.

7. Dieter Wellershoff, *Gottfried Benn. Phänotyp dieser Stunde. Eine Studie über den Problemgehalt seines Werkes* (Cologne/Berlin: Kiepenheuer & Witsch, 1958), p. 139.

8. Lethen, *Der Sound*, p. 144.

9. Gottfried Benn, *Sämtliche Werke*, vol. 2, ed. G. Schuster (Stuttgart: Klett-Cotta, 1986), p. 138. Gottfried Benn, *Selected Poems and Prose*, ed. and trans. D. Paisey (Manchester: Carcanet, 2013), p. 243 (translation varied).

10. Gottfried Benn, 'Bekenntnis zum Expressionismus', *Deutsche Zukunft*, 1.4 (5 November 1933), pp. 15–17.

11. J. M. Ritchie, *Gottfried Benn: The Reconstructed Expressionist* (London: Oswald Wolff, 1972), p. 104.

12. Roland Barthes, *Camera Lucida: Reflections on Photography*, trans. R. Howard, (London: Vintage, 1993), pp. 42–7.

13. Stephen Parker, *Bertolt Brecht: A Literary Life* (London: Bloomsbury, 2014), p. 178.

14. Andrew J. Webber, *Berlin in the Twentieth Century: A Cultural Topography* (Cambridge: Cambridge University Press, 2008), p. 105.

15. Helmut Lethen, *Cool Conduct: The Culture of Distance in Weimar Germany*, trans. D. Reneau (Berkeley: University of California Press, 2002).

16. Julia Kristeva, *Powers of Horror: An Essay on Abjection*, trans. Leon S. Roudiez (New York: Columbia University Press, 1982).

17. Bertolt Brecht, 'Vom ertrunkenen Mädchen', in *Große kommentierte Berliner und Frankfurter Ausgabe*, vol. 11, eds Werner Hecht et al. (Berlin, Weimar and Frankfurt am Main: Aufbau-Verlag and Suhrkamp Verlag, 1993), p. 109. Translation, by permission of David Constantine, will appear in a new collection of Brecht's poems, translated and edited by Tom Kuhn and David Constantine (Norton Liveright, 2019).

18. Lethen, *Cool Conduct*, p. 211.

19. As claimed by Weill in 1929, quoted in Nils Grosch, 'Notiz zum *Berliner Requiem* von Kurt Weill: Aspekte seiner Entstehung und Aufführung', *Kurt Weill-Studien*, 1 (1996), 55–71 (64).

20. Bertolt Brecht, 'Die Lösung', in *Große kommentierte Berliner und Frankfurter Ausgabe*, vol. 12, p. 310. Trans. by Derek Bowman, in Bertolt Brecht, *Poems 1913–1956*, eds John Willett and Ralph Manheim (New York: Methuen, 1979), p. 440.

21. Werner Hecht, *Die Mühen der Ebenen: Brecht und die DDR* (Berlin: Aufbau, 2013), pp. 166–8.

22. Thomas Loy, 'Vom Kanal zur Grünanlage, zum Todesstreifen und wieder zurück', *Der Tagesspiegel*, 12 September 2010: http://www.tagesspiegel.de/ber lin/rueckblick-vom-kamal-zur-gruenanlage-zum-todesstreifen-und-wieder-zur ueck/1931458.html (accessed 23 June 2014).

23. Marc Silberman, ed., *The German Wall: Fallout in Europe* (Basingstoke: Palgrave Macmillan, 2011), p. 8.

24. Lynne B. Hinds and Theodore O. Windt, Jr., *The Cold War as Rhetoric: The Beginnings, 1945–1950* (New York: Praeger Publishers, 1991), pp. 5–25.

25. Gerrit-Jan Berendse, 'Fünfundzwanzig Jahre politische Poesie von Volker Braun: Von einem heftigen Experimentator, der immer neue Wege sucht', *Wirkendes Wort*, 41.3 (1991), pp. 425–35.

26. Volker Braun, 'Die Mauer', *Kursbuch*, 4 (1966), pp. 64–6; Braun, *Wir und nicht sie: Gedichte* (Halle (Saale): Mitteldeutscher Verlag, 1976), pp. 47–9; and Braun, *Gedichte* (Frankfurt am Main: Suhrkamp, 1979), pp. 23–5.

27. Braun, 'Die Mauer', p. 66. Translation: Paul Clements, adapting Charlotte Melin's translation of the GDR version, in Charlotte Melin, ed., *German Poetry in Translation 1945–1990* (Hanover, London: University Press of New England, 1999), pp. 321–5.

28. Adolf Endler, *Dies Sirren: Gespräche mit Renatus Deckert* (Göttingen: Wallstein, 2010), p. 171 (my translation).

29. As Bernd Wagner states, in hindsight, as quoted in Doris Liebermann, 'Die Mauer in der Literatur', *Glossen*, 32 (2007): http://blogs.dickinson.edu/glossen/archive/most-recent-issue-322011 (accessed 18 August 2014).

30. Heiner Müller, 'Mommsens Block', *Drucksache 1: Berliner Ensemble* (Berlin, Alexander Verlag, 1993).

31. Theo Buck, *'Die Adler im Sumpf'* oder *Die missratene deutsche Einheit: Zu Heiner Müllers 'Mommsens Block'* (Berlin: Weidler, 2011), pp. 28–9.

32. Heiner Müller, 'Mommsens Block', *Werke*, ed. Frank Hörnigk (Frankfurt am Main: Suhrkamp, 2005), vol. 1, pp. 257–63 (pp. 257–8). Translation: *A Heiner Müller Reader: Plays, Poetry, Prose*, ed. and trans. Carl Weber (Baltimore and New York: The Johns Hopkins University Press, 2001), pp. 124–9 (p. 124).

33. Gerd Labroise, 'Heiner Müller-Lyrik: Ein besonderer Rezeptionsfall', in *Das Jahrhundert Berlins: Eine Stadt in der Literatur*, eds Jattie Enklaar and Hans Ester (Amsterdam: Rodopi, 2000), pp. 147–86.

34. Frank M. Raddatz, 'Für immer in Hollywood oder: In Deutschland wird nicht mehr geblinzelt', in Müller, *Werke*, vol. 12, pp. 459–75 (p. 468), my translation.

35. Speier, *Poesie der Metropole*, pp. 1–7.

36. Black, *Death in Berlin*, p. 3.

37. David Bowie, 'Where Are We Now?', *The Next Day* (Columbia Records, 2013).

GUIDE TO FURTHER READING

Chapter 1

Birtsch, Günter, 'The Berlin Wednesday Society', in James Schmidt, ed., *What Is Enlightenment? Eighteenth-Century Answers and Twentieth-Century Questions*, Berkeley: University of California Press, 1996, pp. 235–52.

Erlin, Matt, *Berlin's Forgotten Future: City, History and Enlightenment in Eighteenth-Century Germany*, Chapel Hill, NC: University of North Carolina Press, 2004.

Falk, Reiner and Alexander Košenina, *Friedrich Nicolai und die Berliner Aufklärung*, Hannover: Wehrhahn Verlag, 2008.

Feiner, Schmuel and Natalie Naimark-Goldberg, *Cultural Revolution in Berlin: Jews in the Age of Enlightenment*, Oxford: Bodleian Library, 2011.

Förster, Wolfgang, ed., *Aufklärung in Berlin*, Berlin: Akademie-Verlag, 1989.

Goldenbaum, Ursula and Alexander Košenina, eds., *Berliner Aufklärung: Kulturgeschichtliche Studien*, 5 vols to date, Hannover: Wehrhahn Verlag, 1999–2011.

Hermsdorf, Klaus, *Literarisches Leben in Berlin: Aufklärer und Romantiker*, Berlin: Akademie-Verlag, 1987.

Hertz, Deborah, *Jewish High Society in Old Regime Berlin*, New Haven: Yale University Press, 1988.

McFarland, Robert, 'Füße im Steigvers mit weiblichem Ausgang: Anna Louise Karsch's Poem Cycle "Die Spaziergänge von Berlin" and the Pre-History of the "Flaneuse"', *Lessing Yearbook* 36 (2004/5), 135–60.

Selwyn, Pamela, *Everyday Life in the German Book Trade: Friedrich Nicolai as Bookseller and Publisher in the Age of Enlightenment 1750–1810*, University Park: The Pennsylvania State University Press, 2000.

Chapter 2

Becker-Cantarino, Barbara, 'Die "andere" Akademie: Juden, Frauen und Berliner literarische Gesellschaft 1770–1806', in Klaus Garber, ed., *Europäische Sozietätsbewegung und demokratische Tradition*, Tübingen: Niemeyer, 1996, pp. 1478–505.

Clark, Christopher, *Iron Kingdom: The Rise and Downfall of Prussia 1600–1947*, London: Penguin, 2007.

Frühwald, Wolfgang, 'Anti-Judaismus in der Zeit der deutschen Romantik', in Hans Otto Horch and Horst Denkler, eds., *Judentum, Antisemitismus und deutschsprachige Literatur vom 18. Jahrhundert bis zum Ersten Weltkrieg: Interdisziplinäres Symposium*, 2. Teil, Tübingen: Niemeyer, 1989, pp. 72–91.

Hermsdorf, Klaus, *Literarisches Leben in Berlin: Aufklärer und Romantiker*, Berlin: Akademie Verlag, 1987.

Hertz, Deborah, *Jewish High Society in Old Regime Berlin*, New Haven, London: Yale University Press, 1988.

Lund, Hannah Lotte, *Der Berliner 'jüdische Salon' um 1800: Emanzipation und Debatte*, Berlin: de Gruyter, 2012.

Nienhaus, Stefan, *Geschichte der deutschen Tischgesellschaft*, Tübingen: Niemeyer, 2003.

Richie, Alexandra, *Faust's Metropolis: A History of Berlin*, London: Harper Collins, 1998.

Schlutz, Alexander M., 'E. T. A. Hoffmann's Marketplace Vision of Berlin', in Larry H. Peer, eds, *Romanticism and the City*, New York, Basingstoke: Palgrave, 2011, pp. 105–34.

Wilhelmy-Dollinger, Petra, *Die Berliner Salons: Mit kulturhistorischen Spaziergängen*, Berlin, New York: de Gruyter, 2000.

Ziolkowski, Theodore, *Berlin: Ausftieg einer Kulturmetropole um 1800*, Stuttgart: Klett-Cotta, 2002.

Ziolkowski, Theodore, *German Romanticism and Its Institutions*, Princeton, NJ: Princeton University Press, 1990.

Chapter 3

Berman, Russell A., *The Rise of the Modern German Novel: Crisis and Charisma*, Cambridge, MA: Harvard University Press, 1986.

Craig, Gordon A., *Theodor Fontane: Literature and History in the Bismarck Reich*, New York: Oxford University Press, 1999.

Downing, Eric, *Double Exposures: Repetition and Realism in Nineteenth-Century German Fiction*, Stanford, CA: Stanford University Press, 2000.

Forderer, Christof, *Die Großstadt im Roman: Berliner Großstadtdarstellungen zwischen Naturalismus und Moderne*, Wiesbaden: Deutscher Universitätsverlag, 1992.

Holub, Robert, *Reflections of Realism: Paradox, Norm, and Ideology in Nineteenth-Century German Prose*, Detroit: Wayne State University Press, 1991.

Koelb, Clayton and Eric Downing, eds., *Camden House History of German Literature*, vol. 9, Rochester, NY: Camden House, 2005.

Lyon, John B. *Out of Place: German Realism, Displacement, and Modernity*, New York: Bloomsbury Academic, 2013.

Roper, Katherine, *German Encounters with Modernity: Novels of Imperial Berlin*, Atlantic Highlands, NJ: Humanities International, 1991.

Sprengel, Peter, *Gerhart Hauptmann: Epoche, Werk, Wirkung*, Munich: C.H. Beck, 1984.

Stöckmann, I., *Naturalismus*, Stuttgart: Metzler, 2011.

Chapter 4

Fuchs, Anne, 'Why Smallness Matters: The Problem of Attention in Franz Kafka's and Robert Walser's Short Prose', in Ritchie Robertson and Manfred Engel, eds., *Kafka und die kleine Prosa der Moderne/ Franz Kafka and Short Modernist Prose*, Würzburg: Königshausen & Neumann, 2010, pp. 167–81.

Fritzsche, Peter, *Reading Berlin 1900*, Cambridge, MA: Harvard University Press, 1996.

Göttsche, Dirk, *Kleine Prosa in Moderne und Gegenwart*, Münster: Aschendorff, 2006.

Harder, Matthias and Almut Hille, eds., *Weltfabrik Berlin: Eine Metropole als Sujet der Literatur*, Würzburg: Königshausen & Neumann, 2010.

Scharnowski, Susanne, '"Berlin ist schön, Berlin ist groß!" Feuilletonistische Blicke auf Berlin: Alfred Kerr, Robert Walser, Joseph Roth and Bernard Brentano', in Matthias Harder and Almut Hille, eds., *Weltfabrik Berlin: Eine Metropole als Sujet der Literatur*, Würzburg: Königshausen & Neumann, 2010, pp. 67–82.

Schönborn, Sibylle, '" … wie ein Tropfen ins Meer" – Von medialen Raumzeiten und Archiven des Vergessens: das Feuilleton als "kleine Form"', in Thomas Althaus, Wolfgang Bunzel and Dirk Göttsche, eds., *Kleine Prosa: Theorie und Geschichte eines Textfeldes im Literatursystem der Moderne*, Tübingen: Niemeyer, 2007, pp. 197–211.

Utz, Peter, 'Zu kurz gekommene Kleinigkeiten. Robert Walser und der Beitrag des Feuilletons zur literarischen Moderne', in Elmar Locher, ed., *Die kleinen Formen in der Moderne*, Bolzano: Edition Stürzflüge, 2001, pp. 133–65.

Webber, Andrew J., *Berlin in the Twentieth Century: A Cultural Topography*, Cambridge: Cambridge University Press, 2008.

Chapter 5

Donahue, Neil H., *A Companion to the Literature of German Expressionism*, Rochester, NY: Camden House, 2010.

Gleber, Anke, *The Art of Talking a Walk: Flanerie, Literature, and Film in Weimar Culture*, Princeton, NJ: Princeton University Press, 1998.

Hake, Sabine, *Topographies of Class: Modern Architecture and Mass Society in Weimar Berlin*, Ann Arbor, MI: University of Michigan Press, 2008.

Kaes, Anton, Martin Jay and Edward Dimendberg, eds., *The Weimar Republic Sourcebook*, Berkeley, CA: University of California Press, 1994.

Lethen, Helmut, *Cool Conduct: The Culture of Distance in Weimar Germany*, trans. by Don Reneau, Berkeley, CA: University of California Press, 2002.

Uecker, Matthias, *Wirklichkeit und Literatur: Strategien dokumentarischen Schreibens in der Weimarer Republik*, Berne: Lang, 2007.

Ward, Janet, *Weimar Surfaces: Urban Visual Culture in 1920s Germany*, Berkeley, CA: University of California Press, 2001.

Webber, Andrew J., *Berlin in the Twentieth Century: A Cultural Topography*, Cambridge: Cambridge University Press, 2008.

White, Michael, *Generation Dada: The Berlin Avant-Garde and the First World War*, New Haven, CT: Yale University Press, 2013.

Zachau, Reinhard, ed., *Topography and Literature: Berlin and Modernism*, Göttingen: V & R unipress, 2009.

Chapter 6

Adam, Christian, *Lesen unter Hitler: Autoren, Bestseller, Leser im Dritten Reich*, Berlin: Kiepenheuer und Witsch, 2010.

Berman, Russell, *The Rise of the Modern German Novel: Crisis and Charisma*, Boston: Harvard University Press, 1986.

Borst, Otto. *Babel oder Jerusalem? Sechs Kapitel Stadtgeschichte*, Stuttgart: Theiss, 1988.

Brekle, Wolfgang. *Schriftsteller im antifaschistischen Widerstand 1933–1945 in Deutschland*, Berlin: Aufbau, 1985.

Cockburn, Claud, *In Time of Trouble: An Autobiography*, London: Hart-Davis, 1956.

Fischer, Gerhard, ed., *Kästner-Debatte: Kritische Positionen zu einem kontroversen Autor*, Würzburg: Königshausen & Neumann, 2004.

Fisher, Jaimey and Barbara Mennel, eds., *Spatial Turns: Space, Place and Mobility in German Literary and Visual Culture*, Amsterdam: Rodopi, 2010.

Glass, Derek, Dietmar Rösler and John J. White, eds., *Berlin, Literary Images of a City: Eine Großstadt im Spiegel der Literatur*, Berlin: Erich Schmidt, 1989.

Larson, Erik, *In the Garden of Beasts: Love, Terror, and an American Family in Hitler's Berlin*, New York: Crown, 2011.

Schäfer, Hans Dietrich, *Berlin im Zweiten Weltkrieg*, Munich: Piper, 1985.

Schnell, Ralf, 'Was ist nationalsozialistische Dichtung?', in Jörg Thunecke, ed., *Leid der Worte: Panorama des literarischen Nationalsozialismus*, Bonn: Bouvier, 1987, pp. 28–45.

Williams, Jenny, *More Lives Than One: A Biography of Hans Fallada*, Harmondsworth: Penguin, 2012.

Chapter 7

Hammond, Andrew, *British Fiction and the Cold War*, Basingstoke: Palgrave Macmillan, 2013.

Harrison, Hope M., *Driving the Soviets up the Wall: Soviet-East German Relations, 1953-1961*, Princeton, NJ: Princeton University Press, 2013.

Korte, Hermann. 'Wiedergelesen: Christa Wolfs kleiner Roman "Der geteilte Himmel"', *Text + Kritik* 46 (2012), 38–50.

Ladd, Brian, *The Ghosts of Berlin*, Chicago: The University of Chicago Press, 1997.

Lamping, Dieter, *Über Grenzen: Eine literarische Topographie*, Göttingen: Vandenhoeck &Ruprecht, 2001.

Lewis, Alison, 'Das Paradox der freien Partnerwahl in der Liebe: Zum Aufstieg und Fall einer sozialistischen Liebessemantik in Christa Wolfs *Der geteilte Himmel* und Volker Brauns *Unvollendete Geschichte'*, in *Moderne begreifen: Zur Paradoxie eines sozio-ästhetischen Deutungsmusters*, eds Christine Magerski, Robert Savage and Christiane Weller, Wiesbaden: Deutscher Universitäts-Verlag, 2007, pp. 289–309.

Mathäs, Alexander, 'Copying Kafka's Signature: Martin Walser's *Die Verteidigung der Kindheit'*, *Germanic Review* 69.2 (1994), 79–91.

Taberner, Stuart, 'The Meaning of the Nazi Past in The Post-Post-War: Recent Fiction byGünter Grass, Christa Wolf and Martin Walser', *Seminar* 50.1 (2014), 161–77.

Verheven, Dirk, *United City, Divided Memories? Cold War Legacies in Contemporary Berlin*, Lanham: Lexington Books, 2008.

Chapter 8

Brockmann, Stephen, *Literature and German Unification*, Cambridge: Cambridge University Press, 1999.

Carrillo Zeiter, Katja and Berit Callsen, eds., *Berlin – Madrid: postdiktatoriale Grossstadtliteratur*, Berlin: Erich Schmidt, 2011.

Gerstenberger, Katharina, *Writing the New Berlin: The German Capital in Post-Wall Literature*, Rochester, NY: Camden House, 2008.

Huyssen, Andreas, *Present Pasts: Urban Palimpsests and the Politics of Memory*, Stanford, CA: Stanford University Press, 2003.

Ledanff, Susanne, *Hauptstadtphantasien: Berliner Stadtlektüren in der Gegenwartsliteratur 1989–2008*, Bielefeld: Aisthesis, 2008.

Taberner, Stuart, *Contemporary German Fiction: Writing in the Berlin Republic*, Cambridge: Cambridge University Press, 2007.

German Literature of the 1990s and Beyond: Normalization and the Berlin Republic, Rochester, NY: Camden House, 2005.

Till, Karen, *The New Berlin: Memory, Politics, Place*, Minneapolis: University of Minnesota Press, 2005.

Chapter 9

Budke, Petra and Jutta Schulze, *Schriftstellerinnen in Berlin 1871 bis 1945: Ein Lexikon zu Leben und Werk*, Berlin: Orlanda Frauenverlag, 1995.

Gerstenberger, Katharina, *Writing the New Berlin: the German Capital in Post-Wall Literature*, Rochester, NY: Camden House, 2008.

Harder, Matthias and Almut Hille, eds., *Weltfabrik Berlin: Eine Metropole als Sujet der Literatur*, Würzburg: Königshausen & Neumann, 2006.

Langer, Phil C., *Kein Ort. Überall. Die Einschreibung von 'Berlin' in die deutsche Literatur der neunziger Jahre*, Berlin: Weidler, 2002.

Ledanff, Susanne, *Hauptstadtphantasien: Berliner Stadtlektüren in der Gegenwartsliteratur 1989–2008*, Bielefeld: Aisthesis, 2009.

Peters, Laura, *Stadttext und Selbstbild: Berliner Autoren der Postmigration nach 1989*, Heidelberg: Universitätsverlag Winter, 2012.

von Ankum, Katharina, ed., *Women in the Metropolis: Gender and Modernity in Weimar Culture*, Berkeley: University of California Press, 1997.

Weiss-Sussex, Godela and Ulrike Zitzlsperger, eds., *Berlin. Kultur und Metropole in den zwanziger und seit den neunziger Jahren*, Munich: iudicium, 2007.

Zitzlsperger, Ulrike, *ZeitGeschichten: Die Berliner Übergangsjahre: Zur Verortung der Stadt nach der Mauer*, Berne: Peter Lang, 2007.

Chapter 10

Beachy, Robert, *Gay Berlin: Birthplace of a Modern Identity*, New York: Knopf, 2014.

Busch, Alexandra and Dirck Linck, eds., *Frauenliebe, Männerliebe: Eine lesbischschwule Literaturgeschichte in Porträts*, Frankfurt am Main: Suhrkamp, 1999.

Hewitt, Andrew, *Political Inversions: Homosexuality, Fascism, and the Modernist Imaginary*, Stanford, CA: Stanford University Press, 1996.

Jones, James W., *'We of the Third Sex': Literary Representations of Homosexuality in Wilhelmine Germany*, New York: Lang, 1990.

Keilson-Lauritz, Marita, *Die Geschichte der eigenen Geschichte: Literatur und Literaturkritik in den Anfängen der Schwulenbewegung am Beispiel des 'Jahrbuchs für Zwischenstufen' und der Zeitschrift 'Der Eigene'*, Berlin: Rosa Winkel, 1997.

Kennedy, Hubert, *The Ideal Gay Man: The Story of 'Der Kreis'*, London: Routledge, 1999.

Kraß, Andreas, *'Meine erste Geliebte': Magnus Hirschfeld und sein Verhältnis zur schönen Literatur*, Göttingen: Wallstein, 2013.

Lorey, Chrisoph and John Plews, eds., *Queering the Canon: Defying Sights in German Literature and Culture*, Columbia, NY: Camden House, 1998.

Müller, Stefan, *Ach, nur'n bisschen Liebe: Männliche Homosexualität in den Romanen deutschsprachiger Autoren in der Zwischenkriegszeit, 1919–1939*, Würzburg: Königshausen & Neumann, 2011.

Summers, Claude J., ed., *The Gay and Lesbian Literary Heritage: A Reader's Companion to the Writers and their Works, from Antiquity to the Present*, New York: Henry Holt, 1995.

Theweleit, Klaus, *Male Fantasies*, 2 vols, trans. Chris Turner, Minneapolis, MN: University of Minnesota Press, 1989.

Chapter 11

Chin, Rita, *The Guest Worker Question in Postwar Germany*, Cambridge: Cambridge University Press, 2007.

Estraikh, Gennady and Mikhail Krutikov, *Yiddish in Weimar Berlin: At the Crossroads of Diaspora Politics and Culture*, Leeds: Legenda, 2010.

Gezen, Ela Eylem, 'Writing and Sounding the City: Turkish-German Representations of Berlin', Diss. University of Michigan, 2012 (http://deepblue.lib.umich.edu /bitstream/handle/2027.42/94066/egezen_1.pdf?sequence=1).

Göktürk, Deniz, David Gramling and Anton Kaes, eds., *Germany in Transit: Nation and Migration, 1955–2005*, Berkeley, CA: University of California Press, 2007.

Mandel, Ruth, *Cosmopolitan Anxieties: Turkish Challenges to Citizenship and Belonging in Germany*, Durham, NC: Duke University Press, 2008.

Ritchie, Alexandra, *Faust's Metropolis: A History of Berlin*, New York: Carroll and Graf, 1998.

Chapter 12

Barnett, David, *A History of the Berliner Ensemble*, Cambridge: Cambridge University Press, 2015.

Carlson, Marvin, *Theatre Is More Beautiful than War: German Stage Directing in the Late Twentieth Century*, Iowa City, IA: University of Iowa Press, 2009.

Kaes, Anton, Martin Jay and Edward Dimendberg, eds., *The Weimar Republic Sourcebook*, Berkley, CA: University of California Press, 1994, especially pp. 530–50.

Kuhns, David F., *German Expressionist Theatre: The Actor and the Stage*, Cambridge: CUP, 1997.

Osborne, John, *Gerhart Hauptmann and the Naturalist Drama*, revised and updated edition, London: Routledge, 1998.

Patterson, Michael, *Revolution in German Theatre*, London: Routledge, 1981.

Rühle, Günther, *Theater in Deutschland: 1887–1945*, Frankfurt am Main: Fischer, 2007.

Thomson, Peter and Glendyr Sacks, eds., *The Cambridge Companion to Brecht*, 2nd edition, Cambridge: Cambridge University Press, 2006.

Varney, Denise, ed., *Theatre in the Berlin Republic: German Drama since Reunification*, Berne: Lang, 2008.

Williams, Simon and Maik Hamburger, eds., *A History of German Theatre*, Cambridge: Cambridge University Press, 2008.

Chapter 13

Arnold, Heinz Ludwig, ed., *Lyrik des 20. Jahrhunderts*, Munich: Edition Text & Kritik, 1999.

Haxthausen, Charles and Heidrun Suhr, eds., *Berlin: Culture and Metropolis*, Minneapolis, MN: University of Minnesota Press, 1990.

Hofmann, Michael, ed., *The Faber Book of Twentieth-Century German Poems*, London: Faber & Faber, 2005.

Hutchinson, Peter, ed., *Landmarks in German Poetry*, Berne: Lang, 2000.

Korte, Hermann, *Geschichte der deutschen Lyrik. Band 6: Von 1945 bis heute*, Stuttgart: Reclam, 2012.

Leeder, Karen, ed., *Flaschenpost: German Poetry and the Long Twentieth Century*, *Special Issue German Life and Letters*, 60 (2007) 3.

Moorhouse, Roger, *Berlin at War: Life and Death in Hitler's Capital, 1939–45*, London: Vintage Books, 2010.

Schnell, Ralf, *Geschichte der deutschen Lyrik. Band 5: Von der Jahrhundertwende bis zum Ende des Zweiten Weltkriegs*, Stuttgart: Reclam, 2004.

INDEX

Cambridge Companions To ...

AUTHORS

Edward Albee edited by Stephen J. Bottoms

Margaret Atwood edited by Coral Ann Howells

W. H. Auden edited by Stan Smith

Jane Austen edited by Edward Copeland and Juliet McMaster (second edition)

Beckett edited by John Pilling

Bede edited by Scott DeGregorio

Aphra Behn edited by Derek Hughes and Janet Todd

Walter Benjamin edited by David S. Ferris

William Blake edited by Morris Eaves

Boccaccio edited by Guyda Armstrong, Rhiannon Daniels and Stephen J. Milner

Jorge Luis Borges edited by Edwin Williamson

Brecht edited by Peter Thomson and Glendyr Sacks (second edition)

The Brontës edited by Heather Glen

Bunyan edited by Anne Dunan-Page

Frances Burney edited by Peter Sabor

Byron edited by Drummond Bone

Albert Camus edited by Edward J. Hughes

Willa Cather edited by Marilee Lindemann

Cervantes edited by Anthony J. Cascardi

Chaucer edited by Piero Boitani and Jill Mann (second edition)

Chekhov edited by Vera Gottlieb and Paul Allain

Kate Chopin edited by Janet Beer

Caryl Churchill edited by Elaine Aston and Elin Diamond

Cicero edited by Catherine Steel

Coleridge edited by Lucy Newlyn

Wilkie Collins edited by Jenny Bourne Taylor

Joseph Conrad edited by J. H. Stape

H. D. edited by Nephie J. Christodoulides and Polina Mackay

Dante edited by Rachel Jacoff (second edition)

Daniel Defoe edited by John Richetti

Don DeLillo edited by John N. Duvall

Charles Dickens edited by John O. Jordan

Emily Dickinson edited by Wendy Martin

John Donne edited by Achsah Guibbory

Dostoevskii edited by W. J. Leatherbarrow

Theodore Dreiser edited by Leonard Cassuto and Claire Virginia Eby

John Dryden edited by Steven N. Zwicker

W. E. B. Du Bois edited by Shamoon Zamir

George Eliot edited by George Levine

T. S. Eliot edited by A. David Moody

Ralph Ellison edited by Ross Posnock

Ralph Waldo Emerson edited by Joel Porte and Saundra Morris

William Faulkner edited by Philip M. Weinstein

Henry Fielding edited by Claude Rawson

F. Scott Fitzgerald edited by Ruth Prigozy

Flaubert edited by Timothy Unwin

E. M. Forster edited by David Bradshaw

Benjamin Franklin edited by Carla Mulford

Brian Friel edited by Anthony Roche

Robert Frost edited by Robert Faggen

Gabriel García Márquez edited by Philip Swanson

Elizabeth Gaskell edited by Jill L. Matus

Goethe edited by Lesley Sharpe

Günter Grass edited by Stuart Taberner

Thomas Hardy edited by Dale Kramer

David Hare edited by Richard Boon

Nathaniel Hawthorne edited by Richard Millington

Seamus Heaney edited by Bernard O'Donoghue

Ernest Hemingway edited by Scott Donaldson

Homer edited by Robert Fowler

Horace edited by Stephen Harrison

Ted Hughes edited by Terry Gifford

Ibsen edited by James McFarlane

Henry James edited by Jonathan Freedman

Samuel Johnson edited by Greg Clingham

Ben Jonson edited by Richard Harp and Stanley Stewart

James Joyce edited by Derek Attridge (second edition)

Kafka edited by Julian Preece

Keats edited by Susan J. Wolfson

Rudyard Kipling edited by Howard J. Booth

Lacan edited by Jean-Michel Rabaté

D. H. Lawrence edited by Anne Fernihough

Primo Levi edited by Robert Gordon

TOPICS